a copy of [...] [...] by
Pat Nixon!
    Green [...] [...] version
of the tea [...] a similar
[...] folder, [...] whatever you
decide [...] way ...... Love
[signature]

have two trips left – one to N.Y. this week, and then
to Honolulu in May. Enclosing report of recent reading
~~circle~~ with Senator McCarthy. We became good
friends. At one point he said, "Don't kid! If I
had been elected President, you would have been at
the prayer breakfasts instead of Billy Graham!
What a loss!"

    I'm looking forward to your new "book" —
write soon! Our love to all your Glückler, especially
your wife, whose luminous face I often see.

                    Your friend
                    [signature] Oren

P.S. Carol is deluged with requests from Sweden for the
"Teeth-Mother" folder — evidently German Harding had a
note about it in Expressen. (The teeth-mother is really Pat
Nixon) (The foreign poets at a recent conference at the Library of
Congress, by the way, go T, ~~at the~~ White House reception: This —

AIRMAIL

By Robert Bly

Silence in the Snowy Fields (1962)
Hunger by Knut Hamsun (translation, 1967)
The Light Around the Body (1967)
Neruda and Vallejo: Selected Poems (translation, 1971)
Sleepers Joining Hands (1973)
*Friends, You Drank Some Darkness: Three Swedish Poets—Martinson, Ekelöf,
and Tranströmer* (translation, 1975)
Leaping Poetry: An Idea with Poems and Translations (anthology, 1975)
News of the Universe: Poems of Twofold Consciousness (anthology, 1980)
The Man in the Black Coat Turns (1981)
Selected Poems of Rainer Maria Rilke (translation, 1981)
The Eight Stages of Translation (1983)
Times Alone: Selected Poems of Antonio Machado (translation, 1983)
Loving a Woman in Two Worlds (1985)
Iron John: A Book About Men (1990)
The Soul Is Here for Its Own Joy: Sacred Poems from Many Cultures (anthology, 1995)
The Sibling Society (1996)
Morning Poems (1997)
Eating the Honey of Words: New and Selected Poems (1999)
The Half-Finished Heaven: The Best Poems of Tomas Tranströmer (translation, 2001)
The Night Abraham Called to the Stars (2001)
The Winged Energy of Delight: Selected Translations (translation, 2004)
My Sentence Was a Thousand Years of Joy (2005)
Talking into the Ear of a Donkey (2011)

By Tomas Tranströmer

17 Poems (1954)
Secrets on the Road (1958)
The Half-Finished Heaven (1962)
Resonance and Footprints (1966)
Night Vision (1970)
Pathways (1973)
Baltics (1974)
Truth Barriers (1978)
The Wild Market Square (1983)
For the Living and the Dead (1989)
Memories Look at Me (a prose memoir, 1993)
Grief Gondola (1996)
The Great Enigma (2004)

AIRMAIL

The Letters of Robert Bly and Tomas Tranströmer

Edited by
Thomas R. Smith

Original Swedish publication
edited by
Torbjörn Schmidt

Graywolf Press

The original Swedish publication of *Airmail: Brev 1964–1990* was compiled and edited by Torbjörn
Schmidt and published in 2001 by Albert Bonniers Förlag. Original notes and original compilation
© 2001 by Torbjörn Schmidt.

Some of the letters, as noted, originally appeared in *Ironwood* and *Poetry East*.

Letters originally written by Tomas Tranströmer in Swedish (May 27, 1964–January 30, 1970, and
brief excerpts of other letters) were translated into English by Judith Moffett and Lars-Håkan
Svensson, copyright © 2013 by Judith Moffett and Lars-Håkan Svensson. The letter dated October 1,
1966, was translated into English by Robert Bly, copyright © 2013 by Robert Bly.

All poems by Tomas Tranströmer have been translated into English by Robert Bly, except where
noted, and in most cases appear in *The Half-Finished Heaven: The Best Poems of Tomas Tranströmer,*
selected and translated from the Swedish by Robert Bly, and published in 2001 by Graywolf Press.
The poems "Conflict," "Walking Running Crawling," "Sketch in October," "C Major," "To Friends
Behind a Border," and "The Wind Shakes Caterpillars" by Tomas Tranströmer in English trans-
lation © 2013 by Robert Bly. "Twenty-Four Hours" from *Windows and Stones: Selected Poems* by
Tomas Tranströmer, translated by May Swenson with Leif Sjöberg, © 1972; all rights are controlled
by the University of Pittsburgh Press, Pittsburgh, PA 15620; used by permission of the University
of Pittsburgh Press.

Excerpts from this book appeared in the *Kenyon Review,* the *New York Times, Poetry Ireland Review,
Rowboat,* and *Tin House.*

This publication is made possible, in part, by the voters of Minnesota through a Minnesota State
Arts Board Operating Support grant, thanks to a legislative appropriation from the arts and cultural
heritage fund, and through a grant from the National Endowment for the Arts. Significant support
has also been provided by Target, the McKnight Foundation, Amazon.com, and other generous
contributions from foundations, corporations, and individuals. To these organizations and individu-
als we offer our heartfelt thanks.

ART WORKS.
arts.gov

MINNESOTA
STATE ARTS BOARD

CLEAN
WATER
LAND &
LEGACY
AMENDMENT

TARGET.

Published by Graywolf Press
250 Third Avenue North, Suite 600
Minneapolis, Minnesota 55401

www.graywolfpress.org

Published in the United States of America

Printed in Canada

ISBN 978-1-55597-639-2

2 4 6 8 9 7 5 3 1
First Graywolf Printing, 2013

Library of Congress Control Number: 2012953983

Cover design: Kyle G. Hunter
Cover drawing of Robert Bly and Tomas Tranströmer by Monica Tranströmer

Contents

Introduction

Crossways:
Pages from a Literary Friendship

The Friends

In late March 1964, a few days before his thirty-third birthday, Tomas Tranströmer, already critically recognized in Sweden for his first three books, wrote to the Sixties Press in Madison, Minnesota. Tranströmer had caught wind of Robert Bly's press in a British magazine and wanted to see for himself the American literary maverick's poetry journal *The Sixties*. Tranströmer was interested in Bly's journal not only as a reader but also as a writer and translator. In fact, he had already translated poems into Swedish by Bly's close friend and colleague James Wright.

On April 6, Carol Bly typed an initial reply, to which her husband added a note of his own, revealing an amazing and auspicious coincidence:

> Just before your first note came by accident, I went to the Univ of Minn library to get your *Halvfärdiga himlen*.

That day Bly had driven all the way across the state to obtain Tranströmer's recent volume—known in English as *The Half-Finished Heaven*—and discovered upon his return a note from its author.

If initially Tranströmer's interest lay more with Wright's poems, it soon shifted to Bly's. A single letter to Tranströmer, dated July 6, 1964, is included in Wright's selected correspondence, *A Wild Perfection*. If there are others, they remain unpublished; clearly Tranströmer's relationship with Wright, if cordial, stopped short of the intimacy of his friendship with Bly.

By May 1964, Tranströmer had translated a few of Bly's poems, to which the latter responded with obvious enthusiasm. Such was the two poets' curiosity about each other that they soon both actively discussed the possibility of meeting in person. In August Bly announced his intention to include two of his English translations of Tranströmer's poems in a Sixties Press volume, *Twenty Swedish Poets*. That project never came to fruition, though Bly eventually included Tranströmer's "Out in the Open" in the one and only issue of *The Seventies* in 1972.

In the surviving correspondence, Tranströmer's letter of September 3, 1964, marked a new stage in what was quickly becoming a working friendship, the first of many long, fascinating letters detailing the intricacies of the translation process from both sides. In less than five months' time, the friendship between Tranströmer and Bly had developed into something resembling its mature form. Their correspondence would continue for the next twenty-five years at varying degrees of intensity and frequency, until a stroke in 1990 limited Tranströmer's ability to write and speak.

Many English-speaking readers of this book know Robert Bly's labors as poet, editor, translator, social critic, and spiritual father of the men's movement. Bly grew up on a Norwegian American family farm in western Minnesota, earned a degree from Harvard, and eschewed membership in the academic establishment of his day to stake out a contrarian position as a literary outrider and independent scholar. Establishing his base of operations near the old farmstead in Madison, he introduced a generation of American readers to poets from beyond the borders of the United States, including, to mention only the Scandinavians, Swedes such as Tranströmer and Harry Martinson and Norwegians like Rolf Jacobsen and Olav H. Hauge. Bly's vehicle for promoting these and other poets was his now-legendary magazine, in its consecutive incarnations *The Fifties, The Sixties, The Seventies,* and, in one encore appearance, *The Thousands.*

Tomas Tranströmer, five years younger than Bly, was born and grew up in Stockholm. His maternal grandfather was a ship pilot, and his mother, a schoolteacher, separated early from his father. Tranströmer has written insightfully of his boyhood years in a prose memoir, *Memories Look at Me.* Eventually he became a psychologist and, at the time he first made contact with Bly, was installed with his young family on the grounds of a prison for boys at Roxtuna. Worried that Bly might be put off visiting, Tranströmer assured him on May 27, 1964, "Don't be alarmed/frightened! Visitors generally think it an idyllic setting."

A remarkable quality of the two poets' friendship is the swiftness of its evolution from casual beginnings to full-blown engagement. Some of this development, unfortunately, occurs in gaps in what we have of the correspondence. Letters from March to October of 1965 in particular are notably missing. It's evident from Bly's letter of July 8 that they have met. From a letter of July 8 to James Wright we overhear Bly's first impression of Tranströmer while traveling in Sweden:

> . . . he was very nice—what he looked like was a combination of Kierkegaard and Orrin Bly! He had Kierkegaard's long nose and inquisitive profile, and from the back looked exactly like Orrin . . . He was very touching—he knew entire poems of yours and mine by heart, and dozens & dozens of lines, which he would come up with in conversation about a tree or something. He said that *Lion's Tail & Eyes,* even the subtitle Poems About Laziness and Silence, had taught him something incredibly rare—something about *how to live.* He'd bend his head and say this in a dogged way, so I can imagine the pressures in Sweden *against* laziness and *against* silence.

It was the first of many visits in each poet's respective country.

One catches the full flavor of this exuberant, youthful stage of the relationship in Bly's letter of November 20, 1966. Bly is responding to Tranströmer's newly published *Klanger och spår (Resonance and Footprints):*

. . . the book is very good, and I'm enjoying it tremendously. As I
read in it I say, "Well, look at all the things I haven't done yet!" So
it reminds me of poems I might write sometime in the *future,* so it's
a *future* book, the kind I like best. You do some very strange things
in this book. I translated for Carolyn [Bly] your poem about walk-
ing in the woods, and evil shaking his head across a desk, and the
modern building with so much glass, and finally the airport scene.
She was startled and moved . . . The trains that meet in the (station
of this) poem come from such long distances, each of them! That is
what is good! One train still has snow on it, another one has a palm
leaf caught in the undercarriage—

Readers may recognize in the above the seed of an image for Tranströmer's
work that Bly has frequently employed, here in his introduction to *The
Half-Finished Heaven: The Best Poems of Tomas Tranströmer:*

[Tranströmer's] poems are a sort of railway station where trains
that have come enormous distances stand briefly in the same build-
ing. One train has some Russian snow on the under-carriage, and
another may have Mediterranean flowers fresh in the compartments,
and Ruhr soot on the roofs. (ix)

While accurately describing Transtömer's poems, this metaphor also
goes a long way toward defining the affinity between Bly and Transtömer.
Chief among their similarities, both poets are intuitives whose natural
speech is the image. This bond was especially important at a time when
political and academic rhetoric dominated the establishment poetry of
each poet's home country. Transtömer could be speaking for both men
when he wrote in his poem "Standing Up": "no big arm movements,
please, all rhetoric has to be left behind."

Another point of similarity is the two poets' grounding in the natural
world, Bly in the fields and lakes of western Minnesota and Transtömer
in the forests and islands of central Sweden. Both are keepers of an older
way of being on the earth in a time of runaway technological change. As

such, they are not anti-technology so much as rightly wary of change that wrenches human beings out of their ancient rootedness in the physical. Each poet may be said to stand both in the human world and in an interior realm where, as Jung said, the individual life partakes of the totality of existence, in all its mystery and grandeur. To put it another way, Bly and Tranströmer both, as the critic Charles Molesworth has remarked of Bly, write "religious meditations for a public that is no longer ostensibly religious." Interestingly, the political arena is where both poets find themselves on a collision course with the orthodoxies of their respective literary establishments, more ironic perhaps because of their essential political like-mindedness.

In his letter of October 8, 1966, for example, Bly complains that no American editor has shown the courage to publish his ferocious Vietnam War poem "Counting the Small-Boned Bodies": "The little poem is getting to be well-known, though no one will print it. The last to refuse it was the Book Section of the *Herald Tribune* and *Washington Post* this week, who had asked me for poems." For his part, Tranströmer must navigate a narrowly Marxist literary milieu in Sweden. He remarks of one disapproving review:

The whole thing culminated in an accusation that I was legitimizing the idea that "the world might be contemplated as a poem.". . . Generally speaking the young Marxists in Sweden have little tolerance for poetry. One should show decency and stop writing.
(October 29, 1966, trans. JM and L-HS)

In general, the tone taken by these two literary noncomformists strongly suggests what the psychologist Stuart Miller, in his book *Men and Friendship,* identifies as a peculiarly European component of men's friendship, the element of "complicity"—that is, a sense of being united in common purpose and sympathy against the oppressive powers of this world, which in Bly's case manifested as a stifling academic conservatism in the United States and in Tranströmer's, a puritanical Marxist correctness in Sweden.

The friendship of Bly and Tranströmer remains strong to this day despite time and the handicapping silence Tranströmer suffered as a result of his stroke. *Airmail*'s two-and-a-half-decade correspondence tracks the rich multiple threads of that relationship: literary and translation work, personal and family chronicle, political and cultural commentary, all here in abundance and given coherence by a prevailing high-spirited warmth mixed with irreverence in which neither man takes himself so seriously as to be above joking or outright foolery. As the letters unfold, we overhear the two poets inspire and translate each other, arrange reading tours and visits, gossip, and attend the milestones of each other's lives. Above it all, arching like some uncanny northern night rainbow, is a fidelity to art and a delight in the possibilities of the present moment, no matter how politically dark or unpromising it may appear. As Bly exclaims to Tranströmer on December 1, 1965, "How wonderful to be able to live in a time when something fresh can be written! There are endless fields of flowers—many of them are black flowers—on all sides."

The Letters

Viewed as a whole, the correspondence between Robert Bly and Tomas Tranströmer has its own distinct character and arc. The fast-deepening closeness of its authors is mirrored by the mounting volume of letters, reaching a peak in the first decade of the friendship; roughly two-thirds of the correspondence occurs within the first ten years and the last third spans the fifteen years remaining until Tranströmer's stroke. The single highest-volume year is 1970, when Bly and Tranströmer are clearly most energized by their reciprocal translation efforts.

The reader will notice in the letters certain defined stretches of intense concentration on translation work. In this respect, two periods of the correspondence stand out, each centering on major translation projects. The first pairs Tranströmer's volume of Bly's poems, *Krig och tystnad (War and Silence)* in 1969 with Bly's Seventies Press volume *Twenty Poems of Tomas Tranströmer* in 1970. The second pairing occurs roughly a decade later with Tranströmer's selection of Bly's prose poems *Prosadikter* *(Prose Poems)* in 1977 and Bly's translation of Tranströmer's *Truth Barriers* *(Sanningsbarriären)* in 1980.

While the first of these two great periods of translation is exploratory, with each poet learning the other's style, strengths, and weaknesses, in the second period Tranströmer and Bly give much attention to the prose poem medium, with which they are both clearly fascinated. Prose poems such as Bly's "Walking Swiftly" and "Finding the Father" and Tranströmer's "Standing Up" and "Start of a Late Autumn Novel" generate lengthy discussion. A bonus is the draft of Bly's introduction to *Prosadikter,* which to my knowledge has not been reprinted in English since its initial appearance in the May/June 1977 issue of the *American Poetry Review* as "What the Prose Poem Carries with It."

We may remember that at the time these letters were written, the legitimacy of the prose poem, especially in the United States, was by no means universally secured. Today that controversy is mostly a thing of the past, with the prose poem generally acknowledged as "real" poetry. Eventually both poets' interest in the prose poem wanes, though form is still a major topic of discussion. In the 1980s Bly recasts some of his prose poems in complicated stanzas reminiscent of Marianne Moore's ("I am veering back toward form, now," he writes on February 16, 1980, "with a new view of it, supported partly by my amateur researches on sound"), while Tranströmer makes a limited return to the Sapphics of his work in the 1950s ("We will both end up as neo-classicists!!" he exclaims on June 29, 1982).

One of the more fascinating extraliterary features of the correspondence is the discussion of current affairs—American, Swedish, and international— that emerges as a constant in the letters almost from the beginning. These are, of course, the years of the Vietnam War, in which Bly is instrumental in organizing protest readings under the aegis of the American Writers Against the Vietnam War. Tranströmer's grasp of American politics as displayed in the correspondence is extraordinary and humbling when compared with the insularity of most Americans. Of the assassination of Robert F. Kennedy, he observes:

Right after things like that I'm so full of rage and resignation that
poetry becomes impossible . . . to write is to go into reality itself,
where the gunsmoke still lingers. Otherwise I was rather skepti-
cal about Robert Kennedy, terribly split. I'll never know what he
really stood for. Maybe he was very good. But I've put all my eggs,
my American eggs, in McCarthy's basket. Maybe I should also let
Lindsay take an egg. (June 6, 1968, trans. JM and L-HS)

Such examples make clear that a major element in the friendship of
Tranströmer and Bly is an absorbing interest in politics and society as
viewed through the lens of psychology, however speculative that psychol-
ogy may be (especially in Bly's Jungianism, from which Tranströmer stands
at an evident remove). A representative instance of Bly's psychopolitical
speculation on the Vietnam War occurs in his letter of January 14, 1966:

People are wrong though when they think this is the first battle
of World War III—it is the last battle of World War II. The white
race feels guilty and wants to waste now all the riches it took from
the Orient, and if it can do so and at the same time kill large num-
bers of yellow people, so much the better. We are determined to
disgrace ourselves, and nothing will stop us. We are doing it in-
stead of the Europeans for them. The Europeans have disgraced
themselves so much, they are satisfied now. But we still hunger for
disgrace—we howl for it.

We recognize here the psychological dynamic underlying Bly's antiwar
masterpiece "The Teeth Mother Naked at Last." That Tranströmer, by
temperament calmer and less prone to exaggeration than Bly, is willing to
abide Bly's more hyperbolic manner augurs well for their friendship's re-
siliency and longevity.

Thus on one level Airmail serves as a vibrant chronicle of a tumultu-
ous time in U.S. and world history. Bly's running account of his partici-
pation in antiwar activities provides a window into the historical moment

when many American readers first awoke to Bly's defiant eloquence. Bly's December 27, 1967, anecdote of the aftermath of an antidraft demonstration in New York delights in the rebellious high spirits that informed protests of that era:

> Galway Kinnell, Mitch Goodman (Denise Levertov's husband) and I were hauled away with Dr. Spock. We went with Spock first under the barricades (no good) over (no good) around—that worked—and we were all hauled off to jail in the same wagon. Once at the Criminal Courts Building, we were processed, etc. and then tossed in a cell—who should be there but Allen Ginsberg! There were 10 or 12 18 and 19 year old kids in the cell too. When Galway and I came in, they said, Now all the poets are here! Let's have a poetry reading! So we did, and sang mantras with Allen for a while, Allen had brought his Hindu bells to jail with him, and we all had a great time, singing and chanting.

If Tranströmer keeps more distance from the front lines of protest, he maintains a passionate critical involvement with the war and the social turmoil it has engendered in America and elsewhere. His letter of September 2, 1968, gives us a less filtered glimpse of the Soviet invasion of Czechoslovakia than was then available to most U.S. observers:

> I've spent a great part of the past 24 hours in front of the TV and seen tanks roll by from morning till night. I've been able to follow the Czechoslovakian drama from hour to hour—it has made an enormous impression here—I doubt whether you in the U.S. have experienced the events more than 25% of what the Europeans have experienced. Honorable leftists of Sonnevi's type must be having a very hard time. Communists loyal to the party have solved the problem in a radical way by wholeheartedly condemning what's happening—Hermansson, the party leader, requested that we recall our ambassador to the Soviet Union! (No other party has requested that.)

Humor and politics frequently intersect, as in Tranströmer's creative and perhap only half-jesting suggestion of August 22, 1974:

> putting [Nixon] in jail would be too easy a way to get rid of the really sad fact: that the fellow was elected by YOU, the People, by a landslide victory. I think everyone who voted for him should go to jail for three minutes (of silence) instead.

Wit serves throughout the correspondence as a leavening agent. One can't help smiling when Tranströmer (referring to Bly's penchant for designating an easy matter as "duck soup") wryly signs off as "Duck Soup Tommy." Likewise, Bly, after indulging in predictions on the Watergate scandal, dubs himself "The Jeane Dixon of Madison."

Occasional playful jibes in the correspondence over which man would—or wouldn't—win the Nobel Prize ring presciently now. On December 10, 1975, Tomas writes an acerbic account of the Italian poet Eugenio Montale's Nobel ceremony. Maybe, Tomas suggests, Robert will get one when he's eighty.

At times humor masks the inevitable tensions of a long-term relationship. On January 4, 1970, Tranströmer flatly advises Bly to "give up astrology!" Tranströmer's apologetic tone after a 1972 visit suggests a residual strain:

> Sorry to cause harm to your car—how are the brakes now? Better? As soon as I step into your car something happens . . . This was the main reason for not riding one of your beautiful horses, I was afraid to make it lame or something. Good that I did not burn down the chicken house.

For his part, on March 12, 1974, Bly half-comically apologizes for what one gathers was an especially talk-heavy visit:

> After you left, I laughed and laughed to think of all the Jungian fanaticism you had been subjected to in just two or three days . . . At

least half of what I said was absurd, so please do forgive me, forgive all of us—the Sitting Bulls of psychology.

Among the more touching passages of the correspondence are those reflecting the intimate details of the poets' lives, a family illness, the death of a relative, the birth of a child. After the birth of the Blys' son Micah, the proud father writes:

> We'd like you and Monica to be the new baby's godparents, by the way! Yes, we do! We would baptize him, if you agree, while you're here in October, and Monica can be a godparent *in absentia*. Your physical duties would be light, and, spiritually, all you'd have to do is bless him every once in a while. We'd love it if you'd both agree. (May 30, 1971)

In June, the willing godfather reports:

> Monica dreamt the other night that she (as nurse) was called to a woman to help her deliver a child. When she looked into the womb of that woman she found a deep, wide tunnel where a little boy was sitting, serious, waiting. He seemed to be between 6 months and 1 year old. Monica lifted him out but it was impossible to do the usual things you do with newborn babies with him—he seemed too grown-up. He had a very clever look. When she woke up her first association was with your new baby. Congratulations from all parts of us: ego, superego and id.

Friendships have their rhythms and seasons, fat times and lean times. By the late 1970s we notice a decrease of frequency in the exchange of letters; by the early 1980s the era of intensive translation is over. There is less literary substance in the final decade of the correspondence, evident in the proliferation of newsy travel reports and relative paucity of discussion of poems. Tellingly, when Tranströmer's book *Det vilda torget (The Wild Market Square)* appears in 1983, there is no Bly translation. By the late

1980s, the letters are dominated by talk of family and the comings and go-
ings of the two by-now celebrated poets, with fewer glimpses into the inner
workings of their poems. In a real sense, Bly and Tranströmer themselves
have *become* family, prone also to the silences and lacunae of family relation-
ships. Later in the 1990s, Bly will stunningly render the greatest poems in
Tranströmer's last pre-stroke volume, *För levande och döda (For the Living
and the Dead)*, for inclusion in *The Half-Finished Heaven*. "Romanesque
Arches," mentioned in Bly's letter of May 3, 1989, appears to be the last
poem of Tranströmer's he translated before the stroke. Tranströmer's ap-
preciative response on May 14 is worth noting:

> . . . your translation of "Romanska bågar" seems to have the right
> tone. You are probably the only one among my—now rather
> numerous—translators who has the right feeling for this poem
> that embarrasses certain readers and makes others happy.

This is hardly the first time Tranströmer has remarked on Bly's ability
to reconsititute from the Swedish original a successful poem in English. On
February 13, 1974, Tranströmer pays Bly a translator's supreme compliment:

> The good thing with your translations is that I always meet again
> the original emotion I felt just when the poem started. Other trans-
> lators give a (pale) reproduction of the finished poem but you bring
> me back to the original experience.

No doubt Bly's translations have been a major factor in establishing a
wide American readership for Tranströmer's poems, just as Bly has played
no small part in raising Tranströmer's profile internationally, not escap-
ing the notice of the Nobel Prize committee. Christopher Benfey wrote
in the *New Republic:* "For me, a Nobel for Tranströmer, well deserved, is
also a Nobel for his close friend, translator, and collaborator Robert Bly."
As for Tranströmer's translation of Bly's poems and their effect on
Swedish and Scandinavian audiences, we can infer much from Tranströmer's
anecdote on August 11, 1970:

In a small town where I gave a reading, one schoolboy from the audience suddenly went up and read aloud from your (mistranslated) introduction to *[Krig och tystnad]* and asked me about my reaction to your ideas. It was very strange to hear him start: "The great American poet Robert Bly has said that . . . etc." It was in Karlskrona, in Blekinge. The therapeutic influence comes mainly from the honest and sensible effort to bring the inner and the outer worlds together—people are hungry for crossways now.

This hunger for "crossways" on the part of both American and Swedish readers is also the engine that has driven the friendship and collaboration of Bly and Tranströmer and given us these remarkable letters. Though banked lower, the fire of that friendship has never gone out. Bly's enthusiastic response to *For the Living and the Dead* hints tantalizingly that had Tranströmer not suffered his stroke, more mutual translation work might well have lain ahead. One can't mistake the plaintive note in the final letter of the correspondence (dated April–May 1990). "Dear master and buddy," Tranströmer begins his last message to Bly, "why do I always have to write other people than you?"

The Book

In the the late 1990s, the Swedish scholar and author Torbjörn Schmidt began the labor of gathering and sorting the correspondence of Tomas Tranströmer and Robert Bly for what became, in 2001, the original Swedish publication of *Airmail*. Working as Bly's assistant, I was partner to the process, typing and cataloging both Bly's and Tranströmer's letters for our files. To the surprise, I think, of all concerned, *Airmail* became something of a best seller in Sweden. I remember Bly's astonishment as he waved a half-inch-thick sheaf of reviews that had just arrived from Bonniers, the Swedish publisher. "We need to do an American edition," he declared. I gladly accepted the job of editing a collection geared toward readers of English.

Innocent of Swedish, I could avail myself only indirectly of Schmidt's text; however, he proved an invaluable source of information throughout that initial editing pass. I spent a whole summer pleasurably immersed in the original documents, assembling a selection somewhat different from Schmidt's, made even more capacious by virtue of a large cache of letters discovered after the Swedish edition had gone to press. In the end, this selection is my own work, reflective of my knowledge of its authors and my judgment of what does or doesn't fit. The original Swedish volume contains 199 letters—this current version adds close to a hundred "new" letters, twenty or so of which were subsequently included in a Danish edition Schmidt enlarged in 2007. The present volume also includes several previously unpublished Bly translations of Tranströmer's poems, some of them newly completed for this edition. One poem, "Conflict," which I discovered recently in Bly's files, makes its very first appearance in any form in these pages; it is a true find.

I was able to edit this book successfully in large part because, amazingly, Tranströmer had written all but the first three dozen of his letters in English. Bly commissioned translations of most of the Swedish originals by Judith Moffett with the assistance of Lars-Håkan Svensson, translator of the Swedish *Airmail*. Interestingly, since the bulk of the correspondence was written in English, this new version of *Airmail* is closest to the original source documents. I have edited Tranströmer's English very lightly, correcting only obvious mistakes and leaving intact the general flavor of his prose so that you may enjoy these letters as Bly first did.

This new version of *Airmail* also is distinguished by being the first substantial publication in English of any of Bly's voluminous personal correspondence. That makes this book even more revelatory, exhibiting a side of Bly that even his most devoted readers may not know well.

By the end of that first summer's editing, I had a typescript of over 550 pages. My omissions were mostly of routine notes and repetitive lists, itineraries, and so on. I also left out some material that obstructed the main narrative flow and could have confused the reader by referring to lost pieces of the correspondence. This may not be the most scholarly approach, but then this book is not only for academics, though it will certainly be of great use to them. I cared most about the readability of the conversation for the general reader with a lively interest in the multiple themes that give the dialogue between Bly and Tranströmer its unique character. The source documents or copies of them will be available to scholars and researchers for further study in Bly's archive at the Elmer L. Andersen Library on the University of Minnesota campus in Minneapolis.

After I had completed my preliminary edit, the manuscript of this chronicle of intelligent, generative, energetic, and irreverent friendship loitered for nearly a decade in my file cabinet, no doubt because of its highly uncommercial nature. But winds do change. On October 6, 2011, came the announcement that Tomas Tranströmer had at last won the Nobel Prize in Literature, the first time the Swedes had seen fit to so honor one of their own since Harry Martinson's Nobel in 1974. That long-rumored and supremely deserved Nobel Prize has sparked a welcome renewal of interest in Tranströmer's work in the United States. Long in coming but worth the wait, the volume you now hold in your hands is a happy result.

—Thomas R. Smith

A Note on the Translations and Their Presentation

All of Tomas Tranströmer's letters after April 18, 1971, were originally written in English. Three earlier letters, on August 8, 1968, June 14, 1969, and November 17, 1969, are Tranströmer's first English letters to Robert Bly. Tranströmer's letter of October 1, 1966, is translated by Bly. The rest of Tranströmer's Swedish letters are translated by Judith Moffett and Lars-Håkan Svensson. They are as follows:

May 27, 1964; September 3, 1964; March 23, 1965; October 30, 1965; December 10, 1965; January 30, 1966; March 1, 1966; April 10, 1966; April 20, 1966; June 4, 1966; July 20, 1966; September (undated), 1966; October 29, 1966; January 7, 1967; January 15, 1967; March 4, 1967; May 4, 1967; July 11, 1967; August 8, 1967; September 30, 1967; October 7, 1967; December 8, 1967; February 19, 1968; April 19, 1968; June 9, 1968; July 12, 1968; September 2, 1968; December 10, 1968; January 8, 1969; January 18, 1969; May 18, 1969; July 30, 1969; January 4, 1970; January 30, 1970 (latter section beginning "And there is a boat" originally in English); October 27, 1970.

All poem translations are by Robert Bly except as noted. Poems in Tranströmer's letters of April 2, 1971, and April 18, 1971, are translated by May Swenson.

Frequently, in his early letters in Swedish, Tranströmer employed scattered English words and phrases. We were not able to indicate these occurrences of English without disrupting the flow of text, so suffice it to say that, before he began writing to Bly entirely in his friend's language, he had already made many tentative gestures in that direction. Where either poet has used all caps for emphasis, we have retained that feature in our text.

Where occasional excisions have been made by either Bly or Tranströmer in the interest of privacy, I have indicated discontinuities in the text with brackets enclosing dashes. They are not many, and the vast majority of the letters are included in full.

Finally, I have not reproduced many poems referred to in the text that can be easily found in either *The Half-Finished Heaven: The Best Poems of Tomas Tranströmer* or in Bly's own volumes. Several of the poems and translations that have been included are unpublished, unknown, or making their first appearances in this book. I have done my best to match these poems with their original letters. In a very few cases, I have appended poems that merited much discussion in the correspondence. Likewise, I have appended two letters postdating the correspondence that enrich our view of the enduring friendship of Robert Bly and Tomas Tranströmer.

Editor's Acknowledgment

Many individuals have contributed to the making of this book, and some I have thanked elsewhere in these pages. I acknowledge again original editor Torbjörn Schmidt's groundbreaking labor. I would also like to acknowledge the translators of Tomas Tranströmer's early letters, Judith Moffett and Lars-Håkan Svensson. Judy and I, in consultation with Lars-Håkan, were a team of literary detectives, exchanging hundreds of e-mails on these translations-in-progress over the years; it's more than satisfying to see the often puzzled-over, sometimes fretted-over results brought so conclusively to realization. Mary Byers, copy-editor extraordinaire, assisted vastly in enhancing the clarity and continuity of this book. I'm thankful for the intelligent guidance I received from the Graywolf crew, especially associate publisher Katie Dublinski and Jeffrey Shotts, my editor. At times my discoveries along the way (such as the "lost" Tranströmer poem "Conflict" buried in Bly's files) made me feel like an amateur astronomer who has identified a new comet. Jeff Shotts's enthusiasm for those discoveries buoyed me every step of the way, and helped make the challenges of *Airmail* more joy to be relished than hurdle to be surmounted. Gratitude to Ruth Bly and Monica Tranströmer for unfailingly good-natured support over the past years. Thanks to my wife, Krista Spieler, for wholeheartedly cheering on a decade-long effort that for months at a time annexed our dining room to my study. Finally I thank Robert Bly and Tomas Tranströmer a hundred times over for their poems and translations, around which have grown a body of correspondence as readable, engaging, and entertaining as a good biography.

AIRMAIL

The Letters of Robert Bly and Tomas Tranströmer

1964

April 6, 1964

Dear Herr Tranströmer,

We are sending you *Vallejo* and *Lion's Tail & Eyes* under separate cover—and we'll send *Forty Poems Touching on Recent American History* as published.

No, *The Sixties* magazine is not dead. (It will never die.) #6 is the most recent issue, though. Our printer in Ireland says he will have #7 to our subscribers in about 3 weeks.

Thanks again for all your orders with us.

Yours sincerely,
C. Bly

[on same page]

Dear Mr. Tranströmer,

The air rate was so ungodly high we sent *The Sixties* by boat, as we did these. I have been enjoying your poems. Just before your first note came by accident, I went to the Univ of Minn library to get your *Halvfärdiga himlen*. Jim Wright showed me your letter mentioning that you had translated a couple of his poems. That was very kind, and you chose excellent poems. I do read Swedish, and if you'd like to send a copy of the translations to me—I'd love to see them in the first place, and will check them for any mistakes that have crept in, in the second.

Our address from April 20th to August 20th will be

Robert Bly

Mill End

Thaxted

Essex, England.

I'm going to send you from England a translation of your "Paret," which I did a few weeks ago.

Best wishes,

Robert Bly

15 May, '64

Dear Tomas Tranströmer,

Thank you for your letter, and for the translations! I must say I think the translations are excellent. I have no suggestions whatever. You have two of the best poems of J. Wright's book in the Eisenhower poem, and the "I dag var jag so lycklig, etc." Another one I think is awfully good is "The Undermining of the Defense Economy."

As for my own book, my favorite there is "Snöfall på eftermiddagen"!

I am very surprised at how natural the lines sound in Swedish, at least in your Swedish.

I hope that we can meet sometime this summer, fall, or winter. I will be here (in Europe) for a year all told. Until July or August, in England, then perhaps 3 months in Norway followed by three or four months in France. Surely sometime during the time in Norway I will skip over the border! For your part, if you plan to be in England or elsewhere, you are very welcome at our house (wherever it may happen to be!)

I see lots of people translating and studying Charles Olson now. It's part of the widespread suicidal impulse visible in all parts of the world at the present. It's like parsing Latin, also, remarkably good for penance! There isn't much in the *Allen* anthology except Gary Snyder, Robert Creeley, and Denise Levertov. Those three are genuine. Ginsberg is very intelligent, but considerably less a poet than someone like Snyder. The rest of the people are nightmarish. The Allen anthology, by the way, is the one J. Wright had in mind—he had been asked to review it—in the poem on page 36 of the *Branch*, "Depressed by a Book of Bad Poetry, etc."

Here follows a version of your poem "Paret." You may find all sorts of mistakes here. The phrase "Sedan lyftas" I am most unsure about.

The Couple

They snap the light off, and its white globe glows
an instant and then dissolves, like a tablet
in a glass of darkness. Now a rising.
The hotel walls shoot up into the heavenly darkness.

Their love movements grow softer, and they sleep,
but their most secret thoughts go on meeting
like two colors that meet and run together
on the white paper in a schoolboy's watercolor.

It is dark and silent. The city however has come nearer
in the night. With its closed off windows. Houses arrive.
They stand in crowded expectation considerably nearer,
a mob of people with expressionless faces.

All good wishes—
Robert Bly

Roxtuna 27-5-64

Dear Robert Bly,

good to hear that you approve my translations! Still better that you are to visit Norway-Sweden fairly soon. Thinking about your visit, I was suddenly filled with enthusiasm. We have a large house by Swedish standards (5 rooms, bungalow) and you are welcome to stay with us. The summer will be difficult—we are expecting a baby in July and have one child already, my wife has been ill and we will have to hire some sort of help during the first months—but by September things ought to be normal again and a guest room should then be available. We are in the country here, though the situation is somewhat special—in point of fact, it's a prison. I work as a psychologist in a facility for disturbed criminal youth, and the bungalow comes with the position. Don't be alarmed/frightened! Visitors generally think it an idyllic setting. It is located right outside Linköping, 22 Swedish miles south of Stockholm, near the main road between Malmö and Stockholm. A convenient place to spend the night when driving from Stockholm to Malmö or vice versa. Or you can take the train and get off at Linköping, and I can pick you up at the station. So you'll be able to recognize me, I will be wearing a green tail-coat, a false beard, and a straw hat, and reading Nixon's autobiography. Or perhaps some simpler arrangement could be found.

[Editor's note: The rest of this letter is missing.]

25 Aug, 64

Dear Tomas Tranströmer,

I would like some advice from you. I have been thinking of doing a little book for the Sixties Press called "Twenty Swedish Poems." This is roughly my plan so far:

Pär Lagerkvist—"In i mitt hjärtas blodiga hamn"
Karin Boye—Stenarna (Gud hade givit oss tunga själar av sten)
Harry Martinson:—Havsvinden
                  Cotton
                  perhaps one more
Gunnar Ekelöf—Tionfo della Morte (Tre riddare stego ut)
               Monolog med dess hustru
               (Tag två extra gamla, etc.)
               Etudes (I) (Natt och stiltje)

Etudes (III) (En varld ar varje manniska)
Svanen (I) (Jag hörde vildgässs over sujkhuset)
perhaps also an early one such as "blommorna
sover"
Artur Lundkvist—from Freud
Eric Lindegren—Mannen Uten Vag #XXIX (I have doubts on this:
I dislike Lindegren)
Karl Vennberg—We have all done our best
Werner Aspenström—På kyrkogården
one more
Tomas Tranströmer—Paret
one more

Now I would like to have you just comment on this list. Where are the holes? Have I left out anyone extremely important or good? Do you think Lindegren should be included at all? Do you have any suggestions for the third Martinson poem I might include, or the second Aspenstrom? How about the younger ones? Is Eddegren good? I have never read a poem of his, but I hear him mentioned often. I'm most interested to see what you'll say about this plan!

Thank you very much for your last good letter, and forgive my long delay in answering it! Somehow I thought I had already answered it, and was astonished to see it still about. I'm bad on answering anyway. I finally wrote a little poem on it.

Unanswered Letters

Strips of August sun come in through shutters.
Baskets of unanswered letters lie on chairs.
Some foolish man must live here.

[------]
Has your new daughter come yet?!! Or son! We have two small daughters, one Mary, about 2½ (there is a poem about her in Jim Wright's book) and a new one, Bridget, about 1¼. Do tell me how it all turned out! I

will definitely come to see you some time this year. We'll be here another month, and then we go either to Paris for three months, or Oslo for three months (we'll go both places, but the order isn't decided yet). So I do want to know when you will be *leaving* for the United States. How long will you be in that strange Goldwater-ridden nation? Is your family going along?

There is not much to say about James Wright. As he said on the dust jacket of his *Saint Judas,* he has led a "bookish, uneventful" life. Of course that's a lie, but anyway. He was born in Martins Ferry, Ohio, a steel-plant area, not far from where W. S. Merwin, Kenneth Patchen, and Jonathan Winters (our best comic for thirty years) was born. He makes his living as an English teacher (particularly of Dickens) in the colleges and universities, and absolutely refuses to teach any "creative writing" or poetry writing courses. He has refused several offers of "poet in residence" positions, when it involved such teaching; always to the astonishment of the department heads. He is married, and now divorced, with two sons. He has a wild streak in him that makes him a very ambiguous, even frightening, figure in the eyes of the academics. The reason for that uneasiness in their eyes is this: he went to Kenyon College (where John Crowe Ransom was) on a scholarship, and thereby escaped from the steelmill town. Later he took a Ph.D. at the University of Washington where Theodore Roethke was. He began writing poems in the accepted, iambic, traditional manner, which was everywhere in the 1950's, and by many such people was considered the very best in the country in this traditional sort of poetry. Suddenly he renounced the whole thing, and began to write an utterly different sort of poetry, made of mingled streams of savagery and tranquillity. This upset the academic poets considerably, and they still haven't recovered.

[-----]

I hope all is well with you! I have written to Bonniers for your books (the one I was reading belonged to the Univ. of Minn library, and I don't have it here in Europe with me), and so I hope to send you a new translation of one of your poems soon.

with very best wishes,
Robert

3-9-64

Dear Robert Bly,

Thanks for your very welcome letter, and for the poems! I'd better reply right away before three months have suddenly gone by. Naturally I too have begun to write a poem about unanswered letters (with the title "Not to Worry, I'll Write Soon")—it's the insidious old telepathy at work again. But the poem never did come out anywhere; the lines I want to keep were about something completely different, namely the snails that sail forth so majestically in the August night.

For the moment I find myself in a lovely and unaccustomed position. I started my vacation yesterday. I've dreamed about that vacation so much that I'd begun to believe it would never come. I'm the only one of the so-called higher officials who hasn't been away from the INSTITUTION this summer, I've had to sit here "for the sake of continuity." And this institution has resembled Cyprus. Accordingly I haven't had the time or strength to write anything. And just when it looked as if I could, the editor of a collection of Auden's poetry called and barked like a watchdog because I haven't delivered any of the translations of Auden I promised. At night the baby cries. Yes! THE BABY CRIES. It went well, happily. Paula was born in the hospital at Linköping at the beginning of July and was entirely as she should be, despite all the damned uterine complications. It turned out to be a lightning-fast birth that had already started in the car. Twenty minutes after we got to the hospital the baby was born. So it was a happy summer in spite of everything.

I've taken my Saab out of the stable and driven to Kolmården to be alone for a couple of days and have time to catch up with myself. (Kolmården is a woodsy tract between Ostergötland and Södermanland.) I'm sitting in an inn, writing this.

You put some questions in your letter. I think you should let go of the ambition to do some sort of complete Swedish anthology. If you call a book "20 SWEDISH POEMS" you've only promised to display exactly 20 SWEDISH POEMS: twenty Swedish poems which I, Robert Bly, have found and which I think are so good that I want to translate them. How one can translate a poem one dislikes I don't know. Let it be *your* anthology. It's not possible anyway to give a representative picture of twentieth-century Swedish poetry in twenty poems. Gullberg should be included for example: he rhymes and seems almost impossible to translate. Eddegren isn't a big name here, but if you think he's good then translate him. Martinson should suit you and there's an endless number of poems to choose among. Come over soon and we'll go through several kilos of poems. I probably like Martinson best of all the Swedish poets now living. It's hard to say how much of his greatness lies in linguistic nuances that can't be translated. But a poet from Minnesota ought to have a decent chance.

Some of your comments about my translation of "Snowfall" etc. arise from a groundless apprehension. PÅ SJON means "at sea" or "on the sea" ["på havet"] in everyday Swedish. That last phrase sounds "literary" and not entirely natural. It's like this: SJO sometimes means lake, sometimes sea. If you say "en sjö" it always refers to a lake. If you say "sjön" it can also mean the ocean, particularly in such expressions as "på sjön" or "till sjöss" (cf. Eng. sea). Ordinary people, pilots and fishermen for example, don't use the word "sea" ["hav"] at all. You should bear this in mind when you read Swedish texts.

STRÅNA is an awkward, powerful word, entirely in the same class as CORNSTALKS. No, I don't want to use "majsstänglarna" [corn + stalks] by reason of the fact that it brings an element of exoticism into (the Swedish) poem. Majs [corn] is something the Swedish reader has seen Disney's cartoon characters gnawing on or possibly gnawed on themselves from tin cans. What makes translating SNOWFALL so worthwhile is that the poem will strike Swedes as completely natural—a good reader knows right away that this isn't an interesting exotic product by some American but I have experienced this mystery for myself.

BLEKNAR BORT means, exactly, FADE AWAY. If you like we can write TONAR BORT but that sounds a little bit "literary." But I think it's unnecessary. One must have a certain faith in the public's gifts of comprehension.

FARTYG [ship] should perhaps be changed. Not to "stomme" [framework], which God forbid, but to SKROV [hull], maybe FARTYGSSKROV [ship + hull].

I'll translate some more of your poems, at least 4–5. Preferably more. I hope in fact that Bonniers (our great, omnipotent publisher) will bring out an American anthology sooner or later—it's time to be able to read Lowell, William Carlos Williams, Bly, Wright, Wilbur, Levertov and probably some others in a plump selection. Simpson disappointed me a little with his latest book, despite several good pieces. "Redwoods," which would be right up my alley, won't work because of the tree itself, which is wholly exotic (cf. my argument above).

To thank you for the three poems (of which especially "Watching Television" gets me going) I'm sending you three unpublished ones of mine. "About History" is probably to some extent influenced by my work with "the poetry of the Sixties." An attempt to write speechlines, non-rhetorical ones, and not to flinch from the political, the historical. The problem has occupied me for a long time: to write about the reality of the events surrounding us without falling into the dreary rhetorical tradition that possesses even good poets the instant they touch on anything political. They drape themselves in an attitude instead of giving form to things. It's not just a question of taste. Rhetorical attitudes are treason.

Are you coming here before or after the presidential election? That's going to be a terrible night. I mean, it's not enough that Johnson will win, he has to win by a landslide. The ghosts must be decisively defeated. I read with nervousness and astonishment in *Newsweek* a fairly thorough overview of the situation in state after state. Wyoming for instance is considered "SAFE" for Barry. It's said of some other state (Maine, I think) that people there have always been Republicans and they'll go right on being Republicans even if they're against the current candidate. That's what's so incomprehensible to a European. The same men who would have voted for Nelson Rockefeller if he were the candidate, are now working and voting for Goldwater. What is a Republican? What is a Democrat? This is the secret motive for my visit to the U.S.—to try to comprehend such things. My translators (especially Eric Sellin) are organizing a few readings for me as well so that I'll be able to earn my keep (at the university and the YMCA, no, sorry, it was the YMHA). I leave around April 1.

Once again, come and visit Sweden! Monica, Marie and Paula send greetings.

Your pen pal
Tomas T.

23 Oct., '64
50 Rue Jacob
Paris 60

Dear Tomas,

Nå, her er vi alle i Paris! Kan man tenke om en så rar ting! We've been traveling about a bit, having fled from England, like the Hebrews in the dead of the night from Babylonia, and are now settled in an apartment in Paris, recovering on croissants.

Thank you for your fine letter and for the exciting poems! Let me take up several questions in your letter in order—first, I am glad to hear that Paula has come prancing into this world, and is well, even though she cries a bit at night. It is also grand that you have some time off—how long will your vacation be? All the time until April?

Thank you also for encouraging me to go forward enthusiastically with Martinson in my little 20 Swedish Poems, and to read a bit in Gullberg. You are right, one shouldn't worry about covering the ground—just fall on favorite treetops, like some mad snow!

As I expected, the comments on your translation of Snowfall were all nonsense! It is a magnificent translation—I can sense the same *feeling* in it—and the details brought up only show how little someone brought up in one language can know of another. I will mention details like this from time to time on other poems, I expect, but don't even bother to answer them. Just look at them with one eye, like a bird. Only you can judge these things—all I can do is talk—look at them with one eye, and throw them away.

Oh Goldwater is finished! Don't worry about that! His secret is that he never wanted to be president. It is all turning out exactly as he wished. That's why he makes so many odd blunders. (That, and the fact he has the I.Q. (intelligence) of a fairly good football player.)

The Goldwater *backers* are the ambitious ones. Unfortunately their intelligence is not too strong either, proved by their choice of a man so clearly self-destructive. The best description I have seen of the group of people backing Goldwater, by the way, is the description of the "revolted masses" in Ortega y Gasset's *The Revolt of the Masses.* What Ortega thought was a characteristic of a certain part of the *lower classes* (insistence on self, contempt of civilization) has unexpectedly turned up in America in the *middle classes.*

What a fine book that *Revolt of the Masses* is! One of the best books I've read for years. Another man I admire greatly is Groddeck. Has he been translated into Swedish?

I must ring off now, as the English say, take off in a cloud of camel dust, as the Americans say, declare Adieu! I've enjoyed very much the poems you sent. That newspaper out in the weather, on the way to becoming a plant, is wonderful!

Do write—your pen pal francais
Roberto de Rue Jacob

1965

18 March, 65

Dear Tomas,

Oh I'm happy! I have nearly finished my new book! I've been work-
ing on it for several years, and the last months have worked like a North
Dakota farmer, till late at night. Now that is over, and I am ready to travel,
and talk, and here you are, going off to America! I think you said you are
leaving about the first of April.

However, our schedule is a little clearer now. We'll be here in Paris
until May 1st, then in May I'm going to pile the whole family in a car,
and go down to Italy for a month. Then in early June we come up, back
through Paris, and on up to Sweden to see you!

Actually, we will be staying first at Bettna, with our old friend, Christina
(Bratt) Paulston (her first husband was William Duffy, with whom I
started *The Sixties*). She is Swedish and will be at Bettna in the summer
with her family. I could therefore pop up to Roxtuna alone to see you, or
I can bring my family along. We'll let that go until we see how everything
looks at the time.

Now, suppose you aren't back from America in June! Then we'll post-
pone the Swedish trip until July. So let me know how your plans look.

Even though I've been writing on poems, I've also been translating yours! I enjoyed *Hemligheter på vägen* very much, and have translated several there, "Efter Anfall" and "The Man Awakened by a Song Above His Roof" among them. I'm enclosing a first draft of "Efter Anfall" here. I've decided to restrict the TWENTY SWEDISH POEMS to Harry Martinson, Gunnar Ekelöf, and yourself. So each will have about 7 poems.

I have translated 7 of yours already, and I've been trying to get them done so you could take them along with you to the U.S.! I should have them done in a week or so—just have tiny details left—so if you let me know when you're leaving, I will get them up to you.

Meanwhile I want to give you the address of Christina (Bratt) Paulston in New York. You must look her up. She will be at your reading, I'm sure, but if you are in New York for any time at all before the reading, call her, and she'll invite you for dinner, no doubt. She is taking some graduate work in education at Columbia, and lives not too far from where your reading will be at the YMHA. Chris (married to a man named Roland Paulston) lives at 512 West 122nd Street, Apt. 102. The telephone is UN 4-6000, Extension 742. (It's an extension because it is a building owned by Columbia University.) During the day she works at the Asian library, and her number there is UN 5-4000, Extension 2087.

She often says that she hasn't an ounce of poetic feeling in her, though she has more than she lays claim to. At any rate, I think you'll enjoy seeing her.

Your translations of "Laziness and Silence" and "Driving to Town Late to Mail a Letter" are very beautiful! They sound as though they were written in Swedish!

And I could see from *Heligheter* that this mole is an old friend of yours! John Haines now also has a poem with a winged mole in it! We should gather all these mole poems.

So I will stop now, and hope that you will write me back right away, telling me—when you leave, how long you'll be gone, and *where* you are going in the U.S.! There are poets scattered all over the U.S., like magic seed, an especially heavy grouping out in the West, where James Dickey is now, at San Fernando College in California, and Louis Simpson at Berkeley.

Yours always,
Robert
50 Rue Jacob
Paris 6°

First draft only

After the Attack

The sick boy,
Locked in a vision
with tongue stiff as a board.

He sits with his back toward a painting of a wheatfield.
The bandage around his jaw reminds one of embalmers.
His glassy eyes are thick as a diver's. Nothing has any answer
and is grave like a telephone ringing in the night.

But the painting there. It is a landscape that makes one feel peaceful
 even though the wheat is a golden storm.
Blue, fiery blue sky and driving clouds. Underneath in the yellow
 waves
some white shirts are sailing: threshers—they cast no shadows.

At the far end of the field a man seems to be looking this way.
A broad hat leaves his face in shadow.
He has evidently noticed the dark shape in the room here, maybe
 to help.

Invisibly the painting begins to stretch and open behind the man
    who is sick
and sunk in himself. It throws sparks and makes noise. Every
    wheathead throws off light as if to wake him up!
The other man—in the wheat—makes a sign.

He has come nearer.
No one notices it.

3-23-65
Dear Robert,

How pleased I was to hear from you! We'll meet in June, then;
Bettna is only an hour and a half by car from Roxtuna. It's a beautiful first
draft! Just a few details: "glassy eyes"—the boy is wearing glasses, it's the
same as briller in Norwegian; in other words EYEGLASSES → 👓
"He has evidently noticed" etc. I would prefer "He seems to look at
the dark shape" or something similar—you give an interpretation where
my line gives a description only. In the next line "INVISIBLY" might
make for a contradiction later, when the thing in the picture actually
starts moving in a visible way. The seed of this contradiction is already
present in the Swedish text. I am now inclined to change "impercep-
tibly" ["omärkligt"] to "slowly" ["långsamt"] or something of the sort. Or
take it out completely? —In the last line "NO ONE NOTICES IT" is
hard for me to pronounce NO-TI-TICI-CIT-CISS-ITS CIT. Can we
make it shorter, like a lock clicking shut? And can we strike "it"? I'm
very eager to read your translation at the poetical seances to be held
at Columbia University (April 9), Univ. of Philadelphia [sic] (April 12),
Univ. of Wisconsin (April 14), and Univ. of Kansas (April 20–23). I'll
probably have flown off to N.Y. in a few days, so you won't have time
to reply here. But please do so to my Philadelphia address, which looks
like this:

T. Transtromer
c/o Eric Sellin
4106 Locust Street
Philadelphia 4, Pa
U.S.A.

I'll be staying at Sellin's house around April 2–4, and it would be good to have a letter there. If I work up enough courage I'll probably telephone Christina Paulston in New York. Will be in touch soon. In hurry and friendship

Tomas T.

P.S. THE SIXTIES JUST CAME. THANKS!

31 March, '65

Dear Tomas,

Thank you for the letters and the translations from *Ord och Bild* & the fine new poem! I am enclosing here translations of 7 of your poems. The translations vary in quality, alas, and are at various stages of being finished—but I wanted to get them to you anyway while you were there, and with Eric. If you find any errors, you and Eric just change them on the spot. I'll give them all another draft before they are published anyway, so these are more or less provisional translations.

I feel very bad that I am not in Minnesota, & can't greet you, and take you out to my poor old farm! But I've written Jim Wright & he's going to try to arrange a reading in which you & he would read together! That would be good! Anyway, even if you can't, he'll write you & after you're through at Wisconsin, you must jump on a train—it's only 250 miles— and go up to Minneapolis. Jim will take you over to see Allen Tate—the #1 enemy of *The Sixties* in the U.S.—he thinks we're as bad as Mao Tse-Tung—but he likes Jim, and Tate is sort of interesting as an

[Editor's note: Rest of letter missing]

8 July, '65

Dear Tomas,

Here we are, in the old Heimat! old Bleie, whose stones have been stained by Bleie-feet for ten thousand years or so, is still here, supporting apples and cows and some taciturn Norwegians. We are in a magnificent camping place at Lofthus, with the Sørfjord under us, and those wonderful mountains with snow across the fjord. Every day or so I start plunging up the mountain, get halfway up, and then sit down in a sheep-shed for the rest of the morning.

I just wrote Jim Wright and told him about seeing you, and your family, and your taking me to a Moose Museum! It was a wonderful visit to your house. I enjoyed meeting Monica very much. Please give her my best wishes and thanks.

This letter got broken off, and I am finishing it in England. The trip to Norway remained moving, and now we are back in Thaxted. I'm going into London tomorrow, and hope to go out to Devon and see Ted Hughes. Then I want to go up in Wordsworth's country, and walk for a few days.

There's a rather interesting article by Rexroth in the June *Harper's Magazine* called *The New Poetry*—trying to find out what was going on among those under 35, he wrote about a dozen older poets and asked them what they thought. He has some good gags in it too, his certain peculiar pungent sarcasm.

I found in my notebook a little poem I wrote at 4 o'clock in the morning while waiting for the ferry to take us from Germany to Denmark. I'll put it down, as Tao Yuan Ming says, "just for a laugh."

Waiting for a Ferry in Northern Europe

Early dawn, the wind blows around the doors of the car.
A fat Danish bird takes short leaps on the asphalt.
The sun makes boxes of light of the cars parked far off.
And the trucks, leaving the customs sheds with their covered loads.

One of the things I loved best in Sweden was that calm and grotesque St. George in the Stockholm Cathedral. You know it—the dragon's spines and claws leap out in all directions inside the church—in some places he has evidently embedded actual reindeer horns. What I like so much is that it is *not Italian*. The real horseshoes on the hooves—that is instinctual and grotesque, like Dürer & Munch. That's where health lies, I think.

Write us soon. We'll be here until Aug 4th, then to the U.S.A.!

With thanks again for picking me up & taking me to your house—

Affectionately
Robert

Roxtuna, October 30, 1965
Dear Robert,

the other day I finally had that roll of film we took last summer developed. I must say the portrait of you came out well—you'll have it as soon as get another print made. The sight of the Minnesota man's red face exalted with genius made a torrent of questions grow within us like a drumroll: WHAT HAS BECOME OF YOU? (And what has become of America—that's something else I'd like to know.)

Below you will find the first version of "The Condition of the Working Classes." It has a certain verve in Swedish, but it's very possible that I've misunderstood the words in the latter half of the poem. Correct it if I did. "Trapped" in line 1 is obviously a problem. As it stands now it is very dynamic: you really see how the poor bricks are falling into the trap. A quieter and more static version can also be imagined: "Bricks lie trapped in thousands of pale homes."

Did you know that two of your poems ("Sunday in Glastonbury" and that poem that ends with the faucet in Guatemala) appeared in translation in the the last issue of *Clarté*? *Clarté* is the reddest magazine in Sweden, even though the pro-Chinese group has been thrown out of the saddle for the time being. The translator was Lasse Söderberg, an old friend of mine. All I can say is: Welcome to the Söderberg-Tranströmer entanglement! Lasse Söderberg is two meters tall, very fair-haired and quiet, formerly a fanatical surrealist (he has LITERALLY sat at the feet of Breton). We knew each other ten years ago when we were both living in Stockholm. [------] We used to get together occasionally and talk about Life. Afterwards Lasse went to Spain and France and Algeria, married a French woman, and I went to Roxtuna. Since then we've only seen each other once, just to say hello. The reason I'm talking about the Söderberg-Tranströmer entanglement is that Artur Lundqvist writes article after article in which he maintains that I (that *I* in point of fact) have had an inhibiting effect on Lasse's poetical development. He began as a "wild" poet, and with the years has become increasingly sober. I have sometimes almost felt a sort of guilt complex vis-à-vis Lasse, who has never really won the critics over. (He is a very good poet.) What kind of strange portent can it be that he has begun translating you?

My professional life is in the process of changing. I've taken a leave of absence from criminal psychology and am now working half-time for PA-rådet* in Västerås. (A town you must have driven through if you traveled between Stockholm and Oslo.) We'll be moving there in a month. What's good about this is that I get to work half-time and can devote more time to literature. Nowadays I'm doing psychological evaluations of people who are handicapped (physically, psychologically, or morally) with special emphasis on their ability to work. Some are also perfectly healthy people who have wound up in the wrong place. As a memorial to my time of considerably more stress and heavy responsibility at Roxtuna, here is the following poem:

Under Pressure

Powerful engines from the blue sky.
We live on a construction site where everything shivers,

---

* The Swedish Council for Personnel Administration.

where the ocean depths can suddenly open.
A hum in seashells and telephones.

You can see beauty if you look quickly to the side.
The heavy grainfields run together in one yellow river.
The restless shadows in my head want to go out there.
They want to crawl in the grain and turn into something gold.

Night finally. At midnight I go to bed.
The dinghy sets out from the ship.
On the water you are alone.
The dark hull of society keeps on going.

[Robert Bly translation]

Write, man! My address till December 1 is still
Roxtuna Linköping. Monica sends love.

your friend Tomas T.

1 Dec., '65

Dear Tomas,

I'm sitting in a little house in New Concord, Ohio, the house where
Jim Wright's parents live. Also born in this town was—of all people—John
Glenn. Jim is upstairs, writing a poem about Sinclair Lewis. I wanted to
tell you why I've been so close-mouthed. I've just finished my new book
of poems! I've been working on it incommunicado, and just finished it on
Monday. On Wednesday I left for the anti-government demonstrations
in Washington. (There was a convention there too, to organize the anti-
Vietnam-war groups into a national group.) So on Saturday, we all went
out and paraded around the White House. It was interesting. There were
20–30,000 people, an amazing number of them 50–60 years old, also a lot
of entire families pushing baby carriages. The mood was not angry, but the
people seemed confident, particularly over the number of people that had

come from all parts of the country. We sent two busloads, nearly a hundred people, from Minneapolis.

The next day I went up to New York, and Monday night went to a fine reading in NY—John Logan and Galway Kinnell read. I stayed with Christina and Rolland, and yesterday morning saw Leif Sjöberg for fifteen minutes. He gave me a copy of that mad article he wrote about you, saying poetry didn't sell, even though you dressed like a Mad. Ave executive. Sjöberg has a curious attraction to money, like the Congo natives' attraction to crocodile meat.

He told me of a wild issue of *Ord och Bild* that has enraged the King for some reason. Can you send me a copy of that? I should think the King would be getting fairly immune to outrage these days.

Yesterday I took a bus out here to Ohio, and today Jim & I have been jabbering about Jim Dickey and you and other subjects. Jim is on a Guggenheim this year, so he doesn't have to teach. He spent about 6 weeks with us on the farm, and now has come here for a couple of months with his parents. He's still thinking of coming to Europe about March 1st.

Tomorrow we're going up to Kenyon to see John Crowe Ransom, and then I have to give a couple of readings at Cleveland Univ. & Oberlin, and so home! Jim sends his very best. He got a letter from Beatrice Roethke last week, and she mentioned meeting you in N.Y. last year.

Let's see what gossip I heard in N.Y. Randall Jarrell is thought *not* to have committed suicide, but to have been hit by a reckless driver on a lane that had no streetlights. John Logan, who has 9 children, is in the process of declaring bankruptcy. For the last two months he has been living in Oakland under the name of Leopold Bloom to get some peace from his creditors, but it hasn't worked. Don Hall has done a fine play, made up of Frost poems, interspersed with comments from Frost letters. Christina and John Logan and I saw it Sunday. Fine thing.

I've translated your poem called "After a Death," and it looks very well. I'll send you a copy when I get home. "Three Presidents" is about to be published in *Nation,* and I'll send a copy of that too.

Jim feels very strong now, and very happy about poetry. I am too. How wonderful to be able to live in a time when something fresh can be written!

There are endless fields of flowers—many of them are black flowers—on all sides.

Thank you for "Under tryck"! I'm going to translate that too! Could you ask Lasse Söderberg to send me a copy of *Clarté*? I'll have to think a little more about "Condition of the Working Classes" before writing you, but many lines seem to me much like the English, even in tone. I have a new political poem I think you'll like. It has Rusk, McNamara etc. gathering in the woods at night, like the Puritan witches.

Much affection to Monica, whose fine face I remember with joy, and to you—

As ever, Robert

Roxtuna 12-10-65
Dear Robert,

thanks for your letter, which cheered me up. That march on the White House assumes even more personal import for me, when I hear that not only Doctor SPOCK (who has contributed to my children's care from afar), but also you, were in it. The event was covered in the papers here as well, though they dwelt a good deal on the fact that the bus drivers were unhappy about having to drive so many bad Americans around. The picture that ran with the story was the same in all the papers—it showed a Rockwell Nazi going around passing out free gasoline and matches. The coverage somehow implied that the demonstration had been one of peaceful strength, which warmed many hearts over here.

My life will undergo a brutal change next week, when I move to Västerås. Here is my new address: Infanterigatan 144 Vasterås Sweden. All through the fall I've been working two days a week in Västerås and then driving back here. Winter has arrived abominably early, which has meant a constant sliding hither and thither on ice-covered roads, in snow and fog. For me it will be nice to move, but Monica is sentimentally attached to the bungalow here. Then too, I'll have economic problems. The new job is only half-time, which as you can figure out pays only half a salary. The idea is that I'll have time to finish my book, and that it will come out in

1966. I've already begun to be in debt, but not yet so deeply as to think of moving somewhere under the name of Leopold Bloom.

12-14

The day before moving day. They've given a speech for me—the representative of the guards' union spoke for his staff, and it emerged that I "have always shown understanding concerning the problems of the personnel." The inmates have been nice too. Monica is moved to tears by the farewells of the children's playmates. It's terribly cold and snowdrifts obscure the view in all directions. The snow is utterly blue. I wander around, shaking hands.

12-18

Established in Västerås. Every time I sit down, I get out this wrinkled sheet of paper to finish my letter to you. Yesterday I saw Ho Chi Minh on TV. An English reporter (who incidentally was the brother of Graham Greene!) interviewed him, and Ho read his answers from a piece of paper. He seemed moth-eaten, unassuming and imperturbable. I see in the papers where a poll has revealed that more than one in three Americans wants atomic weapons to be used in Viet Nam immediately. My God, one in three. You ride an elevator with three Americans and one of them wants nukes to be used immediately.

Changing the subject, I can't find any copies of that issue of *Ord & Bild* you inquired about. Naturally it's sold out. It must have been the notorious SEX-issue. Deathly serious essays on pornography, illustrated with girls out of porn magazines. I have a hard time believing that the king was furious—the story must have been edited for the American public. It's not entirely out of the question though, the king is one of the financial benefactors of that venerable magazine.

What I have to do now is get going with the poems again. I'm so glad Jim Wright is in good shape. It would be great if he could send me a cartload of poetry again, as testimony that the ground is still fertile and that everything in the world doesn't come wrapped in plastic. I read the Eisenhower poem in Norrköping last fall, as an illustration of how political poetry ought to sound, by contrast with all the damned rhetoric—it was at a recital, as a matter of fact. I've had another reading also, at the University of Stockholm. That one cheered me up a good deal, since four times as many people came as the organizers had planned for—most of them had to stand up for three hours in tropical heat (the ones who fainted were allowed to remain lying down). The organizers made a lot of money for the university by selling cold beer at the event.

Otherwise I've nothing to brag about. Merry Christmas, let's hear from you, and send poems to these arctic regions.

Love from Monica

Tomas T.

1966

14 Jan., '65 [66]

Dear Tomas,

Here it is, a fine snowy morning! I've been thinking of you both and thought it was a good day to write you!

All goes calmly here. I am working on a long poem, and translating Arosenius's *Kattresan* for Mary and Biddy. Photographs enclosed show us in the grip of icy winter!

Thank you for your good letter, and the photograph of that fat American. I'm glad I saw your other little house before you moved—it did have a sweetness. And that strange lake! Now you must write like blazes. We expect poems to flow from you in a never ending stream. As for me, I am getting more and more fond of sleep. A Chinese poet said, "The greatest happiness in life consists in playing jokes on small children."

I am enclosing a copy of a poem I wrote at the Peace March, listening to Martin Luther King talk. Doctor Spock *was* there, and spoke very well! He is a favorite of my wife's. I don't think Johnson really has the guts to pull out. People are wrong though when they think this is the first battle of World War III—it is the last battle of World War II. The white race feels guilty and wants to waste now all the riches it took from the Orient, and if it can do so and at the same time kill large numbers of yellow people, so much the better. We are determined to disgrace ourselves, and nothing will stop us. We are doing it *instead* of the Europeans *for* them. The Europeans have disgraced themselves so much, they are satisfied now. But we still hunger for disgrace—we *howl* for it.

In the old days nations were proud of themselves, as men are. But what will foreign politics be like when nations do not respect themselves?

With these sad thoughts, I stop. Please write soon.

With affection from us all,
Robert

P.S. A question: In "Nocturne" (driving through a village): the melodramatic color—is that from a forest fire or a fireplace?

Västerås 1-30-66
Dear Robert,

thanks for a very stimulating assemblage of words, photographs, poems. Is that the lopsided barn that moves toward the reader at the end of "Snowfall in the Afternoon"? The gable has a face: The poems were fine, of course. Only it's too bad that "redwood" is one of those American trees that can't be translated (like boxelder for instance). You can't translate a whole flora. A kangaroo is comprehensible to a Swede, but a RED WOOD TREE or, even worse, SEQUOIA, never. Naturally I was myself working on a poem about Lofthus when your letter came. However it's not about a waterfall, but about a person who once lived there, namely Grieg. (I've never been there myself.) I see to my relief that Grieg doesn't appear in your poem, so I can immerse myself in its slow downward falling, so beautiful.

Your translation of "After Someone's Death" had such a persuasive tone that I'd like to give it the green light at once. After a closer reading, however, I'm doubtful about some of the details. "It bothers us" line 3: "hyser oss" means "keeps us," in other words we're like prisoners, like inhabitants of the attenuated comet's tail, we're still in it. Admittedly "keeps" doesn't sound too good in and of itself. The Swedish word "hyser" is a bit old-fashioned. Line 6: "Through woods" sounds too big to me. "Dungar" are small thickets of trees or bushes and "the leaves" that are still hanging are quite few. "Where some last-years leaves / still / hang on" would be the literal sense. Finally, "your heart" in line 9 could be misunderstood as "ditt hjärta," which it is not. Does "one's heart beat" sound clumsy? But otherwise the grasp of the whole and the concentration seem perfect— crikey, that poem has to be published for the American people sometime, it seems more persuasive somehow in American than it does in Swedish.

They've been saying for a week now that the halt in the bombing will end. But all we hear, still, is the distant whining of hawks and doves. Hawks and doves . . . They say Rusk is a hawk now. Of course General Wheeler is a hawk. Mr. Mansfield is a dove. I think people in general hope that the biggest dove is actually Lyndon Johnson himself. That's a dove that is so big it looks exactly like a hawk. It has also changed its appearance of late, after having lived on a diet of meat. What to say about Mr. McNamara? He's neither a hawk nor a dove. He is presumably an airplane.

2-1

(The bombs are tumbling down again.) Did I mention in my last letter that I've made contact with another Swedish poet and essayist, Göran Printz-Påhlson, who was a professor at Berkeley (and presumably knows Simpson)? I thought we might do the American anthology together. Printz-Påhlson has translated Wilbur, very beautifully. I thought we could include Wilbur and Lowell, as representatives of a somewhat older "academic" generation, and then run the line out to you. Lowell-Wilbur-(Simpson?)-(Stafford?)-(J. Dickey?)-Wright-Bly. This isn't a representative anthology, of course, but better that the few poets we include have at least five poems each than if we just set up a lot of calling cards with names on them! I've started reading Lowell's *For the Union Dead*. Have you got any advice to offer—is there someone who is BEST? You promised once to send me Dickey's first book—it's twice as important now since his book no. 2 disappeared in the move from Roxtuna to Västerås. In return, you'll get *China in Crisis* by Sven Lindqvist, an old school friend of mine who studied in Peking for two years and speaks Chinese like a Mandarin. He very much wanted to give you the book, and I'm sending it along by surface mail. Some philosophy books (in Swedish) by the same man are coming in the same shipment, extra copies sent to him by the Press when the books came out in mass-market editions. He is a most serious fellow but nowadays also friendly and genial, and has a wife who can play Chinese instruments and cook superbly!

On the subject of ELDSKEN. The reader may decide whether he wishes to understand it as a glow from a campfire or a wildfire.

How is Jim Wright doing? What's his address? I would like to send him a few lines and a book. Has he written any good poems lately? (I would actually much rather translate him than Lowell etc.) If we were to put my Wright translations and Printz-Påhlson's Wilbur translations together, we would have a good title for an anthology: POETRY IN THE AIR— WILBUR WRIGHT'S BEST PIECES.

Now I'm going to drive many miles up through the woods to attend a conference on the treatment of CP (cerebral palsy)—a job that occupies me at my present workplace. It's about finding suitable tests for them. We're meeting at a remotely located institute where these unfortunates are stored and trained. When you first go in you get a powerful shock, but you soon get used to it! The atmosphere is almost religious. All the best from me and Monica.
Tomas.

7 Feb, 66

Dear Tomas,
Many thanks for your letter just received today. Your notes on "Efter nagons dod" are very helpful, and I will do a new draft. The wires, the luftledningarna—I have them as telephone wires. Should they perhaps be what we call "high-tension" wires, that is wires carrying 220 volts of *electricity,* for commercial and home circuits?

I'm enclosing your draft of the Working Class poem, I think "trapped" should undoubtedly be "fangada." "himlarna" maybe should be "himlen." I'm not sure: what I mean is the sky simply, not really the "heavens," which suggests something spiritual in English. The cards are all thrown down *at one time* at the end of the night, usually by the player who dealt the last hand; and he puts them back in a box, closing the flap—more like *låsa*. By stages I didn't mean to suggest the pads from which the rocket rose, but rather the three long parts of which the rocket is made, any one of which is long and narrow like the center aisle of certain long churches.

Now after all this, I must say that I am dissatisfied with the poem after the 5th line, and I think I am going to try to shorten and rewrite the poem. I'll send you the new draft, if I succeed! It's not the translation I'm dissatisfied with, but my own English poem! No, *American* poem! But I'm still dissatisfied with it.

I think your anthology sounds excellent. If you can, I would definitely put in Stafford—the more I read him, the more wonderful I think he is (if you like, I will type up for you the six or seven poems of his I like the best)—the same offer holds for Dickey and Simpson. If you have space to add one more, it should be Creeley. His work is uneven, more so than most poets; but the inclusion of his work would make the anthology absolutely and definitively representative. Maybe I'm wrong: his lines occasionally have great *flavor* in English, but it is done as if by magic, by mirror, and I'm not sure a translation could catch the peculiar throbbing or resonance of his ascetic language. It is like hearing the wavering high pitched song of an old man out in the desert at night alone.

I would like to know which of these books you do *not* have. Those you do not have I will get the American publishers to send you, and it won't cost either of us anything!

LOWELL
  Lord Weary's Castle (1946) (his best book)
  Mills of the Kavanaghs (1951)
  Life Studies (1959) next-best book
  For the Union Dead (1964) worst book

RICHARD WILBUR
> *The Beautiful Changes*
> *Ceremony*
> *Things of This World*
> *Advice to a Prophet* (1961)

WILLIAM STAFFORD
> *Traveling through the Dark*

LOUIS SIMPSON
> *Selected Poems* (1965)

JAMES DICKEY
> *Into the Stone* (1960)
> *Drowning with Others* (his best book) 1962
> *Helmets* (1964)
> *Buckdancer's Choice* (1965)

JAMES WRIGHT
> *The Green Wall* (1957)
> *Saint Judas* (1959)
> *The Branch Will Not Break* (1963)

Just check this list and send it back to me. If you want to read Creeley's work, it is all collected in one book, *For Love.*

As you will see, *For the Union Dead* is uneven. It was described in the United States, in reviews, as if it were the *Iliad.* Lowell's aristocratic birth and his closeness to the N.Y. reviewers combine with everyone's longing to have a great poet *living*—now that Eliot and Roethke and Frost are dead—and the result is an unbelievable chorus of praise. I am attacking the book sharply in the next issue of *The Sixties,* and everyone will say: There's that old grouch again!

I thought there were six or seven good or at least readable poems in the book. The best without question was "The Mouth of the Hudson." (It is a sort of farewell to Williams, who lived just across the Hudson, in

New Jersey, and a sort of rebuke as well to the Beats that grew out of him: "One cannot find America by counting the freight cars.") Also interesting I thought were "The Old Flame," "The Flaw," "For the Union Dead," and in parts at least, "Water"; "Fall, 1961"; and "Night Sweat."

The rest seemed to me bombast, like a bad evangelical preacher.

Yes, that barn was the one in "Snowfall in the Afternoon." The stair in front was added recently. It used to move even better before that! Now the stair looks like its anchor, thrown out before it. I see what you mean about the face. It should have been a face: my father and I built the barn in the '40s.

Jim Wright is staying with his parents: c/o Dudley Wright, 66 East Main Street, New Concord, Ohio. He is on a Guggenheim. I'll send along a new poem of his, and a new poem of mine.

Write soon. My fond hellos to
Monica—
Yours,
Robert

P.S. How strange about Loftus! We stayed there. It's across the fjord from the urgammel Bleie gard.

17 Feb., '65[66]

Dear Tomas,

Christina and I are finally getting ready to print the selected poems of Ekelöf we've been working on for five years or so, lazily. I translated some of Lindegren's essay on him as the main introduction. Then I wrote this little squib to go in the front of the book. Would you glance at it? Does it sound ridiculous or fairly sound?

Yours as ever,
Robert

P.S. No need to return it—just mention it in your next letter.

P.P.S. My best to Monica!

A Note on Gunnar Ekelöf

Gunnar Ekelöf was born in 1907. Many critics consider him the greatest living Swedish poet. He reached out early in his career to two sources outside the Scandinavian tradition: the mystical poetry of Persia in particular, and the Orient in general, and French poetry, especially the surrealist poetry of the late '20's. His poetry also has deep roots in Fröding, Almqvist, and the Swedish fairy tales.

In Swedish literature there is a much firmer division between the proletariat and the aristocratic writing than there is in America or England. There have been a succession of great writers in Sweden who took their place naturally in one of these two groups. Harry Martinson is one of the greatest proletarian poets. It is as if in what James Farrell represents there were poets as sensitive as Wallace Stevens. Gunnar Ekelöf, on the other hand, very clearly belongs to the second group, the writers that are aristocratic, intellectual, elegant.

Some of his poems are made of linked successions of thoughts not easy to follow. These thoughts are embodied in high-spirited and eccentric language. Gunnar Ekelöf is the most difficult Swedish poet; yet, despite the difficulty, his audience is very large. His books of poems are published in editions comparable, given the difference in population, to printings of 200,000 in the U.S. He is an uncomfortable poet, who tries to make the reader conscious of lies.

The ideas which his work returns to again and again have been brought out clearly in an essay by the Swedish poet Eric Lindegren. I have chosen and translated sections from that essay, which appear elsewhere in this book.

Gunnar Ekelöf was elected a member of the Swedish Academy in 1958, and is now the youngest member of that body.

—ROBERT BLY

Västerås 3-1-66

Dear Robert,

　　　　this godawful wolf-winter is grinding to an end at last. Now and then we get a day above freezing, and we have the pleasure of hearing the water gurgle in the gutters and along the roof. Till it freezes again the next day. I've sent wife and children off to Stockholm so that Monica can get out a bit, and so she can parasitize her mama, who has quite a lot of money, for a few days. Our shortage of money is comical—toward the end of the month we go around and shake all our old clothes in the hope that a stray coin might fall out. The poetical deadlock has been broken, however, and I'm hard at work on a poem about COMPUTERS—about the world when computers have propagated themselves and taken over completely! At the same time I'm translating "The Hospital Window" by James Dickey and "Three Presidents" by you. Jackson is easy. Roosevelt fairly easy. Kennedy very difficult. What do you really mean by "I ate the Cubans with a straw"? Did he SUCK THEM OUT with a straw (reed)? Did he eat them with chopsticks like a Chinaman? Did he point at them with a straw and hey presto! they were consumed . . . And in Kennedy, what is meant by "Able to flow past rocks"—I don't understand it purely in the language sense, either. And then all that about the crystal in the sideboards etc., I would be grateful for a more detailed explanation of that! It's such a damned splendid poem, and fantastically exciting to translate.*

I have become culturally active in Västerås through becoming a member of Kulturrådet (The Cultural Council or whatever it would be called in the U.S.). We have strenuous meetings. We aren't paid, unfortunately, but are invited to dinner once a year by Kulturnamnden (The Culture Department?), which is made up exclusively of the city's bigwigs, politicians and the like. My debut in that company was unfortunate—I chanced to fall into a deep sleep after the dinner, in the middle of a solemn debate about the problems of the theater. This was observed by the elders, some of whom came up and congratulated me with heavy irony on my good sleep and a woman in the theater business bade me an ice-cold GOOD-NIGHT in a loud voice. I'm thinking about spreading the word that I suffer from a grave and mysterious illness that causes me to fall asleep abruptly.

---

* The Viet-Nam poem about the ghost train is terrific too!

On Friday I'm going to Lund, the university town in Skåne, to do a poetry reading for the students. The impoverished student union will pay for my lodgings and my publisher for travel expenses. [-----]

A note on a note on Ekelöf! It's accurate except for Part Two, about the proletariat and the aristocratic writing. I read that part with something of the same strange feeling as a Hottentot must have when he reads about himself in a tourist brochure. It's certainly true that one can speak of a "proletarian writer," but that would primarily be a novelist (Ivar Lo-Johansson, Jan Fridegård, Vilhelm Moberg) who—especially in the Thirties—published thick, widely read books in a realistic style, with autobiographical stuff from proletarian reality. It's hardly possible to think of a single equivalent in poetry. The so-called "Five Young Men" (Martinson and Lundkvist, among others) certainly came from working-class or farming backgrounds, but the very two who devoted themselves primarily to poetry quickly took an "intellectual" line. Besides that, "Aristocratic" is misleading—I think you misjudge the number of aristocrats in Sweden and Europe. There aren't all that many, besides Christina of course. Compare your, and all Americans', strange interest in our monarch (he's still reading *Ord & Bild*). In U.S. literature as everyone knows, there is a firm division between the COWBOY-SCHOOL (Robert Bly, Erskine Caldwell, Emerson and Carl Sandburg) and the Hollywood-school (Ray Bradbury, Pearl Buck, W. H. Auden and e. e. cummings).

The most recent issue of the *Literary Review*, to take one example, in which Professor Vowels has invented an entirely new literary school in Sweden, shows that it's not easy to be an expert in the literature of foreign countries.

On another subject, I'm longing like a madman to see a new issue of *The Sixties*. You promised that the issues would come rolling out at high speed this year. Failing that, I could probably console myself with some collections of American poetry. The ones I'd like to have from your list are:
Lowell: *For the Union Dead*
Wilbur: *Advice to a Prophet*

James Dickey: *Into the Stone* and *Buckdancer's Choice*
Simpson: *Selected Poems*
Creeley: *For Love*

    Göran Printz-Påhlson—with whom I will collaborate on the anthology—lives in England and is going to put together a Swedish anthology for a magazine called *Stand*. He may write to you and ask to use some translations.

    With hopes of a speedy reply and the warmest greetings from Monica

    Yours
    Tomas T.

                      Aug [March] 18, 66

Dear Tomas,

    Thanks for your letter! I'm sorry I'm so slow in answering—I've been on a reading tour out West. I'm enclosing a clipping from the *NY Times*—you'll see what we've been up to.

    Herewith a few notes on the Three Presidents: When he says "I ate the Cubans with a straw" he implies that they are so spineless, so weak, so soft that he could suck them all up inside a straw—he wouldn't even need teeth to eat them. Typical American superiority complex toward the South Americans or Spanish-Americans.

    With "able to flow past rocks" I wanted to suggest this: other presidents, faced with the rocks of national habit, for example American anti-intellectualism, could not move. They put the rock of their program in front of this other immovable rock, and the two rocks just sat looking at each other all during the Administration and nothing got done. The strange thing about Kennedy was that he was able to evade American anti-intellectualism, American anti-communism, and he did it by being curiously fluid—he didn't fight with the rocks, he just flowed around them and reformed on the other side. Before they knew it, half the intellectuals in the country were in his Administration.

As for the boulders, the heavy right-wingism, really serious obstacles, he just waited until his flow of water had sufficient momentum, and then he just carried the boulders with him to the valley. He did that at the time of Cuba, and prevented the right wing people from declaring war on Russia or some such stupidity.

By the crystals in sideboards, I was thinking of the fine crystal glasses that wealthy families in Boston will have in oak cupboards, standing in their dining rooms. Kennedy really loved the life of money: he thought himself a part of old wealthy aristocracy, and he thought he glittered like expensive glass. I think he considered the Catholic Church as being in the end an enemy of that sort of life, and that is one reason his interest in the Church was strictly minimal. He didn't care beans for the Church.

Tell me what happened in Lund, when you read poems. [------]

Thank you for your mocking words on my Ekelöf introduction: that is exactly what I wanted! I had some doubts about that aristocrat-proletariat split—I don't know how that idea got into my head—and that's why I sent it to you. I'll have to think up another division now—maybe that between long-headed writers, and round-headed writers. We're always willing to believe the worst of another country.

I write this hastily. Carol sends her very best to you. We've been reading *Sweden Writes,* and Carol says you are the only Swedish writer photographed in it with any strength in the face.

How could that have happened?

I'm sending on a stamp outside for Monica—

Yours,
Robert

P.S. New *Sixties* are coming! Yes! Yes! In fact I've scheduled 5 poems of yours for *Sixties* #9. Payment coming soon.

Thoughts in a Redwood Grove

An old man took me to see a redwood grove.
Fifty redwoods rise in the winter sunset.

The floor is bare; far, far up boughs in the half-dark.
Around me the ground is clean with needles fallen so far.
I sit on a stump, content near great things.
Here the darkness can rest, here it can stretch and sleep.
I see a man stabbed, smelling
Laurel, leaning against an old tree.
My blood spurts out over the shaggy bark and pine brush.
I am dying! My eyes close
Without rancour on leaves. It is all right,
My blood will go to a great hollow under the earth.

Looking Up at the Waterfall in Lofthus, Hardanger

How wonderful to look up and see water falling
Here it seems to come over the edge of the sky
And then drops to a lap, and then the long plunge
    after the slanting blow off the cliff

A deep plunge, loveless,
    floating,
it falls by the cliff
    like tufts of sleep

The sleep that overcomes the truck driver after having driven from
    the coast

The gestures in an animal's eyes when he dies in a room with human
    beings

Like the glimpses the meditator has of something floating under the
    water, neither moving nor not moving,

Seeming to slow as it nears the bottom.

10 April '66

Dear Tomas,

You're getting to be a slow letter writer again! I'm busy, with Galway Kinnell, organizing anti-government readings. We'll have a large rally in Chicago this Saturday for a thousand people or more. The Buddhists are trying desperately to kick us out of Vietnam—I hope to God they succeed.

We are printing up the contents of a typical read-in as a booklet to be called *A Poetry Reading Against the Vietnam War*. It will be out May 3rd. I'll send you a copy.

I'm getting ready to publish soon *Three Swedish Poets* also—it will be 7–10 poems apiece of Martinson, Ekelöf, and Herr Across-the-River. The royalty on such a Sixties book is $150 usually, so I'm dividing it up to the three of you; $50 apiece as permissions fee. I hope that will be all right. Check enclosed here.

Jim Wright called a couple of days ago—he has been on a Guggenheim grant living in N.Y.—but has got a job for next year teaching at Hunter College, and was happy about that—he'll be able to stay in New York, to which he has taken an enormous liking. He'll never get to Europe at all this year. He said he had written a poem that day, and chortled happily.

Harpers has decided to publish my new book, after fierce fighting between the old and new guards there. Don Hall sent a postcard that arrived yesterday to tell me. I was gone all day, poking about at a lake nearby, and so Carol read the card. So, to tell me then, she put a up huge sign in the driveway, that said: DRIVE SLOWLY! HARPERS' AUTHOR LIVES HERE. That was sweet.

My best to Monica & to you—
Affectionately,
Robert

10-4-66

Dear Robert,

The other day we got a Christmas present from you! A very beautiful Joan Baez record—she's often running through my head. It made us very happy. Otherwise I mostly play Brahms, myself, on the piano. It affords a certain comfort, the rolling resigned and bearded progressions one is able to squeeze out of the instrument. It's Truth, my lad, truth, nothing helps right now but that. In Saigon, Da Nang and Hue the truth is being written right now in such large letters that it ought to force itself on the attention even of the blinded masses that nourish themselves on *Time* magazine. It was fine to read that you and others are doing your best in Oregon and elsewhere. I hope you have no objections to BLM running a notice about it—I met Lars Gustafsson the other day and he had also gotten a photostat from the *N.Y. Times.* Powerful poems!

Here is a first draft of the 3 presidents. A few uncertainties: does Roosevelt want to be a stone that rushes around at night, in which case he goes at a fairly violent speed, or does he only want to walk around at an ordinary walking pace. (I imagine him, huddled, concentrated, moving as fast as a hunted bear.) And Kennedy: the air *invisible, resilient* [osynlig, stärkande], that's something I'll probably change. Air is always invisible anyway. Were you thinking of *clear* air? "Resilient" really means "spänstig," but the latter word sounds so athletic in Swedish. Then there's that damned sideboard, actually a *petit* bourgeois thing in Sweden. I shall consult a furniture expert.

My reading in Lund turned out not to be a success since too few people came. The ones who did come were however all young, except for one gray-haired person who was head of prisons for the southern district and had come to honor an old jailer at his reading. [-----] Afterwards we went to the home of a young poet who played Bach on the clavichord. The young people buzzed like bees, had plans to print pamphlets and magazines.

Great fun to meet so much spiritual activity in this POP-Sweden! I provided the address for *The Sixties,* some of them wanted to subscribe.

I too have appeared in a political context, less heroic than the ones where you appear unfortunately. See the enclosed clipping. According to another paper the confusion following the reading was great. The leading Social Democrat in the town council thought it was a *Temperance* lecture.

My face sends his warm greetings to Carol.

One thing we've forgotten to talk about in our letters is your book of poems. More than a year ago you wrote that it was finally finished. Since then, silence on the subject. Reasonably the book should have been out months ago, been praised and disparaged already by your friends/enemies in the press. Here one stands in the presence of something mysterious, something almost frightening in American cultural life. That unbelievable d e l a y i n g of everything serious (förhalande = delaying). It's as if they had all eternity before them. Am I mistaken? My publisher in Kansas who's supposed to be printing a modest brochure with three poems wrote in October that they were to appear "for Christmas." After that I got a Christmas letter informing me that they would come out in January. After that total silence. In a famous magazine *(The Sixties)* I read: "We invite poets to send translations of his [Hernandez's] work. THE DEADLINE IS JUNE 1, 64." What's interesting about that last sentence is that the issue of the magazine came out in Spring 1965. Etcetera. Must the business of publishing serious literature be a subsection of archeology? Sucking up the Cubans once with a straw wasn't enough apparently, a load of MAÑANA had to be taken in as well. In short, I hope your book is published soon and that you become a Guggenheim fellow and come to Europe to see us which would be great, say

Tomas *[in longhand]*, Monica, Marie and Paula *[typed]*

[in longhand:] Now I'm going to put Joan Baez on again.

[in longhand at the top of the second page:] I like Joan Baez, The Presidents, and does Robert really understand Swedish? Monica

4-20-66

Dear Roberto,

congratulations! I assume that the switch from Wesleyan Univ. Press to Harper's implies a great triumph—a sort of Oscar for poets. Your check for 50 dollars was as welcome as it was unexpected. There was a certain amount of discussion before I could get the bank to give me the money, but they did and I immediately bought a little bottle of Seagram's VO—the rest of the money goes to the family: paper dolls, oranges, socks etc. —It's hard to get hold of a Chicago newspaper here in Västerås. How did the read-in go? I eagerly await a report. Greetings to the family!

Tomas

29 April, 66

Dear Tomas,

The Three Presidents translation looks wonderful! A note on your questions: Roosevelt wants to run around at night, with totally senseless energy, rushing all over the grounds, like a murdered chicken.

The descriptions of the air are really a description of Kennedy: he was "invisible" in the sense that he loved to act in secret, even act nobly in secret, and then announce it later with delight like a boy. The air around Johnson is not invisible—it is full of soot, hurricane clouds, and ordinary Texas mud. "Resilient": you might shift a little to a meaning of "resilient" that applied to Kennedy: he was mentally agile and *flexible*—he had not only one rabbit in his bag, but a number of rabbits of various colors. He was rarely at a loss for an act: he could usually think of *something* (at a press conference as well as in foreign relations). For the "skapet" choose any form of furniture or even closet that suggests something aristocratic or at least wealthy. You are right: a middle class suggestion must be avoided. What do they call those huge pieces of oak furniture in castles? I see them sitting around in European castles, dark, lowering, with ornate doors, holding God knows what.

The reading in Chicago and Milwaukee went well! Paul Carroll read a fifteen minute poem, called "Ode to the American Indian." He had typed it all on one long sheet of paper, which lay in curls and heaps at his feet. Everyone turned pale. I'll send you some clippings of them when I get home from this next group. The reporters, who were political reporters, seemed to be astounded that poetry was read all night. They couldn't understand that.

Tomorrow I go to the East for ten days of read-ins. Tuesday at Harvard, Wednesday, Columbia, Thursday three different schools in upstate New York—Jim Wright, and Galway and I go by airplane, hopping about like World War I aviators—Friday, Queens College, Saturday, Oberlin, Sunday, a big one in Philadelphia; Ginsberg will be there too with his long Indian beard and saffron Buddhist robe.

I'm glad you like Joan Baez! I love her voice, so dark and well-like. And wonderful passion in the songs! She has refused for years you know to pay her income tax out of protest against the war.

Write soon,   our best to Monica and the little across the rivers!

Robert

4-6-66

Dear Robert,

I've forgotten whose turn it is to write, yours or mine. Thanks for your last letter in any case! I'm terribly curious about your experiences on those propaganda tours (saw something in the *Times Lit. Supplement* about them—the lead story). Among other things I've been uneasy at the thought of those airplanes you travel in "like World War I aviators." Eric Sellin sent the program for Philadelphia—a splendid collection of names. Are there any poets or other cultural figures who take the other side, who do readings to express their support for an aggressive policy in Southeast Asia? — In spite of everything I have a feeling that a slight climate change has taken place in the U.S.; one can't look upon developments so totally pessimistically anymore. Maybe it's just that summer's coming, I don't know. It could also be McNamara's speech on China. Naturally the Oregon primary was a bad blow; I was unhappy as a wet dog all the next day. When the Viet Nam anthology comes out (remember it *should* have appeared the 3rd of May) you ought to send me some copies that I can send on to some reviewers in the press here—we give all too little publicity to the American opposition to the war. There's nothing to be done about the professionally anti-American intellectuals (of the Artur Lundkvist type) but the shy and shamefaced friends of the U.S. (me, for example) ought to have a little encouragement. —I also hope that you pull back now and then into idleness and silence, so that the YOGI gets a chance to blossom and not just the COMMISSAR.

For the moment I'm developing a big activity, or at least that's how it feels. The job here in Västerås is going fine; I've also taken on some probation work (I am on a small scale a probation officer), in order to reconnect with the old criminal psychology, and am writing the last two poems in my fall book, which will be called *Klanger och spår* and come out on October 13. I sent you that long poem about Grieg, didn't I? —I'd been thinking all along that I'd write it in the third person: "he" did this and that etc., but while working on the translation of the three presidents I discovered that it would be more natural to say "I."

Thanks for your influences.

From time to time I make a road trip up through the forest, which is completely different from forests down in Östergötland. A poem follows.

Open and Closed Space

With his work, as with a glove, a man feels the universe.
At noon he rests a while, and lays the gloves aside on a shelf.
There they suddenly start growing, grow huge
and make the whole house dark from inside.

The darkened house is out in the April winds.
"Amnesty," the grass whispers, "amnesty."
A boy runs along with an invisible string that goes right up into
     the sky.
There his wild dream of the future flies like a kite, bigger than
     his town.

Farther to the north, you see from a hill the blue matting of fir trees
on which the shadows of the clouds
do not move.
No, they are moving.

"drake" = "kite."

Best wishes in every way to you and the family. And write for God's sake!

Your friend,
Tomas T.

11 July, '66

Dear Tomas,
    Thank you for your letter! Yes, I have dropped back into my old soli-
tary habits now with great joy, brooding by reedy lakes, and reading un-
reliable psychoanalysts in the grass. The poem you sent, "Oppna och Slutna
Rum," was lovely. I had a note from Printz-Påhlson the other day asking

for some of my translations of your poems, which I'll send soon. (I heard that small pamphlet of your poems had been printed in Kansas—a friend of mine saw one—but the pigheaded Frankensteinian three legged printer did not send me one.) Göran Sonnevi wrote in a letter recently that your "impact upon younger poets has been great and maybe a bit dangerous." I love that word "dangerous"—they're afraid they might be drawn too close to poetry—as to the oven door! Sonnevi said he thought your new book would be very good, judging from your reading at Lund.

How did you like the new *Sixties*? Jim Wright grumbled a little over my joke that in his nature poems even the ants are well-read, but I think he's forgiven me now. He is staying here with us now, and Louis Simpson is arriving tomorrow. We haven't entirely finished the roof yet on the little shack in the woods where Louis will sleep. He just wanted to come and talk about poetry for a week, so I'll have to go back to talk for a week! Jim is fine as a guest—he just broods silently, and wanders about like a rock with hair.

The mood on Vietnam darkens. Galway wrote me an anguished letter today. We had said a lot of harsh and wildly insulting things about Johnson during the read-ins, and Galway mentioned that he had always had some reservations about that, maybe Johnson did have a streak of honor. But now, he said, I see that all that we said was flattery.

Johnson is going to try to win this summer. But the disgust for him is so deep now in the country that he may be the first president in Am. history not to be reelected while in office.

Do write! My best to Monica.

Affectionately, Robert

Runmarö 20 July '66

Dear Robert,

How happy I was to hear from you, to hear that you hadn't been cast down by all the hellishness that's been going on. It seems from your letter as if people in general in the U.S. were against the policy of aggression against Vietnam. It seems that way in Eric's letters too. But then these damned polls, as soon as Johnson announces some new escalation there's actually a big jump in his popularity. I had so set my hopes on the Buddhist uprisings, that they would indicate to the American people how hollow the talk is about South Vietnam's being *a little country that is asking for the protection of the USA.* But no. Then came the primary in Oregon. New cold shower. Then the bombs rained over Hanoi-Haiphong. Strong popular support. Now the reporters are saying that 90% of the American people are going to insist that North Vietnam be turned into a moonscape if the poor aviators are put on trial. You can understand that it feels good in many ways to get a letter from you when one lives in this atmosphere.

I'm on vacation and have retreated to the island in the Archipelago where I spent all my childhood summers and where my forebears have their roots. (I'm descended from pilots and other sea-folk.) The family's doing fantastically well. They all swim, fight mosquitoes, get lost among tall trees or lie babbling in the sun.

I have now turned in the whole manuscript of my fall book and am sending you the last two poems. There's a section in the first of the poems that touches on my transatlantic relations in a very personal way.

[-----] On another topic, I'm waiting impatiently for *The Sixties,* which you apparently think I've received. No. I really hope the pigheaded etc. printer has sent it. But if it's been sent by surface mail it'll be awhile longer before it gets here. I have in fact discovered that the boats bringing the mail from the States obviously ply their way with the help of oars. Not only is it heavy and laborious to row straight across the Atlantic, besides that the oarsmen are badly paid and go on strike from time to time en route.

I read with surprise that Prinz-Påhlson has contacted you. Truly energetic! I only hope it doesn't mean that I'm now appearing in the English magazine *instead of* in *The Sixties.* I mean that to be published in *The Sixties* now seems to me to be a significantly greater honor, fully comparable to arriving at Valhalla and drinking beer with the great heroes.

I'm working on Lowell's poem about the mouth of the Hudson. What is the Negro sitting toasting? Is it some sort of popcorn? What kind of atmosphere is there around this special food?

Stafford is great, Simpson is good.

Stafford is giving me a lot of trouble. He has a sort of genuine poetic spark even when the poems are a little bit bad. Hideously difficult to translate. Entirely too close to their own language to really be translatable. The word "swerving" for example in "Traveling through the Dark." Simpson on the other hand would be rather easy to translate. I often think his poems are "better" than Stafford's but they lack that mysterious quality, unfortunately. Perhaps he's too much of an extrovert to suit me. I have only one of his books: *The End of the Open Road*. What do you like best in that?

What's become of John Haines? He might be something for Swedish readers—the nearness to the North Pole. Also your poem about the Oyster must have something to tell us. What a wonderful MAD-poem!

In a few days the family and I are going to Gotland to visit some good friends. We'll stay with a family with the prosaic name of Svensson. Svensson himself is Gotland's only psychologist, but he is really less interested in psychology than in such subjects as music (he plays the organ, French horn, cello, oboe and trumpet flawlessly), birds (he instantly identifies by song every bird in this country), fossils (a rather useless knowledge) and the ornamentation of the Viking era. He was at one time very interested in Indians (particularly Rorschach-testing of Indians) and corresponded with a professor in Kansas. He is very modest and quiet. Monica sends her warmest.

your
Tomas T.

8 August, 66

Dear Tomas,

Be sure to get the *Life* magazine from a couple of weeks ago (the date must be around middle July) with the article on James Dickey! He brags that he made $25,000 on poetry last year! The truth is *Life* could only find one poet in the U.S. who was in favor of the Vietnam war, so they wrote an article on him, instead of reviewing *A Poetry Reading against the Vietnam War*, which I know they were also debating doing.

Thank you for your letter! I'll try the couple of questions about the Lowell poem. I've never heard of toasting wheat-seeds. I think the attractiveness of the sound is one thing that drew Lowell to that food. It is definitely not popcorn. The scene is a wharf area, with some unloaded or abandoned freight boxes standing around. I knew a man in New York who used to sleep on the wharf in a large packing-crate. The Negro is probably in the same situation. The only food he is able to pick up on the wharf are some grains of wheat which have fallen out of torn sacks being loaded on ships. He has used some coal fallen out of sacks in the same way, and made a fire in an old barrel.

The most alive word in the poem is the first use of the word "ticking," which suggests the faint sound of ice-cakes rubbing against each other as they all float downstream.

Stafford is marvelous. I love his poems.

I intend to publish translations of your poems *both* in *Stand* and in *The Sixties*! Their readership doesn't overlap very much, since very few people in the U.S. read English magazines. I'll just postpone your publication in *The Sixties* a few months, and all will come out all right.

I like "I det fria" very much, though I am not convinced yet if or how the third stanza fits into the poem. It seems to stand off a bit, but it's possible I haven't really understood the movement of the poem yet either. I have to think about it. The center section is strong, with its "rotter, siffror, dagrar," and the wonderful line with the man leaning over the table. Is he simply shaking his head, as if to say "no" or is it a more violent motion? Or a more ambiguous motion—?

I'm enclosing a translation of your fir forest poem. I've probably fallen on my head!

Here is a new poem of my own:

As the Asian War Begins

There are things that cannot be seen,
Or are seen only by a minister who no longer believes in God,
Living in his parish like a crow in its nest.

And there are flowers with murky centers,
Impenetrable, ebony, basalt. . . .

Give us this day our daily bread.
Give us this day a glimpse of the moon,
Our enemies, the soldiers and the poor.

Love to all in your family! Mary, who is four, just came out to my study (an old chickenhouse) and said, "Come back to the nest! It is supper-time!"

So I close here,

Yours,
Robert

Aug 17, 66

Dear old Tomas,

Thank you for the letter and translation! I have chained myself to the typewriter here, with a cache of carrots to keep me in foodstuff, and am going to answer your letter! "the drawn pilot":

"Drawn" is used in this sense only of the *face,* and it means a face that shows a lot of strain and perhaps fatigue. The face of the pilot shows both fatigue from his flying, and an emotional strain, perhaps from fear of being shot down while he was bombing, perhaps from his awareness of the people he has killed. The word "drawn" was probably applied to faces like that sometimes because when a man is under strain the skin of his face does seem sometimes to be drawn tight over the bones, stretched over the bones like a drum head. It suggests "pale" also.

I have changed the title slightly, and you can adopt the new version if you think it best:

"Asian Peace Offers Rejected without Being Heard"

Changing "without publication" to "without being heard" helps for some people to connect the idea of the poem with the owl at the end, who seems to be the only creature in the U.S. with good hearing, hearing good enough to hear a peace offer.

If you like the earlier version: "Det finns fil kander in departemente" better than the repetition of Rusk, go ahead and use the earlier version for those two lines. Let the rest of the poem go as it is in the final version. I dropped "Liberal Arts graduates" because it was too long in English, a bad mouthful.

The ghost train goes back to a legend of the west. One of the earliest trains that went through the Rockies was buried in an avalanche of snow. Now, when the snow conditions are such that another avalanche might be possible, trainmen swear they have seen the ghost train appear again on its tracks, heading toward the place the disaster occurred, as a warning to the trainmen.

I like the translation very much!

"Snurriga" is a wonderful word. I was thinking of the Walt Disney film about the eccentric or mad professor, and all those Hollywood movies, really anti-intellectual operas.

Did I ever send you this one:

Counting Small-Boned Bodies

Let's count the bodies over again.

If we could only make the bodies smaller,
The size of skulls,
We could make a whole plain white with skulls in the moonlight!

If we could only make the bodies smaller,
Maybe we could get
A whole year's kill in front of us on a desk!

If we could only make the bodies smaller,
We could fit a body
Into a finger-ring, like

A Keepsake Forever.

(A Keepsake Forever is the way a diamond engagement ring is advertised in the U.S. So it is as if the Asian body in the ring were something for Americans terribly sentimental, "your bit of eternity.")

Affectionately,
Robert

Västerås, Sept. 66
Dear Roberto,

　　your letter came at the last possible minute, I crashed into the garage, drove 70 miles to Stockholm, burst into the Bonniers building, wrenched open the door to BLM and there, inside, sat Lars Gustafsson bent over the final proof of the September issue. I was just in time to put in the word HÅRJADE for DRAWN—an exact equivalence. Lars was worried. People at the press who had seen the Bly translations and Ferlinghetti's "Where Is Vietnam?" (his magnum opus without a doubt) had muttered something to the effect that "there could be trouble about this . . ." It'll be interesting to see the reactions.

The issue, by the way, contains the now well-known polemic between Weiss and Enzensberger about "engagement"—where Enzensberger with full justification calls Weiss "an MRA from the Left." The attempt of the Communists to monopolize "engagement" and sail forward on outspread indignation makes me angry, as so much else makes me angry right now.

Thanks for the tip about buying *Life*. The presentation of Dickey put me in mind of that character in Salinger who thinks he has to crush thirty bones in a person's hand when he shakes hands, so that nobody will suspect him of being homosexual.

Charles Whitman was in the same issue. Did you see the photo of the little boy standing with his daddy's guns on the beach? There are secret threads running through that issue of the magazine. What you say in "Plaintiff" (?) about the drift towards masculine brutality goes IN MEDIAS RES. But why should the masculine be so self-evidently associated with the brutal? Come off it! To be masculine is to be a man, period. The rooster has a red comb on his head and goes cock-a-doodle-doo, the hen lays eggs. Why do so many men in the U.S.A. doubt deep down that they are men? Why do authors like Mailer love to hang out with boxers, grateful to be allowed to brush up against them? Monica had bought a little outfit for Sellin's one-year-old boy. But a good friend who had lived many years in America advised us not to send it because in the U.S. it would be taken for a GIRL'S outfit—a clear distinction between boys' and girls' clothing is made at one year old. Later I heard that the Sellins didn't bother about such things, but by then we had already given the suit away to a little Swedish hermaphrodite. It does seem so far out that at one year old you already have to start getting used to signaling your sex through certain attributes. It's not enough to rest secure in the fact that you have a penis and all in good time will grow a beard. You have to get off a shot from time to time, hit somebody in the kisser, be "violent," or make a lot of money. Though I have to say that in my personal experience the American is gentle, friendly and cooperative. And that he's often short of cash.

But not as short of cash as I've now begun to be. Dreadful! Good grief! Despite the fact that I have a salary from the state of 25,000 crowns (about 5,000 dollars) a year as long as I live! This sum is guaranteed. If I earn 10,000 I get 15,000, if I earn 20,000 I get 5,000, and so on. Right now I'm earning about 30,000 from my job, and therefore don't get an a single öre [smallest coin]. But in 1968 I'm thinking of taking a sabbatical just to write and read and travel and eat . . . And besides that I now get a secure old age!

One of my old patients at Roxtuna has shot a police officer to death and has been hunted through the whole of Sweden by great throngs of policemen, newspaper reporters, and mobs of people. Another has caused a scandal by publishing a book in which he "exposes" the Swedish prison system. One of his bits of bravado was when he posed as "Tranströmer, a psychologist from Linköping" at a hotel in the country. Who am I really? I've been brooding a lot lately about my six years at Roxtuna. I ought to write something on the subject, but what? I can't get away from the problem of criminality, though it's extremely nice not to have to work with it professionally any more. The whole business has shrunk down to the fact that I do testing at an institute up in the woods north of Västerås and it's fantastically pleasant there.

Yseult Snepvangers has not sent Dickey's book as she wrote she would (Creeley's came instead). But her name is splendid. Pure baroque. (I also have a weakness for names with grandeur of a more sublimely simple style, classic simplicity: JOE POOL represents a good name in that genre.) Somebody at Wesleyan has also written to inform me that Ignatow, Simpson and Haines are on the way. I'm especially looking forward to Haines.

Your translation of "Open and Closed Spaces" is written in very good Blyish indeed. I've got only two changes. The sleeping man is too active in your version ("He takes the darkened house . . .") No, the house is not out and the man inside is lying still. Then we have the words "an invisible string which goes STRAIGHT UP in the sky . . ." That would mean this:

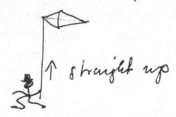

But you can't fly a kite like that. Correct position is this:

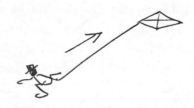

But what "snett up" [on a slant] is in English I don't know. About "Lamento":
The first section should be present tense: It lies there. TOMRUMMET
[void] is a neutral, physical Swedish word. Means a near vacuum but with-
out the scientific associations. I want an "empty" word too. "Universe"
is perhaps too rich in associations with astronauts etc. I don't know how
you would characterize "void" in English, but that's the word you find in
dictionaries. KAPPSÄCK [backpack, duffel] can pretty much look any old
way, it's something one has on long trips. It doesn't have any connotations
of luxury though. I was thinking of a fairly ripped, lumpy thing. Not any-
thing "shiny." Your suggestion works fine. Section 3: "A rustling" could
mean "prassel" [rustling]. But I had thought of VISSLING [whistling].
Perhaps a whistled signal from a bird or from an agent or from a football
referree—we don't know. Finally the cherry tree at the end: their branches
shake against the trucks in a friendly and at the same time somewhat vig-
orous way. "Slap on the back" [Klappar om] is what the team in a game
does to a runner who makes a goal or what relatives do when they greet
one another at the station. The translation that appears in *Sweden Writes*
is bad—"brush" is considerably better. The main thing is to get an im-
pression of robust tenderness, a lightly humorous effect in a dead-serious
poem.

Wonderful to move over to blyish. Maybe the poems will actually be as alive
in English as in Swedish. The language isn't the main problem. The problem
is the other stuff, the landscape, the associations. A thing like keepsake for-
ever would be impossible to translate, and with it that whole excellent poem.
I think it's your strongest "political" poem, because in an intimately vision-
ary way it propels itself into that which is truly relevant in a modern democ-
racy: collective sin, collective detachment. [------]

Did you know that *The Sixties* has a counterpart in Norway now? A young
man in Lambretta, Jan Erik Vold, who visited me the other day, talked
about a magazine called *Profil* that he and several others publish in Oslo.
He is some kind of enfant terrible in Norwegian poetry. I got some cop-
ies of the magazine and by God it not only lacked collections of examples
of dead and living poetry (waxworks of the sort that used to appear in

your magazine) but also had a symbol in the shape of a woollen mitten which is bestowed upon bad reviewers etc. Among the editors was a young American named Noel Cobb, who is evidently a student of yours. Voilà. You ought to look at Vold's own poetry if you're preparing a Norwegian anthology. It's possible that you would find it too abstract, but it means something new for Norway, that's very clear.

Warm greetings from the whole family are clinging tightly to the underside of the mail plane's wings, trembling at high altitudes.

Your friend
Tomas

Västerås 1 Oct 66

Dear Robert, deep fisherman,

Each day there comes new mail from *The Sixties,* Wesleyan, and yourself. There are all sorts of gifts in the exchange of letters—wonderful. It's as if it is fall and fruit falls from the trees. A special thanks I should give to you for *Ducks,* which I hope will become a bestseller, something like *Gone with the Wind.*

In about ten days I will get my new book and send it by boat to you with an issue of the Norwegian magazine which I mentioned to you in an earlier letter. Noel Cobb has been evicted from Norway on grounds of experiments with marijuana!

Will you be so kind as to glance at this poem? Someone has translated three poems of mine which you don't have. I haven't sent the Swedish text, so you'll have to judge it on the basis of the American text alone. Does it sound OK? Also my translation of Lowell's old Hudson poem. In all haste,

Tomas

P.S. There have been many exciting reactions to the BLM issue. It generally seems to be considered one of the best numbers people have seen.

P.P.S. I have begun to get in trouble with some of my best friends. One supports the American Vietnam politics and other has become so completely communist that he seems eager for indoctrination, declares himself opposed to Amnesty because it points too much at the imprisonments in the East, etc. Both speak with a kind of brutal tone. Our old friendships tend to become thin. That's the background to this:

Conflict

After a political argument or wrangle, I become lonesome.
An empty chair opens out into the night sky.
There is no way back. My friend leaves the house.
A heavy moving van rumbles by on the road.
My eyes rest there like wide-awake stones.

(translated by RB)

8 Oct, 66

Dear Tomas,

Your letter just came; let me answer the questions first. The translation of Lowell sounds marvelous. I have doubts only about the very last lines: I'm not sure the pictures in Swedish have the same *mood*. At any rate, this is the mood in English: the shore of the Hudson rises rather steeply in some places, so the other side, with its factories, sometimes gives the effect of rock-ledges in Africa or some sunny, rocky place, like so:

"Branns" may be a little too active. Oddly, there is no color of *red* in the lines at all, just a hideous passive yellow, like a huge yellow snake sunning itself in some prehistorical landscape. The landscape is not "ett landskap" I think but rather "the landscape." For the moment, this landscape is considered to be *the entire landscape* of America—it stands for the whole countryside. The last line then is a brutal and despairing attack on the United States. What it has done with the countryside the Indians left he considers "unforgivable."

Thank you for the *Dagens Nyheter* poems. You know it turns out Hjorth turned down Sonnevi's translation of "Asian Peace Offers" in April. Sonnevi said, "When I met Lars Gustaffson he was quite embarrassed when he realized that BLM had refused the very same poem in April." Sonnevi thought your translation of Asian Peace Offers was good, and in fact thought "the latter part of it is better than mine." He didn't understand the word "yrseldarrar" in the first part, but that was the only word he disagreed with. I don't know why he didn't like it—he didn't say.

[------]

Would you send me a copy of that BLM with the Vietnam poems in it? They never send me anything, and I would like to see the issue.

The three translations of your poems into English, done by this mysterious "X," are curious. It's clear that English is not the native language of the man who translated them. It's strange—in many cases the rough meaning is perfectly correct, and yet the *associations* are off, so it is like unintended dissonance in music. The lines go smoothly, and then suddenly shudder, like a car with the brakes on. Phrases like "then there was a fastness" or "news-sheets" (he means newspapers), or "special cast of countenance" (he means a "certain look on the face") are like boulders that grind against the bottom of the car and, eventually, take off the oil pan.

On the whole, I am surprised at how well they are done—knowing that English is not the translator's native language—in some ways, amazing—and yet, finally, they are not good translations because an air of unreality hangs over the language all the way—exactly the opposite of the mood you want to give, and do give in Swedish. In short, the poems seem to be accurate, but are not written in English.

I wonder who "X" is? Goran Printz-Påhlson? If I guess right, you have to tell me!

Thank you for "Konflikt." I know the feeling well. The Vietnam war here has split families, as well as friends, as nothing else in American history has done since the Civil War. About angry tones of voice: of course all Westerners have so much aggression in them that they are ready at any instant to destroy their own psychic balance and friendships by means of fierce abstract arguments. Christian fundamentalists use up their aggression in the U.S. in arguments about love. So everyone fights his own Vietnam, killing women and children right and left. Do you know Yeats's poem "In Memory of Eva Gore-Booth and Con Markiewicz"? Whitman is another poet who really understood how wrong all this was.

Yet all of this doesn't help reduce the pain.

We gave an anti-Vietnam poetry reading at the University of Michigan at Ann Arbor Sunday. Galway Kinnell came in from Portland, and Don Hall read also, and W. D. Snodgrass (who read only poems of Randall Jarrell—bad poems); then we had a great actor named Will Geer, who read sections of Whitman, as well as Mark Twain's *War Prayer*, a really powerful piece. My wife was in the audience, and all the time I was introducing and reading "Small-Boned Bodies" a group of male students near her was cursing and grumbling, against me and against the poem. They hate the suggestion that America is being brutalized. The little poem is getting to be well-known, though no one will print it. The last to refuse it was the Book Section of the *Herald Tribune* and *Washington Post* this week, who had asked me for poems. So the poem has never been published over here.

Would you do me a favor? A publisher is interested in my translating from the Swedish a novel by P. C. Jersild called *Calvinols resa genom världen*. Is this novel any good? Would you give me your opinion of it? I don't want to translate anything unless it is really good—otherwise it is a waste of time. I'd rather not even spend the time looking at the novel unless there was some possibility of real quality; so your opinion would be very valuable to me.

You didn't mention in your letter if you wanted the new translations into

English returned to you or not. I'll keep them here, meanwhile, and if you do want them, just write me a note and I'll return them immediately.

Write soon!

Robert

Västerås 10-29-66

Dear Robert,

In a fit of recklessness I'm sending the book by air mail so you won't have to wait till Christmas. As you know, literary life in Sweden is played out in the daily papers and where well-known authors are concerned you get reviewed the same day the book comes out. In other words my sentence has been pronounced. In the most influential paper, *Dagens Nyheter,* one of the younger critics wrote that I was unalterably the same, somewhat worse now however than in my first book from 1954. He praised me too, but for the initiated it was immediately clear that I've been knocked off my pedestal. It's like in China—if Chou suddenly stands number 5 after Mao instead of number 3, it means that Chou is half dead. The expert understands that. However, the stupid general public* has bought my book (1100 copies were sold the first two weeks). In *Aftonbladet* Björn Håkansson wrote a critique that gave rise to a small debate. The headline of his contribution was "The Solitary Picture Collector" (which has certain associations with somebody who collects pornographic pictures). He

---

*O blessed, silent poetry-reading public, I love you!

moralized quite powerfully. My poetry strolled through the world "like a well-heeled tourist. But are we what it wishes to find? No, not us. It wants to find pictures; pictures for a solitude which is populated with pictures. If one of us gets to be there too, it's as a blob of color." . . . and later "If one sees only the general in the individual and in history only things and conditions, one legitimizes a passive, contemplative attitude toward the world around oneself, which perhaps provides a yearning experience of amazing distance and cosmic peace but at the cost of all motivation to engage in events and change the world." The whole thing culminated in an accusation that I was legitimizing the idea that "the world might be contemplated as a poem." As you notice, I very nearly fell victim to the Cultural Revolution there! Generally speaking the young Marxists in Sweden have little tolerance for poetry. One should show decency and stop writing. I'm also sending you a considerably more benevolent review—you're mentioned there too, probably owing to the fact that Hedin is a good friend of Sonnevi, who may have gossiped. Outside Stockholm the better critics have generally observed that the new book contains a lot of new subject matter, something that often conduces to artistic uncertainty. But they have in fact noticed that it isn't exactly the same book as "17 Poems."

This has been an egocentric message. I hope to get one just like it when your book is published. It feels good anyway to be able to get out and confront "the intellectuals." They turn their serious, reproachful faces toward me: YOU ARE NOT SOCIALLY ENGAGED. I reply, stammering, that I have worked full-time for 6 years in social work on an unstable front in society. Doesn't count! they answer—YOU HAVEN'T WRITTEN ONE SINGLE ARTICLE DECLARING YOUR POLITICAL POSITION; YOU ARE—O U T.

Thanks for your comments about Lowell—I will take at least two of your remarks ad notam.

    With good wishes
    Tomas

P.S. When I'm feeling strong I'll read Jersild. But it is very desirable however to start reading novels in old age.

20 Nov., 66

Dear Tomas,

Thank you for your book! I have been eating it up like those wonderful dates that come with pictures of camels on the package—in one of your earlier lives you were a camel—(that's why you're able to go for miles through the desert) (that's why you know where the oases are—cf your Monica!) Anyway the book is very good, and I'm enjoying it tremendously. As I read in it I say, "Well, look at all the things I haven't done yet!" So it reminds me of poems I might write sometime in the *future*, so it's a *future* book, the kind I like best. You do some very strange things in this book. I translated for Carolyn [Bly] your poem about walking in the woods, and evil shaking his head across a desk, and the modern building with so much glass, and finally the airport scene. She was startled and moved. And with her true sense, which never fails, excited by something new, that is moving forward, just at the edge of the forest. The trains that meet in the (station of this) poem come from such long distances, each of them! That is what is good! One train still has snow on it, another one has a palm leaf caught in the undercarriage—

Oh you're a bloody genius!

So here, I lift a cup of tea to you! It's 11:44 A.M. Congratulations and thanks!

By the way, did you notice that your *Hemligheter på vägen* cover was used as the model for *A Poetry Reading Against the Vietnam War*? Yes. I sent it along to the printer, and told him to imitate your cover exactly, even to the color! He did.

I enjoyed Bengt-Erik Hedin's essay—I'd love to see more reviews, if you have extra copies of them—it gives me a sense of what Swedish criticism is like.

I'll send you the most insulting review I've ever gotten—it's wonderful, he objects to everything about me except the size of my shoes!

Jim Wright is reading in New York tonight. He has a fine new poem on Leopardi, which will be in the next *Sixties,* along with a poem about our poaching activities.

Lowell and his friends are not all pleased by my article on Lowell's poetry in the last *Sixties* (the red one). It is the only really harsh criticism he has gotten for about ten years, and I'm accused of not bowing to the golden calf. I am very much in the doghouse in N.Y. now, but it's a cozy doghouse, I don't mind!

Thursday about 10 of America's hoarse and chain-smoking larks go down to Houston for a sort of songfest in the bare trees of Texas. We'll all be sitting about there on the branches . . . I'm looking forward to it, mainly because Gary Snyder will be there, whom I've never met. Also there will be Robert Creeley with his one eye, Don Hall with his huge stomach, W. S. Merwin with his 55-year-old wife, May Swenson with her lead-soled boots for stomping on male poets, Carolyn Kizer with her cynical Washington smile (she is rumored to be a mistress of Pres. Johnson's) etc. etc.

Write soon! Warm wishes to Monica & yourself from the Minnesota frontier.

Yours, Robert

1967

Västerås 1-7-67

Dear Roberto,

    some German professor is doubtless going to publish Robert Bly's *Briefe* in 16 volumes someday. Don't let this vision of the future scare you off writing a speedy reply to this letter! I need a little transatlantic blood transfusion.

During the fall I've been working on psychological assignments, among other things for an institute for people with CP. I've also been suffering through a Vietnam depression and reading reviews of my book. I'm very interested in hearing what people are saying about the Viet Nam war right now. In Europe opinion has turned against the U.S. In Sweden, for example, according to Gallup only 8% support American political policy. From what they write in the Swedish papers, it doesn't appear that there's been any change of opinion in the U.S., rather that the hawks' position has become stronger after the election. Typical of the obvious pessimism concerning anything about America is that the local paper in Västerås wrote that the election of Hatfield in Oregon was a triumph for official policy—Duncan was described as a dove! I was completely horrified of course and called the paper's foreign editor and pointed out the error. He apologized again and again. He had—like Homer—dozed off for a while. That anyone who was elected should be a dove naturally seemed so improbable, especially since Rea . . . R . . . (I'm having trouble getting the name out) R E A G A N won so big. %+)/11R(%&!!! How did the vote go in Minnesota?

And now for something less meaningful. From my last letter you will probably have gathered that this time I got some pretty negative reviews. Most have been positive but in *Aftonbladet,* in some ways in DN, in BLM, and a few more, other notes have been struck. A long article about cultural life in BLM was written by a specialist in POP (Leif Nylén) who unfortunately felt he had to assert that TT in his "passivity," "resignation," lack of ideology etc. has to be included in "den förbrukade litteraturen" (used up literature). A sort of grotesque Tranströmer-debate* ensued. My defenders were plainly more numerous than my antagonists. I have at this point been defended both by old Communists and by right-wing authors. Mainly they've disliked the fact that I haven't reconstructed myself enough, that I'm not interested enough in the mass media, McLuhan, POP or "Concretism." The other accusation is that I'm insufficiently socially and politically "engaged." Now it happens that I have in fact been doing social work full-time for 7 years—you're perhaps thinking that would grant me a kind of exemption—ah, then you aren't familiar with the current Swedish cultural climate. The political accusation consists of the fact that I'm not directed by ideology; this year one should preferably be a card-carrying Marxist. Instead, suspect elements of old-fashioned individualism, including religiosity, have been detected. I don't think it's possible to give a sense of the present Swedish cultural climate to any foreigner. I'm sending an article from DN as a sample all the same.

Another item from DN is the photo of the T family that appeared at the end of an article. You're not getting the article itself, however—it actually embarrassed me: the reporter had taken it as his mission to present me as an extraordinarily "engaged" person!

---

*And slow—replies come at 14-day intervals in papers in both Sweden & Finland.

You can't tell from the picture in the paper, but I am at the moment 110 years old and long to be allowed to retreat for a period of meditation. Naturally, I'm longing most of all to write some verses again. Getting to read something good that was written this year, by you for instance, would be a sort of stimulus in that direction. I'm told there were poems by you in *Poetry.* Send them for God's sake!

Västerås has suddenly become a cultural city, since the editor of BLM, author, philosopher, lecturer, Father of Swedish Literature and Bly-translator Lars Gustafsson has moved here. He lives in a special writer's residence in the old part of town. He has just visited Berlin, where he read his own work on TV. There he shared a lodging with Kenneth Rexroth, who displayed a strange knowledge of modern Swedish literature. Among other things he said that he very much appreciated Tranströmer's translations of himself (I've never done any) and Lars G's poems in French (Lars has never been translated into French). Now it happens that Lars has so much on his mind at the same time that he often mixes them up (he believes for example that some of your poems are written by L. Simpson) and if Rexroth is of the same type, the strangest collisions are bound to occur. —On the subject of what you said in your latest, I've brought up the subject of BLM's Vietnam-poem issue with Lars, and he says he's sent it to you.

Warmest greetings to the family. I was happy that old "Out in the Open" was appreciated. It's a sort of intercession for the U.S. among other things, and may all the prayer mills grind day and night for the good and hidden powers.

Yours,
Tomas T.

Västerås 1-15-67
Dear Robert,

     your translations arrived in the mailbox while I was sitting eating breakfast with a visiting Finnish poet and author of children's books. I ran my eye hastily over the letter and told the abovementioned party (since he asked) a few things about its contents. Stephen Potter couldn't have arranged a better situation. For a moment he seemed to believe that this was what ordinarily occurred at breakfast in my house: that the foremost poets of the continents send me their translations and suggestions for publication. My delight, however, couldn't be concealed for long.

And now the commentaries: "Track" seems wonderfully aptly translated. "Lamento" also—"hug" is a good variant for "klappa om." "Summer Grass" is more like a Fantasia on a theme by TT, but fully acceptable, perhaps better in its English version than in its Swedish one. "Kyrie" good, possibly with the exception of "loud steps"—the Swedish words "tunga steg" [heavy steps] are not in the first instance a description of SOUND but of a kinesthetic experience. "A Winter Night" probably can't be translated so that the rhythm is retained. One can choose: either to make it over some and have the rhythm intact or to do as *Sixties* always does in cases of this kind. I think now that you have in any case, and in spite of being so literal, succeeded well in preserving the dactylic quality of the poem (*Sixties* doesn't like iambics either!). The final lines should maybe be reduced somewhat, "feel" and "entirely" probably aren't strictly necessary? Maybe "entirely" should stay in for the sake of the rhythm. Feel?

"From an African Diary" sounds so good in your English version that I wonder if it wasn't conceived in English from the outset and the Swedish text isn't a kind of translation. One thing is Swedish however, and has caused a misunderstanding. HÖTORG ARTIST is something special that you don't know about. Hötorget is a square in Stockholm where formerly (and maybe also now) bad art used to be sold cheap. The sort of landscapes with pines and red cottages, portraits of gypsy women, sunsets. It refers in other words to mass-produced, conventionally painted pictures in oils which were sold cheap by vendors on the street. HÖTORG ART has gradually come to stand for cheap, mass-produced, conventional art. HÖTORG ARTIST, in other words, is the same as the German "Kitschmaler." Kitsch would be the German word, but what is the English? Well. When I was in Africa I discovered that there is hötorg art there too. Vagabond salesmen in Uganda, Burundi and the Congo sold pastels cheap—I bought one. The strange thing was that the human figures in their stereotypical form were thin in these pictures. There's the idea of the first line. Instead, you've conjured up the picture of emaciated Africans in the marketplace. The meaning, in other words, is: On the paintings of the bad congolese artist the figures move about skinny as insects.

"A tourist" in section 2 corresponds to "turisten" in the original version of the poem, which I must have sent you sometime. In the book I've changed it to "utlänning"—the foreigner. The episode is autobiographical (the place was Bangui in the Republic of Central Africa). I probably changed it from "tourist" to "foreigner" for reasons of vanity. I didn't like to consider myself a tourist! (Besides, it was preposterous that anybody would be a tourist in the Republic of Central Africa.) —In the last section you have the plural for some reason, the students, but in Swedish it's one student. Dare I believe that the German plural ending -en ("ach die Studenten, die Studenten") has influenced you? (In Swedish the plural would be STUDENTERNA.) Under the title of the poem I've put "(1963)" in the book version—it's best to date things in these times.

"Allegro" is all right except for line 8. I don't become a man who takes it all calmly, no I MIMIC ONE.

1-25

I've gotten a book, very well known in Denmark, by Poul Borum, called *Poetic Modernism,* which goes through the most important poets from Baudelaire to Eugen Gomringer. One chapter is entitled "Young America" and includes the names Berryman ("who for heaven's sake must not be confused with the frightful women's-magazine poet John Betjeman"), Lowell (his *For the Union Dead* is explained as being "somewhat weaker"), Plath, Snyder, Ashbery, Levertov, Creeley and Bly. Of the last-named he writes "clear, deep and funny and necessary poems." You are further praised for translations "based on relevance and not on formalism." "Poem in 3 parts" and—"Über allen Gipfeln" are quoted.

I get some pretty words myself and am placed between Yves Bonnefoy and
Ted Hughes. The American names are actually, from the Nordic view-
point, original, among other things because the Beatniks are only men-
tioned as "amusing."

Till next time!
   Your friend
      Tomas T.

                           20 Feb, '67

Dear Tomas,
   Thank you for your notes on the translations! I wonder if "thumps"
would do for "tunga steg." We sometimes say "My heart is thumping," and
there is always a little bit of fear in the phrase. I'm not sure if "A Winter
Night" will ever succeed—my first draft was worse than this one. But it's
like walking on a moving wire! The poem sways back and forth in a lovely
way, and I fall off! I'm not sure, by the way, exactly what motion the caravan
has as it starts off from Lapland. I'm not sure of the suggestions around the
whole event. Are there camels in this caravan? It must be a good old Arab-
type caravan with face veils and Richard Burton and everyone in it—?
   I missed the "Hötorgskonst" completely. We call that "tourist art" or
"sunset art" (sunsets are the favorite subject over here—I'll have to think
farther).
   I've written for Borum's book—I want to see what he says about you!
This guy must be intelligent!
   We did our Napalm Poetry Reading in N.Y., showing color slides—
unbelievably harrowing things—of napalmed children in Vietnamese
hospitals—between the poems. There was tremendous emotion in the au-
dience. Several times when I read comments from State Dept spokesmen—
the State Dept is trying to keep the burned children out of this country,
and will not give them visas even to be treated by plastic surgeons here so
far—the audience hissed with anger at the State Dept.

I'm in the process of reproducing the program, prose quotations, slides, and poems now, so it can be shown in many colleges at the same time. We really don't need *poets* for this program—only a good reader and slide projector.

We also took a truck out in various places in N.Y. that week with sound equipment, a short skit about the war, 15 poets, and magnified photographs of the burned children. It was wild. The negroes were very polite. The most unruly audiences (they were street audiences) were upper middle class white areas. On Thurs, when I wasn't with the truck, they all got beat up by a bunch of Cuban exiles, all the sound equipment smashed, etc.

So at last I'm home, and can bounce on my knee our new son, Noah! We both liked the name Noah because he was a friend to the animals. Everyone said, can't you find a good Norwegian name for him—Lars? or Olaf? or Eric? I said, how about Jeremiah? So they shut up. Noah was 9 pounds, 2 ounces, and has a majestic scowl.

Thank you for the photograph from DN! Carol says you look lovely with your hair long, and you are to wear it that way always. You have caught us all in your fixed stare in the photo, and look like the Ancient Mariner, about to tell us of tremendous sea serpents you have just seen, ghost ships with all the men in chains, etc. We'll never get out of the room until you tell that story!

Believe me, Susan Sontag is the greatest bore in the world. Jim Wright out of sheer self-protection, takes a drink every time her name is mentioned. She represents HELL AS (COMPLICATED) BOREDOM. We have your whole Pop art crowd in the U.S. too—but the concrete business is drowned out here because, obviously, one of those concrete poets—they are men made of Lego bricks—can say nothing meaningful about the Vietnam war. So the crisis tends to undermine these buildings built on sand. Interestingly enough, the poets in the U.S. that have proved themselves most able to write strong poems about the situation the United States is in are the *romantic* poets—Denise Levertov, Robert Duncan, Galway Kinnell. That fact has been a shock to the Susan Sontag crowd, as well as the Marxist crowd. The professional leftists haven't written or done a single memorable thing on the war.

Don't bother yourself with the attacks on your work—Machado used
to get the same thing, and now all his critics say, "Gee, I was wrong!" The
only way to read articles on your own books is with one hand over your
mouth to keep from laughing.

Louis Simpson always keeps his attacks around for six months before
reading them—by then, the book seems like someone else's, and you can
cheer them on more! more!

Of course, Sweden is smaller than the U.S. A criticism in the U.S. is
like getting hit with a stone thrown from far far away. It was probably an
accident. I suppose in Sweden you have the feeling the stones are coming
from nearby—Someone is throwing stones at me! You can almost see the
expression on their faces. (faces of the stones.)

Write soon! And send some poems! Everyone says your poems are the
best thing in the New Directions annual. And they are!

My best to Monica,

Yours,

Robert

Västerås 3-4-67

Dear Roberto,

thanks for two missives: your letter with poems, animals, friendly
words and now today some pages from the *Nation*. But first, loud trum-
pet blasts from us to herald the birth of your son Noah, friend of the ani-
mals! However did you keep from telling us he was on the way? Our best
wishes to him—if those are even needed for a baby that weighs so much . . .

It was fine to read about your tours with the burned Vietnamese
children—one seizes upon every reminder that the U.S.A. has a con-
science with the most urgent gratitude. All the same, it feels good that you
are back in Minnesota just now, safe from furious Cubans and the bad air
in New York.

The present degradation of the official U.S.A. torments me as if I were an
American myself. Why? What kind of poor, suffering, tortuous thread is

it that runs between me and the wrinkled devil's masks in the Pentagon? Johnson has now lost everything but his face, it stands by itself in the desert wastes, completely hollow. One who is frightened to death of losing face will eventually lose everything except his face.

Your poems were truly a great and life-giving injection from straight across The Great Water. It was impossible not to translate the turtle poem, it happened seemingly all by itself. The first section is problematic, though, I'll have to think further about it. MAD is difficult to translate. It also sounds strange in Swedish that WE wake up like a sea urchin. Does PASS mean a mountain pass or a ford (are we wading in blood?) But the rest of the poem lifts and carries so delightfully well, it's both Dante and Walt Disney. Here in short is a first draft:

A Journey with Women

1

Floating in turtle blood, going backward and forward,
We wake up like a mad sea-urchin
On the bloody fields near the secret pass—
There the dead sleep in jars . . .

2

Or we go at night slowly into the tunnels of the tortoise's claws,
Carrying chunks of the moon
To light the tunnels,
Listening for the sound of rocks falling into the sea . . .

3

Waking, we find ourselves in the tortoise's beak,
As he carries us high
Over New Jersey—going swiftly
Through the darkness between the constellations . . .

4

At dawn we are still transparent, pulling
In the starlight;
We are still falling like a room
Full of moonlight through the air . . .
            (RB original)

I would also like to translate the ultimate and last draft of "The Peace March" whenever it comes. I want your translation of "African Diary" for the magazine *Transition* (since "Hötorg art" has been corrected). I saw Mr. Rajat Neogy from Kampala when he was here—he is the editor of that Ugandan magazine—and he wanted it because "you really got something of Africa in it." There was a convention of African writers in Stockholm recently. I was there for one day, mostly in order to see Rajat, who is an old pal of mine. Unfortunately I was forced to hear Swedish writers stand up and sing their tired old refrain—macabre. They confessed their sins (for belonging to the colonial race, for being Swedes, etc.) in an aggressive manner that astonished the Africans and made natural contact between them difficult. Lundkvist painted Sweden very black, and also informed them that a large percentage of the Swedish people were "supporting the American war in Viet-Nam." According to the latest Gallup poll, precisely 8% of them do. I should have gotten up and said so, but was too cowardly of course.

When I read the words of encouragement in your letter I have the embarrassing sense that I've complained in some letter about having gotten bad reviews. No, it was only from a few directions that I was accused of having represented a "used-up literature" etc. and it feels quite good to be able to sail against the wind for a while. I'm not surfing on the waves of success this time, but still, poets may swim against the current if they can. I'm getting shouts of encouragement from many directions. Yours are worth the most, however.

                Best wishes from us
                Tomas T.

P.S.

The *Nation* was very interesting. What you say about "the iciness of de-sensitization" was entirely true and essential. Likewise I dream about that grasshopper's leap.

But the poets had better shave off their beards before they visit the Bronx! They ought to come disguised as Bronx housewives. An esteemed, well turned out senator, or Dr. Spock or some baseball hero with a Colgate smile is worth several hundred beatniks in that context. It's such an important matter.

In a few hours I will go to bed in a sleeping car and wake up in Malmö in the morning. I'll mail this letter in Copenhagen and continue on myself to Fredericia on Jylland, where I'll read my own work and talk with students at a folk high school [folkhögskola]. At the end of March I'm going to England for the first time in my life. Shall I convey greetings to anybody there? It will be a short visit—I'm going with a good friend who'll be selling computers! Write soon.

Best wishes to the 5 in Odin House! TT

Västerås again, 5-4-67

Dear Robert,

I've been back in Sweden for 10 days and am already longing to be abroad again. I liked London, it's an amazingly pleasant city for being so big. Most of the Englishmen were chubby little rascals (without much humor), the food was good, the sun shone. I also visited Göran Printz-Påhlson in Cambridge, where he sat sighing over the strict class system in the old English universities. It's pure apartheid—he's not even allowed to walk on the lawns because he isn't a Fellow. I drank beer with some of his students— one of them by the way had translated me in *Adam*. They were exotic figures, which one might expect since they were studying Scandinavian languages. One of them spoke excellent Swedish. Pronounced the words not with an English but a Portuguese accent. Another had a Beatles hair-cut and used to take part in the Hötorget (sic!) mods riots in Stockholm in the summers. It would almost have been nice if they had had a little plastic and marshmallow in them.

In London I called Carroll up. "Oh Hello Mr Transtromrrrr, how nice of you to ring, we must get together, I should publish your poems in my press," he began without preamble. I was completely unprepared for this and purely reflexively (reacting out of my Swedish psyche) I started to say that that was surely impossible, oh no, etc. —I all but said I was a totally worthless writer. Against the next occasion I'll practice the correct response in such a circumstance, such as THIS IS A DAMNED GOOD IDEA or something of the sort. Unfortunately we never did meet, we weren't free at the same times—it's too bad, for he seems like a nice person to have a pint with. However, I met Michael Hamburger and he was exactly as good as you had described him. He was the only Englishman I came in actual contact with.

In Stockholm we're having THE TRIBUNAL—I suppose you've heard about that. It's one of those typical things that make you feel like you've got a big crack straight through from your scalp to your crotch. What's tragic about it is that it could be a good thing—if it weren't dominated by people who have hated America for many years and who can't inspire confidence in those it really concerns, above all in the U.S.A. Then there's all the courtroom terminology . . . As things stand now, facts that have been thoroughly and patiently gathered together aren't going to have any effect when they're presented, because it will be all too easy to dismiss them as "propaganda." Then there's the fact that the Tribunal has led to such atrocities as Tage Erlander (a person who happens to be our Prime Minister) almost apologizing on American TV for the Tribunal's being allowed to come to Sweden. However, Sartre gave a good speech on Opening Day, and maybe some of the information can get through, even if presented by one-eyed fellows.

Hatred flourishes. A writer my own age—and previously a very close friend of mine—said recently at a meeting that it would be a great misfortune if Johnson stopped the bombing of North Vietnam, since hatred of the U.S. would then diminish (I didn't hear this myself, it was reported in the paper). This is the Year of the hawks, on all sides.

I would rather sound a little less gloomy. Eric Sellin wrote in his last letter that it was of course always nice to get a letter from me, but that what I wrote always had the effect of deepening the gloom he felt about the world situation. I'm also sending you a fantastically gloomy poem (though it has a hopeful curl at the end). I have trouble getting going (it's that CRACK) and have to write some shit out of my system first. I hope that soon, in the spring, in the summer, something will happen: the bung will fall out of the barrel and My Life's Work will come pouring out, something tremendously long and tremendously concentrated ah . . .

Send more little magazines and signs of life! The portrait gallery of famous American poets was fantastic. What mature physiognomies! I'd quite like to have a beer with Donald Hall. (I notice that I often return to the subject of beer*—one of Sweden's faults is that we drink too little beer here.) Monica and the little ones say hello.

Your friend,
Tomas T.

10 June, '67

Dear Tomas,

    Here it is, lovely wet old spring. It has been raining for 10 days, and my Norwegian soul (or my mildew) is just beginning to feel comfortable. I'm

---

*A result of the England trip.

home for the summer—no more hopping about! I just jump around inside my head now—leaping from ear to ear, jumping on the sofas inside my brain—springs poking out in all directions, legs fallen off—

I'm glad you met Michael Hamburger. He's awfully ethereal compared to his extroverted, meaty name. A sweet man.

I just sent back page proofs on my new book—it will be ready in another month or so, and I'll send you a copy then.

My translation of Hamsun's *Hunger* is out too, but I won't send you a copy—it's better in Norwegian!

The Stockholm trial got almost no publicity here. I have the clear feeling by the way that we are losing—not only politically, but *militarily*—in Vietnam. The Marine commander has been removed. Letters I get from soldiers in Vietnam (who write poetry and send me some at times) are full of disgust and despair—much more so than a year ago.

Thank you for the wall-stumbling-along-in-the-street poem. Very odd. It is frightening when the empty houses gather as an army.

Write soon. Forgive my long gaps—I'll send some poems next time.

Runmarö 7-11-67 A.D. MCMLXVII
Dear Robert,

as you see, I've moved out to our cottage on the island in the archipelago for the next while. We're on vacation. I forgot my typewriter but have found an old one from the beginning of the century, in one of the houses in the village. The type is hard to read, but has a sentimental value of its own. The keys are trembling with age—an old man's trembling fingers—he's a faithful old worn-out worker called CORONA. Me, I feel significantly younger than I did last year at this time, better than for a good long while, actually. Now something will finally get done! I'll start by finishing a first version of your wonderful president poem. By now Sonnevi has published at least three of your poems in the Swedish press, I only two (it's 3–2 in Sonnevi's favor). His latest was "As the Asian War Begins" in our only young writers' magazine, *Komma*. It's a good translation. [------] I can also inform you from Sweden that there is another Viet-Nam conference in Stockholm and this time I've contributed a little sum of money, which I didn't do at the [Bertrand] Russell Tribunal. The person who made the biggest impression this time was Dr. Spock. Has there been anything in the U.S. press about this conference? Spock asked the Swedes to come up with something besides demonstrations in the streets to influence opinion (in the U.S.). Maybe we should do something for the tourists? I've thought myself that a torrent of sober, well-brought-up letters to the editors of *Time* and *Life* from all over Europe might do some good.

Today the big trees around our house are full of wind. It's blowing so hard that green caterpillars keep falling into my coffee cup. I love the constant sound of it, the rising and falling—it only goes to show that I'm no real sailor. My grandmother (who was born in 1860) always got melancholy and uneasy when the wind moaned in the trees. She would think of the people in small boats out on the water hereabouts. Grandfather, who was a pilot, took himself to and from the big boats in a little rowboat with a sail. Once, in the 1890s, he was hired to sail a Stockholm gentleman from Runmarö to Stockholm. The passenger turned out to be Strindberg. My grandfather could only say about him afterwards that he was "a nice man."

Dear Robert, let me hear from you soon! Every time you go poaching with your Swedish net you should think about your Swedish readers and friends and remember that it's time to send something over. Monica sends her best, as do I, to the whole family.

Tomas

P.S. I'm enclosing a poem,* which jumped into me during a car trip in Dalarna, right before Midsummer. Of course, from a *Sixties* point of view it's a scandal, since it is mostly iambic. —When is *Sixties* coming out, by the way? The greedy public waits impatiently to snatch the new issue out of the bookmonger's hands!

---

*Do you have log driving in the U.S.A.?

Krylbo 8-8-67

Dear Robert,

I write in haste to hurry you up—I would like to submit "3 presidents" to a magazine and want to know if you approve of it or if you want anything changed. I'm also sending you some documents from Sweden. Lasse Söderberg's translations are of a rather good quality, particularly the first poem. In addition I have the pleasure of telling you that Söderberg is more than six feet tall. My own poem is a relapse into the Tranströmeresque "archipelago style" which can't be condemned too harshly. I'm only sending it as a testimonial to what a beautiful vacation I had, out among the islands.

I'm writing this during a work trip to a BORSTAL in the forest.

Have Myrdal's articles appeared anywhere in the American press? What he writes is purely self-evident, but since he seems to have a—perhaps undeserved—reputation in the U.S., maybe they could do some good.

Warmest greetings
Tomas

7 Sept, '67

Dear Tomas,

Forgive my slowness! I get slow and lethargic in August, like the sap in trees, and besides, I've been sick! (Read Alan Watts—his *Nature, Man and Woman* is a wonderful book—if it's not in Swedish, let me know, and I'll send you a copy in English.)

Your translation of "Three Presidents" is wonderful, and I haven't a single criticism. If you are doubtful about "resilient"—I could say this— the line suggests that the air is mentally very quick. It can choose from many alternatives, and is flexible, and able to think fast. If a rock comes up in its path, it just doesn't run head-on into it, like a bull or Lyndon Johnson, but it may sidestep it, go around it swiftly.

Thank you for the Myrdal articles and the new poems! I love that blue lamp. Two nights ago a friend, a potter who knows Swedish, came by heading for San Francisco and we spent the whole evening huddled happily over your *I det fria*. I like the poems immensely, and am determined to translate it. So I have some questions for you, Dad.

1. Is the bulpong tarning a *cube* (as they are in the U.S.) or just a *rectangle*?
2. By *stark* do you wish to suggest "uncompromising"?
3. In "De myllrar i solgasset" do you want the English reader to see the *crawling action* of ants (or insects) or their *busyness*?
4. The man who "sitter pa faltet oah rotar"—is he sitting down? on a chair? What is he doing? Raking? Or digging with a stick?
5. The "ogonblicksbild"—that word isn't in my dictionary! Does it refer to the shutter action of a fast camera?

Does the letter put the *speaker* in the position for a while of the *man digging* on whom the shadow of the cross falls? The image of the cross in the airfield is a *wonderful* image, but something very ominous clings to it.

Write soon!

Your old friend

Västerås 9-30-67

Dear Robert,

it was good to get your letter, thanks! I had an uneasy feeling that something had happened to you, that you were sick or something of the sort. (I don't have such a romantically dreadful idea of the U.S. that I believed you'd been arrested!)

[------]

In other news, we've acquired a pet, a guinea pig named Tyra. Our guinea pig became very good friends with the English poet Jon Silkin, who was here fourteen days ago—he was in the process of putting together a Sweden issue of *Stand*. (He was very satisfied with your translations of me.) After a day or so I drove him to Uppsala and left him with the co-editor of BLM. First we visited a fairly notable novelist that Silkin wanted to include. The novelist just sat like a depressive Buddha, mumbling that he hadn't written anything worth reading. In other words he had been smitten with political sickness. Swedish literary life is filled primarily with people who beat their breasts, damn literature, and promise to mend their ways. Many sleep with *Mao's Little Red Book* on their bedside tables. I speak of the cultural scene of course; society is otherwise becoming increasingly bourgeois and we will have a conservative victory next fall. I feel in great need of that book by Alan Watts, Robert! It's not to be found in Sweden. (However there's another one, on Zen Buddhism, checked out of the library.) My contact with the universe nowadays consists primarily in walking around in the woods hunting mushrooms (MUSHROOM-POWER!), woods that unfortunately aren't so far out that you can't hear the breathing of industry. But there are mushrooms everywhere, even a few yards from the cathedral and library in the middle of the city. They say there are some unusually big fat mushrooms in the churchyard . . .

And now your questions about old "In the Open." Bouillon cubes in Sweden are usually shaped like this: in other words not cubes exactly but four-edged in any event. ("Rektangel" evokes surface, not volume.) Birgitta Steene, who made a first version of the poem, translated it "auburn box." STARK just generally means strong; here the closest word would be *concentrated*. She translated "Myllrar i solgasset" as "teem in the blazing sun," as I recall—I haven't got the translation here. The word myllra in Swedish gives a rather strong feeling of urgent crowding, however, something rather physical and also with certain associations of anthills (as you will recall, we have large anthills in this country). And then the man who sits ROOTING AROUND. Root [rotar] is a rather weak word, it means that he pokes, touches, or digs in the soil, but you can't really see what he's doing—the distance is great. I don't remember if I was conscious of this then, but after the poem was written I couldn't help associating it with the Vietnamese peasants. Halberstam describes in his *Making of a Quagmire* how he flies at a low altitude over the landscape and how some farmer pretends not to notice the plane, because the Vietnamese peasants have now learned that if they leap up and run for cover they'll be shot, as they will then be considered to be "Viet Cong." As it happens I read Halberstam after writing those lines; it gave me a sort of déjà vu experience. But that last part of the poem is in no way invented, it is SEEN, it is *The Lion's Tail and Eyes*. If the airplane cross in the first lines is something dangerous, threatening, negative, I understand the cross in the concluding lines as something positive, helpful, but at the same time violently elusive-recursive, something nearer to us than anything and also something we can only glimpse for an instant, not hang on to. Commenting on all this gets to be rather rhetorical and feeble, it must be seen, and you can probably see better than anyone else.

Write soon! (I will write soon myself.)

Best wishes, happiness and prosperity!

Your friend   Tomas T

2 Oct, 67

Dear Tomas,

Here I am sitting, proofs of a little Ekelöf selection in front of me, about to make a ghastly mistake that will make me the laughing stock of the American Scandinavian Foundation forever! Help me!

In *Strountes,* Ekelöf has a poem about the dead slipping out of the cemeteries at night. The word "knäsatt" is what I don't understand. What does it mean?

The first six lines go this way:

Når de slipper ut genom körgardsgrinden
en pasknatt, en pasknatt
Når de döda gar ut och betitta staden
en manskensnatt, en man-natt
Da är det evig hemlöshet some gör sig knäsatt
knäsatt hos andra döda

Now Christina told me the odd word "knäsatt" meant *sitting on the knees of.* So the last two lines above are now translated:

Then it is the eternal homelessness that is sitting on the knees
the knees of the other dead

But it doesn't really make sense! Is that what it means? My dictionary
seems to say the word means something like "legalize," as if one would say,
"We're going to get this common law marriage legalized."

But if that is so, then the eternal homelessness seems to be legalizing *itself*.

Could it be:

Then the eternal homelessness is taking its rightful place
taking its place with all the dead

Or

Then the eternal homelessness takes its rightful place
Takes its place in all the dead

Did the Harper book, my new one, come yet?

Please answer very soon—I'll have to commit hari-kari if I make such an
idiotic mistake and get the knees in these tangled up . . .
Thank you!
Robert

Västerås 10-7-67
Dear Robert
  you're getting two letters at once. While I was in the middle of
writing the other letter (which is in this envelope), your much-longed-for
book arrived, and then two days later this SOS about KNÄSATT. I've
been reading the book on a recent train trip through southern Sweden

(I've been lecturing on the testing of criminals), reading and heating my imagination—it is—OH—it is fantastically good . . . but first

KNÄSATT [knee + set]

a word which is very seldom encountered, a word with a curious, half-bureaucratic, half-aristocratic atmosphere. It is met with most often in parliamentary debates of the more solemn sort, in phrases like "we of the committee have not chosen to knäsatta the principle concerning taxation of . . ." etc. It means ACCEPT, more or less. MAKE YOUR OWN. LEGALIZE. Originally it must have meant ADOPT—that is, you took a child and sat him on your lap, and that meant you made the child your own. But nowadays the word appears only in its abstract, symbolic meaning. And that, as I said, is rare. The very fact that it appears so seldom, and that KNEE in and of itself is so concrete a thing, makes the effect rather curious. The knee constantly presses through the abstract meaning. This is particularly true in the context in which Ekelöf uses the word. It floats constantly between the bureaucratic-abstract "knäsatt" and the extremely macabre and tangible knees of the dead (skeleton knees?). Besides that, it's a half-rhyme with "moonlit night" [månnatt]. In Swedish the effect is that of a strange kind of qualified nonsense. This poem can't be translated. It plays constantly on nuances within the language, that is, the Swedish language. As I fancy the poems of Lewis Carroll can't be translated. Would you be able to do something with Legalize and Legs? "Taking its rightful place" is of course not wrong in its way, but it would be like arranging a Chopin scherzo for a military band. I hope I haven't discouraged you? Go on Bob, go on.

It was wonderful to be able to sit reading your book while I rolled forward through a rainy Sweden. I had longed to have it for so long, and imagined that some damn businessman at Harper's had moved the publication date back six months or so in order to rush Svetlana's memoirs through, or something else that would sell. But here it came after all. What surprises me a little is that it turned out to be so strong as a whole, that in fact it is a book, with a rich, composite but still integrated spirit. Many little eddies that yet are part of the big whirlpool. Even poems that individually have struck me as strange (for example "Watching Television") have a strong meaning in their context here. And the poems do not die after many readings, they are resurrected during the night and are just as remarkable when one returns to them. Later on I hope to be able to send you some words of criticism as well, but here at the beginning I only want to trumpet forth my mole-like gratitude.

You must write very soon and report how it has been received. Not that it makes much difference as far as the poems are concerned, but it's interesting to me to see how literary life of the U.S.A. operates. A man who ought to have certain difficulties (or maybe it's all too easy for him) in writing his criticism is James Dickey. I was quite shaken by your dispute in *The Sixties,* it was as if the unhappy fellow was being hurled from the Tarpeian Rock by some majestic lictor clad in a suit of armor made of flowers but with a stern, set face. I've never managed to read *Buckdancer's Choice* myself. The poems are so swollen, so many words . . . It's like being a child and sitting with a gigantic serving of porridge in front of you. Besides which I lost interest in Dickey, a bit, after the interview in *Life.* Anyway I'm thinking of finishing that poem about Pappa in the hospital window. That's the end of letter no. 2. Now read letter no. 1.

12-18-67

Dear Robert,

it's hard to write, since my youngest daughter wants to be here too—she's spreading herself across the whole table. Well, what I want to say is BREAK YOUR SILENCE and tell me what happened to your wonderful book and what you think about the wonderful book I and (I hope) Bonniers will publish . . . Is "War and Silence" an appropriate title? Has Bonniers written to you? I've heard nothing myself about the project other than that Lars G. was able to get at least one of the press's mighty editors to go along with the idea. Of course I'm living pretty isolated (snow coming from all sides) but in the morning I'm going to Stockholm to meet some colleagues. The fact is that every year a literary grant is given out by the newspaper *Aftonbladet* and everybody who ever got a grant (I got one in 1958) is invited to a big lunch that usually breaks up around ten o'clock at night in thick fog and slurred discussions. You get to meet the new grantee—nobody knows who it is but I suspect that this year it's going to be Sonnevi, who has published a collection of poems and hasn't gotten any of this autumn's grants as yet. So if it's Sonnevi I'll have a chance to drag him into a corner to discuss the project—we do need to know whether we're translating the same poems. And if we are translating the same ones, which version should we use? Etc. I have no idea how frequent your contacts with S. are and what you yourself think of our respective translations. I only met S. once (in Lund) and he seemed to me to be an honest and serious fellow. My picture of his own poetry is very diffuse, owing to the fact that I haven't read his latest book apart from certain political fragments, which haven't really convinced me. (But his translations of you are good.)

To comfort myself in my own melancholy I've been translating yours. Stanza 2 is the problematic one. What does "wooden rail" mean. What does "slip off" mean. Does the crown slide off the chest/coffin or does it sneak away? I'm satisfied with stanza 4—sounds very convincing in Swedish.

What I actually wanted to do was wish you a Merry Christmas and Happy New Year. It seems I never get around to sending out my greetings in the snowstorm! I'm standing here waving a lantern.

> Together with me 2 spoiled children and one
> heroic wife send their best greetings
> Your friend
> Tomas T.

27 Dec, '67

Dear Tomas,

Forgive the silence! I spent almost all of Nov. in California, giving readings to make enough money to get the Neruda and Jiménez books away from their respective printers, who (wisely) refuse to send me a single book until they have the soiled American dollars in their inky hands. The trip was hectic and exhausting. Then on Dec. 5th, I went to N.Y. for the demonstrations at the Induction Center there. Galway Kinnell, Mitch Goodman (Denise Levertov's husband) and I were hauled away with Dr. Spock. We went with Spock first under the barricades (no good) over (no good) around—that worked—and we were all hauled off to jail in the same wagon. Once at the Criminal Courts Building, we were processed, etc. and then tossed in a cell—who should be there but Allen Ginsberg! There were 10 or 12 18 and 19 year old kids in the cell too. When Galway and I came in, they said, Now all the poets are here! Let's have a poetry reading! So we did, and sang mantras with Allen for a while, Allen had brought his Hindu bells to jail with him, and we all had a great time, singing and chanting.

I'm sending on a newspaper clipping showing your American translator there at 6:30 AM, just before we started to go under the barricades.

I've also enclosed copies of some letters published in the *New York Review of Books* last week. The whole issue is causing a lot of stir and uneasiness—I was the first writer to turn down a govt grant, and it had the effect of throwing the problem out for public discussion. I'm getting attacked by the right wing for being "ungrateful for the blessings he has enjoyed as an American," and it's interesting.

Also a copy of my play—just typed up, and probably very bad. I'm serious, it's probably awful.

I haven't heard from Bonniers! Wonderful idea! I'm all for it! I can't judge the resonances in a Swedish translation, but I hereby give you my Swedish power-of-literary-attorney, I appoint you my Swedish agent, translator, and father-in-law (as you are already my brother), and *you* decide about the translations—whatever you decide will be fine—will be law!—with me. Take as many or as few of Sonnevi's translations as you like.

I have two new poems on the Vietnam War which I'll send you from N.Y. I got an apartment in N.Y. for my wife and children in Jan & Feb, and we're leaving tomorrow! So in January & Feb. our address will be

126 East 36th St.

New York, New York

On March 1st, if I have enough money, we plan to jump on a boat and go to Europe. We'll be in England (at Thaxted) March, April & May, then go up by my relatives in Norway June, July & August. So you must come to see us, or I'll come to see you! ! ! ! ! ! !

You asked about reviews of *The Light*—it's being attacked from all sides so far! The mingling of "inward life" and political or social poetry has really infuriated the reviewers so far. They insist one of the two sides or areas must be false, "affected"—possibly *both!* They're willing to accept either of these two sorts of thought in its own book, specialized, etc, but not *together,* as if there were some connection. I'll send you some clippings later on.

"Melancholi" is lovely in Swedish! I'm very glad you chose that one. On your questions:

Strophe 2 takes place entirely at a funeral service in a country church. The "wooden rail" is the varnished and polished altar rail, behind which in the old fashioned immigrant churches, the minister stands when he reads the Gospel or preaches, or gives communion. There is a gleam from this polished rail, a reflection from the overhead church lights. I was thinking of a funeral service for an old farmer who had lived on the farm next to ours when my brother and I were children. He was warm and wonderful. At the services in the country, the minister at some point, while the casket is standing in front of the church, will go to the pulpit and read off the date of birth of the dead man, the year he got married, and to whom, and then, strangely, they describe where his life *took place.* "In 1927 he moved with his wife and children from Brown County to Lac Qui Parle County, where he resided until 1948 when he moved to Yellow Medicine County, etc." It would be something like "flytta" in Norwegian.

During the reading of those dates I imagine the dark funeral wreath suddenly slipping off the shiny coffin and falling to the floor.

In strophe 3—we are someplace like Italy or Spain—an entirely different kind of church. Catholic, run by the rich—the poor outside are sitting around the outer walls of the cathedral, with their knees drawn up,

They are leaning *more onto* their knees, out of hunger, than the man I've drawn here but that is the idea.

I don't find any changes at all to suggest in "Direktorens död," "De som äts av Amerika," or "Förtryckt av världen"—they all sound wonderful.

I know in "Smothered by the World" the "death outside the death" is not very clear. But for the purposes of the poem, physical death is regarded as almost comforting compared to the other death, that takes place in life, with the executives and others being shoved out of inner life, and forced to live on the *other side* of the wall, in the cold, in the outer world. So the hairy tail that howls should give a true feeling of anguish that the executives feel, who know of their own spiritual death, and are not *numb,* but howl with anguish.

Write us in New York! Love to your sweet wife and children

Robert

1968

Västerås 2-19-67 [1968]

Dear Robert, defender of the barricades,

     I must pull myself together now and write to you, whom I think of so often. Monica and I ABSOLUTELY WANT TO SEE YOU THIS SUMMER—it's one of the few good pieces of information from the world, that you're coming to Scandinavia. Please try to stay out of jail! Here comes another bit of news (which by now is a month old): Bonniers will publish the book with your poems in translations by me, Sonnevi and Lasse Söderberg. It will probably be out this fall—we being speedier than other, larger countries, once we get rolling. You ought to write the foreword yourself. We can look through the whole thing together one last time if you come here early in the summer. (I'll drive to Norway and pick you up!) Shall we all have a big children's party?

Thanks for the play! I am shaken. It's such a horrifically inspired thing. Whether it's "good" or not I can't tell. I hope it's good! At any rate there's poetry in it that's as strong as poems of a similar sort in *The Light* . . . I have one reservation. It concerns the idea of people in different colors. They can't change their color, they are like that from beginning to end. I've become hypersensitive to such things of late. There's a totalitarian streak in that kind of coloration, though it's fine from a dramatic point of view.

I think your book can also mean something positive for the poor Swedish poets, who lead a withering existence. The climate here is completely different from the one that seems to hold sway in the U.S. When I read your attacks on THE NEW CRITICISM etc. it's like a message from another planet. Here it's the other way round—what's wanted is political poetry, which doesn't mean that poetry should take political reality as its subject but that poetry, no matter what it's about, should speak a language of political cliché. Just now the always-latent contempt for poetry is booming right along. When you appear before students these days you're always accused of "taking up a reactionary attitude" if you read a poem with some animals or blades of grass in it. And if you write a poem that touches on politics, that's wrong too, because you haven't used the correct political clichés. Some of the most influential debaters in Sweden sound—when they make their declarations—like prosecutors in the Sinyavsky trial—it's completely grotesque. At the same time the whole country is becoming more and more bourgeois! Intellectual life is getting to be a sort of totalitarian reserve. The moral motivation is of course the Vietnam war and let us lay on top of all LBJ's other—and significantly grosser—crimes this little one that he has made the air hard to breathe for someone who wants to work through sensibility, imagination, and self-knowledge in poetry. I hate this damned war with all my heart but I haven't therefore begun to declare myself a fighting Marxist or begged forgiveness for writing about blades of grass and animals. I haven't given any money for weapons to the NLF either, only to humanitarian or peace movements, which the real NLF-warriors despise. Of course I believe that the Vietnamese people prefer the NLF to the marionette generals of the Saigon government many times over, and of course I want the U.S.A. to withdraw from the country. But to join an NLF group here in Sweden means that one doesn't primarily desire peace but victory— never mind how many people are exterminated, or that one is affiliating oneself with a program that wants "more Vietnams worldwide"—the program of the Havana Conference, in other words. It also means that one condemns all compromise and approves in advance the bloodbath of the opposition that can follow a total NLF victory. What I believe in, would like to fight for, is a coalition solution where the NLF plays a large but not a total role (that's actually the NLF's own recent official line). But that sort of standpoint is considered "lukewarm." In this climate it's all or nothing. Anybody not 100% for is "self-evidently" 100% against. Have I given you a little picture of the climate? All you can do is follow your own crooked conscience, wait for the moment of truth and hope you won't need to be ashamed one day of how you lived through these years. God *damn* it, how I long to see you by the way! Let me hear from you as soon as possible—I'll write soon again but want to get this off in time to catch you before you leave for Thaxted. Monica and the kids are fine—I hope your family is the same. And write poems!

Your friend   Tomas T.

Västerås 4-19-68
Dear Robert,

I sent a super-urgent message to you in New York a fortnight ago and also wrote then that I would send one to England at the same time in case you should be there. The problem is that you have disappeared, like Livingstone. I never got around to sending anything to England— here it comes instead. Let's hear from you! Write to Bonniers* and say where you are! Write to Göran S. and tell him how the Vietnamese children's fund will work! Write to me—above all—and tell me how you're doing! Enough for now, it feels pointless to write more when I don't know whether you will ever get these messages in bottles, urgent letters, emergency flares, tootings in the fog. We won't talk about the world, way too much has happened. But we're finally past the NADIR, I think. It feels like that anyway.

Your friend   Tomas T.

---

*As I mentioned in the previous letter it's now 100% certain that the book will be published and that it will happen either this fall or spring 69—probably this fall.

23 April, '68

Dear Tomas,

Your letters just came, both in the same day! After two months of talk in New York, I lapsed into hermitical silence, not even replying to fences or puppies. But I'm going to start writing letters again, today! So I'll write to you first. We are in Thaxted, in a little cottage across from a flock of geese! They talk all night themselves, in low and hoarse voices, like New York divorcées. I have been reading Taoist books, which give off pure and clear sounds, like flutes. My voice is—alas—half way between.

I'm looking foward to seeing you and your sweet women folk this summer! It will definitely come to pass! But when I'm not sure yet. We have some uncertainty about *when* we can be in *this* house, etc.

How wonderful that Bonniers is going ahead with the book! I'll write them today, as soon as I finish this! The poems I'm sure are better in translation than in the original, and I'm entering the country under false pretenses. I'll have to get a forged passport too! Thank you for encouraging this book! I'll never criticize Sweden again.

We're all happy here, in this odd and un-American country. But the happiest day we had was the day Johnson QUIT! How fantastic! It meant that the peace movement had won! It was already impossible for him to give speeches anywhere except at military bases, and the planners of the Democratic Convention in Chicago had already decided they could not bring him to the hall through the streets—the hippies would have covered his car with urine and calf blood—he was to have been brought to the roof by helicopter. Even that was not entirely safe.

I tossed my private grenade at the National Book Awards ceremony. What a scene! A huge elegant hall with chandeliers, panelling and speeches guaranteed to be of the most impeccable boredom, politeness and obsequiousness. Each of the 6 winners had 500 words they were allowed to say. George Kennan's, just before me, was polite and standard. When I got about ten sentences into mine, I literally saw faces full of shock and disbelief—the first time I've ever seen it. The mink-coated crowd went wild with rage. The rest, about ⅔ of the audience, enjoyed it to the tips of

their toes, or so they told me. At the end, I called up a young man from
Resistance out of the audience, gave him the $1000 check, and then re-
peated Spock's crime, urging him not to enter the U.S. army, ever, etc.
Mayor Lindsay was on stage—he had opened the proceedings—and this
put him in a spot. A public official must leave the stage if a law is bro-
ken in his presence, or he is condoning the [breaking of the] law. But if
Lindsay had left the stage, he would have gotten booed by the crowd; in
any case, he stayed—I'm sending along some extra clippings etc people
have sent. You needn't return them. Also a copy of the speech.

This speech might be published at the end of the selected poems if you
think it's a good idea. Harpers is thinking of doing it, but it probably has
more meaning to the U.S. literary community than to Europeans. See what
you think.

Do you still want some sort of preface from me? What should it say?
"Unaccustomed as I am to speaking in Swedish, gulp, cough."

Thank you for the clipping with the review of *Ord om Vietnam*. Your
description of the climate in Sweden—"either write political verse or we'll
turn you into a grasshopper"—is eerie—it is a stage we haven't gotten to
yet. But the Swedes move faster in such things because the war means *less*
to them. The English are the same. Their riots are unreal, and their sup-
port of the NLF is so much oatmeal.

The European failing is always the drive to <u>polarize</u> everything—utter
good or utter evil. Only the Taoists know clearly how dumb that is!

"Bend and you will be upright,
Curl up and you will be straight,
Keep hold of emptiness and you will be full.
Grow old and you will be young,
Have little and you will get larger,
Have much and you will get confused."

The two ends meet! So making poles—allt or intet—is trying to stop the
world. As the Taoists say, "If you do that, you'll be lucky if you don't cut
your hand!"

I'll stop jabbering now. Write me right away, and I'll write back. My love to your family—forgive my thick-tonguedness—

Robert

Västerås 6-9-68

Dear Roberto,

I'm finally sitting here, writing to you on my old black office typewriter. I've found a house for you! It's in downtown Västerås, an old part of the city. Usually the writer Clas Engström lives there with his wife (who is a sculptor) + a son and a little adopted Indian girl. They will be away all of July and Clas has put the house at my disposal. You won't need to pay any rent but you can of course leave them your two poetry collections when you move out. But we shouldn't hang around Västerås, just have it as a base for various outings in different directions. The land right around here is depicted in the enclosed poem—destruction of nature is ongoing—farther north you're in the woods.

I've just come back from a trip to my old haunts—Östergötland in other words—I had a psychology assignment there and seized the opportunity at the same time to take a few days off for writing. But the whole thing was wrecked by Kennedy's murder. Right after things like that I'm so full of rage and resignation that poetry becomes impossible—working at my job goes well, however—the job is a kind of escape from reality! But to write is to go into reality itself, where the gunsmoke still lingers. Otherwise I was rather skeptical about Robert Kennedy, terribly split. I'll never know what he really stood for. Maybe he was very good. But I've put all my eggs, my American eggs, in McCarthy's basket. Maybe I should also let Lindsay take an egg. After all, he belonged to the part of your audience that put up with what you said (so damned well) and it shouldn't be held against him too much that he called in sick the next day.

The prospect of this evening has put me in a bad mood. What's happening is that a journalist from the local paper is coming here to finish an interview with me. He has previously managed to misunderstand, or maybe not misunderstand but caricature, my reasoning and viewpoints to such a degree that I don't recognize them any more. So that the interview will finally be finished I've chosen to invite him to dinner, I thought it would all go a little easier that way. He has let it be known that he is a teetotaler, so I will try to soften him up with food instead. Nearly all the people who write in the newspapers about culture in Sweden these days resemble wolves that lie in Grandma's clothing, waiting for Red Riding Hood. Some years ago they were like Santa Claus coming with presents. In both cases representatives of the pseudo-world. I myself want to be a MOLE that digs itself out of all this, right through illusion and into reality. He needn't have golden wings, though that's fine too, it's enough that he's alive and can dig.

Write soon. I want to hear about your address in Norway, travel plans etc. We send greetings and long to see you!

Your friend

Tomas T.

7 July, '68

Dear Tomas,

Thank you for your letter, and the enclosed letters, which just arrived! The thing that amuses me is that the FBI is unable to open and read my mail over here! That is a terrible frustration to them—they're falling behind on various plots.

The Sixties is being printed in N.Y. now—I've sent page proofs back—and so will be out *sometime*!

I just read a book—prose poems—of Jan Erik Vold, who visited you. [------]

We're leaving here the 14th of July, and will be in Oslo the 15th. But my host there has stuck me with a lecture on "modernisk Amerikansk poesi" at the Oslo Summer School on the 16th, so that we probably won't get to Sweden until the 18th or 19th.

But it seems to me you said that you had your vacation until the 20th, so I'm worried that we're bringing you back from Runmarö sooner than you would have come if I had not poked my nose into Sweden. It would be very easy for us to stay a day or two longer in Oslo, and arrive in Västerås on the 20th or 21st, so that you and your family could be in Runmarö for the time you had planned! Please write me in Oslo about that! Our address there will be c/o Skardal, Sørkedalsveien 229, Oslo 7. Telephone 24-58-68.

We'll arrive in Oslo night of 15th, then the 16th I'll be at the University during the morning and part of the afternoon, and on the 17th among relatives, probably at the Sørkedalsveien house.

I don't know how far it is from Oslo to Västerås, but it's probably more than a day's drive! So it would be easy for us to drive on the 20th. Please let us know—looking forward very much to seeing all of you again!

Yours, Robert

Runmarö 7-12-68

Dear Robert,

I've come back to Runmarö now after having left Mamma in the hospital in Stockholm. In other words, for the next few days things are under control. When I came out here your most recent letter was waiting. It's a good plan to come on the 19th or 20th! I'll call Sørkedalsveien sometime on the 17th and we'll fix the details. I hope my sad and stress-fraught note from Stockholm didn't scare you off!

I enclose a letter from Mr. Hall which has been injured—not by the FBI but by me—it got mashed in my briefcase.

Jan Erik Vold has sent greetings to me on two occasions. He rides a motor-cycle and wears a complete diving suit—he looks—from a distance—like a minor character out of some James Bond movie. When he has taken off his motorcycle outfit, he's pure friendliness. Awhile back he wrote some good poems but I don't connect with his latest phase at all—his texts make me feel so troublesomely old-fashioned.

It's rainy and windy out here. I'm devoting myself to escapism on the sofa, reading Sherlock Holmes—the great comforter. Regression!

Till we meet again! See you in a few days
Tomas

Runmarö, undated [August 8, 1968]

Dear Bly's! (because I write by hand I try some English—to make life less complicated for you and the FBI-people—if Louis Simpson too is under supervision). Oh we miss you! The cave is almost empty but summer goes on. Paula is fat as a broiler and Emma learned to swim yesterday. I have been back to Västerås and working with a few unreal city-clients for 2 days, then returning to the island. In the mail I found a large swarm of letters for you (which I will forward to Madison) and the magazine *Motor* for me. Passing Stockholm I visited Bonniers and handed over the list of books—they will send you soon I hope. I got some news about Martinson—he is not so ill after all—he was ill this winter but has recovered and would probably be interested in getting some support—send him *Unicorn*! Address is simple: Gnesta, Sweden. They did not know about your translations except for the Ekelöf book—Bonniers is of course interested in novel translating primarily, businessmen as they are. But they should know! They always say that there is no interest in Swedish poetry abroad. So send them a *Unicorn* too.

In Västerås I watched television from Miami Beach for hours. A paradise of fools! but the small excerpt from Lindsay's speech was not bad. The rest was more terrible protoplasm of stomach-and-muscle rhetoric, which causes severe attacks of suffocation among nervous-system-listeners.

Mother feels a little better now. But she is losing her hair. "Hair does not want to stay on a sick person," she said.

5 hugs to all of you from us!

Vännen   Tomas

[on envelope]

THE WIND SHAKES CATERPILLARS DOWN FROM THE TREES—ONE LANDS ON MY SHIRT.

Västerås 2 Sept. 68

Dear Robert,

first a catastrophic message from Lars Gustafsson—he has been instructed to start setting up your book "within 14 days" and it's therefore necessary that you send the poems to me, or to Bonniers, in the order you want them—and that you send them by air. Preferably with a foreword—though I think the foreword can be sent a week or two later if you haven't had time to write it.

I've sent the "three presidents" to the Finland Swedish magazine *Horisont* but haven't heard back from them yet.

As you will understand, I've spent a great part of the past 24 hours in front of the TV and seen tanks roll by from morning till night. I've been able to follow the Czechoslovakian drama from hour to hour—it has made an enormous impression here—I doubt whether you in the U.S. have experienced the events more than 25% of what the Europeans have experienced. Honorable leftists of Sonnevi's type must be having a very hard time. Communists loyal to the party have solved the problem in a radical way by wholeheartedly condemning what's happening—Hermansson, the party leader, requested that we recall our ambassador to the Soviet Union! (No other party has requested that.) Among the NLF groups a number of members have requested that the movement be expanded so as to oppose the Soviet Union. In other words it would be an anti-U.S.–anti-Soviet movement. From the humanitarian point of view such a thing would be perfectly logical, but from an ideological one it would be absurd (you know North Vietnam's position). The whole thing is a boiling cauldron.

In Västerås the flag is at half-mast.

We often think of you and miss you.

Love to Carol!
Your friend   T

18 Sept, '68

Dear Tomas,

Sorry I've been away! Part physically & part spiritually! I didn't realize deadline was so close! Enclosed find poems with order indicated, approved STAMP

I'm working on foreword, it will appear in 10 days or two weeks (I'll bet!)
Love to you and your beautiful, graceful, bird-like
branch-like wife and family!

Robert

21 Oct, '68

Dear Tomas,

I'm sending some literary curiosities here in an old *New World Writing* (1959!) with my first political (glumpf) (and my last, some would say) poems. Also a little book of interviews from 1963 that has had a lot of influence one way or the other. A new *Stand* with some of my ranting, and two *Kayak*s. #12 has my criticism; and I've asked George to send you #13, which has the critcism of me for my criticism!

I got a lovely bunch of books from Bonniers—the *only* thing they didn't send were the prose books I needed to get an owl eye view of you

African-Swedish poets. For example there was one paperback on poets of the '50's with an article on you, and another paperback I think with an article on your parachute poem. How could I (sob) get copies of those?

I had a marvellous week alone by myself in the woods, and I wrote some moonlight poems I'll send you this winter—and I wrote an outhouse poem the other day! But now I have to put my harness on, stick the bit in my mouth, and start pulling the manure spreader. Tomorrow I start off on a long tour to get money for us through the winter. I decided to put all readings into the fall this year, so I will have Dec, Jan, & Feb all to myself, utan program!

Then we'll write long letters to each other, and "settle all difficult interpretations."

(I did a draft of the introduction last night and will send it to you from my tour.)

Love to you and Monica
and Paula and Emma!   from usn's
Robert

Västerås 10 dec. 68

Dear Robert, Caruso of 78 RPMs,

I've received a strict order from Bonniers to write to you immediately and remind you of THE FOREWORD TO THE BOOK. I've gotten the proofs, but the foreword, where is that? We now have to have it by January 1. You are good at forewords (Take for example Neruda). Or shall we ask Carolyn Kizer to write it? I saw in the paper that she was here recently making a good-will visit to Swedish writers and institutions.

These last few days the most wonderful pieces of mail have been dancing down into my mailbox. Ah what a lot of fun I've had with *Kayak* and with various books. Most of all I like the letters from *The Sixties* readers. Harry Smith takes the cake. I will beg a few publishers for some books to send you, a CHRISTMAS PACKAGE, which by the usual swift surface mail can be expected to arrive around March. (The Cutty Sark isn't running any longer.)

[------]

In November—right after I'd gotten myself back together after the damned Presidential election—I went to Berlin for an "author symposium" with Professor Walter Höllerer. We sat and philosophized around a long table for four days: Lars Gustafsson, I and two Swedish prose writers and 30 German docents and professors and authors and thinkers and linguists and observers from the Swedish Institute etc. etc. I didn't even understand the title of the conference! Erklärbarkeit und Nicht-Erklärbarkeit der Welt als Axiom für die Literatur? The food was good. Afterwards there was a reading: I had bad German translations with me. They were improved by a bunch of Dichter und Denker and were finished 5 minutes after the reading was supposed to begin. I stumbled out of a taxi and up to the podium and read "Nach einem Tod" so that there wasn't a dry eye in the house. "Im Freien" was read by a Mr. Jürgen Becker. Nothing by one of the novelists (Enquist) got read, the other, Jersild, got a terrible presentation by his translator who after having read (in a pathetic voice) for 40 minutes suddenly broke off and said with an anguished expression on his face: "Ach meine Damen und Herren, Entschuldigung, the text is just too long, I'll have to skip over part of it"—whereupon he skipped to three lines from the end and fell across the finish line. It went in other words the way it usually goes when Swedish literature is presented abroad. Even so we are considered to have had a certain success—especially Enquist whom the audience escaped hearing: his book was purchased direct. I myself was courted by Professor Höllerer's poetry series editors, by Rundfunk and by *Akzente*. I'm even going to appear in Suhrkampf. It's my (problematic) translator who tells me this—what do I know? I do hope so, I do absolutely want a reason to travel down to the continent again soon and eat Sauerkraut.

Our household economy has gotten even worse of late and I've taken on a few extra jobs—among other things I'm leading a group-counseling session for social workers in Västerås: they sit and unbosom themselves under my tactful guidance. It's dark and cold as hell but my 1966–67 depression has in fact released me and I feel quite energetic.

Now we would very much like to hear from you. Love to you all! Sometimes I walk with a stiff right leg and think how nice it was to have Biddy hanging on to it.

Your friend
Tomas

P.S. Poems enclosed. Give me a fatherly advice—should I say "I" instead of "he" in "The Open Window"?

T.

30 Dec, '68

Dear Tomas,

I can't describe what weather we're having—fantastic! No mail goes out for days, and we don't get out of the yard for days. It's like a medieval village!

At last, here is the introduction stained by snow. Tell me what you think—should some be dropped? It seemed egotistical to write an introduction to my own poems, so I stole some paragraphs from older prose—the second section is new. I did the best I could.

I'll write a longer letter soon, with some poems—thank you for the two lovely poems!—I must trudge out with this—Gustafsson has been threatening me—I'm frightened of the snow gods—

love as ever,
Robert

Crossing Roads

Poetry's purpose in its recent growth is to advance deeper into the unknown country. In order to penetrate into this country poetry must learn to sleep differently, to awake differently, to listen for new sounds, to walk differently.

What is the unknown country? It is the change in inward life which corresponds to the recent changes in outward life. In the last hundred years, outwardly, colonialism dies, engines are born, the religions lose power, business takes power, the falcon and the eagle weaken, fear of the mother increases. The change has been thorough. The change penetrates deeper than we believe. Poetry has been able to describe that inward change better than fiction has. Neruda tells us more about modern life than Faulkner; Rilke tells us more than Mann.

All around us are huge reservoirs of bypassed emotions, ignored feelings, unexplored thoughts. As Rilke said to sculptors, there are hundreds of gestures being made which we are not aware of. The purpose of poetry is to awaken the half of us that has been asleep for many years—to express the thoughts not thought. All expression of hidden feelings involves opposition to the existing order.

****

New poetry then embodies hidden feelings, feelings that are almost inaccessible to the eyes and hands of the Western ego. Spiritual joy rises from levels of the personality far beneath the ego; the impulses that cause the Vietnam war rise from levels of the American personality far beneath the American ego. What is necessary—for an American poet—to write political poetry is inwardness.

When we first write political poems, we hope to use our opinions, to build the poems out of our opinions. But all our opinions are like the tin cans that lie around some modern woodcutter's house in the forest. The longing to kill Asians—it is a longing, not an opinion—lies far down in the soil of Westerners, tin cans rot at that depth, there is too much acid in the soil. But poetry finds those longings there, they are almost indestructible. The love of solitude lies at the same depth, nothing can make it disintegrate.

What I value in poetry are the mysterious lines that cross, roads that start out in political energy and end in spiritual energy, roads that start out in solitude and end in human love, roads that start out in primitive energy and pass through compassion and on into spiritual energy, passing many other roads on the way.

ROBERT BLY

1969

Västerås 1-8-69 [January]

Dear Robert,

Good! I've translated the foreword and sent it to Bonniers. Those are good, strong formulations, which I have perhaps not been able to do full justice to in Swedish. One section is less persuasive than the others: the one beginning "when we first write political poems" and ending with "The love of solitude." This is owing partly to the Swedish. "Längta," which is the only thing "longing" can be translated into, is a positively charged, rather weak and sentimental word in Swedish. For that reason "The longing to murder Asians" ["Längtan att mörda asiater"] has an odd sound. The whole discussion of that dark urge to murder Asians is confusing among all the tin cans. I understand what you mean, but it's possible that the whole discussion will sound strange to a Swede. I'll ask some Swedes. You can decide yourself whether or not it should be dropped. The conclusion with "what I value in poetry" proceeds very well in Swedish and hangs together well with what goes before "When we first write polit . . ." so as far as continuity is concerned it works fine to drop the tin cans and the deep longings. Decide right away and I shall obey. I don't know when the book will be published but we need to hurry. Lars G. called last night and said he thought it would be out in a month. He has just come home from Israel and is writing a "25-page essay on my experiences," after that he flies to Vienna where he will lecture on Swedish literature "a follow-up to what we did in Berlin," after that he goes to London to "take part in a film on Bakunin's life" etc. He is developing an activity combining those of the octopus and the albatross. The snow lies deep now in Västerås which resembles a Siberian town more than it does a medieval village. I'm longing very much for some new poems from you, a longing that comes from the deeper regions in my personality.

Love to you, Carol and the kids
Tomas

15 Jan, '69

Dear Tomas,

My dear wife tells me that we both are wrong. I'm wrong for putting those tin cans in that paragraph in the first place, and you're wrong for being willing to drop the whole paragraph! She says there is a third way— redo the paragraph!

So that's what I have done, a very limping, prosaic job, leaving out my beloved tin cans, scattered about the Grimm Brothers house.

Here is the new paragraph to replace the old:

When we first write political poems, we hope to use our opinions, but what is useful for poems are desires. The Americans have a desire to die, as many other national peoples do, but we also have a desire to kill Asians—it comes out of our earlier incomplete massacre of their relatives, the American Indians. Americans have a grudge against all people with black hair. The desire to kill lies very deep in the personality. But poetry finds those desires there, they are nearly indestructible. The love of solitude lies at the same level, poetry is glad to find it.

Now do what you wish with it! Rewrite it, or cut it, or cancel the entire book! If you think these particular opinions, like the desire to kill Asians, and its relation to the murder of the Indians, are so outré, so foreign and unbelievable in this brief exposition, that it will make the Swedes think me an utter fool, then I suppose you should leave them out. I'm so used to the idea that it sounds perfectly reasonable to me. This you have to decide!

I'd rather have it in, but I can't tell how it might sound in Swedish, or to Swedes. At least it turns the discussion of the war away from Imperialism and the Sonnevi Marxist clichés.

In my next letter, I'm going to send you a whole bunch of miscellaneous poems. Here's my only one line poem.

Poem in One Sentence

So many things I love have been sent to Grenoble with the
    sea-urchins.

I'm not sure that could be translated. "Sea-urchin" is such a marvellous word in English—it's one of those spiky round things, you know, but "urchin" is fantastic.

Yes I definitely think you should use "I" in the "Open Window." Yes! I don't understand three lines: "Sa mycket han tyckte om, har det nan tyngt?" (This is a question I would never be able to answer!) Also, the final two lines are a puzzle. I don't see how the *horse* got in there.

I think I can translate the cement piping poem—it is a rich thing! But I need a little help with "dödläge"—deadlocked? or condemned (as we say, this building is condemned, a thruway is coming here)? I'm not sure, either, of the associations the translation of "lagardar" ought to have.

Love to you all! I'm enclosing your first check from your poems floating about on the American waters, in my translation at least: this is for "Kyrie." We have some more photographs from Runmarö we will send soon.

Tell me how your mother is. I think of her often, but you haven't mentioned her in your letters.

Yours affectionately,
Robert

Västerås 1-18-69
Dear Maestro,

quit brooding about what I wrote about your foreword! Anyway it's too late. Bonniers has been gripped by The Great Panic and decided to bring the book out on February 7. At the last instant I was able to correct some craziness they'd written about you in a little biographical blurb on the back cover—among other things that you've been a Lecturer in Norway. Nice that you'll be coming out so soon. I'll send clippings from our politicized critics. Bonniers is also going to start a new literary magazine for the younger generation. The entire editorial board is made up of eager Communists and the Editor-in-Chief explained on the radio that literature was a "fucking dusty word" and that we should only hold debates. We already have approximately 50 such magazines (*Marxistiskt Forum, Zenit, Tidsignal* etc. etc.) so why not one more? There's reason to believe that you'll be regarded as an extreme reactionary (though not because you named the name of Rilke—there probably aren't many people who know who he is anymore). Thanks for Misan's mittens! They came the other day and were a great success. I'll write again soon.

Love to C, B, M and N.
Tomas

Västerås 5-18-69
Dear Robert,

I've been waiting for 3 months for the promised ONE-LINE poems by you. They certainly do take a long time to write down. How are you? Are there problems? Is the old family firm *The Sixties* bankrupt? I feel so well and lively now that I want to see all my friends blossom on all sides of the oceans. Unfortunately I haven't got much poetry to show, but here comes something anyway, my newborn prosepiece "The Bookcase"—I find it awfully good. It is very European.

War and Silence has gotten reviews—very benevolent for the most part—in many local papers, but the big papers—with the exception of *Aftonbladet*—

haven't written anything about it. Miserable lazybones! Nearly everyone who's written about the book has focused on the foreword—it was obviously an excellent foreword, very effective in its subtle authority. The poor youngest generation of Swedish poets truly needs all the help it can get. The youngest are often aggressively polemical and judgmental in their attitudes but suffer from an absolute lack of inner self-confidence.

Tomorrow I fly to the wonderful island of Gotland where I will give a lecture for some social-work codgers about the criminal behavior of young people. On the same trip I'm reading poems in a High school in Visby (the medieval city, with a wall around it). I won't be paid anything apart from my expenses for travel and lodgings. Navigare necesse est.

Our best regards to the family! Hug Carol "she-almost-bet-the-old-man" Bly.

      Tomas

P.S. (on the train) The above letter is no longer current since Franzén has done a big write-up for you in *Dagens Nyheter.* Enclosed.

The biographical detail that always turns up is that you were "menig i flottan" (private in the navy)—it's presented as if a great military secret were being exposed.

Västerås 14-6-69
Dear Robert,
      here comes a new collection of Swedish country-papers' writings about your book. I could not find the long and praising review in *Expressen* (Sweden's biggest and probably worst paper) but it has appeared anyhow.

Do you realize that you have not written a line to me since beginning of February? That fact should hit you like a flash of lightning. From Sonnevi I have heard that you were alive as late as in March and some good pictures Carol sent in April show a poet who I with some difficulty can recognize

as you. In the latest *Kayak* you are described as "the energetic editor"—
that gives me some hope for the future. The best in *Kayak* was your prose
poems.* I have not read "sitting on some rocks" before. I should like to
translate them but I can't just now, because I am lately too interested
in prose poems myself—I don't want to get influenced. Monica thinks I
should write prose—I have some hidden talkativeness inside me that does
not come forward in ordinary verse (the hidden Stomach, within . . .).

We are preparing for Runmarö now—I bring the family to the island
in the next week but I can't get vacation myself until July. Yesterday I
was making tests and interviews in the borstal Sundbo up in the woods.
I have introduced something new in Swedish psychology: OUTDOOR
INTERVIEWING—the client and the psychologist sitting in the grass—
the problems, the vocational guidance, the drug addiction questions etc.
evaporating in the burning sun—Scandinavia is for the present the hot-
test place in Europe.

Warm greetings to Carol and the children! Send a few lines and tell if you
are going along well—it's *important* for me to know!

Yours
Tomas

24 June, '69

Dear Tomas,

After my spring disturbance—remarkably long this year—I am my-
self again! (I mean the public nightmares.) I am back now writing poems.
When you didn't write me for so long about your mother, I had guessed
that she was in the hospital once more. And then suddenly I knew that

---

*Actually I have not read all of the stuff in the issue.

she had died: I woke one morning, and looked over at my bedside table, and suddenly realized that she had died that night or the day before. And a couple of days later your letter came. I'm glad I got to see her old neighborhood, and your old apartment—those rooms are some of the vividest places to me in Europe now. I remember them so well.

I am enclosing copies of first drafts of two translations, which I hope you will comment on! The *Twenty poems of T.T.* is about to go to press, at last! (We've had no money.) I predict for it a sale just under that of the King James Bible! I'll do a special promotional pitch for nervous system types. "Tomas Tranströmer understands *you*! etc. Just fill out this coupon . . ."

I'm also enclosing several foolish attempts of my own. Did you get the *Tennessee Poetry Journal*? There are a few new poems in it. You're right, *Kayak* was a dead loss this time except for some prose poems (which, according to a letter George Hitchcock received from Elizabeth Bishop, I stole from some prose-poems of *hers*! . . . I really stole them from you and Francis Ponge, but with my Minnesota accent, no one can tell . . .)

The press releases etc enclosed will help explain why I've written so seldom this spring. I think I visited about a total of 30 colleges this spring (they all flow together into one golden stream).

Another reason I don't answer your letters is that they often have in them reviews of my book—praise, even! I can't quite explain it, but there's a special joy in piecing out my prose laboriously from a language you only half know. Reading something about my poems in Swedish, for me, is just like finding my name in the Bible! The thought of someone in a Swedish town reading my poems, and even understanding them, sends me off into lovely Wizard of Oz trips, I float along, bumping into doorframes, falling asleep in the middle of the day, setting up dormouse parties in the cellar, eating strawberries under the full moon etc.

I am still reading Erich Neumann, and learning, or seeming to learn, a great deal from him. His book *The Great Mother*—he is the Sheldon of the psychic underworld—made all the blizzards here this winter luminous, and now I've started on his *Origins and History of Consciousness.* If you can't get those books in Swedish, let me know, and I'll get the English versions for you. He wrote them in German, in Palestine.

I'm so surprised to be writing a letter that I think I'll stop right here, and wait for you to write back! Carol, and Mary and Biddy and Noah are all well, and we all wish we could go to the island right now!

Write soon,

Affectionately

Robert

P.S. I'm going to London on July 8th for some poetry conference. I'll be there two weeks, spending some of the time with the Tibetans in Scotland. I wanted them to invite you too, and they promised to next time! Meanwhile, the man in Austin, Texas, who was running the visiting-European-writers program to Austin resigned, and no one has been appointed to take his place yet. I'll suggest to Nixon that he invite you for a poetry reading at the White House. Would you mind sharing a program with Billy Graham?

Black Ants

Green sparks fly north, south, east, and west!
What the moon does, we never know.
But we study old strawpiles
    for the love that is in them.
The moon rises through water!
      and the luminous cloud
hugs to itself particles of death-earth!
Don't hesitate!
Gobble down the grave!
And the green hill flies up to swallow you,
Your arms and legs get free
Out of your mouth comes
    the luminous cloud of black ants!

Love Poem

It is the feminine and this windy December night.
There is a mother with teeth,
"Do not be frightened, children!"
But the birds have eaten the womb-shaped, owl-shaped seeds we
   dropped in the moonlight.
The fish dives.
It comes up carrying a gold ring!
This love is like a sun held inside a tiny solar system—
like the moon kept in a pouch.
"Do not be frightened, children!"
Some will die,
others will lengthen out years on islands,
but this night blows against hubcaps.
Men will die for the night.

Picking Mushrooms in Late Summer in the Western Half of the Island of Runmarö with Tomas Tranströmer

The mushrooms loom in the grass like extremely stupid thoughts.
They are skies from which parachutes never fall.
From us, too, sometimes a poem falls, sometimes not.
Delighted to be together, we are out in the summer woods, picking
   mushrooms.

Rowing at Dusk in the Baltic

for Tomas

The sea rolls away flat as a womb.
West of us pale sunset water.

East of us eastern darkness.
The utopia of ducks swims away along the white water.

July 1968

25 June, '69

Dear Tomas,

I was looking over with pleasure again the book you—*mainly*—put together: *Krig og tystnad*! It's interesting to see these poems all jumbled together, and the translations—I noticed one of the wise men picked out your voice particularly—are wonderful.

I did find one sentence in the introduction which may be a misunderstanding: "Det som gör det nödvändigt—för en amerikansk poet—att skriva politisk poesi är uppmärksamheten inat." As I understand that, it suggests that if an American poet looks inward, he will naturally, even *necessarily,* write political poems. I meant that what an American poet must possess <u>before</u> he can write (good) political poetry is inwardness. "What is necessary—for an American poet—to write political poetry is inwardness." What the poet needs to get down to those "levels" far below the ego is the diving apparatus called "inwardness." My sentence omitted the phrase "to have."

Lovely night here—windy! Yours, Robert

Here's a poem from this winter I found in my notebook:

Standing by the Plow Buried in Snow

More snow coming, and a basketball game tonight.
Car horns heard from the town a mile away.
The girls all taking their hair out of curlers,
    as the snow comes sideways through the confident twigs in near
        dark.

Västerås 7-30-[1969?]

Dear Robert,

thanks for the letters, poems, clippings and *Issa* (which I'll send to a select group of friends). It was so good to hear from you—I was seriously worried that something terrible had happened: that you were in the hospital (after a car/plane crash), that the family was ruined, that you were in jail or that the post office in Västerås had stolen all the letters from America in hopes that there were dollars in them. I also had a psychological (paranoid) explanation for why you never wrote: namely that after 200 unsuccessful attempts to place my poems in American little magazines (with one success: in Albuquerque!) you had concluded that I was impossible as a product and ought to be forgotten as quickly as possible and that you were brooding about how you were going to be able to inform me of this in a friendly and tactful way. ("Well, dear Tomas, ähmmm . . . I . . . I . . . have something to tell you that is not entirely pleasant . . . your poems have failed completely in this country but you are a wonderful pianist . . .")

A few weeks ago the winter number of the BLY magazine from Tennessee arrived. I had a hell of a lot of trouble deciphering Allen Tate's microscript but the others went down like butter. I remember most of the poems from that manuscript of yours that I read on Runmarö but I'd forgotten that "A Small Bird's Nest" was so good. I don't know why I'm so strangely affected by those intense nurses from the Crimean War. Immortal poem! Your two newest ("Black Ants" and "Love Poem") are darkly fascinating—"Love Poem" totally incomprehensible. "Black Ants" makes me happy in an ecstatic black-and-green way.

It's a hot summer night. I can't manage to write as long a letter as I'd meant to when I began, but I'm sending a huge stack of clippings from this country; pay special attention to the last clipping ("Concerning Tranströmer") which gives the ideological starting point of the representative young scribe. (Comrade Zhdanov nods from his mausoleum in a friendly way.) I'm also sending a moderate scribe who has reviewed *War and Silence* in BLM. (Never mention the terrible misinterpretation I made in your foreword. You are quite right. I must have been influenced by the cultural climate in Sweden. *Pitiful!*) Love to Carol and the children! I'll write again soon.

Tomas

Västerås 12-8-69
Dear Robert,
             every day a new thump from the postman. One day Stafford *(Tennessee Poetry Journal)*, the next day *Naked Poetry*, the next day *Café Solo*
     thump
             thump
                   It is wonderful, I am rich. Probably tomorrow the invitation from Nixon you announced. I would definitely turn down Billy Graham. The only proper partner for me at the reading is Hammarskjöld's ghost.

I am very fond of your mushroom poem. There are too few mushroom poems. You have dubbed me an old Chinese.

I could not resist the Devon barn piece, I had to make a first version of it (full of mistakes).

From the *Naked Poetry** I found out that Merwin could be translated into Swedish. I will try some pieces. The pictures of the poets are—as usual (look in the Scandinavian picture gallery I sent you)—the faces are often so (I have to look in the dictionary) . . . pretentious, presuming, presumptuous (look at Mezey himself). How blurred and humble your own portrait looks in this collection, it looks like some necessary figure in an old picture from the foundation of DADA in Zurich 1916 or something like that.

I send you a pamphlet and a document from the Swedish situation. Peer poets—no stamina.

Love to the family!
                          Yours
                              Tomas

17-11-69
Dear Robert,
        I am hammering on my typewriter again. Now, when the big march is over you can perhaps have time for a letter, and for answering it too. You were 300,000 in Washington the newspapers say. Good! I have been a nervous spectator of course—fearing that something would go wrong and give Nixon a reason to use all his Sturmbrigaden. It must be difficult to have 300,000 rotten apples in the barrel. (Maybe I use the wrong words—I have no dictionary here.) Göran Sonnevi called me the other day and read in the telephone some lines from a new and—as it

---

*Who is this "HOLDERIN" you are talking about? Could it possibly be HÖLDERLIN?

                    your friend TRANSOMAHR

sounded—very strong poem of yours. He was translating it but said that he wanted some help from me with "the Buddhistic parts." Send it!

I spent 2 weeks in Eastern Europe in the end of October—2 of the most exciting weeks of my life. I was a cultural agent for the Swedish Institute and my mission was to establish links behind, through and beside the official bureaucratic lines. The contacts with countries behind the Iron Curtain have been too official, we have an exchange program but often get the politrucs instead of the real people. As I speak understandable German, am not a Marxist and not a conservative, not too young and not too old, not too unknown and not too well-known, not an official man and not too wild etc. I was chosen for the job. I have been working with translations from Hungarian (together with an exiled Hungarian poet) so I have some knowledge of Hungary, and Budapest was the main goal. In the last minute the Hungarians knew about my arrival and transformed me into "official guest of the Writers Union" and that meant that I was met at the airport by an energetic woman ("the interpreter") and a big official schedule to run through. The interpreter complicated the situation in some quarters of course but she was tired in the afternoons so I could see my private addresses alone. I was glad to have the professional psychological training—Hungary is complicated. I met about 8 composers, 13 poets, 3 editors, 2 publishers, 1 director of an institution for delinquent boys, 20 ordinary people etc.

One of the men I wanted to invite to Sweden was János Pilinszky. You have met him in the poetry conference in London this summer. Pilinszky lives in one room in a flat in central Budapest (like most poor Hungarians he can't afford a flat of his own). He is a wonderful guy, we spent a memorable evening together (without interpreter). His official position is weak and it is not granted that he could be allowed to go to Sweden (he is a pious Catholic and his wife has deserted to France). He spoke warmly about you—he was surprised that he could have such a good contact with one of those Americans who scared him first with their strange clothes and complete freedom of acting. Between 1948 and 1956 he was forbidden to publish one line of his own. Another man who was forced to silence during this time was Sándor Weöres and he is the other poet I will propose for invitation to Sweden. I have translated 5 of his poems for a radio program and for BLM. It was moving to meet these people who could keep their human integrity when treated like Pavlovian dogs for many years.

But the mood in Hungary today is relaxed when compared with Czechoslovakia. In Prague I was not an official guest but I had a letter of recommendation to the head of the foreign section of the Writers union (which until now has been miraculously intact—as in the Dubček days). The letter was written by the Czech lady whom you met in my house in 1968 and she wrote that I was a non-political poet. That is of course not completely true but it was useful as a *recommendation* in Prague! The head of the foreign section of the Writers union was a kind but very nervous fellow who spoke in 5 telephones and had a badly hurt right hand. He tried to give some official optimism for the future but his eyes were contradicting it. Then I was let free to meet anybody—and I did. I spent many hours discussing, and met the most massive and united pessimism. Writers, workers, members of the party, bourgeois people . . . all were reacting the same way. They were nice and understandable and they knew that they represented 99% of the public opinion but they were completely convinced that the remaining 1% were preparing terror, purges as in the old days. The climate had hardened just before my arrival when Husák closed the frontiers. They were desperately eager to keep some link with the rest of Europe so I suddenly felt the ridiculous character of the Swedish Institute, Cultural Exchange and such things disappear. I hope to be used some way in the future contacts. Sweden is in a position that gives opportunity to do *something*. Very little but something.

My family is all right. Emma [------] is very active: dancing, playing the flute, riding (she is mad about horses). The small one, Paula, still has round cheeks and is uncomplicated, her father's best support. Do you know that Carol wrote a wonderful letter to Monica and me some months ago? We were so happy to get it and we are always longing to see you all again. Warm greetings!

Tomas

10 Dec, '69

Dear Tomas,

Yes, the Washington march was marvellous. The *New York Times* correspondent estimated 650,000. I had been there for other marches, and there were at least 3 times as many this time. The A.P. wire said from 250,000 to a million, with no way to judge inbetween. Of course all the U.S. newspapers put down 250,000, and forgot the rest of the sentence. There were wonderful signs—you remember Agnew saying that the protestors were all "effete snobs." One sign said, "God is an effete snob." A joke around Washington was, "What is effete?" "That's what Spiro Agnew puts in his mouth." In the middle of the rally, Dick Gregory came on a minute, and said, "What makes me nervous is Nixon going abroad! That leaves only Agnew in the White House, and he's just the type who'd make a crank call to the Kremlin on the hot line!"

Coming down off the Monument Hill at 5 in the afternoon when the rally ended, I wandered with a friend off toward the Justice Dept— there were about 5,000 of us in a three block stretch in front of the Justice Dept about 5:30—most of them curious strollers, or kids who didn't know Washington and were looking for their buses. Nixon wanted to do something to impress the Legionnaires in Nebraska, so at 5:30 without warning the police suddenly started lobbing tear gas—(actually the CS gas used in Vietnam)—they must have exploded 25 to 30 canisters, in us, on top of us, and when we started to head for fresh air, ahead of us, in the air, so we'd have to run through it. Children screaming, women vomiting—wild scene. I had a tear gas cough all night. We're all little lambs in Agnew's pasture.

My long Vietnam poem—that must be the one Göran means—was sent to you months ago! I sent it to you first in June or so! I remember you didn't mention it, so maybe it went astray. I've got a new title for it now, "The Teeth-Mother Naked at Last," and it's being printed this week. I'm printing 1,000 copies free to be given away by the Resistance at their offices. If you don't have a copy, tell me. I'll send a copy of the printed version—(many changes in it since the copy Göran received, and about eight new lines on "the teeth-mother")—anyway, as soon as one arrives here.

I spent all of November out on the road, gathering money for the winter. James Wright and I gave a reading together in mid-Nov at a huge opera house in Pittsburgh—it was a joy. Christina Paulston was there—she and Rolland live near Pittsburgh now—she was stunned, by the way, at how much the Swedish versions in *Krig og tystnad* sounded like the original poems. She thought your translations were the best, but all were good; and she said the poems sounded as if they had been written in Swedish. (Of course, that's possible.)

Did you receive a copy of *Field*? Please send me the address of János Pilinszky. I'd like to write him a note, and maybe send him the new poem. What language did you use in talking with him?

I'm home now for the winter. It's such a joy! I've moved over to an abandoned country schoolhouse, which I'm using this winter as a study. It has tall windows on two sides so I can see the snowy trees. I'm working on my new book, which will be called *The Shadow Brother*. It will have the long Vietnam poem in it, and the short prose poems that were in *Morning Glory* etc. Then off and on, I work on poems for a new book of Snowy Fields poems (Son of Snowy Fields) which will be called, I think—

Doing Nothing for a Thousand Years

In the evenings we all tell troll stories, and watch Laurel and Hardy movies with a projector Carol got me for Christmas last year. The family are all troll-sensitive, shining-eyed, mad for narratives. Noah told me his first composed story yesterday. He came up and said to me: "A dog went poo-poo on the road, and then he died!"

I said, My goodness, Why did he die?

Noah said firmly, "Because he went poo-poo on the road!"

So there it is, a narrative, involving even the Western genius for cause and effect.

Tomas, I want to know your birth-date. I'm studying astrology.

I end with a little poem I found yesterday in a notebook, must have been written last winter:

Doing Nothing Poem

My toes call over the dark peoples.
This poem will unwind from inside the reindeer's horn.
At that call the seas gather themselves
Together, as a man leaps out of bed!

(I guess the reindeer's horn would have to be an antler, but I'd like a horn
that wound around, like a seashell, or a snail shell.
Write soon!
Robert

P.S. There was one beautiful moment in the Wash. rally. About 3:30, some
screamers got up. Women's Liberation types, who wanted to burn down
the Justice Dept, and castrate themselves, or something, and the rally
could have turned ugly. Suddenly the M.C. said, "We have a statement
here, signed by 80 members of the Cleveland Symphony Orchestra, sup-
porting the Moratorium . . . As a matter of fact, 4 of them have just ar-
rived from Cleveland, and they're going to play us a string quartet now."
We were all stunned. So 600,000 people sat down. And over the loud-
speaker system—a sensitive system, that cost $18,000 for one day—the
4 musicians played a Beethoven String Quartet. It was so marvellous, tears
came to everyone's eyes.

I felt strange—in some sort of time-warp. As if we were all at once pro-
testing against Napoleon!
R.

1970

1-4-70

Dear Robert,

I'm writing in Swedish this time to keep you in practice. Thanks for a long and shimmering letter! But the letter with the long Vietnam poem has gotten lost in transit. Probably it's been hijacked by someone and has flown to Cuba. I don't know what "Field" is either. Is it a contraction of "Snowy Fields"? How fantastic it must be to travel around the whole U.S.A. and storm against the administration and give public readings. And then disappear into the wilderness to do nothing for a thousand years. Politician and Guru in the same person, traveling together like Laurel and Hardy.

By surface mail (since I'm poor and stingy) I'm now sending my German translation and Ekelöf's posthumous book—he wrote it while he was dying of lung cancer. The good thing about the German translation is that Michael Hamburger wrote a letter to me (after 3 years) in which he started to intimate something about the possibility of my being invited to England. He asked me to send the best *English* translations I had and I then discovered that I haven't got any copies of the translations we did together on Runmarö. Can you send a few of the best?

I'm an idiot! I forgot about Pilinszky's address! But I'll very likely get a letter from him and will make a note of the address then. He speaks French and German very well, not English.

Tomas Tranströmer was born on April 15, 1931. The exact moment I don't know. For God's sake, drop astrology! We have enough misfortunes threatening us as it is.

I'll write again soon but am sending a new poem. The word "sisu" probably isn't in your dictionary. It's Finnish and is used mostly in the context of sports, especially when describing Finnish athletes. It means something like "tenacity."

The family sends best wishes. We long to see you all again someday, go sailing around the world! In any case it's good that you exist.

Tomas

undated (postmarked January 13, 1970)

Dear Tomas,

I answer your letter soon! Meanwhile I send you copies of some translations right away!

Field is the name of the best new poetry magazine—out of Oberlin—which has 3 of your poems in the first issue, you are as popular in Oberlin as Sophia Loren! I've told them to send you copies. They told me they had sent you a check too. Did that arrive?

American poet confused by the world

16 Jan, '70

Dear Tomas,

I found a letter of yours with two poems and a translation of the Barn in Devon!

So I'll answer a couple of questions there while I am at my "writing-machine," as you Europeans call it.

This was a stone barn I found while walking in far south England, where there are these marvellous green hills that simply plunge straight into the Atlantic! They roll about a bit like a woman's stomach and then down they go! I really think the sense of a woman's stomach must have been in my head even then, because the barn had an overwhelming feeling of a place where we prepare to return to life again, rest a bit before we return to the womb and are born.

In "järteckan" I wanted to suggest that the hoofmarks in heavy dung outside the door are not to be taken as a symbol that the body is filthy, or that life is rotten; they are no symbol of fleshly evil.

The "doors" are those wooden separations, that cattlemen use when they are separating cows into two bunches: two men stand behind it, one man behind each end, and either move it in front of the cow's nose as he comes up, discouraging him to go back, or open it suddenly so the cow goes through. They are easy to lift, usually about eight or ten feet long. They usually have fresh wood showing somewhere, since they are leaned against walls, and knocked down by the cows later, one of whom always steps on it, and cracks off a piece.

Anyway, the "gate" or whatever you call it, looked so useful, so humble, so lacking in egotism, that it was holy, like an altar. (I'm thinking mainly of those small table-altars on which the Buddhists set their flowers and incense and Buddha-statues.)

"Flopping down" suggests the way a cow lies down, without thinking of manners or whether anyone is watching: it's a wonderful sight.

The stones that make up the walls of the barn evidently turn at night into the walls of the womb, dark, and to the infant, invisible.

I have just started with "Preludier," but I have a couple of questions already. The pronouns in "Två sanningar" are difficult for me. In the second stanza, does "den" imply a human being, or one of the two "sanningar" mentioned in the stanza before? I'm not sure I understand the third line of the second stanza, "Vad some helst, etc."

I don't understand "det" in "Och det är en bat."

Does the fourth stanza take place completely *away* from the boat landing—in a house in the middle of the woods, for example—or does it take place near the water?

Does this boat hook hit any of the dancers? (I know what you'll say: "Why I really don't know!")

The poem about your old apartment and your mother's apartment is very moving at the end. The telescope, the Quaker thought, and the doves cooing are marvellous.

In that poem, I wonder if you could give me a literal English version of the second sentence—"rader sorg" throws me into confusion.

I've done a new version of the rocket-shaver poem! Will send it soon. We think a lot about rockets over here—must have to do with the American virility-complex. Shaving of course is a clear reference to castration-desire—Freud told me that only yesterday. I use the old blade-razor myself—Aaaaaaaaaah! (Of course if your shaving poem is really a castration poem, it makes the pilot's remark more sensible: "You're seeing this for the last time!")

(By the way, I still have one question on that poem: "I kamerans barndom." Does that mean the early days of the camera when everyone had to hold still for so long; or does it refer to the way children pose so stiffly for photographs?)

Give my love to your beautiful, good, and desirable wife, och flickorna...

(be careful with those razor poems)

Den Norske Medicine-Man
Robert

20 Jan, '70

Dear Tomas,

I've enjoyed your Hen Poem! The seam to the Africa scene may be a little too prominent—I'm not sure. I'll have to read it ten more times. Also when you say "ette minne" it sounds like the world-traveller bragging. (Naturally those of us who haven't been to Africa are envious, and hate to have you reminding us of it.) Couldn't that scene be a *dream,* instead of memory? (We all have dreams!)

"Enligt reglerna"—does that mean "according to the rules"?

I'm not sure how to understand two phrases particularly: "sanninger fran 1912," and "ett balansnummer."

But I like it very much! It is eerie, and mysterious, and all the hen section is true to hens. I love hens, and I get terribly cross if writers don't get true hendom into their hen-lines. You have done beautifully!

Field should come soon. It is 40 below here this morning. I am working hard. How lazy I am! That must be a Capricorn failing . . . or maybe a Norwegian-no-longer-having-to-grub-out-trees-in-the-cold-rain-failing. There's no doubt, the Norwegians have got it too good over here. I've got to do more work! It's a disgrace! One book every five years . . . laziness!

Write soon!

Your slothful friend,
Robert

Västerås 1-30-70
Dear Robert,
    GOOD GRIEF!
    Wow!
"The Teeth Mother" has come and I'm knocked out. It is incredibly strong, it's as if Walt Whitman had been with you, whispering in your ear to give you strength to write on. I've read large parts of the poem before in various versions but this compilation is superior. (Except the beginning

of section II with the Roman knives—I can imagine that the version in
The Light Around is lying underneath and providing resonance.) The poem
lives both in its details and as a whole. Most remarkable is VI since it is
so naively direct and yet strikes so deeply into the soul. But after this you
can't write anything else about Viet Nam. This poem has the character of
ULTIMATE, LAST, FINAL STATEMENT. The strangest thing about
the poem is that in its incredible bitterness and sorrow it makes the reader
feel such love for life, the earth, everything that moves. Strange. Lucky for
you that you live protected by snowstorms and all those miles of prairie
in Minnesota, so that fame won't get to be too trying. It must be dreadful
to fall into the clutches of that great American fame, all the microphones
being thrust at you etc. How do you deal with it? DO YOU HAVE A
STOMACH OF THE RIGHT SIZE BY NOW? WHEN A PERSON
GETS FAMOUS HE DEVELOPS HIS STOMACH AS AN ACT OF
SELF-PROTECTION.

I've just driven Emma to the stables and seen to it that she got her favor-
ite horse, a black pony by the name of Sotha. The children ride round and
round on the sawdust for almost nothing. Monica is home doing home-
work. She's actually begun to study so she can apply to nursing school in
a year or so. Svärmor (mother-in-law) is living in the house for the time
being to watch the kids when we're both away. I am somewhat over-excited,
owing to the fact that I'm getting ready for a new trip at the expense of the
Swedish Institute. Monica says that trips behind THE IRON CURTAIN
give me the opportunity to develop the latent paranoia I have. I CAN
SMELL A TRAP AT A FAR DISTANCE.

Thanks for the transcriptions of the poetry translations! When I made
copies to send to Hamburger I discovered something that's probably a
mistake. In "Night Duty" section II you write "The language marches im-
perfect step with the boots" but in Swedish it goes "the language marches
in step with the boots"—should be "in perfect step." What I mean of
course is that voices on the radio and in politics and public life in gen-

eral speak a language that marches all too well with the executioners and therefore I, we, must seek a new language that does not collaborate with the executioners.

No. 2 of "Preludes" should go more or less like this in rough translation:

Two truths walk towards one another. One (of the truths) comes
    from the outside and one from the inside
(and at the place) where they meet you have a chance to catch sight of
    yourself.
But he (the person, the one) who sees what is going to happen cries
    in despair:
"Anything! (May anything happen, I can take anything except *that*)
    if only I escape knowing myself."

What it means is of course—you have the truth of your inner world (you Robert must understand that) and there is the truth of the outer world. When there is a confrontation of the two your true character is exposed, at this confrontation you get a glimpse of "WHO I AM." And most people are afraid of that, they want to have the two worlds apart. They can take a lot of suffering, build endlessly defense mechanisms and barriers, even risk their life to escape knowing themselves. "Vadsomhelst" is a typical Swedish colloquialism. "Vadsomhelst, if only my boy gets well" says a mother in desperation to the doctor, for example. It's a contraction of something much longer, for example "Anything [Vad som helst] would be better than not to . . ." Or "I can stand anything [vad som helst] except not to . . ."

[Editor's note: The following seems to be a continuation, though something may be missing.]

And there is a boat trying to put in (trying to land), trying exactly along here. It will try thousands of times. From the darkness of the wood comes a boat-hook, pushed in through the open window, in among the party guests who have been dancing until they were are warm (getting warm by dancing) eller warmed up by dancing . . . The boathook is something totally foreign in the party milieu, it's something from another world, perhaps from Gallilee, it's frightening, a bit comical also, it's religious. I don't know whether these modern party guests are struck by it, maybe I'm the only one who actually sees it come shooting mysteriously in through the window (as if a boat were floating out in the darkness of the forest, trying to land).

Part III.

The apartment where I lived most part of my life is going to be evacuated. Is it now empty of everything. The anchor has let go (has got free, has loosened lost its grip—on the bottom of the sea)—although there still is (a state of) mourning, it is the lightest flat in the whole city. The truth does not need furniture etc. "råder" means "prevails." You know it is shortly after a death and I am mourning but at the same time a *lightness* is experienced. You have to leave all this, what is of value is transformed in a sort of light perhaps. For the last time I see my old apartment just as naked as it was when I saw it the first time: blown out, empty. Light only, memories are vanishing . . .

From the other poem ["Open Window"]: "I kamerans barndon" means the early days of camera when we had to sit still for many seconds to get pictured. This is a beautiful expression in Swedish—we often say "the childhood of the car" etc., it gives an atmosphere of tenderness to these technical things. I have never heard the expression "the childhood of the atomic bomb" but it could be possible. In Swedish.

I went through The Teeth-mother together with Monica this afternoon. (a prima vista translation) The words I did not know I replaced with my own inventions, I read aloud. We were very moved. The only thing I am skeptical about is the title.

(Monica has large front teeth but she is definitely not a teeth-mother.)

(Cartoon caption: A memory of Africa has just popped up . . . J.M., trans)

About the Hen poem (its title is now "Upprätt"—"upright"). The African memory is authentic—I have been to Chad and I must tell it! Few Swedes have been there. (I have longed for such a long time to tell it.) I am glad you have the right sense for hens. I had 4 hens last summer. "Enligt reglerna" is "according to the rules"—the poultry house is a society with strict rules, and the poor birds follow them in an almost neurotic rigidity. They are our sisters. —"sannigar från 1912" is simply "truths of 1912," those years before World War I, when ladies had large hats with (ostrich) plumes, bourgeois rules etc. "Balansnummer" is "balancing act." The poem is partly a protest-poem against the prevailing mood in Swedish intellectual life. What I say is that finding the truth, being honest etc. is a difficult individualistic act of balance, you have to put off the rhetoric, all slogans and mustaches and prejudices and . . . Just like being before Death. (But I did not introduce Charon in the poem.)

Thank you for telling the *Field* people to send their magazine (it has not arrived yet) For some strange reason I am always published in NR 1 issues. Are you starting a whole plantation of magazines around U.S.A.? I like to be present in the babyhood of a magazine. Tell Carol the kindest greetings from us. Give everyone a royal HUG [KLEMM], as it's certainly called in Norway. Your confused

friend
Tomas

Västerås 4-2-70
Dear friend,

since you are my impresario I must have some orientation about all these magazines you have. I love the effete snob magazines I have seen and am very happy to be buried in them. Yes, if we had only ONE of them in our poor country! The enthusiasm you see in a line like this—from Mr DiPalma—"I want to make *Doones* nr 3 something more than just another collection of contemporary poems and translations," this enthusiasm is real, it is good, not the usual tired businessman attitude of most people in the book-publishing trade. Another thing he wrote made me a little nervous: "what you had to say about Tranströmer interested me." What have you written? Have you tried to make me interesting? Until I get *Field* I expect biographical notations like this:

> Tomas Tranströmer is a 67 year old Maoistic sewing machine repairer of mixed Lappish-Jewish origin from Kiruna. He now is a political refugee in Norway.
>
> or:
> Tomas Tranströmer is 14 years old and has written 3 novels but in Sweden he is best known as a composer. His chamber opera "The Quiet Don," based upon Sholokhov's novel, will soon be performed in Baden-Baden.
>
> or:
> Tomas Tranströmer died recently in Mexico. He also published novels under the pen name of B. Traven.

After many years of silence Leif Sjöberg sent me a letter and told me that he was working for a magazine called *Stony Brook*. From some advertisement-quotation he sent I understood that this was the best thing ever printed, anywhere.

Your translation of "Outskirts" seems to be excellent. The last line is probably not a quotation from King James Bible (it sounds to me more like the uttering of a New Jersey mafia leader) but it is good anyhow.

It is almost midnight. Good night!
Yours
aff. Tomas

9 Feb, '70

Dear Tomas,

Would you check this translation, oh master? It is wonderfully exciting in English. I recited it to Carolyn, and her eyes shone like children's eyes listening to pirate stories . . . of course we love to hear about the Russian Revolution over here—it makes us shiver deliciously in our beds . . . But it is a marvellous poem!

"imperfect step" is a typing error by my forbannade typist, R.B.; he should have typed "in perfect step."

Your remarks on the new poems were very helpful. Of course I understand how it is with you world travellers—your memories of Africa just come bursting out, they can't be stopped, it's like a person with a high fever shuddering, he just can't stop it . . . like pain in a gall-bladder attack . . .

Of all things, a check came today from Bonniers for 100 English pounds, for the "advance" on something called *Poems*. It must be *Krig og tystnad* they are talking about. And here I thought the Swedes were efficient!

Thank you for your words on "Teeth-Mother." (The Teeth-Mother is the Great Mother in her Medusa, or teeth side, positively a metaphysical being, and no slander of living women intended!) (Monica is the Great Mother as GOOD Mother, anyway, she is the Mother With The Blue Cloak the old painters used to paint in the 16th Century.) I appreciated your words on the poem so much. I worked on it so long, that now I am indecisive about it, and lack confidence.

Tell me about your new trip! I leave next week for Ann Arbor, where I'll be a writer in residence for the students for 2 weeks—mainly I'll fill their minds with thoughts about the Great Mother.

STUDENT FILLED WITH GREAT MOTHER
THOUGHTS BY R BLY, FLOATING OVER
DETROIT . . .

> Write soon—
> your friend
> Robert

15 Feb, '70

Dear Tomas,

Check this over, will you? It's a paragraph I added to the introduction made for your book. The rest of the introduction is in *Field*, which you've—I hope!—seen by now.

Are these facts and details right?

> As ever,
> Robert

P.S. Can you get me a copy—glossy—of that elegant undernourished photo of you taken by the Italian dame for your German book? I like it! And maybe we can work it into your American book!

Praise praise praise
(see *Field*)

New section

I feel in the poems an increasing psychic depth as they go on. The poem called "After a Death" is surely some sort of brief masterpiece, and more moving than any poem written by an American poet on President Kennedy's death. Tomas Tranströmer's foster father died at nearly the same time, and Tomas has said that both deaths became mingled in the poem. He mentions in the last two lines the Japanese armor that stands in the Stockholm museum near a model of the warrior who fit into it. To say of a man's death, "The samurai looks insignificant beside his armor of black dragon scales" seems to me magnificent.

I think "Out in the Open" is a weird and interesting poem also. It is neither a nature poem, nor a political poem, nor a religious poem. One of the poem's purposes, evidently, is to draw from all these three sections of psychic experiences without choosing between them; and Tranströmer has said as much in a note he wrote for a Scandinavian anthology that included the poem.

more
Praise
(see Field)

Signed
Coleridge

Västerås 27-2-70

Dear Robert,

I am a little shocked by this Tranströmer boom that suddenly comes. I got a nice letter from my Latvian translator the other day, the letter was certainly read by many censors but went through . . . And this morning *Field* arrived (airborne—the previous sending was lost in the Sargasso Sea). And the other day some fellow wrote a praising piece about me in *Dagens Nyheter,* without provocation—my first thought was: "By Jove, I must have published a book again!" I have not the right stomach for taking in PRAISE in large quantities but I will try to read your beautiful introduction again and make the necessary cold comments . . . Well, I was born in 1931, not 1930 (I am still young!—Life begins at forty and I am not there yet). I have some doubts about your line "Someone sent me a clipping recently, which recounted the adventures of a youth" etc. . . . I want to see this clipping! Mythomania could be good for *Field,* but not for an introduction in 70s Press. Actually I have only read the story in a police report and not recently (5 years ago). Maybe "recently" according to *Sixties* standards (when will the next issue of your wonderful magazine appear?). In the new section of the introduction—the part you sent in the letter— you must change "T.T.'s foster father died at nearly the same time." It was not my foster father, it was my uncle. My biological father, who is still alive, would be very hurt. (My parents were divorced when I was 3 but my father has followed my development from a distance and I am going to send him the book when it appears.) About the Japanese armor. I don't know if there is a model of the Japanese himself beside the armor in the museum. I think I imagined him standing there. So far the corrections.

Nothing written about my poems has made me so glad as your railway station metaphor—it is so beautiful in itself, a poem, and I can only hope that it is true too. I have always loved your characterizations of this type in the Crunk pieces.

The problem is that the railway station is empty for the present, the trains are delayed and the station master attacked by angry passengers. So I hurry to give my

APPROVAL

of the old Balakirev-poem. A few details. "and the plough was a bird just leaving the ground" is much better than the original text, where it stands "en fågel some störtat" (a crashed bird). So use your version. "The crew came up from below" is more doubtful because it is written "ice-locked, lights out, people on deck" in the previous stanza. "Besättningen kom fram" means they were coming towards him. As a whole it sounds good in the English version—yes I have read all the lines, if you have dropped a few it could not have been important ones.

I have been very busy the last weeks, doing testings and interviews with cerebral palsy children in an institution up in the woods. It is the most interesting part of my present job, it has a little of pioneer scientific work in it and the contact with the patients there is rewarding too. We write long reports about every individual case, trying to make a map of his, her, particular brain. It is a good institution, friendly, even tolerating sexual relationships between the handicapped. They are often glad to be brought there—some have been more or less hidden by their parents and isolated in many ways. Modern urbanized civilization is less tolerant than the old village society.

Spiro Agnew troubles me.

Your effete station master

Tomas

Västerås 19 April 70.
Dear Robert,
        many thanks for wonderful sendings of books, magazines, ghost-portraits of famous Americans etc. A special thanks for the poem "walking in spring ditches"—this type of poem (almost impossible to translate) is for me, together with the big, passionate Teeth-mother-poetry, your unique contribution . . . to . . . MANKIND. The old boards, old ditches, old cows, old shoes eating the grass, whales, gods! (My English is not good enough.)

I have just arrived from [the Soviet Union]. The Swedish Institute again paid the trip: Stockholm-Leningrad-Riga-Tallinn-Leningrad-Stockholm and the idea was that I should establish contacts on different levels

(primarily personal) with people in the former Baltic countries and try
to start some cultural exchange. We are nowadays almost completely iso-
lated from these countries that are so geographically and historically close
to us. After all Estonia and a big part of Latvia once belonged to Sweden
and the people there have a favorable memory of us because we abolished
feudalism there in the 17th century—feudalism was reintroduced after the
Russian occupation in 1710. (These facts are of course suppressed in the
offical Soviet history-writing.) The countries were independent from 1918
to 1940 when they were given to the Soviets after the Hitler-Stalin pact.
After a period of deportation came the Germans, a new ruthless occupa-
tion followed and after the war the Russians were back and they are now
Soviet Republics. Yes, you know all this of course. But you can imagine
how strange it is to BE THERE, to see the "old town" of Riga that—from
some distance—looks exactly like the "old town" in Stockholm and to re-
alize that in the 1930s regular boat-trips went from Stockholm to Tallinn
3 times a week, and now it takes 15 to 20 days for a letter to arrive. (The
censors are many.) To get to Riga I had to take a flight to Leningrad, stay
there overnight and the next day take Aeroflot to Riga together with enor-
mously mesomorphic Russian military men and to be housed in a hotel
famous for its hidden microphones.

It started with some poems. A man in Riga translated me into Latvian
and 2 poems "Telpas: Kas vala, un telpas, kas ciet" (Öppna och slutna
rum) and "Par vesturi" (Om historien) were printed together with some
Lindegren and Ekelöf in a poetry book *Dzejas diena*—printed in 30,000
copies and sold out in a week in a country with less than 2 million Latvian-
speaking inhabitants. My translator was sent to Sweden in 1965 to study
Swedish for a year and after that to work on the Riga radio—they have
regular sendings in Swedish. When he returned he was not sufficiently
cooperative so he got fired and now he is playing viola in a musical com-
edy orchestra for 85 rubles a week. He is married to Vizma Belševica, the
most gifted poetess in Latvia, now dangerously in disgrace for something
she has written. So they are a controversial couple and I love them. She
is very heroic, he is more simply human. He had translated many poems
of mine that could not be published for the present ("Allegro" e.g. is im-

possible of course but more astonishing is that "Den halvfärdiga himlen" is suspected—because of the line "våra istidsateljéers röda djur"!) So at last I am regarded as a dangerous political poet! They arranged an un-official reading in their home and I met some 15 poets, musicians etc. from Latvia. The next day I was identified and Swedish-speaking official people came to the hotel to take care of me. One was a very nice chap, the other was like a character from an early Graham Greene novel. We talked about cultural relations, ice hockey etc. Every night in Riga the telephone called, at midnight!, and when I lifted the receiver someone rang off. That did not happen in Tallinn so I regard Estonia as less controlled than Latvia. Another difference: in Tallinn the churches are still churches, in Riga most of them are transformed into cafés, planetariums, lecture-rooms (or other would-be-wise temples). (They say the Estonians are more willing to enter the Party, climb, and rule it from within—they are more practi-cal than heroic.) Anyhow the voyage was useful, I think, some ways for communication have been opened (for books, records and ultimately per-sons). Surprisingly many were studying Swedish more or less by them-selves, from old books. They are longing for contact with us and we have been indifferent for so long—with exception of a few crusaders operat-ing with reactionary exile organizations. Unofficial contacts are opposed both by the reactionary part of the exile organizations (who look forward to the "liberation" of the countries through a third world war) and by the Soviets who want to keep them isolated, inside Russia. I will give you a probably bad poem I wrote there, functioning within the special emo-tional situation. I gave it to my friends before leaving Riga, for them to read when they get colorless letters from me in the future. It is very impor-tant that the receivers could not be identified so I called it simply:

To Friends behind a Border

I

I wrote sparsely to you. But everything I couldn't say
swelled up like some old-fashioned hot-air balloon
and disappeared finally in the night sky.

II

Now the censor has my letter. He turns on his light.
My words, alarmed, fly up like monkeys in a cage,
rattle the bars, hold still, and show their teeth.

III

Read between the lines. We'll meet two hundred years from now
when the microphones in the hotel walls are useless
and can finally fall asleep and be trilobites.

(translated by RB)

"Ortoceratiter" is a special type of fossil, often found in Baltic limestone; they
are a little like fossil microphones (from the Silurian age). This is the end of
the travel report. Love to Carol and the children! I will send you a new "book"
(11 poems only) before the end of the month—it is not printed by Bonniers,
we have made it ourselves in the so-called "Författarförlaget"—a death-blow
to commercial, capitalistic, feudalistic book-printing. Good night.

Yours Tomas

26 April, '70

Dear Tomas,

Thank you for the marvellous letter about the Latvian trip! It's all
so strange—the telephones ringing late at night in Riga . . . and no one
there—The Europeans really have developed these claustrophobic anti-
people technological harassments far beyond what we have done here. I
think it's because Europe became over-populated first. More and more
I think that many curious events such as burning down banks, telephone
harassment at night, seemingly rational, are actually rat-reactions that
come when the cage gets too full of rats. As Neruda said in 1934:

It so happens I am sick of being a man.

I like "Till vänner bakom engräns," but I long for more anguish between Parts II and III, anguish as clear as that marvellous hostility made clear in II with the ordene sum "visar tänderna" to the censors.

I don't want to take the long view, and be rocked asleep, that *soon*.

I'm getting tired of being a *speaker*—but I only have two trips left—one to N.Y. this week, and then to Honolulu in May. Enclosing report of recent reading with Senator McCarthy. We became good friends. At one point he said, "Just think! If I had been elected President, *you* would have been at the prayer breakfasts instead of Billy Graham! What a loss!"

I'm looking forward to your new "book"—write soon! Our love to all your flickor, especially your wife, whose luminous face I often see.

Your friend,
Robert

P.S. Carol is deluged with requests from Sweden for the "Teeth-Mother" folder—evidently Gunnar Harding had a note about it in *Expressen*. (The teeth-mother is really Pat Nixon) (The foreign poets at a recent conference at the Library of Congress, by the way, got at a White House reception: This, a copy of *The Collected Poems of Elizabeth Bishop*, signed by Pat Nixon! How's that!) (The mind boggles)

Göran says that you and he may do a Swedish version of the teeth-mother. It would be nice to have it in a similar folder, free, or at a very low price. But whatever you decide is fine . . . The Swedes are rich anyway . . . love, Robert

Västerås 2 May 70

Dear Robert,

one of the reasons why ectomorphs seldom succeed in politics is THE PHYSIOLOGICAL OVERRESPONSE. Nixon's Cambodia speech is sitting like a FISHBONE in my throat, I simply can't eat these days, only small amounts, I feel sick, I can only hope that you and all wise people have strength to take up the fight, without desperation, with a quiet, effective, white-hot fury against this latest bestial stupidity.

My life is confused just now. Today I got my new book. I'll send it in a week. I absolutely don't give a damn what they write about it. Tomorrow I'm going to Budapest—invited to attend a "Journées de la Poésie à Budapest"—the Hungarian Writers' Union thinks I'm a big cultural personality in Sweden! What a mistake! But they've sent plane tickets and I'm going. My fugitive friends have urged me to go—otherwise they'll just invite some Party poet from Bulgaria. I've never been to a deluxe conference of this kind before; it makes me ashamed. Voznesensky is coming too. The discussions will be carried on in French, Russian, and Hungarian. Since I am phenomenally bad at French, I'll just sit there like an idiot. But I hope to be able to sneak away from the program and see my friends from the earlier visit.

Maybe my appetite will come back. In any case I want to live long enough to see Nixon lose the next presidential election. He darkens the sun. Otherwise there's plenty to be happy about in the family circle.

Our household has been augmented by two dwarf rabbits. We escaped a dog this time. But how it will be when summer comes I don't know. Probably the house is going to resemble Noah's Ark more and more. Your son would feel at home here.

I LOVE YOU ALL.
                    Tomas

Västerås 10 June [1970]

Dear Robert,
            I am longing very much for news from you. Good news, I mean, to hear that you and Carol and the children are well.

In the meantime take this little book and these clippings from the Swedish scene. I am in the ridiculous position of being FAMOUS again.

They love me again, even the Marxistic hard-hats. Why? The small book is now printed in 7000 copies, about 5000 are thought to be sold already.

It is full summer—I rush directly from my poor clients into the water.

Love from all of us

Tomas

20 June, '70

Dear Tomas,

I keep waiting for your new book, but all I get are new books of Göran Sonnevi! That's OK, but his books don't have enough lairs, mole-nests, skulls full of wet straw, interiors of horse-ears, soggy cities under wet stones etc. (Man does not live by air alone.) Oh, how wise I am!

Tell me how the Budapest journey was! Did you see Voznesensky? I'd love to write to him, and tell him how much I like his poems.

I postponed my new book three or four months, while I struggle this summer with yet another draft of my long poem on Great Mother Fears.

If you send me some new poems, I'll send you some! We are all well, staying home. J Wright has gone to Vienna, Louis Simpson to England.

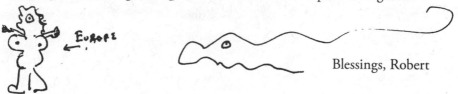

Blessings, Robert

29 July, '70

Dear Tomas,

Your new book did come! And I like it very much! So much that I'm thinking maybe I should just translate the whole thing, in the same order you have it, and have it printed as a little pamphlet. Then, when you come over here next, on a triumphal reading tour, like Charles Dickens, you'll have *two* books on the market!

I enjoyed the reviews also—the Marxist critics seem to have collapsed, and have stopped attacking you as a medieval pope—That is ominous—bad news for the Left—I'm afraid they're losing their morale.

Only the small town critics, as in Örebro, are still malicious, holding up their poisoned end, or pen, or whatever it is.

You asked how we are—we're all very well! I go swimming every afternoon with the children, teaching them to dive, and I resemble Julie Nixon more each day.

Tonight there is a parade—of pets for the children, who must dress their pets. Mary is taking an extraordinary chicken we have—extremely interested in the human race, contemptuous of the company of other chickens, insists on roosting each night on one of the outdoor stairs, alone—his name is Orville. So Orville's wildest dream comes true tonight—he's going to be dressed as a human being! Or nearly so—he gets some Raggedy Ann doll clothes . . . I suppose this piece of good luck will completely unbalance him, and we'll have to send him to the psychiatrist. Hubris is no doubt dangerous in chickens, he may end up as a delinquent, a demonstrator, a "bum" . . . probably able to make love only in garderoben . . .

Please write, and send me some news from the island . . . and from your dear family . . .

Robert

Runmarö 11-8-70

Dear Robert,

I am writing to you on a dirty piece of paper—we are short of paper here in the Island because I have been struggling with a very LONG poem (about the Baltic—from all points of view). It is raining today and we are a little upset because Monica, Great Mother, is ill, she should remain in bed, she has a sore throat. She is probably exhausted too—we have had an endless stream of visitors, mostly children with insomnia problems, and sometimes grown up people with emotional problems—the place has been overcrowded—the latest guest is a cat who refuses to leave the house. This summer we have 6 chickens, 2 guinea pigs, 2 rabbits and outside 1 hedgehog and 1 owl who is sitting all the night in a pine at the north-west corner of the house shouting WHZIII . . . WHZII.

It was good to get your letter. I am of course very positive to the idea of making a pamphlet of "mörkerseende." But the title in English seems to be "dark vision" and that sounds very commonplace pathetic. Perhaps something like "dark adaptation" would be better. What has happened to the 20 poems? 10 months ago you wrote "your book is being printed now" and a simple arithmetic calculation gives the result that if your printing capacity is 2 poems in one month the book would be almost completed now. But don't hurry! In the meantime I have got these wonderful magazines. The latest was *Kayak*—an old dream of mine has been fulfilled! I felt like being represented in Madame Tussaud's museum. I hope Mr Di Palma (is that the name?) will send his mag when it is brought out.

Do you know that Birger Norman (a nice man and a sometimes good poet) has written an essay about you and Senghor in a Christian cultural magazine called *Vår Lösen*? I will send it as soon as I can find it—I have only read it in a library. I think the little volume *Krig och tystnad* has made a strong impression, even influence, on some people here. In a small town where I gave a reading, one schoolboy from the audience suddenly went up and read aloud from your (mistranslated) introduction to the book and asked me about my reaction to your ideas. It was very strange to hear him start: "The great American poet Robert Bly has said that . . . etc." It was in Karlskrona, in Blekinge. The therapeutic influence comes mainly from the honest and sensible effort to bring the inner and the outer worlds together—people are hungry for crossways now.

I hope you will not destroy anything in "Teeth-Mother" when you rewrite it. Be careful. The only weakness in the poem is the title. But titles are difficult. Sonnevi has a large manuscript ready but can't find the title—he has a list of about 200 proposals, mostly of the type "Och nu," "Här är språket," "Dag för dag," "Ordet är vitt" etc., dry constructions—and he is not satisfied, so the book will be delayed or printed with the absolute capitulation title of "Dikter 1963–70."

I go back to Västerås this afternoon. By train. My old car, my dear Saab, is dead. Not far from Enköping—a town between Stockholm and Västerås—the brakes suddenly did not function. The liquid in the brake system went out in half a second and I was pressing the pedal in vain. My car ran into the car in front of it and crashed. I had my safety belt on and was not hurt. But the front of my Saab was transformed into an accordion. It could not be repaired. The car I hit was possible to repair and the driver was not hurt so after all I had good luck.

The problem is that I have no money to buy another car. Let us not talk about it. Read instead my last (latest) poem about roads. It was written reluctantly—I wanted to concentrate on the Baltic poem instead but the typewriter did not agree. A few words: "grävlingens fotspår" = "the tracks of the hedgehog." "Strömbrytare" is the button you press in order to get electric light.

I hope to hear from you soon. Love to Carol and the children! From us all
     Tomas

P.S. The abdominable pig that has replaced Odin as an emblem for Seventies Press—is it Särimner, the pig that was killed every evening in Valhalla, eaten by the dead Vikings and risen from the dead the next morning?

Västerås 7-9-70

Dear Robert, it is urgent so I am writing with red typewriting this time! I have sent the following 4 translations to the magazine *Böckernas Värld* (which is Bonniers attempt to reach the train-riding audience, the mag is sold in all shops at the railway stations, small tobacco shops etc.). It is a popular magazine but not too popular—I myself e.g. have been published in it. They pay well. I hope you will get something too, but I can't promise. Another reason for publishing the translations is that the original poems are so good. Especially I like the Canadian Thistle. As you can see, I have changed some words. "Tumbleweed" does not exist in Swedish (or in Sweden) and—as a matter of fact—the Canada thistle, *Cirsium arvense, is no tumbleweed.* So I have brought the tumbling to the line with "in front of me" and have invented the word "trasselväxt." Onomatopoetic. There are some small changes in the other poems too, have a look at them and give the confirmation or proposals (the latter I can bring into the text at the proof-reading stage). I hope your reaction will be fast, because they want to print the poems soon. Sweden is waiting.

Love to you 5
from Tomas

Sept 14 70

Dear Tomas,

I've got a new typewriter, so I must write to you on it. It's wonderful to be able to get new toys, at my advanced age. It's an Olympia. The Germans really know how to make typewriters. But who can type on them?

I'm delighted you're printing some of the prose poems, and you always have my permission to print them, in any form, with or without writing me, any poems of mine. But I will make a few notes on these, most of them minor indeed.

"Renaissance Painting"

It's a lovely translation, swift and clear. For myself, I've always been a bit dissatisfied with the last stanza, and in the second edition of *Morning Glory,* just now being printed, I've altered the last stanza. I'll type the new version here, and you can use whichever version you please.

The rocks have not been forgotten by the sea either. They are the old brains of the sea. They glow for several seconds every morning, as the old man who lives in a hut on the shore drinks his glass of salt water.

I'd like your opinion, too, on which version is best, of this final paragraph.

"The Hunter"
(The old Central Post office in New York used to have inscribed above its Corinthian columns: NEITHER SNOW NOR HEAT, NOR HAIL NOR SLEET CAN KEEP HIM FROM THE SWIFT COMPLETION OF HIS APPOINTED ROUNDS)

I love the translation.
His answer is a sensitive point. I can't feel the implications of "gärna det," so I'll have to talk about the English. His answer "Why not?" is affectionate and faintly rude at the same time. It's the answer that a parent might give a child, if the child asked if it could take a cupful of water out of the sea. Or suppose there is a woman who loves you, and she is lying on a sofa, and you ask her if you can kiss her—she says, "Why not?" smiling.

At the moment, the Japanese man has a firmer grip of reality than the other person, stunned by the octopus-reality.

The octopuses are found in shelved rock, at low tide.

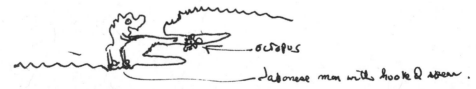

octopus

Japanese man with hooked spear.

"Helicopter"
Again I've changed the last stanza, but the Swedish sounds excellent, and I think you've solved some things in the Swedish I was dissatisfied with in English, so let's leave yours exactly as it is.

"Canadian Thistle"

It turns out the weed was not a Canadian thistle at all, as you have surmised, but what is called in the Midwest, in a slang term, "a Russian thistle." They are the Texas and Oklahoma tumbleweed, and in the Thirties, during the Depression, they used to blow all the way from Oklahoma to Minnesota in the fall, maybe traveling a thousand miles over the prairies. So they were very exciting to me as a boy. They look like this:

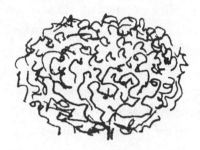

When mature, they get round and wonderfully dry and brown, break off at the stem, and roll around to drop their seeds. Very clever of them.

With the "amazing arrows" I was thinking, I think, of arrows like those in Irish fairy tales, or in the story of William Tell, enchanted arrows with powers that humans do not have.

I'm not sure if the "tumlar" should be in the line with "främfor mig" or not . . . I don't want the reader to get the impression that the weed is actually moving on his desk. It is stationary, but has so much complication of branches that precisely in standing still, it looks as if it were moving. The image should suggest a lion, much contained energy . . .

I gave the printer of your book a deadline of October 15th. And I hope he can meet it. He is setting each page by hand, and a Swedish girl in Milwaukee is reading proof on the Swedish—I hope she can read!

We are now in Inverness, which is more like Runmarö than any place we have ever been. I go to the sea every day, and drink my morning glass of salt water.

Love to you all!

Robert

Our address: Inverness, California 94937

23 Oct, '70

Dear Tomas,

Just a note to establish friendship again! We've come out to California for the winter—a lovely foggy little town north of San Francisco—and so all is turmoil, but settling down. Our address is Box 452, Inverness, California 94937.

The crazy printer in Milwaukee says he will have your book done by Nov 15th. After it's out a few months, then we're going to get you over here! Either in the spring, or next fall! Maybe you'll stubbornly refuse to come either time, but I'll start thinking of some readings anyway. In a couple of them, I hope I can be with you—you read the poems in Swedish, and I'll read them in English—or the other way around! Swedish with a heavy Sioux accent.

Do write me some more about the implications of the word "Mörker-seende." Does this touch on the ability some people have to see in the dark? Cats can do it, they say. How about a man with a searchlight? "Getting Used to the Dark"?

What an interesting story that was to me of the boy in Karlskrona! I should live so long! I can imagine it was startling to you to have him refer to me as if I were some mythical figure from the Arab Middle Ages, said to have visited Tibet and discovered Victoria Falls.

Do send me a copy of Birger Norman's article if you can get one. Senghor . . . egad.

Don't insult the PIG. You know what happened to Odysseus' crew on the island of Circe.

I like the light-switch poem. All the same, you're a stone-fetishist!

Your admirer,
Robert

Västerås 27 Oct. -70

Dear Robert,

I just got the proof of your prose piece plus a request from the editor not to change anything, even if I'm not entirely satisfied. The maga-

zine is being done by the grace of the publishers (Åhlén & Åkerlund) of the
Bonnier Concern's weekly magazine, and changes in the proof would hardly
be allowed. I might leave "tumlandet" [tumbling] alone this time, though
I'll change it the next time the poem is published, in a book for instance
(I'm thinking about bringing out a collection of my translations sometime).

All well with us. The only one who's been feeling bad is me. I've been
sick for 14 days and have been forced to stop smoking. For a week I also had
to stop talking. (The vocal cords did not produce tones. Hs&%?TCHZZX
was the sound.) After penicillin etc. I've now gotten my voice back, or
more accurately a new voice, much stronger, like an opera singer's.

The literary establishment in Sweden is in the process of falling apart.
BLM won't be published once a month anymore, but only four times a
year. The controversy rages in the papers. The magazine has lost its reader-
ship since it was taken over after a military coup by a group of extreme left-
ists who paint honorable old novelists as "Fascists" and wax enthusiastic all
but exclusively over books about Albania. (Albania and North Korea are
in.) Lars Gustafsson is however still editor-in-chief at BLM, but his role has
begun to resemble that of Vittorio Emanuele in Mussolini's Italy.

The cultural life of Sweden is and remains a scene for fools. Help me
out of this! Release at least 20 of my poor poems from the cage of the
Swedish language! You wrote that October 15 was the deadline. But surely
a tornado has lifted the roof off the press and scattered the papers.

You never write anything about how the magazine *The Sixties* is doing.
I long for a new issue the way a prisoner of war longs for a package from
the Red Cross.

We love you all
Tomas

I am still working with my l o n g (talkative) poem about the Baltic. In the
meantime this small piece in the old style.

Sketch In October

The tugboat is freckly with rust. What's it doing here, so far inland?
It is a thick lamp, gone out in the cold.

But the trees have wild colors: signals to the other shore
As if somebody wants to be rescued.

On the way home, I notice inky mushrooms poking up through grass.
They are fingers of someone asking for help,
someone who has wept for himself a long time down there in the dark.
We belong to earth.

(translated by RB)

DICTIONARY:
Bogserbåt = tow-boat

Bläcksvamp = horsetail-mushroom

Västerås 1 nov-70
Dear Robert

Heavy snow today, cold, I am really longing for California! I did not know that you were staying so long in Inverness so I recently sent a letter to Madison—it will probably arrive some day. I was happy to hear that the delay is only one month. The delay for the 20 poems I mean. Do you really think the small volume can bring me over there? And who is going to pay the ticket? Shall I try to apply to the Västerås' cultural funds? Anyhow, if there is a genuine interest from some audiences to hear us read ourselves in broken languages I will welcome it as a wonderful opportunity to rejoin the Bly family and to hear your new stories, especially in rural surroundings. And to see the hectic law-and-order-life in some big places too. In *early* spring it is possible—in May I am ordered to go to military service again, a so-called refresher training! In the autumn I am ready to cross the ocean too. Perhaps autumn will be best, I don't know, we must meditate . . . As for "Mörkerseende," it is a technical term for the ability to see in darkness. An Englishman told me that the word should be "dark vision"—that sounds very pathetic to me. "Dark adaptation" sounds more like the Swedish. The "mörkerseende" develops when you get used to the dark, after half an hour outside the lamps it is beginning to function at its best. Don't smoke when driving in the dark, nicotine impairs your mörkerseende etc. —I phoned Birger Norman and asked him to send his article to Inverness, he will do that. He is a poet and journalist, about 50, self-educated, a mild but sharp critic of the political establishment in Sweden, he has written a wonderful TV-play about personnel policy in a big Enterprise, a very funny play, and a documentary book about one of our few revolutionary episodes—the Ådal riots in 1931, when military were firing at workers for the last time in Sweden. He comes from this part of Sweden, now an area of diminishing population. —Did you vote for Hubert Humphrey? —What happened to Raymond DiPalma and his magazine? (I was almost saying "Raymond DiPalma and his orchestra"—sounds like somebody in a TV show.) Full stop.

In a hurry but affectionate

Tomas

8 Nov, '70

Dear Tomas,

I'll ask some esteemed loonies in the literary world which time of the year they think most propitious for your descent—April or early October—and then I'll set to work arranging some readings, and parties. If I'm lucky, I'll figure a way to get travel expenses—your air fare—from some overfed, understaffed Scandinavian Cultural Foundation. But I do think maybe applying for Västerås funds might be useful too. If you get two travel grants, one could be used for travel *inside* the United States, which is costly too, especially the medical expenses incurred every time you step out of the railway station at night—bandages, arm splints, etc. We'll have a good time—if you had travel expenses, you could even get out to California and see the soft underbelly of the United States.

I just came back from three days in the poet-hothouse at the State

Univ of Buffalo. They get wonderfully excited there, and read everything they can find. After a reading one night there, a young man came up to me and asked me, "Are you going to do any more translations from Swedish?" with his eyes shining. It was very beautiful. I said Yes, yes, yes, and he thanked me, and rushed out into the night (trying to see the stars through the Buffalo smog, probably).

I think mörkerseende is simply night vision. Cats have good night vision, horses do not.

I have a question for you—what are the two best articles written about you in Swedish? Can you send me a copy of each? I think I'll try to get them translated and printed here—several people have offered to do it.

[closing lost]   Robert

12 Nov, '70

Dear Tomas,

Almost every day now I'll send you a new poem translated from *Night Vision*. Here is the first. As you see, I don't understand "sisu." (You sent me some notes on the poem, but I stupidly left them in Minnesota.) I'm not sure either about SARA. (What it means, or why it is capitalized.)

Meanwhile I have a few questions about other poems. Please be patient (be kind to your web-footed friends):

In "The Bookcase," I'm not sure why the mercury pellet is described as rising. Doesn't one usually see a mercury pellet sliding along a table horizontally? I have difficulty imagining it climbing. I'm not sure I understand if you mean there to be a connection between that and the inability to turn the head. And for the first of those two phrasings, which sentence do you think is closer to the muscle-feeling of the Swedish:

You couldn't turn your head away.

or

You couldn't get your head to turn.   ?

A second sentence I don't understand—this time it is really vocabulary—

is the last sentence of the second paragraph. I don't understand "bär av," unless it means "wear off." And the bookcase is still stronger—than what?

****

In "Preludes": in Part III, I can't understand the grammar of the clause beginning "trots att." (unless it means: "despite the continuing circumstances of grief, it is the lightest apartment in the whole city.")

In the sentence beginning "Saker" I can't understand the words "med om," though I understand the meaning of the sentence.

Forgive my new typewriter—its mother was frightened by a Latin manuscript, and it doesn't believe in pauses . . .

In "Med älven," there are "igenkistrade ögon." Are those eyelids stuck together by some sort of glue or are they merely pressed together (temporarily) by their owner?

*****

I just went in for lunch, and told Carol about the hen poem, which I managed to recite for her. When I finished, she said, "Tomas is marvelous. The whole poem is a revelation. And Tomas is a storyteller too, that's what's so good—so it is a revelation with story telling." Or story telling with revelation.

Your hard-working friend . . . I'm the only person

in California working! . . .

Robert

Standing Up

In a split-second of hard thought, I managed to catch her. I stopped, holding the hen in my hands. Strange, she didn't really feel alive: rigid, dry, a white ladies' hat full of plumes that shrieked out the truths of 1912. Thunder in the air. An odor rose from the fence-boards, as when you open a photo album that has gotten so old no one can identify the people any longer.

I carried her back inside the chicken netting and let her go. All of a sudden she came back to life, she knew who she was, and ran off according to the rules. Henyards are thick with taboos. But the earth all around is full of affection and of sisu. A low stonewall half overgrown with leaves. When dusk begins to fall the stones are faintly luminous with the hundred-year-old warmth from the hands that built it.

It's been a hard winter but summer is here and the fields want us to walk upright. Every man unimpeded, as when you stand up in a small boat. There is a link to Africa I remember: by the banks of the Chari, many boats, an atmosphere positively friendly, the men almost blue black in color with three parallel scars on each cheek (meaning the Sara race). I am welcomed on a boat—it's a canoe made from a dark tree. The canoe is incredibly rocky, even when you sit on your heels. A balancing act. If you have the heart on the left side you have to lean a bit to the right, nothing to be in the pockets, no big arm movements please, all rhetoric has to be left behind. It's necessary: rhetoric will ruin everything here. The canoe glides out over the water.

What a wonderful poem!

[on envelope]

Thank you for "Skiss i oktober." But "speak for yourself," as my Grandmother used to say when I told her we were all descended from apes.

"Jag är jordens." Or am I wrong? I don't know.

Sorry to hear about BLM. Soon *The Sixties* will be the only magazine left alive? I worked on *Seventies* 1 last night. You're all over it.

12 Nov, '70

Dear Tomas,

Please comment! I couldn't get in "too long" for the stairway because of the adjective problem in English. I could try "lengthy"—but the sound is not so good.

The problem in the final stanza was to keep your repetition of "glömma" in "glömskans." We can't do that in English—"forgetfulness" and "oblivion" are both extremely weak and won't join with a strong word like "hell." So you can see how I tried to solve it.

For "snabbt snabbt" I can also say "quickly quickly" or "swiftly swiftly" but the first implies very short steps, and the second a kind of gliding motion.

I love the poem.

Your friend,
Robert

Västerås 18-11-70

Dear Robert,

I got 2 letters from you today, thank you, I am for the present confused and rather happy—suddenly there are not only unpaid bills covering my table. The other day I got the whole *Mörkerseende* in French—translated by a professor in Lyon and yesterday he wrote me that he has found a French publisher too. More sensational than that—some fellow is translating me into ICELANDIC. I also got a letter from Mr Leif Sjöberg in N.Y. ordering me to send immediately and by air my collected works to Miss May Swenson—he did not tell why. Is she going to criticize your translations somewhere? I think she is the same person as the poet May Swenson (whom I have not read), or is it a common American name? It sounds so incredibly Swedish. —

The letter from the professor in the solid brick house in Tennessee was shocking—I return it hereby. I did not know that Tennessee was that bad. (But it is in accordance with the election outcome, when Albert Gore was fired and replaced with a Nixon man.) Shall we make a reading in the Deep South? I have studied the election results carefully. A professor in Vermont has made a list of all the congressmen and given them an anti-war score from 0 to 100. I have gone through the list and looked after what people have been re-elected. For Minnesota there are 2 extreme doves: Fraser (100) and Karth (86). Both were re-elected. The moderate dove Blatnik (with a score of 70) was re-elected too. So was the hawk Zwach (25). The worst man in Minnesota with an anti-war score of only zero is NELSEN—I have not found out if he is re-elected or not. But another hawk, Langen (0) was fired. Were any of these people from your neighborhood?

Let us turn to the more pleasant battlefield of translating problems. I am very fond of your "Standing Up" version. I have the impression that you have caught the right tone—at the same time it should have the relaxed storyteller mood and the deadly serious mood of exposure before death.

I like the liberties of your translation. The start is almost SEXY "I managed to catch her!" The word "sisu" is the problem. It is a Finnish word, often used in Sweden in some special connections. Most frequently by sports journalists. It means "tenacity," "stamina" and "fighting spirit"—not the theatrical fighting spirit of General de Gaulle but the silent, stubborn, discrete Finnish unconquerableness. I think the word got into our language during the Finland/Soviet war 1939–40 when the Finns were holding back a nation 50 times bigger than their own. But today the word is used mainly when describing sporting events, especially if some Finn is fighting. I think it is the first time the word has appeared in poetry, it gives a pleasant shock. It gives these trivial sports associations but at the same time the word is exotic, like the word "taboo" in the previous lines.

The Sara people is not a problem. Sara is a tribe in Chad. The scars on the cheeks are the signs of the tribe members (you can see it on the present, bad, president François Tombalbaye, who is a Sara). It has nothing to do with Sara in the Bible. "Tribe" is a better word than "race" here—it is not a special race, just a group among the Sudan negroes. I think the reason why I capitalized the whole word SARA was that if I wrote "Sara" I would think of the woman's name, but "SARA" makes more exoticism.

The Bookcase. Robert, I think you are too proud. Don't despise your helpful friend, the dictionary. "Kvicksilverpelare" has nothing to do with "pellets." "Pelare" is the same word as the English "pillar." So it is an enormous column/pillar of mercury rising (as inside an enormous thermometer—when you have fever). I don't know enough English to judge about the two proposals for head-turning expression. It means simply you must not turn your head away. "Bär av" is a typical spoken language expression. "Nu bär det av" a mother (or father) says when sitting with her child on a sled, just when they start sledding down a slope. In American films they often say "here we go" in such situations. Perhaps you should translate it "now when we set off" or something like that. Your last question "and the bookcase is stronger—than what?" is probably not to be answered. I don't know. Well, it is unclear in Swedish, it could mean "the bookcase is still more powerful than I have succeeded to describe in the previous part of this damned poem."

Preludes. "Trots att det fortfarande råder sorg" is just a contrast to the lightness of the apartment, because mourning, grief, is associated with heaviness.

"Saker jag varit med om här" is a spoken language expression. It means simply: Things (events) I have taken part in (experienced) . . . "Saker" does not mean pieces of furniture, playthings, concrete substantives, it means *events.* Like "thing" in "a strange thing happened to me yesterday etc."

Standing Up again. You missed the word "varsamma." Unimpeded but careful, when you stand up in a boat you have to be careful. The word "varsam" has nothing to do with cowardice, it is used when you take care of small babies or tiny animals, it has a certain tenderness around it.

Have Bonniers sent you *Böckernas Värld* with the prose poems? I am not responsible for the introduction about your life and work. It was *not* a very good introduction but I have seen much worse.

Love to you all! A word of praise from Carol's lips is more dear to me than praise from hundreds of Pompidous. Monica sends her best greetings.
    Tomas

P.S. Med älven. Their eyes are stuck together with some ideological glue.

Västerås 19-11-70

Dear Robert,

the messages go quickly down the long Atlantic mailroad in these days. I think your version of "The Name" is excellent except for one thing. You write "the Hell of unconsciousness . . ." But it is not "unconsciousness," it is oblivion. I have in the previous part of the poem written: "I'm *fully conscious,* but that doesn't help." Well, then you can't call it "unconsciousness" a few lines later. I don't think it is important that "glömma" and "glömska" are related. You say that "forgetfulness" and "oblivion" are "weak" words in English. "Glömska" is rather weak in Swedish too. I think the problem is that in English the strong word "hell" comes first, and the weak word "oblivion" afterwards, so you get an anti-climax. In Swedish the weak word "glömskans" comes first and then as a terrible crescendo the strong word "helvete." Then you get a climax, not an anti-climax. Is it possible to say "oblivion's hell"? Another solution would be to use the words "wide awake" instead of "fully conscious" in the first part of the poem. That is all for tonight. Warm greetings

Tomas

20-11-70

Dear Robert,

Umph . . . Well, let us start the translation business again. Today we have "Breathing Space in July" or "Breathing Space July" as I prefer to call the poem (did you notice that?).

Monica thinks that your translations are a little better than the original texts. The poems grow a little. For instance this poem is bigger in space. You have translated the whole scene, from the Swedish archipelago with its small, gray bridges to a Californian scenery with "ocean docks," it's the Pacific no doubt.

I think the first stanza is wonderful.

The second stanza is "Californian." I don't know if I shall object to the "ocean docks" or not.

The third stanza sounds very good but the man is not necessarily r o w i n g (do you ever row in California?). Actually I wrote the stanza after a trip in a *motor boat,* around whole Runmarö.

That it is a *kerosene* lamp is never written in Swedish, but I think it is good to have it there. So no objections. But I am not sure what the "chimney" is? In my childhood we had, roughly, 2 types of kerosene lamps

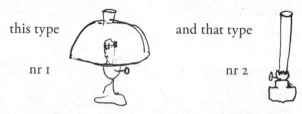

this type   and that type

nr 1   nr 2

I have the former in mind, when reading the poem, but I have the suspicion that you have the latter. "The chimney" must be the glass pipe of nr 2. I imagine the islands/moths crawling over the s h a d e of nr 1. Could it be called "chimney" too? Love   Tomas

20 Nov, '70

Dear Tomas,

Here are "PRELUDES." It's hard to decide on the pronouns for the first two stanzas of part II. And this is just a first draft typed up to see how it looks.

I'm not sure if you'd like the suggestion on the wall paintings to be:

The outline left behind on a wall when a picture that has been there
a long time is removed

or

Perhaps the pictures are *still* hanging there on the wall.

Help me with this!

BOSWELL

Preludes

I

I shy from something that comes hurrying katty-corner through the
    blizzard.
Fragment of what is to come.
A wall gotten loose. Something eyeless. Hard.
A face made of teeth!
A wall, alone. Or is a house there,
even though I can't see it?
The future . . . an army of empty houses
feeling their way forward in the falling snow.

II

Two truths approach each other. One comes from inside, the other
    from outside,
and where they meet we have a chance to catch sight of ourselves.

The man who sees what is about to take place cries out wildly:
    "Stop it!
the hell with it all, if only I don't have to know myself."
And a boat exists that wants to tie up on shore—it's trying right
    here—
in fact it will try thousands of times yet.

Out of the darkness of the woods a long boathook appears, snakes in
    through the open window,
in among the guests who are getting warm dancing.

III

The apartment where I lived over half my life has to be cleaned out.
It's already empty of everything. The anchor has let go—despite the
continuing weight of grief it is the lightest apartment in the whole
city. Truth doesn't need any furniture. I have made a big circle around

my life and come back to its starting point: a room blown empty. Things I loved so much now appear on the walls like Egyptian paintings, scenes from the inside of the grave chamber. But they are more and more blown clean. For example the light is too stark. The telescope held up to the sky. It is silent as a Quaker's breathing. All you can hear are the doves in the back yard, their cooing.

24 Nov, '70

Dear Tomas,

May Swenson is a poetess of very dubious ability whom I know fairly well. Her parents were Swedish, from the country, converted to Mormonism by Mormon missionaries, and so transported to Utah!!! where May Swenson grew up. She's lived in N.Y. for years now. She is very anti-man. I remember an incident from the gathering of poets at Houston several years ago. Don Hall was there, round and full of childish, stomach-type charm and warmth as always. Two young girls—about 15—who called themselves the Houston Society of Young Poets, had taken a liking to Don's face, and had presented him with a balloon. It was a sort of formal reception, in a ballroom, and Don looked lovely, walking around with his blown up balloon floating about him. He suddenly came to me, mad as a wet hen. I said, What's the matter? He said, "May Swenson pricked my balloon!" (She had just put her lighted cigarette against it, looking him in the eyes, and popped it.) He said, "That's the meanest thing I've ever seen a human being do!" He was crushed.

She belongs at the same time to an elegant, conservative, rather decadent we-like-rich-folks literary set in New York—they're always on prize committees of the American Academy of Arts & Letters and such things— and so I'm sure she *does* like your poems, and also thinks it would be a *favor to you* to rescue you from the barbarian, Robert Bly—

So let her go ahead—you really can't stop her anyway. And maybe you can improve her translations a bit. It will be interesting to see what she does.

For "The Name"—try this:
But it is impossible to forget the fifteen second battle in the hell of noth-
ingness, a few feet from a major highway, where the cars slip past with
their lights dimmed.

Sometimes patients in hospitals will describe the "sense of nothingness"
they felt while under ether.
Both "oblivion" and "forgetfulness" are impossible, and never used in
spoken English any more. Do you think "the hell of nothingness" would
be a possible solution?
I enclose "At the Riverside." I'm not sure I understand the visual sug-
gestions of "snurrar trögt och hjälplöst hän."
I hope you're happy having mocked me about the mercury thermome-
ter. Capricorns are very sensitive to mockery—spiritual hemophiliacs . . .

Yours as always,

Robert

P.S. Would you send me another copy of *Mörkerseende*? I want to use it as
a model for the pamphlet, and my copy is wroten on (to speak in Anglo-
Saxon). Thanks.

25 Nov, '70

Dear Tomas,
I've now finished the first draft of *Mörkerseende*! Here are the last two,
"Traffic" and "The Bookcase."
I need some help on Bookcase. Check the tenses carefully through-
out. The last sentence of the second stanza is still very difficult for me,
even though I know roughly what it *means*. The problem is that there are
so many shades of meaning, which I can turn the reader towards by slight
alterations in the English, and I don't know what to do. Would you write
me a few sentences, discussing each part of that three part sentence (begin-
ning "Man kan tydligen inte resa"), and its relation to the rest of the poem.
I'm sending the third draft of Traffic. I had a lot of trouble with that
poem; I think it looks fairly good now. "Mr. Clean" is a man in a white suit

who appears in television commercials, I think for household cleaning products, useful as I recall for kitchen sinks, toilets, etc. He is a cartoon character.

In this draft I tried "chassis" (I haven't checked the spelling of the plural)—a word used mainly for car bodies, but taken over from the French word for, I expect, carriages. The old Chevrolets always had a small metal plate by the running board saying "Chassis by General Motors," meaning someone else may have made the motor and tires. "Vehicle" is no good, implying wagons.

For the horsechestnut tree shall I use "melancholy" or "sinister"? The first is passive, the second active.

For "periscopet," do you want us to see a periscope on a submarine, or some general kind of telescope?

I'm going off next week now to Indiana and Ohio, to get the money for the next month, and when I get back, I'll try to absorb your various comments, and type a complete draft, which I'll send to you to read when you have insomnia.

I haven't seen *Böckernas Värld.* Maybe it was sent by boat.

On Minnesota elections: Zwach is the man from our county and the neighboring county. He is a total dope. Odin Langen is from the far north, and represents pulp-cutters, Indian-haters, and poachers. Fraser is a pretty good man, representing the university community in Minneapolis plus a lot of suburbs, the kind in which there is always a poster of Che Guevara in the teenager's bedroom, pinned over Early American Wallpaper.

Today is Thanksgiving. Nixon had hoped to have the prisoners of war rescued from North Vietnam at a Thanksgiving dinner *in the White House today.* Wouldn't that have been marvelously sentimental? An orgy.

What an operation! Right out of Batman comics! No one can over-estimate the effect of comic books on weak minds.   Love to all,

Robert

The Bookcase

It was moved out of the apartment after her death. It stood empty several days, before I put the books in, all the clothbound ones, the heavy ones. Somehow during it all I had also let some grave earth slip in. Something came from underneath, rose gradually and implacably like an enormous mercury-column. You must not turn your head away.

The dark volumes, faces that are closed. They resembled the faces of those Algerians I saw at the zone border in Friedrichstrasse waiting for the East German People's Police to stamp their identity card. My own identity card lay for a long time in the glass cubicles. And the dusky air I saw that day in Berlin I see again inside the bookcase. There is some ancient self-doubt in there, that reminds us of Passchendaele and the Versailles Peace Treaty, maybe even older than that. Those black massive tomes—I come back to them—they are in their way a kind of identity card too, and the reason they are so thick is because people have had to collect so many official stamps on them—over centuries. It's clear that a man can't really travel with heavy enough baggage, now that it's starting to go, now that you finally . . .

All the old historians are there, they get their chance to stand up and see into our family life. You can't hear a thing, but the lips are moving all the time behind the pane ("Passchendaele" . . .). I think for some reason of that ancient office building (this is a pure ghost story), a building where portraits of long dead gentlemen hung on the wall behind glass, and one morning the office workers found some mist on the inside of the glass. The dead had begun to breathe during the night.

The bookcase is even stronger. Looks straight from one zone to the next. A faint sky, the glimmery skin on a dark river that space has to see its own face in. And turning the head is not allowed.

Traffic

The semi-trailer crawls through the fog.
It is the lengthened shadow of a dragonfly larva
crawling over the murky lakebottom.

Headlights cross among dripping branches.
You can't see the other driver's face.
Light overflows through the pines.

We have come, shadows chassis from all directions
in failing light, we go in tandem after each other,
past each other, sweep on in a modest roar

into the fields where industries are sitting on their eggs,
and every year the factory buildings go down another
eighth of an inch—the earth is gulping them slowly.

Strange paws leave a print
on the glossiest artifacts dreamed up here.
Pollen is determined to live in asphalt.

The horsechestnut trees loom up first, melancholy
as if they intended to produce clusters of iron gloves
rather than white flowers, and past them

the reception room—an out of order sign
blinks off and on. Some magic door is around here! Open!
and look downward, through the reversed periscope,

down to the great mouths, the huge buried pipes
where algae is growing like the beards on dead men
and Mr. Clean swims on in his overcoat of slime

his strokes weaker and weaker, he will be choked soon.
And no one knows how it will happen, we only know
the chain breaks and grows back together all the time.

Västerås 27 nov 70
Dear Master,
    you have now translated 8 of 11 poems. You can see the light at the
end of the tunnel.
        "Preludes": I think nr 1 and 2 have found very good English solutions.
        The prose part, nr 3, has some mistakes in it. "Saker jag varit med

om här" means "events from my earlier life that have happened here":—
this is too long and clumsy but it is the meaning of it.

Monica and I once visited the inside of a pharaonic tomb (the
Sakkara pyramid) and in the very chamber where the dead king was previ-
ously put there were paintings on the walls, showing episodes from his life.

In this text I see the paintings from my life getting more and more
vague until they disappear completely. As if you were showing a film and
you gradually draw up the black blinds (curtains), letting in the light from
outside—when the curtains are completely away you can't see the pro-
jected film pictures anymore—the light is too strong. The text should be
something like "but they are more and more effaced, since the light is get-
ting too strong. The windows have grown bigger (larger?)"

"Kväkarandakt" has nothing to do with "breath." "Andakt" means "de-
votion." As you know the Quakers are silent during their divine service.

> Affectionately
>
> (I don't sign—you
> know perfectly well who
> is writing)

(I am sitting in a train, shaking.)
More about Swedish pronouns in the
next message . . .

Västerås 29 nov -70
Dear Robert,

the gossip about May Swenson was invaluable. Do you think I have
to visit this conservative, rather decadent, we-like-rich-folks set? Perhaps
I can meet some of the Buckleys there and change history. The other day
I fell asleep before my TV during a long film made by Peter Orlovsky. It
was a film about Peter Orlovsky's brother, who was just released from a
mental hospital. The brother was autistic, sitting so quiet behind Ginsberg
on a stage where a poetry reading was performed. I felt much sympathy
for the brother. I did not see how the poetry reading ended—I fell asleep.
In the night I had a dream about my future readings in the U.S.A., I was

surrounded by shouting barbarians all the time. I looked in vain for some *holy* barbarian (you).

Tonight I had another dream, probably influenced by your letter about the Swenson set. I was not reading this time, I was listening to another man reading, it was not poems, some sort of prose, interrupted by passages of sheer onomatopoetic noise, sneezings and so on. I did not see the performer first but suddenly I saw him—it was Melvin Laird!

"Med älven" (I have to talk at some length about this text, like a professor.

The Swedish word "älv" is the provincial word for "river." Especially it is used when speaking about the northern rivers in Sweden, the northern rivers that often are wild currents, with rapids. "At the riverside" is too calm—the nearest translation should be "with the current." I think the first lines are too calm in your translation. The Swedish text is packed, the statements are simple but the rhythm is rather violent. Listen:

Vid samtal med samtida såg hörde jag bakom deeras ansikten
     strömmen
som rann och rann och drog med sig villiga och motvilliga.

It is very irregular, it is like Gerard Manley Hopkins's sprung rhythm. It starts with alliterations. By chance it could be that in English too:
Conversations/contemporaries
A word-by-word translation would be

Conversing contemporaries I saw heard behind their faces the stream
     going on going on dragging with it the willing and the unwilling
"Samtida" does not mean "men of my generation":—it means "contemporaries" (even if in this text I mostly think of my generation, my friends).

I want to have the "saw heard" together without a "no" (I am both seeing and hearing the current).

I liked first "what is for and what is against" because it was a strong formulation, but I am doubtful now. Well, it should be WHO are for and WHO are against, of course. But the polarization is not mature yet. The unwilling are not definitely against, they are reluctant. They are taken by the stream, some with enthusiasm, some reluctantly, but the reluctant ones are not actually fighting against. Is "the willing and the unwilling" impossible in English?

"Varelsen" in the next stanza is singular form, "The Creature." What sort of creature? Probably I have in mind an allegorical person, the collective mood as a person. It is vague, I admit. I was partly thinking of my old friend X who was so happy at last to have found a reason to let go, to feel hate and 100% enthusiasm in left wing politics (after having spent his years brooding over the construction of Durrell's Alexandria novels or R. P. Blackmur's theories of criticism). But "the creature" is probably a thing where you may project many things.

If you are very convinced that the plural form "creatures" is better I accept that.

But the line "Allt stridare vatten drar" is mistranslated. "Stridare" is a form of the *adjective* "strid," not the substantive. It means *rapid*. The sentence is in translation: "More and more rapid water is pulling."

"Några få människor borta i byn" should be something like "one or two men drown there in the village" OBS: "by" means "village" in Swedish—it is in Norwegian that it means "city." There was a village situated near this very bridge, and I could see a few men outside their houses far away. (So we are back—after visiting the General Assembly, Kosygin, etc., we are taken back to the village, and the rapids and the bridge . . .)

The description of the timber floating is made in 2 stanzas that are terzines à la Dante (with rhymes and everything—you are surprised!). "And huge masses of water plough by under the narrow" is a line of its own, then a gap, then the first terzina:

> förbi. Här komer timret. Några trän
> styr som torpeder rakt fram. Andra vänder
> på tvären, snurrar trögt och hjälplöst hän

then the second: I am iambic too!

> och några nosar sig mot älvens stränder,
> styr in bland sten och bråte, kilas fast
> och tornar upp sig där som knäppta händer

of course I don't dream
about a translation with rhymes. No reader has yet, by himself, discovered
the rhymes here.

"Vänder på tvären" means "turn cross-wise"—they are floating like B.
The A timbers are the "torpedoes."

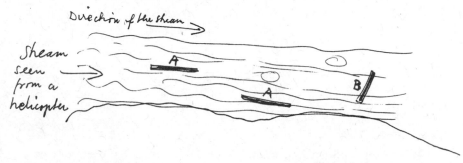

But these logs are not "safe" as you wrote. They are helplessly sluggishly
turning in the stream. A Scotsman, Mr Robin Fulton, has translated this
poem and his translation of these lines is:

> Some logs
> shoot right out like torpedoes. Others turn
> crosswise, twirl sluggishly and helplessly away
>
> and some nose against the river banks. . . .

The folded hands need an expla-
nation. The logs are piling up. Like that ⅃ on the banks of the current.

The logs often resemble the fingers of folded hands. So *the pile* is the folded
hands. I have the impression that in your translation it is the solitary log
that folds its hands.

OK, do you accept all this? I am a little tired of my poem now. For
the ideological background you can look into my letters of 1967–68, if you
have kept them. The moral weakness of the poem is of course that I am

standing at a bridge, looking at it, and not struggling in the waves. But I was standing that very day, in June 1967, in Floda in Dalecarlia, looking at Väster-Dalälven—it is a documentary. But if you change the title from "At the Riverside" to "With the current" you bring me a little more into the water.

Your Old friend, professor
Kenneth Burke

10 Dec, '70

Dear Tomas,

An annoying thing. You know your book is being handset, so I get no proofs. All is done now but four pages that have the longest poem, "Balakirev's Dream." A sudden appeal from the printer, who stopped printing as he noticed one more stanza on the Swedish than in the English. Somehow, I, or a typist, left out this stanza in English:

Droskan gled dit över isen och hjulen
spann och spann met ett ljud av silke.

Neither of us noticed it! You didn't either! (And your own poem—what a disgrace.) Now my notes are all in Minnesota! So I've retranslated the lines so:

The carriage rolled away over the ice, the wheels
spinning and spinning with a sound like silk.

Will you let me know by return mail if that is accurate? With all the problems, you'd think we were printing *The Decline and Fall of the Roman Empire*! I'm sorry we're so slow and hopeless (the printer is worse than I am, honest).

Your friend,
Robert

14 Dec, '70

Dear Tomas,

Thank you for your very good notes on "Traffic" and "The Bookcase."
You're right about Mr. Clean. I'll try "brood" and "sitting on eggs" with
a couple of wise women, and see what happens. Isn't the link with think-
ing odd in both languages?

I know the power the word "pass" has in Europe. The word "passport"
has no power at all in English—I suppose because most Americans travel
so seldom over borders. It has the feeling of some honorary document, like
a graduation certificate from Sunday School. So if I compared a heavy tome
to a passport, they'd just yawn. I will try to get the *identity* (that's what our
raw nerve is) card enlarged somehow to a book, or pamphlet, at least!

I was sure that "rummet" was "space!" The idea of space looking at itself
in the dark skin of a river is nice. But "the room" makes a good and scary
image—horizontal, rather than vertical, and more to the point, in the poem!

Carol says Louis Simpson will adore this poem, so I must send it to him.

I'll do my last corrections and then set about getting them in maga-
zines and a pamphlet. The tour will be duck soup. I'll have acceptances in
a couple of weeks.

I got up at 5 this morning to work, and my little shack where I work is
too cold this morning (temperature went down to 35 Fahrenheit last night,
Polar for California stoves, summery for Minnesota), so I'm writing in-
side, on the dining room table, the floor covered with cheerful toys, and
fragments of cotton batting—(Mary and Biddy spent 2 hours yesterday
making a Santa Claus costume, with beard, for Noah, and putting him
in it—he looked as if he'd just seen the Pope, and would bless us shortly).

Love, Robert

Västerås 20 dec 70

Dear Roberto,

these lines will reach you after Christmas, so happy (ending of the)
Christmas to you and pope Noah and the rest of the good family! I hope

to see you in 1971—if, if, the expression "duck soup" means something good. You wrote "your tour will be duck soup" and I have not found an American slang dictionary yet, so I don't know if the expression means YES or NO.

Best new year greetings to the Printer (the hand-printer, not the foot-printer). He is no stakhanovite, but observant. I think your translation of the missing 2 lines in "Balakirev's Dream" is excellent. I hurry to make my confirmation.

I told a few friends about the translation and they began to look at me with some suspicion now. Recently a young Norwegian truck driver got headlines—he had inherited 1 million crowns from an unknown relative in the U.S.A. He was interviewed etc. A week later he disappeared—it was found out that the poor man had invented the whole thing.

This translation business is slipping out of my control. What is Leif Sjöberg doing? A student in Göteborg, who has written a small thesis about my poetry for his examen, got a sudden message from Leif Sjöberg (he had never heard about him before) *ordering* him to send *by air mail* his thesis, the reason was that Leif needed some inspiration for a "foreword to the translation." What translation? I have not yet heard anything from May Swenson. You will hear from me soon, I am afraid.

Love

Tomas

28 Dec, '70

Dear Tomas,

I'm on a plane about to land in N.Y., where I'm going to read "Teeth Mother" tomorrow night to a mob of 3000 howling academics—here for a conference of college English teachers—who will no doubt throw their old Miltons at me. The Hilton Hotel (where the conference is) would not give us a room in which to hold this antiwar reading (can you imagine— after all these years), so we are holding it, of all places, in the Ballroom of the Barbizon-Plaza.

I typed up last night all my work for the last three months on my long poem—the Mss amounts to about 40 pages now. I'll no doubt, for common decency, have to remove some of the worst pages. The writing goes most of the time very easily like duck soup, but we will have to wait and see if it has as much flavor.

The plane is down. The concrete has a cement-headed foreman. I must go and check in.

Love from your old
mushroom picking friend,
Robert

Västerås 30 dec 70
Dear Robert,

I must have your fatherly advice (big-brotherly advice), and very soon! Yesterday I got a recommended letter from the USA which gave the explanation to Leif Sjöberg's cryptic small messages about translations. The letter was from a Mr Samuel Hazo, director of "International Poetry Forum, Carnegie Library, 4400 Forbes Avenue, Pittsburgh, Penn." I quote the start of it:

Dear Mr Transtromer:

As Director of the International Poetry Forum, I am happy to inform you that you have been designated by a jury of your peers under the general chairmanship of Mrs. Ingrid Arvidsson, Cultural Attache of the Swedish Embassy in Washington, D.C., the winner of the Swedish Award for poetry.

The Swedish Award is the third in a series of foreign awards established by the International Poetry Forum. The purpose of each award is to recognize a poet of a country whose literature is not widely known outside of that country. The awards preceding the Swedish award have been the Turkish and Syria-Lebanon Award.

The award itself provides for publication of a bilingual edition of a selection of the winning poet's work by the University of Pittsburgh Press. It also provides for a cash prize of $1,000. With the help of Mrs. Arvidsson, I have invited the distinguished American poet May Swenson, who is of Swedish descent, to translate your poems in collaboration with Professor Leif Sjöberg, who will also write an introduction to the book. This of course, is contingent upon your willingness to accept the award and to concur in the choice of Miss Swenson and Professor Sjöberg.

The rest is a description of how Mr Hazo is going to Sweden in the summer of 1971 and wants to present me the award at a ceremony in the Swedish Institute etc. And that the book will be brought out in the fall of 1972 and I will be invited to the U.S. at that time.

What I urgently must know is if this International Poetry Forum is something I should reject for moral reasons—I mean if it is responsible in any possible way for the Vietnam War, chemical warfare etc., like the grant you rejected—you sent me the correspondence with Carolyn Kizer as you remember. I trust your opinion here Robert. I have never heard about the International Poetry Forum before, I don't know if it is paid by the CIA or Donald Duck's uncle or . . . Simply, I want to know if I, when accepting, am used as a propaganda man for the Nixon administration or not. You are the man to know that. I am not rejecting it for secondary reasons— e.g. that I object to an introduction by Leif, or the translations made by Swenson etc.

What is the meaning of "a jury of your peers." Does it mean a jury of a representative selection of Americans, or Swedes, or just poets?

warmest greetings

your paranoiac Syria-Lebanon friend
Tomas

1971

6 Jan, '71

Dear Tomas,

If I were you, I'd accept! The International Poetry Forum is a simple poetry center set up to help bring culture to Pittsburgh, Pennsylvania: it is like those "Flor D'Italia Opera Houses" that used to be set up in the 19th century in Nevada mining towns. (It's amazing how large they were, by the way—the buildings still stand, and they would import a European soprano every winter for a grand recital, when the miners would all take a bath.) You see, we've advanced quite a ways.

Samuel Hazo is a sullen Catholic academic, with an oily manner, who has the knack of getting money out of rich Pittsburgh widows at teas set up for the purpose. With his tea-gotten gain, he has set up an office in the Carnegie Library in Pittsburgh, and for five years or so, sponsored a series of poetry readings each season in a marvelous theater (or opera house) in Pittsburgh. James Wright and I read together there last winter, and I just say it was a good place to read: a large audience, and the audience used to hearing poetry. I had a 103° fever, but it was a pleasant memory. In the last two years the International Poetry Forum, no doubt suddenly becoming conscious of its own name, has taken to awarding prizes to worthy Turkish-Lebanese poets from Västerås. They print a credible book, and the award, though it hardly comes from a house that suggests the avant-garde or anything liberal or anything non-institutional, nevertheless has no—so far as I know—CIA or germ warfare links, and in fact no gross drawbacks.

I'll give you a couple of pieces of advice on practical matters.

First, be sure they understand when you sign the agreement or whatever it is that they are not receiving *exclusive permission* to translate and publish the poems chosen. In other words, it should be clear that other people after May Swenson will be able to translate and publish the same poems she has chosen. This is called in English "non-exclusive" translation rights. The Rilke estate got itself into serious trouble by granting exclusive rights to certain English translators of the poems they wanted, and the result is that no one can put out a selected Rilke now (with younger translators) because the older translators will not release their rights.

Second *the public reading* in Pittsburgh. We don't know at this point whether May Swenson's translations will be any good or not. If her translations are no good, the public reading of your poems at Pittsburgh in the fall of 1972 will be harmed no matter how sweetly you warble them in Swedish. So when you're writing them, you might just drop in a sentence to the effect that in the public reading at the Forum you would like to use also some translations of Eric Sellin and Robert Bly, who were the first, etc etc. Then if May Swenson's translations turn out to be terrible, you can use half at least of our translations; or, if Swenson's are OK, you can use just a single translation. That will give you some leeway, and won't put you entirely at the mercy of the OFFICIAL PITTSBURGH TRANSLATOR.

On the whole, I think it's a nice stroke of luck. The International Poetry Forum also sponsors a prize each year for a first book by a new American poet, and the contest is drawing more and more attention each year, so the young poets are aware of the Forum.

The "jury of your peers" is bureaucratic language meaning you are not to inquire who the jury *were*. I would guess it was Mrs. Arvidsson, Samuel Hazo, Leif Sjöberg, and possibly Russel Vowles, with maybe Göran Prinz-Påhlson.

The $1000 is nice—it's too bad he can't send you the check right now, and just give you flowers when he comes to Sweden this summer!

Congratulations! Inform the Lebanese colony in Västerås . . .

Yours faithfully,
Robert

21 Jan, '71

Dear Tomas,

Thank you for your letter to the Pittsburgh Benefactors. It wasn't exactly a cry of joy, and I'm very curious how this inhibited Catholic will respond to it. You did everything but warn him he has to take off his shoes before he enters your house! But it's too late now—he's already promised you the dough, so what can he do? I think it's good for him too— Americans seem to have an engrained conviction that everyone will fall over backward at their gifts.

Everyone about here has been working very hard cleaning oil off birds. They now realize that you mustn't wash them with detergents, but only with mineral oil, which helps to preserve the birds' own natural oils. And 85% are living this time if brought to a cleaning station. At the last oil spill 90% of the birds washed died.

This is just a note to tell you that the best pamphlet series we have, published by Lillabulero Press, in Ithaca, N.Y., has agreed happily to publish *Night Vision* right away. They'll have it out by April 1st. It hasn't been decided yet whether to include the Swedish or not. If the Swedish is left out— and I think that would be all right in a pamphlet—they might be able to sell the pamphlet for 50¢ or 75¢! I've suggested they follow the same general design as in *Mörkerseende*, large type, lots of open space. The editor, William Matthews (he wrote the piece on me in the *Tenn Poetry Journal*

toward the end—and is the best critic we have about the age of 30—) will
write you.

Your Boswell faithfulus,
Robert

Västerås 14-2-71

Dear Robert,

Thank you for letters and magazines! I had just finished 5 pages of
my "long" poem, growing slowly like a crocodile, when I got your mes-
sage that you had typed 40 (!) pages of a new work. Oh. And it is proba-
bly good, not like the FILIBUSTER poetry of the late James Dickey type.
My own effort is a serious excercise in filibuster poetry writing, an attempt
to give the small talkative fellow inside me a chance.

But 40 pages!

You ask me about Mr Hazo's reaction. My letter was not meant to
be unfriendly, it was meant to be straightforward. I had to prevent—at
this early stage—them from making the prize a Swedish-American official
friendship demonstration with official people etc. I was told that 12 per-
sons from the Mellon foundation (mostly rich men) are doing Europe and
Sweden in June, they are visiting Stockholm and are going to be present
at the ceremony when I am receiving the prize. Actually they had already
invited themselves to a dinner paid by the Swedish Institute for the occa-
sion. The official American people here are always stressing the good rela-
tions between the U.S. and Sweden, there are small differences in opinion
about the Indo China war, but that is of no importance, we have so much
in common, look at the cultural exchange etc. . . . That is their attitude and
I did not like the idea of being used as an example of wonderful coopera-
tion demonstrating that different opinions about the Indo China war
are of no importance. What now happens is that the Swedish Institute
will treat them as welcome *private tourists,* no flags, no embassy people
present at the dinner etc. The ceremony I have to swallow (difficult for a
cerebrotonic person with no viscerotonic "love of polite ceremony"). Well,
Mr Hazo's reaction was that he phoned Ingrid Arvidsson in Washington

and complained a little. She got irritated (she seems to be very much for smooth cooperation between the U.S. and Sweden) and asked the Swedish Institute why I was troublesome. I had to discuss the matter with her. From Mr Hazo I have heard nothing. He probably regards me as a difficult person. Mrs Arvidsson seemed very anxious that the good benefactors should not be hurt. She has sent a lot of material too from the Poetry Forum—even Dan Berrigan is included! Sometimes I find the U.S. very confusing.

From Leif Sjöberg and May Swenson I have heard absolutely nothing.

It seems to me strange a cultural life that depends upon the benevolence of rich people. It must create a disgusting combination of submissiveness and rebellion in the mind of the artist. How does it work? I want to hear your wise point of view about it, your observations. If you are a poet, like Mr Hazo, do you feel embarrassed, flattered or angry together with the rich? Is it a business-like attitude you develop or an Uncle Tom mentality? Or are the circumstances of no importance, can you have a matter-of-fact acceptance of the conditions?

How is a small publisher like Lillabulero Press organized? Can it work independent of benefactors?

It has been a hard week with too much work—50% of the psychologists at our institution are ill and I am in command, I have had no time for anything but testing. And now on Sunday the MIGRAINE arrives, it grows and grows, in a few hours I will be in bed with the facial expression of one of the old Spanish painter's martyr portraits. Write soon dear Robert and give Carol my warmest greetings.

Tomas

24 Feb, '71

Dear Tomas,

I just saw your letter. I never *see* the rich! Those bristles and bad manners you see sticking out of *The Sixties* are there partly to prevent that blob-like embrace, which has suffocated many a good Midwest farm boy.

One reason *The Sixties* has been liked by the kids is that they know I get no money—nor it—from the benefactors, or the rich in general. Lillabulero Press, I think, is independent as well. It's a "small press."

But you can take one embrace from the rich here and then flee—embraces by the rich in a *foreign country* are amusing, like visiting the Australian section of the zoo.

Your friend,
Robert

Västerås 21-3-71

Dear Robert,

Thank you for the acceptances from Berkeley etc. I will use them when I have my next talk with the Writer's Foundation. It is strange having you as an efficient impresario—it is as if Dylan Thomas was arranging a reading trip for John Malcolm Brinnin. What I should like best is to give a few readings. Enough to have a reason to visit the U.S.A. and you and Carol and the Pacific. To give lectures about modern Swedish literature would be almost impossible for me. I am no expert on that, and I am often against my fellow poets here. In the final selection of reading places I think I would favor those who are not particularly interested in "Scandinavia." Geographically I would favor Hawaii and California.

Simply I want to see new areas and meet my friends. I want to read to people who are interested in the kind of poetry I write and who don't care if the poet is Swedish, Lebanese or Byelorussian.

I have got the proposed Publication Agreement from Pittsburgh University Press. I look forward to long and taxing negotiations. It is a contract between an analphabetic South American boxer and a Chicago boxing syndicate. It starts:

"Grant. 1. To grant and assign to the PUBLISHER the sole and exclusive right to publish or to cause others to publish the work in all forms in all languages (!) throughout the world."

So that was the type of agreement you warned me about. I don't understand what they think they gain by pressing for exclusive rights. It is not *Love Story* I have written. If some other person translates me in a magazine or another book that will simply—if we are lucky—stimulate some interest in me and give an impulse to buy the Pittsburgh book. I will try to convince the publisher. Probably they don't know about *The Seventies* and Lillabulero editions. Shall I tell them? My immediate reaction is to deny exclusive rights. If after half a year of fruitless negotiations they threaten to withdraw the prize I will give them 2 years of exclusive rights and exclude the better poems from the final selection. I hope to hear from you soon.

Love and Peace

Tomas

26 March, '71

Dear Tomas,

I called Hazo and talked him out of the "exclusive rights" business. The editor of Pittsburgh Univ Press called me back, and they intend to rewrite that part of the contract, asking for only *non-exclusive* rights, and, of course, dropping their request for rights in other languages, which was a mad idea to start with. So hold firm.

In the conversation, Hazo apologized for asking May Swenson—it seems he did no research and didn't know that Eric Sellin and I had already translated you. He wanted to "get something down on paper" right away, and so asked May Swenson, who was the only American poet with a Swedish name he could think of. She, alas, does not really known Swedish, and Leif Sjöberg is having to prepare interlinear prose trots for her.

In fairness, Eric Sellin is the one they should have asked. He first published translations of you in that New Directions Annual, and they were *good* translations.

You might ask for Eric, even at this late date. He would do a better book than May Swenson, I'm sure. Maybe they could work together— each doing half of the poems chosen. That would bring some money to

Eric, and would also recognize the work that he has done on you, and his early faith in your poetry.

Why not? You have some rights in this matter. I think it was crazy of Hazo not to ask your opinion before assigning a translator, but I think you could still *add* Eric, if you think it's worth it.

Love from this
sunlit madhouse
Robert

Västerås 2 april -71

Dear Robert,

I feel a sudden need to write to you, just for no reason at all. I get sick of reading about the popular war hero William Calley. He is swelling and swelling in the newspapers. He is swelling to the status of a National Symbol, like John Kennedy was in the good old days.

Let us talk about other things. I have in front of me a huge pile of May Swenson translations. She is translating faster than I can read. Her letters are *kind*. No balloons pricked yet. She assures me that she will follow my advice. I have the impressions that she can do good things out of my school-boyish poetry (my first 2 books, now almost completely translated by her). Let me give you an example. Is it good?

> Unmoving, the ant in the forest keeps watch,
> seeing nothing. Nothing heard but the ticking
> of dark greenery, nightlong the murmur deep
> > in summer's gorge.

> The spruce tree at point, like a clock's jagged
> hand. The ant aglow in the mountain's shadow.
> A bird screams! At last. Slowly the cloud-cart
> > begins to roll.

I yesterday answered positively a Miss Dzintra Bungs (wonderful name) in N.Y. She invited me to read for the Baltic students in New York, when

I arrive. I could not get a fixed fee, but I was promised the net profit of the program. She had read me in Latvian.

A book is planned with translations from some younger American poets, not yet translated into Swedish. I was asked to contribute and I have the idea to translate W. S. Merwin—the poems I have seen seem quite possible to do in Swedish. But I don't know. How is the man? I want you to open the door of your wonderful treasury of gossip. Some characteristic anecdotes etc. about W. S. please.

Love to Carol and the small ones.

Tomas

10 April '71

Dear Tomas,

As you see your book is printed now! It is just being bound now, and the dust jacket being printed. You'll probably get a few paper copies in the mail, with the first try at the dust jacket on them—but I don't like the jacket, and intend to change it.

But it does exist!

The May Swenson translation is *not good*. (Except for the last 2 lines, which are fine, even excellent.) The first six lines all have archaic sentence order—you sound a bit like an 1824 English romantic

"Nightlong the murmur deep in summer's gorge."

"Summer's gorge" is literary and "poetic," and the sentence order is simply miles from spoken English. "The spruce tree *at point*" means nothing. The only thing a reader can see is the spruce tree stretched out like an English hunting dog, about to flush a partridge.

The ant *aglow*—"aglow" is not 19th century but 17th century. You'll have to make it clear to her that you write in 20th century Swedish, and ask her to work on them, making the English more contemporary and spoken.

I think Merwin would be fairly easy to translate, but I'm not sure you'd *receive* anything from his poetry. He radiates psychic cold, like an extremely literate lieutenant. I'd try Gary Snyder (poems from *Riprap*) or William Stafford. I think they're both in *Naked Poetry*. Must go! Do write!

Love, Robert

Västerås 18 april 71

Dear Robert,

Thank you for the book! I always liked the typed letters of the previous 60s books and I am happy that I got the same. Even the abdominable pig-head looked sweet. But no man is perfect and the printer was probably drunk when he typed "Out in the Open" (or perhaps he is a hawk and did not like My Message) so he transformed a building into a wood-stack. When the last copies have been torn from the hands of the booksellers in Omaha and Tulsa by voracious readers and you have to print a new edition you might correct the lines in this poem a little . . . Such accidents also happened to Shakespeare, so I don't want to be finicky. The translations in general make me happy. I did not see before that the translations of my "Solitude" and "Slow Music" were so wonderful. I have one reservation: the end of "Out in the Open"—you put "Force" instead of "Violence." For me "Force" is not negative, it is a neutral, even positive word. Or what are the associations in the U.S.? Have you been debating about "Violence" so much that the word has been worn out?

Can you ask the editors of the *Seneca Review* and *Doones* to send me the issues where I am published? I'd love to see those small magazines—I have never heard about them before.

Your action on the exclusive rights battle was effective. You must have frightened them! I sent Hertzel a long, extremely pedagogic letter about the question before I knew of your telephone speech to Hazo. "There are 2 sound ways of looking at a verse translation. You may regard the translation as a proposal, one of many equivalent aspects of the original text. Another way of looking at a translated poem is to see it as a poem in its own right, in this case a poem in English (this is especially valid if you have an excellent poet-translator like May Swenson). But none of these 2 approaches is compatible with the idea of exclusive rights to translate a certain poem . . ." etc. I also tried to convince him that as many (good) translations as possible would stimulate the selling of the

Pittsburgh book. Forgive me for putting in the line about May as excellent. It is bad that her translations have this 19th century touch. My earlier poems often are old-fashioned in respect to meter but the language is simple 20th century language always. Now May is very un-academic about meter—if she felt the need to follow the original meter I could understand that the language could be forced into some awkward archaisms. But as it is now . . . well, I can't see these archaisms myself, I don't know enough English. Perhaps you are too harsh. I will give you another example of her translation.

Sailor's Yarn

There are bare winter days when the sea resembles
ranges of mountains, humped in gray feathers,
a moment blue, then long hours of waves that, pallid
as lynx, seek and fall their grip on the shore's gravel.

On such days wrecked ships leave the sea to seek
their masters, seated in the city's noise, and drowned
crews drift ashore, more transparent than pipesmoke.

(In the north flits the real lynx, with shining claws
and dream-blue eyes. In the north where day
lives in a mine both day and night.

There a single survivor is permitted to sit
by the northern lights' oven and listen
to the music of the freezers-to-death.)

Anyhow I have accepted her and I am not going to have Eric included in the Pitt book even if he has been mistreated. But at the reading in Pittsburgh I will read some of his translations and give him credit.

[------]
Would you cast a glance at another May Swenson poem of mine:

Evening-Morning

The moon's mast has rotted and the sail shrivelled.
A gull soars drinkenly over the sea.
The jetty's thick quadrangle is charred. Brushwood
                bends low in the dusk.

Out on the doorstep. Daybreak slams and slams in
the sea's gray stone gateway, and the sun flashes
close to the world. Half-choked summer gods
                fumble in sea-mist.

"Drinkenly" is not in my dictionary. Is it a 16th century word for intoxicated olympic gods or something?

Monica is studying. She has been a nurse-pupil since January and is at school (hospital) all day and doing lessons at home all night. The other day she made her first post-mortem dissection. No one fainted. The girls are tough nowadays. In Sweden nurses are more thoroughly educated than in most countries—they often have to do a doctor's job in the country—we are short of doctors. When she is examined (2 years from now) we hope that she can have a job as a school nurse, half-time. Paula broke her arm on Easter Eve, when trying to fly a kite, I have just recovered from a suppuration in the upper jaw. The economy is bordering on bankruptcy. The weather is bad. We send our most hearty greetings.

                        Tomas

Västerås 21-5-71

Dear Robert,

the day after tomorrow I leave Västerås for Northern Sweden. The military authorities want to refresh my memory about warfare during some weeks. I will send you a message from the bush later—I don't know if I am supposed to be crawling with camouflage-painted face through barbed wire or if they will let me sit calmly day after day in a forgotten bunker. But if I disappear you have at least the included 2 documents: 1: My statement about the spiritual situation in Sweden ("Den skingrade församlingen") and 2: the first two parts of my attempt to write The Long Poem, called "Baltics." The poem will have 4 or 5 parts. It started when I found my grandfather's almanacs from the 1880s, where he had noted down the ships he was piloting. The 3 ships/captains/draughts etc. quoted are from the almanac. Then I found out that much of my life had some connection with the Baltics so I started to give a jumbly sketch of many things—even my visit to Riga is there, fragmentarily, in part 2.

I don't know if I am strong enough to stand Carol's condemnation of the Mormon Lady's translations, when it comes. There must—for Heaven's sake—be *something* good in them. May is doing the complete Tranströmer, without hesitation, and from that GESAMMTWERK I am supposed to make a final selection. Leif Sjöberg is impatient because my comments arrive much slower than her translations—"you must be in love with your own poems" he wrote reproachingly. Oh no. I am not in love with them, I just have a gloomy paternal sense of responsibility for them. Beside, the last months have been taxing, with Monica running to her hospital work at 0615 in the morning.

We send our best, summer warm wishes! If you drop me a note to my Västerås address Monica will send it forward to my military address.

Din gamle vän
Tomas

30 May, '71

Dear Tomas,

I just found an old letter of yours, which I propose to answer! I hesi-
tated myself between "force" and "violence" in "Out in the Open," and I'll
think it over again when the time comes to reprint. In that same poem, I
cannot find the building that got turned into a woodstack! Give me more
on that. Actually I took the only copy of your book I had up to Carol in
the hospital yesterday, so she'd have something good to read. She gave
birth to a little (of course he was little) baby boy yesterday morning at 6:30!
It all went very fast, and two days ahead of time, and she is very happy
about the boy! Just before we went to the hospital, when we were still not
sure it was time to go, I closed my eyes for a bit, and saw this sign over
and over again, in various colors, and I felt it was the sign of the new boy.
It looked like this:

It was a pair of wings, spread, with two crescent moons underneath. I don't
know what it means, but I think it's a magic baby. I've always thought so.
After all, two mediums in 1968 predicted his birth (or another child at
least). We'd like you and Monica to be the new baby's godparents, by the
way! Yes, we do! We would baptize him, if you agree, while you're here in
October, and Monica can be a godparent *in absentia*. Your physical duties
would be light, and, spiritually, all you'd have to do is bless him every once
in a while. We'd love it if you'd both agree.

He is strong, and kicked a lot in the womb, weighed over eight pounds,
and looks very calm indeed. We haven't decided on a name for him yet, and
plan to wait a bit for that.

About May Swenson: Obviously some poems are going to slip into

English for her better than others. Sometimes she goes two whole lines without 16th century English coming in. Since she is doing the entire Gesammelte Werke, I think this is a time to depend on your friends a little. Let the whole group come in, get them all gathered together, then in consultation with your American-speaking friends, choose the ones to be finished. Carol and I would be happy to vote in this matter, and maybe Eric or someone would help too. Once that choice is made, then you can also depend on us to make suggestions on which lines need to be modernized a bit. I'd rather let it go, and let her just do the whole thing, and know nothing about it all until it was printed—but I do hate to see your—particularly your—poems mangled.

Perhaps you can sort of gather alternate versions of clogged lines over the summer, and then talk them over with May when you come in the fall, maybe on your way home. We could go over the poems chosen, one by one, while you're staying with us in Minnesota.

I will write you soon about the tour, since we need to settle dates soon. Would you like to come for 2 weeks or for 3? Would you like it to be in early October or later October? How many readings would you like to give? Suppose you stayed two weeks . . . Would you think 6 readings would be about right? The truth is you've had so many acceptances you can give as many as you want to. At the moment, I'm discouraging Scandinavian departments, and, following your sensible suggestion, encouraging colleges interested in a simple *poetry reading*. I have to go through the papers soon, and settle on an itinerary.

In your letter, you sent along a copy of May's translation of "Sailor's Yarn." I can see two things here she is doing that she hasn't thought through. In the attempt to gain music, she is working with sound in rather obvious ways. For example, the last line of the first stanza of "Sailor's Yarn" goes:

as lynx, seek and fall their grip in the shore's gravel.

That line really doesn't make any sense in English, and evidently she did it that way in order to get the two "g's" in "grip" and "gravel," following what she imagines to be your three planned "F's." (Her "k" in "seek" is probably intended to suggest a third "g.") But I don't think these consonant repetitions can be constructed as easily as all that in translations. Here she has had to lose the grip on the meaning, and the reader's assumption then is that the meaning is not important to you either.

Her second mistake I mentioned earlier: the tendency to translate without care for contemporary usage. "In the north flits the real lynx." She is just translating word for word, but it happens that in English now the verb in such a sentence *never* comes before the noun. No one says: "In Washington run the demonstrators." You should remind her to adopt English sentence order, forgetting what the sentence order is in Swedish.

Related to that error is her habit of using "seek" instead of "look for," "pallid" instead of the simple "pale." It's the same habit turning up in nouns. (By the way, in the last stanza of this poem: are those "de ihjal-frusnas" the ones who have <u>been</u> already frozen to death, or are they the ones who are freezing *others* to death? May has it the second way.) (In her English, the music seems to be coming from extremely ominous types, sort of living refrigerators walking about the far north.)

"Evening-Morning": this one is better. "Drinkenly" doesn't exist—she means drunkenly. Several problems: "charred" means the bruggan has been *burned*. It doesn't *look* like coal, but is ruined. If you want that, it's OK. "Brushwood" implies dead twigs and branches, such as would be gathered for a fire. As I understand it, you really mean just the living bushes etc near the water.

"Slams" doesn't have as much movement back and forth as "slar." Instead of movement that is *seen*, we basically *hear* the sound of a door slamming, as when one person is mad at another. "Flashes" is not quite "sprakar": flashes is rather mechanical, and implies a light that flashes on and off every few seconds.

But I think this one is not bad, and with a little work, will be OK.

I think I'd better stop. Write when you can escape from your war duties, and preparations for Ragnarok. *Newsweek* reported this week that the

Swedish army has issued hairnets to its soldiers, so I figure the last days are approaching.

    Love to you all from all of us, especially our new Gemini baby!

Robert

4-6-71

Dear Robert, I am writing this hiding behind the army equipment. Up to now I have only fired 4 bullets in this war, but it is a constant hurry and confusion. In the night I lie in my sleeping bag like a frozen sausage in its plastic cover, in the day I am grilled. That will last 8 more days, then I am free again, eating at tables, playing the piano, reading books, translating mad poems about Hawaiian crabs, patting my children etc. Most unreal. It is difficult to say something intelligent. But writing to you like this is helping me to hold on to my identity. —I got a long letter from George Young (in Hanover, N.H.). He is going to Finland this summer (these frequent voyages from the U.S.A. to Finland are a mystery, somebody should make an investigation). He is working for the idea to make a president of Ralph Nader. What a strange American idea! Ralph Nader is too good, and has too little stomach-mentality to be a president. And if he was elected he would be assassinated very soon. A wonderful target for solitary madmen or big oil company conspirators. Let him live. I want everyone to live and be happy. And go fishing. And listen to Scriabin. And visit Byelo-Russia. And fill his pipe with sunrise. Goodnight mankind. Goodnight arriving new family member in the Bly house. Goodnight Robert and Carol and the girls and Noah. Goodnight.

Tomas

[June 71]

Love to little  from his godparents.

Monica dreamt the other night that she (as nurse) was called to a woman to help her deliver a child. When she looked into the womb of that woman she found a deep, wide tunnel where a little boy was sitting, serious, waiting. He seemed to be between 6 months and 1 year old. Monica lifted him out but it was impossible to do the usual things you do with newborn babies with him—he seemed too grown-up. He had a very clever look. When she woke up her first association was with your new baby. Congratulations from all parts of us: ego, superego and id.

The other evening I was presented with a SCROLL and a MEDAL in Stockholm. Monica and I borrowed money from friends to get to Stockholm, dressed in clothes from my old well-paid Roxtuna days and mixed with the rich in a restaurant. Representatives from Pittsburgh are doing a visit in Europe this summer to study cultural policy and they wanted to make a big celebration of the Pitt prize. I had forbidden the presence of official people (from the U.S. Embassy and the Swedish Foreign department) so it was a completely private thing, only some people from the Swedish Institute, the rich, Monica and I. Many speeches. Mr Hazo looked extremely exotic and magnificent. The rich were nice and got a sudden affection for Monica so she was invited too to Pittsburgh! The agreement details I shall discuss with Mr Hazo on Sunday—it is now very favorable.

In these days the Writer's Foundation is determining if I get the autumn voyage or not. I will probably have a "yes" from them. I have asked for a ticket from Stockholm to Los Angeles and back plus some financial support for the family during my 3 weeks' stay in the U.S. I will let you know at once when I get the definite answer from them. I want to go in the middle of October. You will hear from me very soon.

Love
Tomas

P.S. From now on my address is Gatan *13038 Runmarö*.

22 July, '71

Dear Tomas,

Forgive me for being so slow to answer.

My brother was killed in a car accident not far from his farm about three weeks ago. I have lost most of my energy, and can't seem to get anything done. All I want to do is to be with my children, and I waste day after day.

His two older girls were in high school and out of it, but he left a boy 14 and a girl about 8. The boy did nothing but sob for three days straight—in farming, a man and his son tend to be very close. I don't know what I can do now, if I can be of any use at all. We were never close intellectually at all, and I suspect his widow considers me as his "opposite," and will always be suspicious of me.

Our new little boy, Micah, is fine. Carol sends her love.

I like your National Guard Camp poem. I've translated the first two stanzas today with Mary—and she has already memorized them.

A porgy is a saltwater fish, which we often found in fish markets in England—*Pagrus pagrus,* sometimes called "scup" in English too. Several varieties are loosely called "porgy." It's a small, affectionate, non-threatening fish.

Love from us all
to you and Monica and
Emma and Paula
Robert

27 July, '71

Dear Tomas,

You're right—this is the first good translation the Mormon feminist has made. I've made a few minor suggestions—don't tell her they come from me! I'll be the invisible advisor, communicating to you as Madame Blavatsky's advisors used to, from "somewhere in the hidden Himalayas." They are said to have been living for four hundred years "in caves on the slopes of Tibet," etc.

I like your translations of "Spiritual Death" and "The Sleeping Woman"! And I'm pleased that you liked them! With the word "loggolve"—threshing floor—the reader should pick up the feeling of the threshing floors in the Old Testament, such as the one Ruth slept on or a threshing floor where Tammuz or Adonis dances would be held in Mesopotamia. The poem has a modern feeling in English, except for that line, which suggests

Mesopotamia, and the last line, which suggests a Middle Ages witch in a fairy tale woods . . .

(And I think it's true psychologically, that if a man dies, spiritually, his wife will then—almost as if by natural process—become a witch.) (I thought I'd praise my own poem!)

The word "acquarious" in "The Sleeping Woman" is almost a pun, since it simple means the water is watery, but its liquid syllables do help the water to flow along . . . "Akvarieaktigt" may have an oversurplus of consonants—I can't tell. It might be possible to use a word connected with the astrological sign Aquarius, since that was also drifting through my water-longing head.

I'm going to try your Snowmelt poem—the *Times Literary Supplement* writes me that it wants some poems of yours for an issue this September— but you'll have to help me with the last line. Is the bird sailing past death or the dead or the *grave*?

Each will produce a different mood in English. Also, is the bird flapping, or floating on extended wings? Is he an eagle, a crow, a mythical Persian bird, or just a bird? "Fugel" has such a lovely open sound in Swedish. I see why you all use it so often. But it doesn't help with color!

A friend in N.Y. sent me this clipping from the *N.Y. Times* of last Monday. I certainly dislike the idea of adding an "e" to all Swedes' names! It's like adding water to milk. [My name is mentioned, and Lars is evidently meaning to insult me, but I couldn't tell for sure. (Did you see the *Time* magazine article on American poetry in mid-July? Look at it! It's wonderful.)] I see you've been laying the groundwork for a new golden age with metaphors sharp as needles. This is dangerous work! Always wear gloves.

Your friend,
Robert

Västerås 4-8-71
Dear Robert,

good to hear from you again, but the news about your brother and his family made me very sad. The catastrophes with cars are the modern equivalent to smallpox, almost every family has some victim. About the same day as you lost your brother, a woman was killed in a crash in Yugoslavia, a woman I had been very close to in 1954–55. (She was killed the 7th or 8th of July.)

xxxx

About "loggolvet." It is a Swedish word with a lot of old peasant life aroma. It is not biblical, just old, simple, rural. I looked in the Book of Ruth to see what the Swedish Bible has for the place where Ruth was lying. It gave "tröskplatsen," a hopeless word without biblical quality.

xxxx

Lars Gustafsson's presentation of Swedish poetry looks exactly like a chapter from one of these books about Sweden, written by mildly interested and informed Anglo-Saxons who have some fixed idea. Interesting to see how writing in a foreign language can change the outlook. As for you, it was probably meant to be the highest possible prize—you are compared to Enzensberger, Lars's hero. I must go to the library and ask for the *Time* issue. I will write when I have seen it.

All good things for the Blys and their

numerous children.

Tomas

August 15 [1971]
Västerås

Dear Robert,

a black day. I just left my TV after having seen our discus-thrower Ricky Bruch make a fool of himself and all Swedes in the olympic stadium of Helsinki, where the european athletic competitions are performed. This fool, Bruch, a human broiler, stuffed with hormone pills and talking like Cassius Clay, did not throw his damned discus longer than 59 meters—in small unimportant competitions he usually throws it 66–68 meters. He is nr 2 in the world in his art (only Jay Silvester is better) but as soon as it comes to important, international games he loses his nerves completely and the whole nation cries.

[-----]

In the competition for fools I think I will give the palm of victory to the author of the *Time* article about U.S. poetry. I found it at last in the library. I suppose this presentation falls into the category of "middle class thinking" and it is always wonderful to see almost perfect expressions of such things. *Time* probably thinks that it has done a good service to poetry by giving "publicity." Anyhow, I feel very safe, knowing that I am patronized by an authorized polemical roarer, when I come over to Your country in October.

Talking of roaring: I think the liberties You took in translating "Snow Melting Time" will help the poem survive in English. So I like your solution. The *Times Literary Supplement* is an improbable place to appear in. Do You really say they wrote you and ASKED for a translation? Of course I agree to it.

Tomorrow George Young from N.H. will visit me, I just talked to him by the telephone. I heard at once from his voice that he is no fool. So I look forward to seeing him.

Love from us all. Write soon!

Your friend

Tomas

About the snow-melt poem . . . It is a small thing only, but the snow-melting of 1966 was big—it had been such a long and hard winter and all of a sudden it was summer, water overflowing.

Tumbling tumbling water, roar, old hypnosis . . . The Swedish word "störtande" has more water in it . . . it is a current, perhaps a cataract. You are on the bridge. Further away a churchyard for old, dead cars. The water is overflowing it too, glittering behind the empty shells of the cars (also, perhaps overflowing human beings, glittering behind *their* masks—e.g., the faces . . .). I am standing on the bridge, in a slight dizziness. Gripping the bridge parapet. The bridge is like a large bird of iron sailing past death. "Segla" in Swedish is a calm word, no flapping. The type of bird: albatross. But larger. And of Iron. Sailing past death.

Drawing on next page.

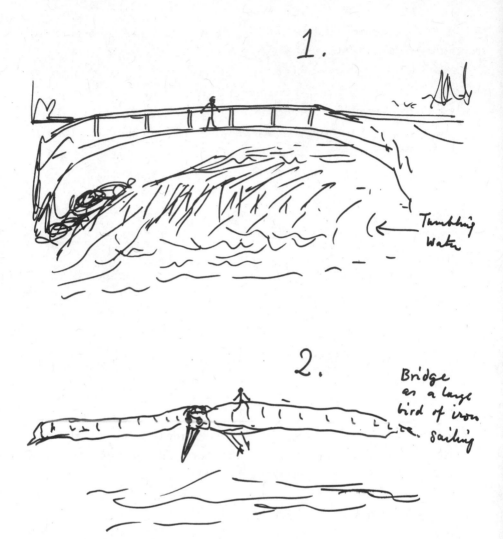

1 Sept, '71

Dear Tomas,

For an anthology of Swedish poetry I've prepared, I've had to write a note on Aspenström. Would you read it and tell me if it's utterly absurd . . . All I have of his is his *66 Dikter,* published in Svanens Lyrikkclub in 1964. And what's even worse, in the introduction there's a sentence I can't understand at all! I attempt to translate the exchange he sets down between Mayakovsky and Esenin. Mayakovsky says:

"For my part I think the stanza beginning 'I walk alone out on the road' is a campaign to get girls to go for walks with poets. A person walking alone is bored, you see! O, would that poetry were given such powers that it might urge people to join together in cooperatives!" I can't grasp the meaning of the second sentence at all. The other two I took a guess at.

Your faithful blockhead,
Robert

3 Sept, '71

Dear Tomas,

This is a letter about your Tour. Notice the colorfully marked sheet I have enclosed, indicating the schedule, subject to any modifications you have (within reason) (or without). I have told them all the fee will be $250, and if the Swedes pay the air fare, as they evidently are going to do, and if you don't spend too much on whiskey and doughnuts, you should be able to go home with about $2000–$2500 after three weeks of labor.

Here is the way it looks:

1 Sat–Sun — October 16–17—special poetry weekend at Cornell College set up for you by Wm Matthews, hopefully John Logan and Jim Wright will both be there also, a sort of minor festival.

2 Tuesday — October 19th—The Academy of American poets very much wants you to come and read there at the Guggenheim Museum on Tuesday night. Jim Wright will probably introduce you (unless he has a class that night—we haven't been able to get hold of him) and will maybe read the translations. Two disadvantages: they can only afford $150, and you would have to come back to New York from Ithaca. That's not hard, and you could

come by train, either on Monday the 18th or Tuesday the 19th, but you would have to *fly out* to Cleveland the next morning, for your reading at Oberlin on Wednesday.

The Academy is about to print its fall program, and so this is the only place that needs an immediate answer from you on this day: Tuesday, Oct 19th. Could you send a cable to

> Elizabeth Kray
> Academy of Poets
> 1078 Madison Avenue, NY

and just say: "Yes I will be there," or "No I can't come on the 19th."

It might be fun to have a reading in New York; you'd meet some of the New York poets etc. etc.

3 Wednesday   Oct 20th—I'll join you at Oberlin for the reading there. That should be fun. It's the best small college in the U.S.

Then we will come back together to the farm in Minnesota, and you will spend the weekend with us, and Micah's baptism will be Sunday.

4 Monday   Oct 25th—We'll drive together to St. John's Univ in Collegeville, Minn, an excellent Catholic college, and read there. I'll read translations for you.

5 Tuesday   Oct 26th—We drive to Gustavus Adolphus, another college in Minn where the Swedes hang out, but you're being asked by the English department, and will not have to answer any questions about the Swedish economic system. On Wednesday we part company and you go to:

6 Thursday   Oct 28th—You have a reading in Boulder, Colorado, sponsored by the Scandinavian Dept. It's the only one

I accepted, but it was the only way to get you easily into the Rocky Mountains. Boulder is a lovely place, just at the east edge of the Rockies, as they rise straight up out of the plains.

Friday, Sat, Sun—You now have three free days, which you can spend any way you wish. It would be easy to rent a car in Boulder and drive alone to Pocatello, Idaho, if you'd like to. Or you could drive part way and catch a plane the rest of the way. This is marvellous western country between Boulder and Pocatello, and you'll go straight up and over the best part of the Rockies, if the passes are still open.

7 Monday —reading in Pocatello, Idaho. Very good feeling of what Idaho is like.

8 Wednesday, Nov 3rd—I want you to see San Francisco, so am arranging a reading at San Francisco State, which is the poetry Hub of San Francisco. Lots of freaky poets around here, and the only beautiful city in the U.S.

9 Friday —If you want to go to LA and Disneyland, a reading on the 5th at Univ of Cal at LA.

Then you could either fly directly home, or if you'd like to give one more reading in the South, I can arrange one in North Carolina very easily. Or maybe you'd like to hit the South the next time you come. Let me know on this last point. I didn't want to commit you until I knew how much time you had.

So if you do accept the reading in New York—and I think it would be fun for you—that makes three readings a week, for three weeks. If you'd like me to add one more, either during the three weeks or after, nothing would be easier. I arranged these mainly so that you'd see the Western U.S. a bit. Tell me how the schedule sounds!

Love from us all!
Excitedly
Robert

Västerås 13-9-71

Dear Robert,

Your planning is beautiful. Especially I like the generous time with you and Carol and the 3 silent days between Boulder and Pocatello. But probably I will not have time for North Carolina this time. I hope to do it when I come to Pittsburgh next year.

But my visit to the traveller's bureau here was a disappointment. I told them that I was going to give a few readings and they telephoned the U.S. embassy and they said that my readings are regarded as WORK in the U.S., so I have to ask for a "certificate of eligibility" from all the 9 places and after that I could hope to get a special sort of visa. I alarmed the Swedish Institute and they had never heard about this problem before—many Swedes give lectures without such certificates and a mild panic expanded. I just now wait for a telephone call from Mr Walldén . . . well here the telephone call arrived . . . Mr Walldén (my favorite bureaucrat* at the Swedish Institute) is telexing Mrs Arvidsson in Washington (you might hear from her very soon, probably as early as the day before yesterday) and something called "Sverige-Amerika-stiftelsen" seems to be entrusted with permission to give a general "certificate of eligibility" and when that arrives I can go to the embassy and get my visa etc. Bureaucrats! Rats! As I am no drug addict or TB patient or member of the Communist Party I have some hope to be able to do these readings after all. Let us take

---

*Actually he is no bureaucrat at all. If you want to do anything in the Swedish-American field, turn to him.

it for granted. In the meantime, many thanks for your wonderful job and good planning.

Enthusiastically,

Tomas

P.S. I forgot the Aspenström problems. Your introduction is reasonable. But I doubt he has translated Hart Crane.

"Den ene har tråkigt ser ni" means word by word THE ONE (means "one of us," means "I") has a tedious time. Means "One of us is bored, you see."

What is absurd is the story you told about Sonnevi's Viet Nam poem. A sailor's yarn. Palme was never inspired by this poem. The truth is that he did not know that the Vietnamese should take part in the demonstration together with him. When Palme arrived, the Hanoi ambassador was there, smiling, and it was too late for Palme to get out. Keep strictly to the truth when writing introductions especially when you have to do with such serious fellows as Sonnevi!

Your always faithful,

Tomas T.

20 Sept, '71

Dear Tomas,

I don't deliberately try to tell lies in introductions, you know! Some Swede told me that story of the electric effect of Sonnevi's Viet Nam poem. But how did you see that one? I only sent you the Aspenström, as I recall. I hope you'll return the Aspenström sheet if you still have it, since it's the only copy I have at the moment (and it's obviously a GREAT WORK). I don't know a thing about W. A. but Leif says he translated Hart Crane. If I can't believe the Swedes, then what will I do? Chasms of unbelief yawn.

There's a rumor in Iowa City that you have agreed to come to Paul

Engle's International Writers Visiting Program for 4 months next year. Is that true? Goodness, such popularity! TLS for Sept 10th carries two poems of yours—I trust they sent you a copy.

We're broke here and eating tomatoes.

Your friend, Robert

Västerås 25-9 [1971]

Dear Roberto,

here is the Aspenström introduction back again. I kept it, yes, I did. People have a fantastic ability to remember that they sent me some letter or manuscript, sometimes 3–4 years ago and suddenly, they ask for it back. Recently a literary forestry officer from South Sweden wrote me that the manuscript for an autobiographical novel, written in advanced William Faulkner prose with phonetic spelling of spoken language etc., had been stolen from him in France. He asked me immediately to return the 3 pages from it he sent me in 1968. Earlier this year a psychotic Västerås lady demanded I return a confused letter written with a lipstick and smuggled out of a mental hospital in 1967 etc. I keep everything! The problem is always that I don't know WHERE I keep it. But I have a U.S. box where I keep all transatlantic correspondence and one IRON CURTAIN box where I keep the East European things. But the Swedish letters are dispersed, crawling like cockroaches everywhere in the house. Even my own poems sometimes get out of sight.

I have received a "certificate of eligibility," a general one, covering all places where I will read, from the State Department, so I sent it forward to the U.S. embassy, asking for a visa.

I have never been asked to come to Iowa. And if invited I have to say no thanks as long as Monica is studying and my children are in school. I would welcome such an invitation 10 years from now. But it is nice to hear that I have readers in Iowa. I definitely have a better reputation abroad than in Sweden. I am inclined to suspect your translations are better than the original poems. That does not disturb me. What matters is that the texts give people something, if you or I am responsible for their experience is irrelevant.

Thank you for the 20 poems, they arrived the other day! I was happy to have that drawing ("man with a kerosene lamp standing upon a reindeer") on the front page. I also like the brown color, unsentimental like hard bread. But too much praise on the cover! My wife thought it to be accurate but personally I think I am nr 7 or 11 on the ranking list of 20th century Swedish poets. Most literary officials in Sweden would think I am nr 24 or 29. Your own reputation is in danger! Let us forget all ranking lists. Everyone is a world champion in his own art!

      Goodbye!

      Your friend

          Tomas

30 Sept, '71

Dear Tomas,

I've finished my new book! O glumphious joy! I think I'll call it *Sleepers Joining Hands.*

Beacon Press, who is printing the Swedish anthology, reports that I have only 2 poems of Aspenström's in the anthology and they think that's too little. Would it be an imposition—Yes it would!—to ask you to suggest six or seven poems from his *66 Poems* (it's the only book of his I have) that you think are solid? If his best poems aren't in that book, tell me, and I'll order them from Sweden.

Tomorrow I go up to the north woods to be alone a week!!!!!!!!!!!!

Every word I say on the jacket of 20 Poems is the exact and literal truth— Monica knows that.

      Signed, Coleridge

23 Nov, '71

Dear Tomas,

You'll probably get an inquiry from the Kansas City Poetry Forum— it's one of the best audiences in the U.S.—including older people as well as students—about your reading there next year. I've just received a letter from Samuel Hazo—who it turns out was sleeping lightly by his telephone the last month, waiting for a call from THE SWEDE,—(the contemporary GRETA GARBO)—and Hazo declares that he plans for you to appear in Pittsburgh "sometime between October 20th and November 20th, 1972." So if you do want to add other dates, why don't you choose a period somewhere around there for your next raid, and I'll just funnel offers on to you from time to time.

I read some of your poems at the Univ of Iowa last week, along with Voznesensky's, and used that as an entrance, attacking them for asking neither of you for the students to hear, and then going on to other 4-4-4 generalizations. As you can imagine, my muscle portion delighted in the smell of gunpowder, and I believe the generals on the other side are a bit jumpy . . .

Noah was with me down there . . .

He's sitting on the floor now, opening offers from Time Life to subscribe for all of Beethoven's work . . .

Love from us all,
Robert

Västerås 26-11, [1971]
Dear Robert,

Monica and I are sitting here radiating the warmest we can to you all 6. Go immediately and kiss Carol and Mary and Biddy and Noah and (especially) little Micah! After that read quickly my version of "Hair" and write your comments. I must have it back soon—the editors of the anthology are impatient. (Explain the last 2 lines—what is a hornblade? What does the mammoth do there?) Translating it was a joy. I have a need to call people and read it aloud.

Martinson published a new book today. I have ordered it and after reading it I will send it to you by air with my favorite poems marked.

Love

Monica ♡ Tomas

12 Dec, '71

Dear Tomas,

Would you be a good old horse and stare with your divided vision at these feeble attempts to English Harry M.? I'm stumbling along in the dark of Swedish, my Norwegian spectacles not bifocal . . . liable to call a toothbrush a barn . . .

I'm also enclosing "Hair," which arrived while I was away, and so is late returning! I think it's marvellous! I love it!

Notes on two lines enclosed . . .

Oddly enough, I had a haircut today . . . a hug for Monica and Emma and Paula,

Robert

Some Notes on "Hair"

1. Melankoli should be capitalized—it is the name of Burton's book of the 18th century, *The Anatomy of Melancholy*. You have to imagine rather illiterate nails who live under the tumbledown porches of those Negro slum houses in Baltimore—the word row-houses picks those up sometimes for Americans—there is a curious sort of slum street in Baltimore with all the houses, 19th century, exactly alike. These nails roll out into the street, and manage to slow up the Secretary of State on his way to the airport, by giving him a flat tire. So "catch" means merely "touch" or "tag" as when children say in a game: I caught him!

The implication of the last line there is not only that he has threads to deliver, but that somehow the main purpose of the trip, emotionally at least, is precisely in order to threaten or humiliate the premiers of poorer nations.

- - - - - -

2. "All those things borne down by the world"—this doesn't have to do with being *born*, but with being *carried* down, as when a drowning man is carried down to the bottom by the weight of his boots.

The world itself is like the heavy boots, which bear him down, and the corpses are imagined as being light for awhile, but finally the weight of death pulls them down too.

"Veins clogged with flakes of sludge" presents a scene somewhat like the scene in "Traffic" in which Mr. Clean tries to swim. "Sludge" is a word that could be used both for the goo in sewers and also for the black stuff that appears at the bottom of oil pans in automobiles. The use of "flakes" with it is a bit odd, but sometimes that heavy sludge will flake off, that is come in thin flat pieces. The veins of the "worldly" man are imagined full of this stuff, instead of cholesterol.

3. "Ordovician" hair is a bit weird. Ordovician is a favorite word of mine. I found it in a geology book, and have used it ever since. It describes one of the ages of geology—the Silurian Age, the Ordovician Age, etc. Don't try to make any sense out of it—here was no hair in the Ordovician age, but the reader does get the feeling of extremely *old* hair. The word has a peculiar air of triumph about it in English, and so fits the line.

In the next line hair is imagined as a ship that carries the holy, who are all shouting like mad, joyfully over the river of the dead to the other side.

4. What is lying in the bureau drawer (the same sort of chest of drawers one would find in any bedroom) are golden pins—the same sort children use to pin together bits of paper or tailors use to pin together seams before sewing—only they are gold. "Glory" should emphasize not the power but some immense light, as if you would be half blinded if you caught sight of the pins. In the next line, "power" suggests the ability of the shaman to heal, or the ability of Christ to raise the dead.

5. "At dawn the Stalinist"—you can drop out "at dawn" if you want to; I added it when typing it up, and it doesn't seem to add much. In fact, I think it just clutters the pictures.

— The singer—again someone like Judy Garland—is on a transatlantic ship and tries to commit suicide by climbing out the porthole.

— The "lograft" is not a large mass of tree trunks, but rather a raft carefully made of logs perhaps by some explorers lost on the shores of the Amazon; they have made the raft in the hopes of getting back to civilization, but they did not see the huge waterfall ahead of them, and the raft breaks up as the current begins to speed up, and they themselves are about to be killed.

— The spider line should give the feeling of a single gleaming filament, gleaming because the morning sun is hitting it, and the spider goes up it with such speed that the watcher becomes dizzy. It is "blinding" because we have a curious phrase in English, "his speed was blinding," meaning he went so fast the eye could hardly catch it.

6. The last stanza: This is Senator Kennedy's plane falling in an orchard in Massachusetts, when he was almost killed. It's as if there were something mysterious in the Kennedy lives, full of black magic. Occasionally when sawing a log with one of the mechanical saws, the blade will hit a heavy knot-place in the log. Even if you weren't looking at the log, you would still know you had hit that place because looking down into the pale heap of sawdust, you would notice a dark place in the sawdust. I give one more example of "magic": the "hornblade" suggests in English some of the earliest knives made by cave-age man. This is at the time of the Cave-Painters, who are trying various magic procedures to kill the mammoths which they need for food. I imagine a hornblade made well, but which had a single nick in the blade.

Every time this blade was taken along on a hunt, the mammoth escaped, because he escaped through that nick on the blade!

27 Dec, '71

Dear Tomas,

I just had a thought about the relationship between Martinson and you . . . He is the Father, and you the (more spiritual) Son, —and Ekelöf is the Holy Ghost!

Yours,
Robert

Västerås 31 jan [Dec.] 71

Dear Robert, Sta Claus, Scandinavian Moses,

the little Indian dolls did not like to leave Minnesota so they run away from my luggage. I am glad you picked them up and—good timing—they arrived on Christmas Eve! They refused to say anything about Voznesensky so I have to ask you directly for a colorful description of your adventures with this (crying?) Russian.

We had a terrible Christmas. The Hong Kong flu hit Emma [------]. She is all right now, starts her horsemanship tomorrow.

www

I have lost my collected Martinson. So, just now, I can only speak about the *Nomad* poems in your translation.

"Landscape" seems 100% good.

"Creation Night" good except for line 4. The Swedish text is more direct, primitive, and naive. "We twisted together [in order] to make God." That would be a word by word translation, I think. "Slingra oss samman," legs, arms trunks etc.—naturalistic description—"threw ourselves to-gether" sounds to me more like Madame Bovary and "create the divine" is Madame Blavatsky. The line should have matter-of-fact ecstasy.

"March Evening"

"Crying, crying" is OK, if there is no "weeping" in it. I don't know how an American reads it. What do you say about a bird? "Calling"? "En snölykta" is something we simple Swedes make in the winter, outside country houses, sometimes. You make a pyramid of snowballs

FIVE FOOT MAN

Snow balls

and inside this small building—there should be a good space inside—you put a candle and light it. Then the candle is mysteriously shining through the snow walls, the walls made of snowballs. I am sure there is still some old Swede or Norwegian in Minnesota that make "snölyktor" outside his house.

a "snölykta" cut through

The 2 last lines "Och aldrig kom resanden hem
        men i lykta och stund låg hans liv"
                         sound like a song, maybe a
sailor's song—I think the first line is actually taken from some ballad.
Difficult to make the English short enough here.
        And the passenger never got home
        but in lantern and instant his life was
                         does not sound very natural, I
must say. Perhaps you should try some variation of
        And the passenger never got home, his life
        remained in that lantern and instant.

                I will write soon. Do the same!
                Love Tomas

1972

Dear Tomas,

It is New Year's Day! I took a long walk last night, and came to an abandoned farm. Surprisingly, there were bales of new straw outside the barn. I went in . . . forty or so calves breathing heavily in the near dark. Such abundance! I hope that will be like the new year . . .

I'm translating more Martinson, and his new book has come, thank you! I think I'll do "Henhouse" and the troll poem ("Berget i Skogen").

I have a bill here for $16.50 for a call to Sweden. That must be yours! If you don't pay, we'll call you collect.

Have you collected by the way from the various American colleges? If not, let me know, and I will send them a dainty reminder.

We have skates and are all going skating this morning, maybe to Muskrat Pond! I found out how muskrats make those houses. They first make a sort of mountain of reeds and mud and leaves—and then *eat out* the rooms they want! They edit it, so to speak.

Love from us all,
Robert

Västerås 18-1-72

Dear Robert,

the last weeks I have been too busy with my psychology—I was, together with 2 other colleagues, elected b o s s of the Västerås branch of PA-rådet. Yes, we rule the office as a troika, the troika elected by the people who work here (so called "företagsdemokrati"). It is not much to boast about, makes me more busy though.

I called Bonniers and asked for the Friberg and Sjöstrand books (they just arrived). The lady in the foreign department of Bonniers did not burst out in joy, as I expected, when I told her that Martinson would be published by Beacon. "Has Bly or the publisher asked us?" Probably not. So make sure that the Beacon Press (or you) send Bonniers (and Martinson) the happy message and ask for permission, which they will give, I am sure. She said that Bonniers did not expect any economical gain from it, but they must be *told*. (I suddenly felt the roots of my hair g l o w i n g in anger when I, once again, realized, how ungrateful the job of introducing non-selling good poetry is—the big publishers do very little or nothing for the spread of good poetry, but as soon as someone, by sheer love, does something, they want to be consulted.)

Yes it is ungrateful. Especially when some guest star makes a transatlantic telephone call for 16.5 dollars and runs away. Don't call me collect! I will give your family full compensation! Just give me some respite, as soon as I sit down in the street with my begging hat in front of me, it gets so full of snow I have to retire, waiting for better weather.

Every week some new letter arrives from the U.S.A. with the nicest greetings from readers. Last week I got one message from a Mr Schuler in Mount Carroll, Ill. Yesterday I got one from a girl in New York, telling me that 20 copies of the Seventies Press edition was sold out in a certain bookshop in N.Y.C. "right away." She had pasted a golden star on the letter "for that." I am sending them warm thanks on ugly postcards from Västerås.

And now to work.

Your translation of Martinson's

F a l l

"Hårdknutna plöjare" means "hard knot(ted) ploughmen"—I think a word by word translation would be best—"hårdknutna" gives the impression of psychologically rather stiff-necked, inward-minded, tough, strained men, physically probably a mixture of mesomorphs and ectomorphs (no big stomachs here). "Repa" means "scratch" or "score." "Fold" might be too soft, I think of clothes, sewing women etc . . . I might be wrong . . .

The Birch and the Child

I must say, you chose strange poems. I don't know if I understand it either. What is written is, word by word, "Weakness has grown on (built on) strength, my child, and strength has played with the weak (ones). Today you will pat my birch-bark, tomorrow you will be beaten." —Not beaten with the bark of course, but with a rod. "Far off in the defenseless years, so utterly without heat or cold, a wondering bottomless eye stood (there) in the night and wept over this." It is *one* eye. Whose eye? Might be a small lake. Or the eye of mother nature. Or the existence. That does not matter. I think it is a naive poem about the tragic double character of life and nature, both tender and cruel.

What happened to Voznesensky? Did Berryman jump from a bridge and die? (Harding just told me something like that.)

I will give you new commentaries soon.

Love   Tomas

23 Jan, '72

Dear Tomas,

I happened to read your translation of the octopus prose poem today, in order to give the Norwegians—who are translating the prose poems too—some help with the word for "illiterate," and "mufflers" in another poem.

I found one detail in the Swedish of "Hunter." When I ask if I can put my head in, the Swedish goes "Ja, gärna det." Maybe that does give the feeling of "Why not?" Why not is used in English to answer an extremely stupid question, as when a city boy asks a farmer if he could have a cupful of cow dung, or when a farmer asks an islander if he could take a pail of water out of the sea . . .

Noah is out in the schoolhouse with me, trying to put on a pair of plastic handcuffs—my handwriting is weakening—

> Love,
> Robert

29 Jan, '72

Dear Tomas,

Thank you for the corrections and commentaries on Martinson, which were most helpful, and for the copy of the Alan Ross letter. I'll write to Bonniers one day, so they can feel courted. (Just think what immense breasts Bonniers must have . . . or . . .) We have of all things a poetry-reading class here in Madison this month, and are translating some of your poems. We hit a serious knot with the Scattered Congregation poem! And we must ask the horse himself. The first stanza is marvellous. The begging bowl—is this the ordinary collection plate, or is it some special thing, a relic perhaps from the Middle Ages? Does it go in the aisle, as if it were a collection plate? Why doesn't it go up by itself—because there are no people coming to the churches anymore?

When you say the bells "maste go" under the earth, does this mean:
1) that they have no other place to go
2) that they will have to go there sometime in the future
3) that they are already there, and have to <u>ring</u> now
4) they are already there, and are already ringing besides . . .

> Your stupid farmer friend,
> Robert

Västerås 31-1-72
Dear Robert,

an example of real Swedish handwriting. "The Hunter" is probably included in the anthology I have talked about (edited by Gunnar Harding).

But "Garne det" sounds rather stupid in Swedish too. The renaissance painting is there (in the earlier version which is better in Swedish) and the "Canadian" thistle and "Hair" (wow!) and "For the Reader" (you have not seen that translation but I am 100% right, sir). Then Lasse Söderberg has some translations too. I have 7–8 James Wright and as many W. S. Merwin. The rest is Levertov, O'Hara etc. made by other people.

I am preparing a new Robert Bly book too. You will occupy 25% of a small volume I want to publish. There should be 25% myself, 25% Robert B., 25% János Pilinszky and 25% Vizma Belševica (the Latvian lady I asked you to ask Voznesensky about). The idea is not to make any difference between original poems and translations. So I will only use the translations I really think of as a part of myself.

"Collapsing House" by Martinson seems good. I prefer "In a hundred years they will marry," if it sounds natural.

"The Smelter's Lot"

"Churchyard" . . . why not "burial place"? For me a churchyard is a vast thing around a church. "Lokomobil" is a forerunner to the tractor—an extinct monster nowadays, the name in English is probably "Locomobile" (look after it in an encyclopedia!). "Med opp—nade anahmier" means more than "intestines"—it has the atmosphere of old Dutch 17th century paintings ("Dr X's Anatomy Lesson" etc.). Is it impossible to say "Their anatomies open[ed]"? "Metal foliage" makes me think of a man disappearing high *above* the ground . . . Or is foliage also something that grows near the ground? (The original poem has "mekl grass" as you know.) Today I have been talking to fools only. Write soon! Love   Tomas

Västerås 8-2-72

Dear Robert,

I pause in the terrible and exciting job of making an income declaration for 1971. This is extremely complicated for a Swedish citizen, and especially for a writer with his many odd small salaries from different places . . . In that case the future seems bright. The lawyer of the Swedish Writer's Union had never met this problem before—I seem to be the first Swedish poet who has made a reading tour in the U.S.A.! Is that possible? The next one could be the mystic Mr "Kristoffersson" Elizabeth Kray mentioned. No one here has ever heard about a poet named Kristoffersson. I think it must be Sjöstrand. An exciting possibility is that it is Håkan Berggren himself, disguised with a false beard and appearing before a New York audience, reading his own, till now unknown, poetry. I can see him at his own party afterwards running between the kitchen (for changing clothes, putting on his beard) and back to the drawing room and back again etc.

How is it possible to have a poetry reading class in Madison? You have the dentist Scherer of course and he is a magnificent judge of poetry, as I remember from our evening in his house.

About "The Scattered Congregation":
The begging bowl problem. It is a general begging bowl, could be old, lifting itself up from the floor (like a flying saucer) and slowly going in the aisle. In Swedish churches we don't pass a plate ourselves while taking collection. A chuchwarden is slowly going with a sort of bag net, reaching it to the people who drop money in it. But this is not a bag net, it is a bowl. It is passed as if by an invisible man. I got this fancy once during a sermon. Now I don't know if I would imagine the church to be empty or not.

"Måste gå under jorden" . . . "måste" could be both present and past tense. "Gå under jorden" is both literal and symbolic. Angela Davis had to "gå under jorden" when she was wanted by the police etc. I think the expression is simply "go underground." In Sweden religion is suspect. People (especially intellectuals) are often ashamed of their secret religious beliefs or longings. In the old times religion was organized and honored, at the top of the hierarchy, public, high up (like the church bells). But now the church bells have to go to a more humble position, almost like the first Christians in the Roman catacombs. But they get more strength down there.

I would think the most difficult problem in this poem is the translation of the very first line. "Vi ställde upp" is colloquial, almost slangy. Means "We joined in." Example: "We are going to have a party next Friday, ställer ni upp?" Another example: The sergeant: "I need two men for a dangerous mission out there, ställer ni upp?" It means that you agree to take part in something, in the poem it is to represent the welfare state before a visitor.

Alan Ross wrote me that it is too late to change the title of the London Magazine edition. But the title is *Night Vision and Other Poems,* so it is not too bad, after all. He is a true instant publisher, and that is good.

I am still waiting for the copies of *Night Vision* and *20 poems* and my leftover books mailed in October. Everything must be delayed by the old longshoreman strike. Or are these hardhats making sabotage against Sweden?

Have you written some short poems that you really like yourself the latest months? Please send them!

Love   Tomas

12 March, '72

Dear Tomas,

Thank you for the Worm Digging Poem! It is terrific. I have one or two queries: Does "lätta" suggest "not heavy" as well as "easy"?

"Nära et slott" sounds odd, though it is exactly what the English says. As I recall the dream, a man was working with stones, perhaps on a flying buttress of a castle. I started fooling with the stones in a careless way while I talked, and soon the entire wall of the castle began to come down.

If you prefer, you can leave out "och gick tvärs igenom"—that was added in a late draft, and I'm not sure yet whether the phrase is necessary or not.

"Slott" is correct, I'm sure.

I wonder if "Allegro" *is* in this poem? Let's hope so. My poor poem needs all the joy it can get!

Your friend,
Robert

Västerås 5 april [1972]

Dear Robert,

a friend of mine just convinced me—scientifically—that there is no statistical and political possibility for anyone at all to be nominated Democratic candidate. You will have to stick to your old peace president Trick E. Dixon.

Today a snowstorm. I am angry. Yesterday a rotten critic wrote that my *Night Vision* was an example of the influence of criticism. Tranströmer has become "prosaic" because he was attacked for the previous book and he has now tried to write in a style that would satisfy the Swedish critics. "Actually *Mörkerseende* is written by Tranströmer's critics." Of course I have nothing against his opinion that I am "prosaic" etc., but the attack on my CHARACTER, the idea that I for a fraction of a second could have felt a remote responsibility of being EXPEDIENT, SUBMISSIVE in relation to the people who are ruling this Inferno of Stupidity that is Swedish Cultural Life. AUGH!

Here is your wonderful Hawaiian crab. Can you send me the Voznesensky-reading poem too? And I ask once again. What happened to Andrei in the U.S.A.? I saw in *Life* that Yevtushenko is a good friend of James Dickey. Somatotonia always finds companions when it comes to large audiences, bombs and money.

It was warming to look at the pictures from Madison, I just got them from the photo shop. How good it is to think about you all.

Tomas

Can I trust Leif Sjöberg when he tells me that a new issue of *The Seventies* is out?

8 April, '72

Dear Tomas,

Seventies #1 is out, and should be in this same mail. Enclosed find check for "Out in the Open" in same issue!

By the way, do you remember if you were paid any royalties for *Twenty Poems,* and if so, how much? It seems to me I sent a small sort of check in advance, maybe $50 or $100—but nothing since? Am I right? I'm not saying you'll get any more, just wondering . . .

Thank you for the photographs! They are lovely, and a joy to have. How Emma and Paula have grown! They look so spirited and feminine.

I haven't read your Maui translation yet, Carol has the letter! What appears to be a Hindi poem is actually an account of all your flaws and failures, drawn from interviews with your old schoolteachers, bosses, and girlfriends—it's being distributed hand to hand all over India.

Faithfully,

Robert

Västerås 1 May -72

Dear Robert,

it has been hard times with Nixon still going wrong and a terrible threat against Europe—the CDU efforts to make Willy Brandt's Eastern policy collapse. I have been lying, grinding my teeth, in a transparent coffin, except for some trips—one a reading trip together with Gunnar Harding to Norrkörping and Växjö. In Norrkörping we read from the U.S. issue of *Lyrikvännen* (did they send it to you?) so "Hair" got its Swedish premier (I was making some arm movements too when reading it). I also read the now 4 completed parts of *Östersjöar.* (In the next letter when my energy has returned I will copy nr 3 and 4 for you—in the meantime, take this shorter poem that does not belong to *Östersjöar.*)

I liked the "jump-issue" of *The Seventies* very much. I think, being published there, I have reached the absolute summit of my public life.

The day before yesterday I saw Östen and Ella Sjöstrand in Mariefred (a small town 40 miles from here) just before they left for the U.S.A. They are present at a Scandinavian conference in Madison, Wisc. Are you invited? What a fantastic combination of people: Lars Gustafsson, Eric Sellin, Leif Sjöberg, you, Östen and Ella, plus Prof. Vowles. If you are there, give me a vivid description of the drama!

I hope everything is fine with you and your family in spite of the ugly times.

Love
Tomas

24 May, '72

Dear Tomas,

I've studied "Pa Mauis Klippor" now, and I think the translation is wonderful! So much energy in the Swedish verbs! Superb!

I have a thought about the "arameiska" passage. I think the phrase needs more "s"'s—(I noticed Arabs were especially fond of the letter "s"—) ("w" they hated—and "d" they were just indifferent to as they were to all numerals)—so I think you might use some word for "understand"—i.e., "en demon some forstar arameiska." . . .

I'm not sure he's reading the prayers out of books—maybe the prayers are silent ones he is making up in the same way the ocean keeps making up new waves . . .

Late, gorgeous spring here! We're going tomorrow to visit the Muskrat Heaven . . . the angels with a low IQ . . .

I didn't get to meet Östen Sjöstrand—I was too tired (of humans and distance) after my spring tour to drive the 3 hours into Mpls to see him . . . and besides his *Dream Is No Facade* book was too intellectual . . . and there was too much defense of poetry in it . . . whoever heard of defending a mountain against detractors . . . and saying "A Mountain Is No Facade" or "A Badger is No Facade" . . . the female badger knows that . . .

Thank you from the
Arab nation
Robert

P.S. Do either of your girls collect stamps?

Västerås 1-6-72

Dear Robert,

so good to hear from you. I don't have Martinson's book, so you have to wait a week or so for comments. But I can tell you about the 2 words that are absent in your dictionary. "Kåckel" is an invention by Martinson, an onomatopoeic word, built on "kackel" which is a dictionary word for "cackle." So if there is no other English word called COCKLE I think that would be best—or "cawkle"? "Slutarlika" means "shutter-like." "Slutare" is a part of a camera, my dictionary says the English word is "shutter."

I will try to bring more s's into the Aramaic part of the crab poem. "Läsa sina böner" does not primarily mean that he is reading from a book. A child in a religious family "läser sina böner" every evening and that means simply "saying prayers."

About "Seeing through the Ground." It has one grand mistake in it: Line 7, "almost through it" is wrong. You think that the Swedish word "fast" means the same as the German word "fast." But in Swedish it means "but." And "tvärtom" means "contrary." So the lines mean

"like aerial photos of a city at war
but the opposite"/contrary/reverse. The mole is taking his picture from below, he is a reverse pilot/photographer.

Line 1:

"Rinner ut"—well, maybe "runs out" is the best. It should be the expression you use about a pat of butter in a hot stew. Line 8: "dova färger." "Dova" is mostly used about sounds, dull, hollow, dark sounds. I don't think there is an exact synonym for it in English. Something in the direction of "gloomy." Paula sometimes takes a stamp from the envelopes. I put some strange stamps on this letter, if your children do it. They are—as you can see—the stamps of the People's Republic of Sweden. Love   Tomas

26 June, '72

Dear Tomas,

I heard from Fort Collins today that you were due there on Nov 1st. When are you to be in Pittsburgh? How long will you be in this country? Have you set a date for the Univ of Minn? Will you visit us? Do you want me to set up any other readings? How many readings do you want to do? Do you floss your teeth everyday? What hobbies do you pursue at present? Do you prefer the shoulder strap or the abdomen strap? Do you have friends on other planets?

> Signed,
> Ole Bull

[8-7-72]

Walking Running Crawling

Walk among fallen trees a year after the storm.
Wing-sound. Torn up roots
turned toward heaven, stretching out
like skis on someone jumping.

Thirsty wasps hum low over the moss.
And the holes, they resemble the holes
after all those invisible trees
that have also been uprooted these last years.

I don't even have wings. I pull my way forward
in my life—the labyrinth
whose walls you can see through—
walking running crawling.
        (translated by RB)

Big Brother, will you cast your horse-dealer's glance on this small thing.

My Pittsburgh coronation ceremony is around Oct. 23–24. I don't know how many readings Sam Hazo will arrange, I hope not too many, because if you could arrange something IN THE SOUTH or very near your chicken house, I would be most happy. So if things turn out as I hope there will be 2–3 Pennsylvania readings (Hazo) and the rest in more exotic places (Bly). But I have not heard anything from Sam Hazo about it. I know that the Swenson book is out, I got a review from the *Library Journal,* a kind one. Even you are mentioned:

> Robert Bly's translations of the later poems (in Tranströmer's *Night Vision,* Lillabulero Pr.) are sometimes better, sometimes not; but this [Swenson's] is a generally excellent translation. . . .

Monica sends her best, she asks about the sponsored child especially. Do you succeed with Micah's education?

Runmarö Thunder and rain

from
your old friend
Tomas

8 July, '72

Dear Tomas,

Mary and I are going to the Black Hills today (of So. Dakota) to walk for a couple of days. Then on July 17th I go to Norway to brood for 3 weeks. Will you be in Runmarö all that time? Send me your telephone number.

Love from all your
poor relations among
the savages of North
America,
Robert

10 July, '72

Dear Tomas,

A friend, Bill Holm, wants you to read at Hampton Institute, a black college in Virginia, this fall. If you want to, save a date for that. You could go down from Pittsburgh. He said, "They won't put out money for a white man, but they might for a Swede!"

Micah says ciao,
Robert

Runmarö 28-7-72
Dear Robert,

as you can see we have moved into Runmarö, and are perfectly healthy and almost nudists—the sun is so strong today, the birds are singing, but from the radio: new war crimes.

You ask about Håkanson's "flimmer." It is a noun made from the verb "flimra" which you, in my poem "Track," translated "flicker." So I think it's right to say "That this flickering disturbs me is a fact." "Flimmer" is often used when you speak about the way a wrongly adjusted TV-screen behaves. The poem is not bad and quite translatable.

Martinson's "The Hill in the Woods" will be an excellent translation when completed. I will help you, but I did not have the book, so I wrote to a friend for a photo-copy of this poem—it arrived today. The 3 lines you don't understand are typical Martinson word play with old-fashioned, folklore expressions. I will think it over. A problem is the word "berg," that can mean anything from "rock" to "mountain." "Hill" is probably OK but so soft, such a mild word, while "berg" is full of harshness and scars. The line you have translated "She was mad all right" should word by word be translated "She was hillstrong" or "rockstrong." "Bergstark" is a Martinson invention and very expressive—I think you misunderstood it as "berserk" or something. But the girl is simply stronger than the boys and gave them a beating (she did not have to use a club).

Look at the stamp I put on this envelope!
    Give the whole Bly clan my sponsor blessings!
      Your old
        Tomas
Gatan 13038 Runmarö

30-7-72 [postcard]

Dear globetrotter,

I wrote to Carol and got this incredible name: *Steinshylla*. (You forgot to give me any Norwegian addresses.) You must visit. We are in Västerås now tel. 0954621 021-11 10 45, the address you know perfectly well. Write or call soon. I can even pick you up at the Arlanda airport if necessary (have a car now).

      In a hurry
      your friend Tomas

      Thursday [4-8-1972]
Dear Tomas,
    Your note has just this moment come! And now, alas, there is no more time! I have to go back Sunday.
    I knew you were on the island, and I didn't want to disturb you—you would have had to take the boat all the way to the quai, drive to Stockholm, etc.—it is too much! And go all the way back . . .
    Besides, you might mistake me for one of those Americans—or Canadians—who say, with a wide grin, "I'm coming to live with you this summer!"
    And double besides, I didn't want to wear out my welcome—I want to bring Carol and the children and live with you all a whole week one summer on the island!! (So you see, I am one of those after all . . .)
    I am just doing—up here in Steinshylla's hytte—the last work on my long poem "Sleepers Joining Hands," and I'm all excited and jumping

about . . . I'm too modest to say it's good . . . but I'm proud of it, as I am of Noah and Micah and Mary and Biddy . . . Your godchild by the way is the most forward child seen in Madison for many a year—barely 1 year old, he opened the top of the big record player cabinet the other day, climbed in, *sat* on the turntable, and turned it on! Of course Carol is convinced he's a genius, and tells him so about 45 times a day—it's doubtful if he'll ever achieve humility, like the rest of us . . . Love to Monica—

Your Norwegian country
cousin, Robert

Västerås 9-8-72

Dear Robert,

your explanations for not visiting your old friend Goethe were a bit strained. The risk that we would be so tired of you after a short visit that we would turn down the whole family next summer is really small . . . No, we will love to have you all, yes a whole week, all the 6 humble geniuses, in our guest house. It will be a good summer full of innocent country occupations: fishing, chicken raising, walks in the woods, poem writing etc. Monica was happy to hear about your arrival. But first a gloomy winter. For me endurable because of the U.S. trip. I will be pumped up like a balloon so I can keep myself floating the rest of the dark months.

Write soon and send the smaller works so I can make selection for my next "book."

Warmest greetings
Tomas

1 Sept., '72

Dear Tomas,

I have my notes on your reading schedule from our telephone conversation, but I can't read them! Would you send your schedule so far to me . . . you land on Oct 15th . . . then . . . all is murk.

I went out the night I talked to you with some Norwegian poets to Kjell Heggelund's house and sat around participating spasmodically in the extrovert conversations, and thought, "This is terrible! Where is Tomas? Where is my wonderful introvert friend?" I should have taken a plane to Västerås earlier that day, but I was too stupid . . . but we are looking forward now very much to your visit here. Maybe I'll meet you in Fort Collins, and then we'll drive back to Madison . . . How would that be?

Varma hälsningar
Robert

Västerås 3 okt -72
Dear You,

thank you for all altruistic efforts for arranging readings! I will go to Hampton the 26th. But I cannot do Ann Arbor the 24th. That will give Pittsburgh only one single day and I think Hazo would be definitely hurt in that case.

I will probably leave the U.S. on nov 5th or 6th. My family needs me very much this autumn. We have just now no one to help us with the children etc. Monica works 40 hours a week in the hospital (they use the nurse students as unpaid workers—the whole Swedish hospital system would fall into pieces without that custom). I hope we will get a girl to help us some hours during my U.S. stay, but that is expensive. The conditions last year were much more favorable. Anyhow I am proud of my little overprotected daughters who have managed to take the situation in good spirits. [------] . . . horses, books, flute playing, choir singing etc. fill Emma's day—I am surprised that she has time to go to school. Paula's situation is worse, but she is the ambitious type and her geisha smile easily gives her protection from neighbors.

I am not at all prepared, financially and psychologically, for this reading trip. It is bad that you can't inflate me with poetic self-confidence and poetic identity before I go. As it is now, I will probably stand in the Guggenheim museum bewildered, asking, WHO AM I on the 17th. As I don't want to stand there and say "Well, here I am again with exactly the same old poems as the previous year," you can give me good help by sending the final version of "Seeing through the Earth" and "The Dispersed Congregation," 2 things you have translated—the first one I have only seen in a first draft and the second one never seen. So if you find them, please send them very fast (I will leave Sweden on oct 13th). No, it is probably too late already, send them c/o Academy of Am. Poets, Betty Kray—I will meet her before the reading. She sent a wonderful description of the situation in Pittsburgh so I know pretty well what I have to expect among the millionaires there. I will certainly bring a tie this year.

May all good fairies, trolls and brownies support the Bly farm and its people!

> Your friend
> ~~John Updi . . .~~
> pardon
> Tomas

8 Oct., '72

Dear Tomas,

This is just a note to assure you that the Sam Hazo problem is OK. I offered to change the Ann Arbor reading to sometime the week before, and Hazo said no, it was perfect as it was. If you arrived by noon on the 25th, it would be plenty of time. He sounded rushed—maybe he has a couple of Swedish poets in the house already? He knows too that you go to Virginia the next week.

On your following long weekend, you could fool around the Great Smokies and Virginia; or take a train to Alabama or Mississippi, and rent a car there; or fly to Chicago or Mpls and take the wonderful western train to Fort Collins. If you arrive at Fort Collins by the night of the 31st, you'll be in time.

I carefully set aside these free days which are known as Introvert Days, and are to be spent in solitary anxious, obstinate, confused ectomorph brooding.

Love from us all,
Robert

[20-11-72]

Elegy

> (Is this the same in Swedish as in
> English? In English it implies
> someone dead, also an old classical
> verse habit, and finally a certain
> amount of praise for the dead one.)

I open the first door.
It is a large sunlit room.
A heavy car passes outside
and makes the china tinkle.

I open door number two.
Friends! You drank darkness
and became visible.

Door number three. A narrow hotel room.
Looks out on an alley.
One lamppost glistens on the asphalt.
The beautiful slag of experiences.

Dear Wolfgang . . . please check this for "liberties," that is rape committed by the feeble mind.

The last line is a puzzle—it's not entirely natural in English to have a plural "experiences." Normally it would go "the beautiful slag of experience." . . . meaning that out of the number of experiences, lasting over years (and *experience,* as opposed to staying in your room and listening to television), out of all that experience, a slag remains . . . so we have to talk about plural or singular there I guess. What do you say, Wolfgang?

Västerås 21-11-72

Dear Badger,

        I am calling you from the deep abyss of my gratitude. It is a feeling of gratitude without guilt feelings, though I was a happy sponge in your house. Sorry to cause harm to your car—how are the brakes now? Better? As soon as I step into your car something happens . . . This was the main reason for not riding one of your beautiful horses, I was afraid to make it lame or something. Good that I did not burn down the chicken house.

        It was fine in Minnesota. The homecoming was fine too. Everybody seemed happy to see me again. The whole family was healthy and flourishing. Monica has advanced from the emergency department to the intense care. Now she is an operation nurse (it is difficult to hear what the doctors say behind their mouth veils . . . "twhehh bggg sczzrrrs ssstr . . ." etc. and that makes life a little more nervous).

        An Australian (Keith Harrison) is the next visitor here—did you give him my address? He did not know about your translations.

        How is Franklin? I will write to him, but I would like to know first how his conditions are.

Love and Best
to you all
from Us All
Tomas

26 Nov, '72

Dear Tomas,

Franklin Brainard has heard nothing conclusive so far, and he may be all right. He'd enjoy a letter from you very much. The tests do not indicate that he has gone into the acute stage.

We just finished a two-day "poetry festival" at the annual conference—in Mpls this time—of the National Council of Teachers of English—mainly high school teachers. All the poets acted "like nuts," and had a marvellous time. Keith Gunderson announced that he paid me $17.50 a reading for not mentioning the Mother, and $21.00 if I didn't mention the Reptile Brain. Now, he said, a new figure has appeared, the SHADOW SELF, and he's applying for a grant from the Ford Foundation to pay me and so protect the public from this new danger. . . .

Don Hall has hair to his shoulders, bags under his eyes, and looks exactly like the old photographs of Tennyson . . . It is snowing today on the chickenhouse . . .

Your friend,
Robert

29-11-72
Yes Master,

you are probably right about the plural of experience. In Swedish we often use the word "experience" [erfarenhet] in plural . . . I will now tell you a little about my experiences in the U.S. Okay, first I caught a cold, and then I met Professor Ussachevsky and then I went to Stony Brook and then I watched TV and then there was a snowstorm and then I was in the chicken coop and then we tried to smuggle some bottles of wine into a restaurant in Minneapolis but, surprise, that didn't work out . . . right, those were some of my experiencs in the U.S. . . . But if you ask the question "What was your experience of the U.S. like?" then I have to answer in a more academic way like Hm . . . My experience of the U.S. is that it is a country in constant change, a dynamic environment at once attractive and repellant . . . in short . . . hm . . . a country that makes a visitor feel both large and small . . . hm in any case it's impossible according to my experience to elucidate in so few lines my experience of that remarkable country.

Did you get an idea of the difference between singular and plural or "enfarenhet" in Swedish? So it is OK with singular form in English here when it is OK with plural in Swedish.

About the Martinson foreword . . . I think instead of "Hegel and Breton" you should have "Spengler and Valéry." Oswald Spengler was the topical man in Europe in the 1920s.

All the best to you
                    from your old friend
                              Tomas

1973

Jan 9 -72 [1973]

Dear Robert,

today I had a letter from Bert Meyers and that is the first letter from the U.S.A. since Dec 18 when the terror bombings started. Before that date I had 4–5 letters per week. Does it mean anything? Are people writing some useful letters to the Congress instead? When you read this the bombings might have started again. I thought I had no illusions about Nixon but I was wrong. He is worse than expected. 4 years . . .

So the Christmas was spent in a mood of despair, rage and hopelessness.

In the middle of this I was given a prize of 5,000 crowns by the Swedish Radio. The jury consisted of 5 poets: Sonnevi, Espmark (my favorite), Harding, Alf Henrikson (70 years old) and Peter Curman. I was interviewed in the radio by—of all people—Ingrid Arvidsson, who has quit the Washington job and become cultural boss of the Swedish radio. She answered most of her questions herself so I did not have to say much. I met some radio people and proposed a reading for you when you come here in the spring. I think they will be well disposed towards this offer when it is time.

Everywhere here people are signing a protest against the bombings and an appeal to the U.S. government to sign the October agreement. Lists are in post offices, churches and offices. It will probably have more than one million names when finished around February 1. The first names are those of the leaders of the 5 parties. The protest will be sent to Nixon as one more expression of our ungrateful, malevolent lack of understanding for the efforts of a troubled peace president.

It is a long time since I heard anything from you now. I hope everything inside the family is well, as it is here.

Love to all

Tomas

This is a small despair poem I wrote recently. "Here I come the invisible man . . ." (The saint is Sanct Sigfrid, a sculpture from the middle ages in the Munktorp Church in Västmanland.)

10 Jan, '73

Dear Tomas,

It looks as if I <u>will</u> be over there this spring! Carol signed me up for a very cheap flight (AAA—American Automobile Assn) that leaves Mpls & goes to London May 24th!!! So I suppose a few days later, either before or after I visit my homeland, its fjords and glaciers, I will be on your hands! It would be a grand time to do the final work on Martinson, as well as touch ups for others in the next Beacon book, coming out in August, who will be: *Martinson, Ekelöf, Tranströmer: Selected Poems*, chosen and edited by General Custer himself. You suggested tickling the udder of the Swedish Institute to see if any gold coins fall out, and that seems wise.

My new book is out, but my own copies haven't come. I heard this morning that the *Times Book Review* has already done a review, but won't print it till February, because Harper hasn't got the books in the bookstores yet. No doubt it's written by James Dickey or by Charles Tomlinson.

Do write.   Your faithful dog

SPOT

12 Jan, '73

Dear Tomas,

The war news is so depressing that as soon as your letter came, I translated the poem to have something to do. It's just a first draft . . . please comment on whatever "liberties" you notice. . . .

It's more clear every day that China knocked out McGovern deliberately—I think they like Nixon in there, so that Russia will be busy sending war materials to the victims of Nixon's paranoia. They really don't care if the war is ever settled, and apparently care no more for the North Vietnamese than we do.

So much for Göran's hero.

Congratulations on the Swedish Radio prize! If they had any wit, they'd give you a radio, as well as money. What will you do with your 1,000 dollars? Hire a thousand baby sitters, I suppose. I'm glad to hear Ingrid Arvidsson is out of this country at least. By the way, the other day I got a check from Danish Radio for—of all things—$211—which I needed badly—for their reading "The Teeth Mother" twice on Danish Radio. I had no idea they paid so much money. I wish fervently that you and Göran would finish your translation of "The Teeth Mother" and put it on Swedish Radio!

I'm going to take Noah for a walk out in the snow soon—the fields are frozen now, and the snow so hard packed that you can walk over it . . .

                    As ever affectionately
                         Robert

                                        Would you correct it

December Evening, 72

Here I come the invisible man, perhaps in the employ
of some huge Memory that wants to live at the moment. And
    I drive by

the white church shuttered once more—a saint made of wood
    is inside,
smiling, helpless, as if someone had stolen his glass eyes.

He's lonely. The whole world is now, now, now. The law of
    gravitation that pulls
toward work in the day and toward the bed at night. The war.

"All de andra" I don't really understand—is it everything else,
    everyone else?

"Tagit av" is this simply taken away, or stolen?
It is the Minne that wants to live right now?

Västeras Jan 19 [1973]

Thank you for 2 good letters and welcome in May! The only thing that could
prevent our meeting now is if I get drafted and deported to the Northern
Front again, as in 1971! Around June 1st usually is the best time of the year
in Sweden, sunshine, birds, flowers and fresh green. Monica gets her exam
as a nurse at June 13 and if (IF) the Viet Nam nightmare is over at that time
it will be the best June in many years.

Hope and despair goes up and down from one bulletin to another. It is
like being treated by an expert in brainwashing.

It was nice of you to translate my little poem. About the glasses: yes it is
glasses, spectacles, not "glass eyes." This saint—I think it is Saint Sigfrid,
in the Munktorp church not far from here, has the look of a person who
used to wear glasses but just has lost them: a confused smile is typical
for near-sighted people when stripped of their glasses. I don't think the
glasses have been "stolen," rather just taken away from him. I would pre-
fer "they" to "someone." "As if they had taken away his glasses" suggests

that there is an unfriendly majority of Nixons, Transtömers, Brezhnevs and other modern, brutal people living in secular Now who have done it. "Allt det andra" is simply "everything else" or "The rest" . . . it is a little like "the rest is silence" (the ending of *Hamlet,* as you certainly know Professor). "This moment" might be better than "the moment." I sometimes have the feeling that I have a duty to do for some hidden Consciousness. Why do I have to live through this constant confusion, to see and hear all these things, what does it mean? I sometimes get a little comfort from the feeling that Someone, or rather Something, wants me to do it. "Stay where you are my dear Tomas, don't run away, you have a function even if you don't know what it is." (The same idea is in the middle of the guard duty poem.)

It has been a strange winter because no snow arrived until yesterday. That has not happened for many decades.

Right now an enormous magazine, *Invisible City,* arrived, sent by you. I have never heard from or about the translator, Mr. Kaebitzsch. Probably a *bad* translation. I don't mind.

I saw yesterday that de Gaulle is Nixon's hero. A disastrous example of the American admiration of Europe. I want to see Carol's best story. Good night! Good luck!   Warmly   Tomas

Västerås 28-1-73
Dear Robert,

        a Mr Booth from England wrote me and asked for permission to print 2 of your translations, which of course I agreed to—even if I now, after reading *Virginia Quarterly,* know that they are made by a CULTIST in order to prove an irrelevant point. But I don't blame you Robert. We cannot all be graced with the enormous craftsmanship of a May Swenson.
        Is Mr Booth descended from The Salvation Army?
        Now an important announcement!

From now on I will authorize only one name for the mushrooms mentioned at the end of the October poem. And that name is

INKY-CAP MUSHROOMS

which is and shall forever be the correct name for a *Coprinus comatus* in English. The name in the dictionary ("horsetail mushrooms") is simply wrong and the fool who put it into the dictionary has probably passed away, poisoned by a mushroom he mistook for another.

> Love and Peace
> Tomas

Joan Baez just arrived, warm thanks!

[9/2/1973]
Dear Robert,

a bombardment of mail from Madison has disturbed me in the most wonderful way the last days. *Sleeper* is of course the most remarkable of these things. I read the title poem the other night when I was very sleepy and I did not fall asleep. Why is this fellow's subconscious so engaging? I have had very little time to read this week because of busy life conditions but I carry the impressive red and white tome with me (in the bag with the cucumbers) and next week I hope to disappear into it. (I have been working full-time in my office and poor Monica has NIGHT DUTY—I take her to the hospital at 9 p.m. and pick her up outside at 7 a.m. the next day. So we have a strange life now.) But how good to have a book I really want to roll over in! It was a long time ago . . . I hope you can feel something of the same about Lars Gustafsson's latest! ("Guillevic are making them in France"—that is very bad English, isn't it?) The solution of your Gustafsson problem must be to recommend some other person. Michael Dennis Browne? He seemed to be generous, intelligent, poetic etc. Yes, I looked melancholy when I met Lars because it was in the middle of the Christmas Bombings. I admit. I was melancholy. Good that

someone gets "sad to see it." I am not melancholy now. But too many du-
ties. When you arrive in May/June I will be much more free. I told John
Walldén about your visit and wrote a formal request for 1,500 Swedish
crowns to be sent to you in Norway as contribution for your travel and
living in Sweden. (You will probably get at least 1,000.) You remember
"completing the Martinson translations and visiting the Publisher etc."
You will probably meet some more or less gifted people in Stockholm
who think that you have the key to the American audience—it has not
been mentioned in the newspapers etc. that you have translated me
but there are RUMORS ciruclating about it so be prepared. I know that
the advisory board for literature of the Swedish Institute wants to have
a meeting with you—and you should definitely see them: that is an in-
credible combination of very different people: One crew-cut conservative,
one ecstatic young poet, one politruc, one Newspaper Caesar and so on.
More gossip later.

   I sent the paper about The Minnesota Writers to our boss of the
Writers' publishing house. How is Franklin? Love to you all. Please forgive
this mess. I am hunted by djinns.

                              Tomas

                         17 March, '73

Dear Tomas,
   Beacon has sent me a few queries I can't answer, and I have to pass them
on, with apologies, to you.

   1. Martinson's poem "Namnlöst," why is it called Namnlöst, when
   he mentions her name, Clary, in the poem? Would it be Nameless,
   by the way, or Namelessly? in English . . . (poem from *Nomad*)

   2. One of Ekelöf's poems, from *Färjesång*, the group called "Etyder,"
   is called "Sung." What is that? A Swedish word? or the Sung dy-
   nasty, and therefore not to be translated?

3. For the anthology entitled *Modern lyrik* . . . is *The Modern Poem*
ok? "Spökskepp" I trust is "Ghost Ship."
  "Nomad" I trust is "nomad."

Don't forget to send me the title of your poem about looking for light
switches in the woods . . . looking for fuses on the bottom of rivers is a lot
of fun, too . . .

Your friend,
Robert

24 March, '73

Dear Tomas,

  I don't want to go to Göteborg! I just want to sit in your house and
hear the stones roll through the windows, while all the panes remain
whole. Yes, truly. The only other thing I long for is for both of us to pay
a visit, for a half hour or an hour, to Harry Martinson. As you know by
now, the Swedish Institute collapsed in a disgraceful way under your pres-
sure and awarded me 1,500 Swedish crowns . . . oh joy oh joy! It means I'll
buy a lot of goat cheese in Norway . . .

Love, Robert

I'll come May 1st (or the night of the 31st), and will be with you June 1, 2,
3, 4. I have to fly to London and home on the 5th.

March 25 -73
Spring is early this year. It is the first day without overcoats! This evening
Emma is singing in the cathedral, in a cantata by our friend Werner Wolf
Glaser—she is a member of the choir, not soloist. (The text is—humbly—
chosen by Glaser: Rilke, Schiller and Glaser himself! He has published a
book of poems at his own expense.) He is a brilliant Jew from Köln, a refu-
gee in Denmark until 1943 when he was *smuggled* to Sweden.

The Göteborg reading was for an audience of writers. And some of their friends. They did not use me well. Instead of talking with me they gave small speeches about "the meaning of poetry" etc. One middle-aged lady—a rather unknown poet—was nice and said that *Krig och tystnad* was one of her favorite books. I think she wants to hear your poems primarily. But some of the other ones probably see a glimpse of hope to be translated by you. Especially one former Englishman, Martin S. Allwood (he was not present when I was there but he sent a mesage that you should come, he was so eager to see you). Allwood has started a sort of translation industry and wants to have you in the business, I think. If he is good or not I don't know, but I know that he is prolific. Too prolific. The only possible day for a visit by you seems to be May 30. I leave it to you to decide, but if I were in your shoes (like whales eating the grass) I would *hesitate* to accept.

I have always been fond of the mad Walking in ditch grass poem. So here is a first version. With liberties.

Walking in the Ditch Grass

The spring wind blows dissatisfactions
and mad architects, two-mile long tails,

and my shoes like whales
eat the grass, sweeping through
the grass, eating
up the darkness.

The night is windy. Sleek cows fly
across the sky. Samson
is angry.
So much of women
in this uneven grass.
       (RB original)

Note. So much of women, what does it mean. So much of femininity? Or so many women? Or? Does "sleek cows" mean that the cows are shining? (real welfare state cows?) Does uneven grass mean that some leaves are tall and some are short or does it mean that the grass is rough? Do the cows fly, like aeroplanes or birds, or are they simply running in the sky direction? You see how complicated your poems are, you need a real professor Richards to give lectures about you for months.

Love and peace

Tomas

Västerås 29 3 [1973]

Dear Robert,

I don't know why the title of the Martinson poem is "Namnlöst." Maybe he could not give a name to the poem so he simply called it "Without Name." "Sung" is Chinese, not Swedish. It means "Sung." "Modern Lyrik" means "Modern Poetry." The title of my lightswitch poem is still "Further in"—"Längre in"—I hope to find a better name before the book is published.

The translations of Ingegerd Friberg are not bad. Her fault is that she is too close to the English text—she does not dare to let go—naturally, she is humble. As a good woman she does not know that the name for "firebombs" in Swedish is "brandbomber," not "eldbomber." "Nedhangande grenar gin platsen låg"—is bad word-by-word translation—Gustafsson is better here. "Eremilën" and "Att se in i ett amibile" are good translations. The poem about walking in the woods and the November birch is not bad in Swedish but I think I can do it still better. May I? You will see it in my next letter.

I was hypnotized yesterday. I am not a "deep trancer"—sorry to say—but I can become one probably. The state of mind was fine anyhow and I felt happy afterwards.

I got the Hawaiian magazine. Fine! This young Minnesota poet is good—Louis Jenkins—one of your best pupils. Did I meet him?

It is evening. I am rather satisfied and extremely stupid. Have you ever gotten such a stupid letter from me? My IQ is 78. Good night.

Monica is doing something in the kitchen. The dog is growing and growing. Be careful! Hope to see you soon. Your old 1-2-6 (ectomorph)

friend   Tomas T.

29 March, '73

Dear Tomas,

O wonderful! A chance to talk about my own poem . . . it has five layers, three of which you should avoid, they have caused temporary or permanent insanity in all the readers who have ventured into them, their shoes are later found in ditches many miles from their homes, in the hospital, their noses retain scratch marks for many weeks . . .

"Sleek cows" . . . like cows in Denmark, they are fat, and terribly self-satisfied . . . their skin may shine a little from sheer good health but they are not spiritual beings at all . . . just well-fed and well-cared-for cows . . . I don't know why they're in the poem. Maybe Samson has just thrown them! I doubt that, he was crazy about jawbones of asses, that was his thing . . . In any case, they fly across the huge midwestern sky like enormous passenger airplanes, crossing in front of you from east to west.

"So much of women" . . . I wrote this poem as it was, on a walk in the ditch just west of our house one spring . . . so you have to imagine the long natural grasses that grow in the ditches around there. Eventually some fool farmer comes and cuts them, but this was early enough in the summer or spring so that no one had cut the grass yet, and it was wonderfully thick, around my ankles. So I wanted to end with the mood of that grass, which was so un-super-ego, so un-welfare-state, so un-Nixon. At first the line was "so much richness / in this long ditch grass." No doubt "so much darkness / in the long uncut grass" came in then "so much of the future / in this long ditch grass" . . . but none of them were right. Then I decided that by "the future" what I meant or hoped for was that I would come closer to my own feminine soul . . . and that closely cut lawns must be like crew-cuts on men, and uncut grass is like the long hair of women . . . so it finally settled down, after about a year, to "So much of women

in this uneven grass."

You can still use "long ditch grass," or "uncut grass," or "grass never cut" . . . whatever will make the image clear.

In the original the "dissatisfactions," which are also dissatisfactions the poet has with his own (overly masculine) psyche, or with his present life, are in the plural. The architects are insane, from too much planning no doubt, and are trying to build their buildings from the top floor down, the tails (on invisible animals) are approximately three kilometers long . . . it's just important to have many confident syllables there:

mad architects, two-mile-long tails . . . almost every one of the syllables in that line receives emphasis and a long-seeming vowel . . .

Göteborg sounds horrible. I'll punish them by sending Mark Strand there to read.

Love, Robert

5 May, '73

Dear Tomas,

I am in an airplane on the way to Honolulu! I was supposed to meet Voznesensky here tomorrow, but the Russians decided not to let him come, after he wrote several naughty poems you've probably heard about . . . pulling the ears of bureaucrats and talking of his trips to the U.S. I've just done a few other readings to clear up debts, including a reading last Tuesday at the Donnell Library, where I found many of your fans . . . I read them the new "We got ready and showed our home" poem of yours. The audience clapped so long after the first stanza that I almost decided to give up reading poems of yours at all, and clapped after every
[Editor's note: Some text is missing here.]
a version of the November Birch poem has come, but I don't have it with me, for some reason. So I'll just make a few foolish generalizations. The

poem was written up in Northern Minnesota, where one feels the land much less *used or conquered* by human beings. The spirit finds that exhilarating. I think I used the word "obedient" to describe the farm land around Madison, which I was about to go back to. The farm land is like a cowed schoolboy, who has had all the rebelliousness crushed out of him, no doubt by administrators and psychological counselors.

I know "sodden body" is difficult, but it's related to the poem "Suffocation" in *The Light Around the Body,* when the psyche becomes wholly filled with "worldly" detail, the body grows thick and sodden (as in the opening lines of "Hair"). "Sodden" is used to describe a washrag, for example, so soaked with dirty water that if you lifted it, the water would drip out. It is also used, oddly, to describe a man totally drunk in Ireland. It is then a term of contempt. So it suggests weight, grossness (like John Mitchell's face), an utter absence of the spirit.

A rumor is going around the U.S., started by me, that Harry Martinson is your spiritual father. In fact last week when the *Nation* printed two of my Martinson translations, he was simply identified in the contributors' notes in one sentence as "Tomas Tranströmer's spiritual forefather." That seemed to the *Nation* sufficient justification for his existence, I guess.

Watergate is having powerful impact here, possible only in a nation where the people are becoming rapidly infantilized, and have given over decisions on what is right and wrong to Daddy—how furious they are to have the decisions handed back again!

It means that next time we'll elect a *mother*—look for a Presidential candidate who is a stomach type—he will win.

Write soon.

The Jeane Dixon of Madison
Minnesota
Robert

Västerås 29-6-73

Dear Robert,

here are 2 pictures of the late Mr Trans . . . pardon, here are 2 l a t e pictures of Mr Tranströmer, the Swedish Bard.

I want *to have them back* after they have been used by Beacon Press. It was difficult to get them.

You will get 100 dollars from Författarförlaget soon. Don't complain, it is not my fault that the American economy has been handled so badly that 100 dollars are not worth much today.

From now on my address will be

Gatan, 13038 Runmarö Sweden

The summer started with fantastic sunshine, Sweden was—as the previous year—one of the hottest places in Europe. This week I have been working still in Västerås, with the family safe on the Island. For the first time since the early sixties I have no serious problem to live with and I hope that will be a good position for writing something. What a pity that you can't live on the Island too, this summer!

Hope to hear from you soon.

Love

Tomas

P.S. Do you think it is necessary to *write* to Harper's and Wesleyan? Could you not simply give the permission for publishing? Suppose they say NO. We will publish the poems anyway.

4 July '73

Dear Monica and Tomas,

I told Carol all the details of my visit with you, and she was properly impressed with all the work we did, and all the goodies we managed to eat up, and the walk into the suburban wildness, where there are always fingers of foreigners poking from the ground, asking for a bed. I had such a good time with you all . . . thank you for it. Stockholm seemed very prosaic afterward, and James Tate seemed to be suffering stomach pains from having eaten some huge canary—Gunnar Harding is still hungry, but I noticed some feathers around his mouth. I went into the washroom, and carefully brushed mine off . . .

I've been studying your fruit-poem, though I disappear into a vast abyss each time I come to Salamo . . . perhaps it's the name of one of the new Italian works in Västerås . . .

Carol has sold her story to *New American Review*—that's like being invited to visit the Pope—and is likely to be paid $600 for it!!!!!!! The children's interest in my poetry is fading now—

Love
Robert

Västerås 18-8-73
Dear Robert,

You will have some more money from this rich country soon, the fee for your poems in Författarförlagets Tranströmer book *Stigar*, but it will be only half of the *Dagens Nyheter* fee—there must be *some* difference between the honorable publishing in a Newspaper and the more humble appearance in a Book (as there is a difference in status between a big guy who writes journalism and a small guy who is a poet)! Your poems in *Stigar* are: Ensamhet om natten i skogarna, Sex vinterdikter i avskildhet, Promenad på dikesrenen, Gräver efter mask, På Mauis klipper. Or shorter: *Six winter poems late at night about digging worms in the spring ditches of Maui.*

I read the whole book for a small audience (mostly middle aged ladies of both sexes) in Leksand, Dalecarlia, in July and after the reading I asked if they wanted to hear some poems once again. Well, what happened was that they asked for your poems "I want to hear this winter poem by this wonderful American . . ." etc. So I am trained now in reading your poems (without trying to do a choreographic interpretation of the black crab).

Economy is bad and I am looking forward to the money from Beacon Press. What has happened there? Have Martinson and the widow of Ekelöf agreed? Except for the economy everything is fine, Monica and the children are in good spirits, have recovered from the winter hardships. I have written about 75 lines of *Östersjöar* and sketched about 100 (I can see no end of it) and I could have done more if the weather had not been so good—a fantastic summer heat has paralyzed the brain often.

The house of my mother-in-law at Runmarö will be empty 10 days in June next summer and you can all live there free of cost if you like. We would all be happy if you could.

My visit to the U.S.A. next year will start in Tucson at February 25. It will probably end one month later in Canada (London, Ontario—Steven Osterlund's place). In between—do you think there are some nice audiences in New Mexico or Nevada?

Love to you all. I am eagerly waiting for reports about how you are.

Tomas

18 Sept, '73

Dear Tomas,

I thought you'd like to see the sort of letters your strange countrymen write to total strangers . . . I'm sending you a copy of *Some,* a good new magazine . . . and a little poem of mine enclosed . . . I'm typing up some new ones . . . one about a moth is passable . . . the rest . . . Don Hall has written an article on *Sleepers* in which he says I'm the most "systematic" poet in the U.S.—Snyder is second—that's a stomach type . . . whatever has a skeleton they find to be too masculine, over-reachers—We have a pony here who is a perfect stomach type—his name is terrific for that— PEANUTS—he is only quarrelsome if he hasn't just eaten—his back is so wide and broad you don't know where to put the saddle—that's probably a secret of stomach types—was Don Quixote a pure nervous system type?—his horse too . . . I'm babysitting Micah, he is the sweetest child I have ever seen, even among my own huge brood! Love to Monica—What a good time I had there at her table.

Love

Robert

Lying in a Boat, Troubled

I listen to the hull cut through the water,
water hitting the hull
and being thrown back!
The sound
is the snow falling,
the path down the mountain being slowly obscured.

1974

Dear Tomas,

I've been doing some work on your tour, and things look well! I'll write you tomorrow with the new dates. It looks roughly this way—

Week of Feb 24 [*sic*]—Tucson etc.
                  (through the desert to:)
Week of Feb 3—California!!
Week of Feb 10th—Midwest; Wisconsin\
                etc.—at the end of this
                week to
Week of Feb 17th—MADISON, MINN!
                one or two readings around here
                then east
Feb 25th—Toronto, Ontario.

I'm enclosing several missives, self-explanatory, and a version of the kamikaze poem. Please comment on errors of fact, tone, and taste!

Field wrote me that you had sent them some bad translations by "your Scottish friend," so I tried to rescue them from their dilemma (my solution is always the same) by sending them "Sentry Duty," "Further In," "Elegy," and the kamikaze poem.

Robin Fulton's translation of *Baltics V* is readable, but curiously pale, like someone who has been in a hospital for months with pneumonia or gall bladder trouble—even the hair on the old bull has turned gray— the sea winds move feebly about the cemetery stones, pausing to rest often—

I will close now—a kiss to Monica! A hug for your two sweet girls—

Love
Robert

Västerås 13-2-74

Dear Robert,

I hope you had my emergency message—sent to Mr Galin in New York. The content was: there is no third week in February. I have to be back around 15–16 of February. I have so far heard nothing from the man in Canada so this part can be neglected. And I am so grateful for California. I will—if I don't get another message—buy a ticket: Stockholm-New York-Albuquerque-Tucson-Los Angeles-Cleveland-Minneapolis (or Sioux Falls?)-New York-Stockholm. If I buy it in Sweden I get a 25% discount. Los Angeles can probably be changed to San Francisco without much cost in the U.S., if it is that part of California you are preparing for me.

I will call you from New York (probably one hour after you have this letter).

XXX

Here is such a mess. I am impossible. I cannot find your letter with the "Along the Lines" translation! But I remember it well. The good thing with your translations is that I always meet again the original emotion I felt just when the poem started. Other translators give a (pale) reproduction of the finished poem but you bring me back to the original experience. I like it tremendously. What I am against is that you translate the "words of love" with "word" (singular), I insist that it should be plural. Also I am against stanza 2, the 2 last lines of it. If I am turning my shoulders, but still sitting there, I will be more and more like a corkscrew.

Why not simply "turning slowly"? —I need your translations of the latest poems very much, I have only first versions of some of them—I think you took them back to polish for Beacon Press. What I need is especially: "Looking through the Ground," "Sentry Duty," "Along the Lines," and the rushingwaterpoem with the car graveyard. (Please type them and send me quickly or I'll have to read the Fulton versions!!) ("Headlong, headlong waters" etc.) Type them and send them to Lois Shelton in Tucson. In Albuquerque I have the mad idea to read "Baltics" (exoticism), but not in Fulton's translation but in Sam Charters's (a pupil of Charles Olson!), which you have not seen, and not (yet) condemned. Sam Charters is a good man and he has smelled some sea winds.

They read "6 winter privacy poems" recently on the Swedish radio as "dagens dikt." I was paid 117 crowns for the translation. Did you get anything?

XXX

I am sorry you have to type so much. It is awful to type. But what can I do without the texts?

XXX

Solzhenitsyn just landed in Frankfurt.

Goodbye, auf wiedersehen, love
Tomas

12 March, '74

Dear Tomas,

It was a great joy to see you as always! I did regret that, pressed by circumstances neither of us could control, constant conviviality kept us from the muskrats and what other small fallen creatures this flatland affords. After you left, I laughed and laughed to think of all the Jungian fanaticism you had been subjected to in just two or three days—this fanaticism in changing everyone *is* American, but perhaps when it starts to broaden to Jung, it's going too far! At least half of what I said was absurd, so please do forgive me, forgive all of us—the Sitting Bulls of psychology.

Biddy made a Raggedy Ann for Paula or Emma, and is mailing that tomorrow. We're still reading *Miss Jane Pittman,* to open mouths.

Ruth says that she thinks that in your Baltics poem you are moving in the right direction—I guess broadening the view back toward ancestors—and that since the island belongs to the area of the Mother—or of your mother—you have to walk carefully.

Tell me what other adventures you have had!

Love from us
all and a hug—
Robert

New York 15-3 [1974]

Dear Robert,

a few last words before I take off from that other continent. Thank you for your letter! Everything went fine in Ohio—for me, but not for the people around me. Stuart Friebert got the flu and Tom Lux, who replaced him, yes, his *lungs* collapsed so he had to be taken to a hospital. In Ada no one was sick. When arriving in N.Y. I was supposed to meet Jim Wright and Michael Benedikt. Both were ready but—alas—Jim Wright got suddenly "dizzy" and had to go to bed before seeing me. Now we waited for Michael. He was coming on a bus from Connecticut. But I did not see him either. He got sick on the bus and had to go to bed immediately. So I bring plague to everybody. As soon as I am in the neighborhood people turn sick. I hope you and your family are well. I feel like a poltergeist, but very healthy.

Carl Gustav Jung sends his best and reminds you that because intuition is my strongest side I should write poetry with my fact-grasping part, e.g. collecting more dull facts for Baltics and trying to make the poem still more *flat*. I will try to do that in Part VI.

Love to you all and grateful hugs
from Tomas

15 March, '74

Dear Tomas,

That's strange—Jung had the same effect upon people. Freud fainted once when he was with Jung . . . it sounds as if in this over suggestible country they start fainting as soon as you enter the *city*. First Jim Wright falls over, dreaming you are his father, then Michael Benedikt collapses in the aisle of a bus, convinced he is irretrievably an orphan.

I'm enclosing a brochure, showing where—according to Daniela herself—(an old girlfriend of John Logan's and Bill Knott's)—the Great Mother essay in *Sleepers* is now leading innocent and suggestible feminists. This ought to cheer Lars Forssell up.

Do write.
Love,
Robert

30 March, '74

Dear Tomas,

I hope you are well there! Spring still hasn't come here—and it looks exactly the same as when you were here! I am still working on the same poem, too, so nothing has changed!

A new APR has come out, with a continuation of my Jung brainwashing (archetype-implanting, we call it) and I've torn out a copy to enclose. The rest of the issue, which includes a letter from Louis Simpson claiming he is not a thinking type at all, but, I gather, some sort of universal man, like Goethe, I've sent on by ship mail. I'm going out tomorrow on a 10 day trip, including Kenyon, where the undergraduates talk of the Great Mother a lot, and yet when you listen to them, she seems indistinguishable from the reason! Of course, I must go and straighten them out—with my beak and a cawkle.

I enclose the gruesome news from the telephone company—but this is all of it. Next time I'll do it by letter!!

Love,
Robert

Västerås 30th of April -74

Dear Robert,

I should not write to you now because my thinking function is very weak here, the day after the leaves really came out. It is good, ecstatic spring weather. Monica is preparing a gigantic party—the first for many years. The good mood from the U.S.A. trip is still left. That usually happens: the first 2 weeks after returning I float like a balloon, and then the balloon loses air and eventually I drop, slowly, into the mess of everyday duties, the Swedish cultural politics etc. But this time was different. We went to Madeira, for the first time since 1959 we were together alone in a new place for a whole week. Monica had had a tough time during February–March and she recovered completely on this fantastic island, I started to write and read books. We were completely irresponsible.

Many many thanks for the book of seal poems, it comes in the right moment when I am hungry for good *prose*. I also had the 2 Danish pamphlets. The translations look reasonable.

A rumor says that Lars-Olof Franzén from *Dagens Nyheter* wants to visit you. If he arrives, don't forget to sing the hymns before meals! Give him the full Jungian/Lutheran treatment!

Your community/network discussions in APR are very interesting and with a better thinking function (which will appear in a few days) I will say something about it. I have recommended the book to my colleagues here in the office—I think the ideas are relevant for Sweden too, and not especially for writers and artists but for vast areas of our society. It is a great thing that you have this column in APR. As soon as you happen to read a book that really makes an impression on you, you start to feed the audience with the stuff, like feeding a baby with a spoon.

Love to everybody in the Bly farm.

Tomas

16 July, '74

Dear Tomas,

I'm so glad to hear from you! I was afraid that as soon as you got back to Sweden, you had called in friends, poets and reporters and said, "I now have definite proof that Robert Bly is a Jungian!" (Gasps of horror.) (I have heard that Jung is hated in Europe by amazingly large masses of people.) And you would follow that with a declaration: "I am never going to write to Robert Bly again!" (Loud cheers from assembled Swedes.) "Every time he mentioned with favor a horned animal, such as a moose, he was really talking of Jung." (Cheers "Good job of detective work. Those fellas are subtle, etc.")

I've been reading Jung since an early age, and rehabilitation is difficult now. As Khrushchev said, "Only the grave can cure a hunchback!"

Around here it is hot summer, no islands, no delicious paths through high trees, no swims in the Baltic, no rowboats among the duck utopias. I am learning to play a dulcimer, and Bill Holm comes once in a while with his clavichord in the trunk, and we all have a lovely time then.

Jim Wright committed himself to a hospital for four days, and is determined to end his drinking; John Crowe Ransom died last week, quietly, in his sleep. Ingegerd Friberg (the one who is doing a thesis on my poems in Göteborg), much buoyed up by that *Dagens Nyheter* article by Lundqvist—(I sounded there like a bull elephant, who was a "special friend" of the Mother's—imagining I am an elephant, of course, I liked it)—she brought me a Lapp drinking cup. Don Hall, the stomach type, is writing poems about going to bed with skeletons and things—I don't understand that.

That's all the literary news! At my shack I have your new poem, which I like—do <u>not</u> leave out the "crystallizing" line! It is very interesting, and necessary. I think I'll try to translate the poem—it will probably end up set in Iceland, since my Swedish dictionary is not there!

Love to you all,

Robert

18 Aug, '74

Dear Tomas,

I'm sending along a letter proving that there was one person at least alive in our audience in St. Cloud this spring! It's a very gloomy day here— late August, the grass has nearly given up, little rain, the farmers are crabby at supper time, the tractors break down, the farmers' sons ruin the engines of their $200 cars by racing to the nearby towns, where the girls have their hair in curlers, getting ready to go to the State Fair. Then they get there, and think the boys are vulgar, and rabbits come in and eat all the flowers in the old ladies' gardens overnight. That is what it is like around here. I'm about to go up on the belfry of my old schoolhouse with a book and stay there—no one can find me there, because this being a Protestant country, no one ever looks up!

We do have gypsies here, real ones, and I was once invited to join a band of them—but I knew I would pick the wrong girl and get knifed—

Do write.

Love, Robert

Västerås 22-8-74
Dear Robert,

back again in Västerås after a rainy and cold summer—but I enjoyed it, oh I needed it, and we must go back to Runmarö for a couple of days soon. I completed *Östersjöar* (bad for you Jungians!) and the whole pile will be published by Bonniers in October.

Gunnar will publish one of your APR columns in *Lyrikvännen* and that could give Jung a push forward among your fans here in Sweden. I think his underground position so to say is strong—his books are always borrowed in the libraries, but in the Office Intellectual Sweden he is probably not highly valued—the Junta favors a strange combination of Freud and Marx.*

---

*Jag gillar Jung, tvivla inte på det.

So you are tempting me with the South again. I would love to visit the U.S.A. and I can do it in autumn 75, not in the spring. In the spring I have to stay here and work hard at the office to pay my delayed taxes. But let us do a reading in New York or elsewhere under the supervision of Betty Kray. I think Carleton College in Minnesota will have me too—the nice reviewer in *Carleton Miscellany* wrote me and gave a half-invitation. Don't use the telephone any more, I can write postcards in advance, we have plenty of time.

Another of your fads, the brain-philosophy, had a fantastic confirmation lately—the last months of President Nixon, the reptile brain *fighting long after the battle was lost.* The whole tape story also has something to do with reptile thinking, the need to *roll up,* to protect oneself with winding things. Sam Charters and his wife were visiting us the day he left his President job, 5 pm Swedish time, we were sitting drinking beer outside the shop in Södersunda village, the sun was shining, they looked very pleased, they wanted to see him in jail—I don't want to, I have no real explanation for that, maybe I suspect putting him in jail would be too easy a way to get rid of the really sad fact: that the fellow was elected by YOU, the People, by a landslide victory. I think everyone who voted for him should go to jail for three minutes (of silence) instead.

I have come close to Frida, our dog, this summer. She is absolutely 100% mammal brain, there is not a single atom of other brains in her. The rest of the family is a mixture, as before.

You ask about the photo for the Beacon Press book. I think *there is a stamp on the back of the photo* with the name and address of the woman who took the picture—I don't remember her name but she is nice and married to the poet Walter Höllerer in Berlin. She is definitely not Hungarian.

Love to everybody in Odin House!

Tomas

3 Sept, '74

Dear Tomas,

OK, let's agree on October of 75!! Betty Kray wants us to read together in N.Y. and then you can read in So Carolina for that strange person called GUS SUCCUP. I will avoid the telephone, and pass along to you—by fish express—any hints I hear of places looking for a Nixon sympathizer. I love your idea that everyone who voted for him should go to prison for 3 minutes. The prison would be full of feeling types and sensation types—the intuitive types would be standing around outside smiling.

We're all well here. Carol is working hard on her project to get buses for old people. Ruth is about to get a job, she hopes, as a planner in a nearby town. Sam and Noah come home from school, and leap immediately on their aged ponies, who had hoped for a calm old age, and gallop off in several directions. The ponies usually get a revenge by running them through an apple tree on the way home—last night it was a plum tree. Noah arrived at the supper table all scratched up.

Love to you and Monica
and the girls,
Robert

P.S. I like the Danton poem. I expect it is about your father. Please help me with the waiting room at the end—is it a waiting room in a railway station? or a doctor's office? In what sense do the alleys *bend down* towards it? Is this a slum, or some sort of "gamle by"? It's a wonderful, strong poem.

16 Oct, '74

Dear Tomas,

I'm on the bus to Mpls, off on my first reading this year, to Texas. Last week I got a letter from a student, who said someone there in the physics dept wanted "to photograph my aura." That sounds wonderful, though I have the same fear as the native when the first white man wants to photograph his face. Also the man's name (the physicist) is not Dr. Dostrorski, or Dr. Jonathan Adamson, but JOE PIZZO. I must proceed carefully.

I sympathize with your problem vis-à-vis the Swedish Academy. Nothing is nicer than to be a cricket, living in the laundry chute. We don't have such a severe problem with these official positions in the U.S., because somehow, we produce a constantly hatching supply of Mark Strands, who fill all these positions with alacrity and satisfaction.

Anne Sexton committed suicide last week. She sat in her idling car in her garage, after having been divorced a few weeks before. Menninger in *Man Against Himself* mentions that many people find suicide too unconventional in its naked state, and so they embezzle money or get divorced in order to provide an acceptable excuse for the suicide.

The DEPRESSION mood continues in the U.S.—yesterday Macmillan fired 100 people; today the NFO farmers are shooting calves—the photograph shows a pure muscle type just about to push a calf into a grave-trench.

All the children are well. Your god-child has immense wings. Carol just got back from her two weeks in England. Ruth has a job for a greenhouse, laying sod (rolled up grass) along a freeway, for $5.25 an hour. She lives in a tent, and is gone all week. Before that, she worked for a greenhouse in Montevideo, doing similar physical work, very hard work, for $1.85 an hour, and found the men and boys were getting $2.45 an hour for the same work. So she told the boss off, much to the satisfaction of his wife, and quit. In her new job men and women are paid the same.

Thank you for the notes on "Citoyens." I must get some poems of yours ready, to satisfy the Tranströmer-freaks.

Now I'm in the airplane on my way to Houston—the stewardesses are awful.

Your friend,
Robert

4 Nov, '74

Dear Tomas,

Emergency! Disaster! HELP!

Ingegerd Friberg, the sweet maternal Swedish lady who offered to read the proofs of the Swedish text of *Martinson, Ekelöf and Tranströmer* has found a matter in the "African Diary" poem that needs ATTENTION.

My line reads:

"Those who are ahead have a long way to go."

She says it should read:

"Those who have arrived have a long way to go."

"Arrived" makes the line a little tinny in English, but if it is truly accurate, and the other not accurate to the Swedish, we must do something. So tell me, Wolfgang, shall we change it or leave it?

ZER ISS NO TIME TO VASTE!

Pressed by Father Time

On the train Västerås-Göteborg 13-11-74.

Dear Robert,

I have never been so busy in my life—I am transported from my office to a reading and then back, and then for a meeting, and then to a patient, and then to a reading etc. . . . I will tell you the whole story as soon as this rush is over.

But the emergency . . . Well, strictly linguistically both you and the Lady are right. "Framme" could mean both "Framme-vid-måle" and "Framme-i-täten." But 90% of the Swedish readers would choose the first version. So she has her point. I think I meant that too—the one who has arrived at the goal (independence etc.) still has a long way to go. But your version has more of the *character* of the Swedish line. So I don't know what to say. HELP! Is there a 3rd possibility? "The one who has got there"—It should be clear that the one who has arrived is not the tourist . . . Many problems. If you decide to keep your version I will not blame you but remain always your true friend, supporter, parasite.

Tomas

24 Nov, '74

Dear Tomas,

I trust that you and Monica and the girls are well. Here everything is slanting down toward the waiting-room of THE DEPRESSION— Macmillan fired 150 people the other day, the mayor of N.Y. laid off 1500. I was just in New York, and saw Jim Wright. He has been off the booze since June, and he seems frail, and with such a low energy level, as if he had turned into his own father. I understand that in a couple of years, his energy level will go back up again, and he'll become the son of that father again—but now it is hard for him. He'd enjoy a note from you, I know (in case you have nothing to do), his address is now 529 East 85th St., N.Y. 10028. My father and mother are well, though both frail.

I've been reading your "Allegro" and "Scattered Congregation" on my (last) week of N.Y. readings with great success. I decided to leave "those who are ahead" as it was. Why rock a verbal boat? I wonder if nouns are on the left side of the body, and verbs on the right—or is it the other way around? Who is more like a verb, a man or a woman?

Let me know if Swedish literature improves as a result of my Jung essay in "The Poet's Friend"—or is it "The Poem's Friend"?

> This missive from your friend,
> Robert

Västerås Christmas Day -74
Dear Robert,

I have not been writing for a long time, involved in too many robot-like activities and longing for peace and time to write poems, letters, decent things. It looks dark. I am almost broke (financially) because of the threatening unpaid TAXES. As soon as you have read this, forget it. I am ashamed of talking about it. When we meet in the autumn I hope all this is over and I will be "In the clear" (May Swenson).

The book *Ostersjöar* was well-received by most critics*—I send you a page from a Göteborg paper where they were generous enough to let 2 students review it. One of them is extremely enthusiastic. I met him afterwards, when reading in Göteborg and he—Torsten Rönnerstrand—turned out to be a real JUNGIAN and he loves you too!! (He will probably write to you sooner or later.) He was (mis)quoting you many times.

Your Jungian piece in *Lyrikvännen* has already got off-shoots here—I heard that the magazine has received a Swedish version where we are all nailed in different Jungian directions—can you imagine, Forssell, ME, Ekelöf etc. worked over again in this fashion. I hope they will publish it.

---

*There has been a wide range. One fellow in BLM thinks I am all worthless. Another—in *Gefle Dagblad*—shouts "GIVE HIM THE NOBEL PRIZE... And you [who have] not yet read this book, I envy you, the book will CHANGE YOUR LIFE." So far the sales have been 2,800 copies.

I will make a pause in this nice letter-writing now, must go home and have lunch with the girls and my mother-in-law who has prepared her famous LUTEFISK-GRATIN—an almost Norwegian dish.

xxxxx pause for food xxxxxx

The lutefisk was great. We eat it only at Christmas here in Sweden, but in Norway it is eaten around the year. (Maybe here too when the Norwegians take over Scandinavia—and the other oil sheiks the rest of Western Europe.)

[------]

The meaning of this letter is simply: Have a good 1975! Bless my godson and his family.

From your friend

Tomas

1975

Västerås 4-2-75

Dear Robert,

very nice to have a message from you! We live here in a period of
waiting. I am working a lot at the office—many of my fellow psycholo-
gists have become pregnant (not because of my working here) and there
are many gaps to fill, my half-time job covers most of the week. I am also
busy with readings (see e.g. a clip from a local paper, full of misunder-
standings). I am simply trying to pay my delayed taxes and the waiting
is for the Västerås Grant which can save us all (15,000 Sw. crowns)—Lars
Gustafsson, who is a member of the Cultural Advisory Board of Västerås
has given a speech in favor of me (he is really a friend), describing me
as an international figure—after hearing him another member, choked up,
phoned me immediately begging me to read poems at an exhibition of
his wife's probably bad paintings which I refused, arrogant as I am, and
Monica is working in the Child Psychiatry department of the hospital
where she is attacked by small meter-high 10-year-old experts in karate, I
repeat, Monica has an interesting time but I see too little of her so if we
get the 15,000 I will kidnap her for a week or so and fly to the South with
her, with all taxes paid and a good conscience.

I have half a dozen unfinished poems and only two "finished." The first is
embarrassingly small and goes like this:

Hemåt

Ett telefonsamtal ran ut i natten och glittrade på landsbygden och i
förstäderna.
Efteråt sov jag oroligt i hotellsängen.
Jag liknade nålen i en kompass som orienteringslöparen bär genom
skogen med bultande hjärta.

And the other one is on the next page. The Swedish word "torp" is loaded
with old associations, means "a crofter's cottage" (or is it simply "croft"?).

I, and Harding, and Forssell and Lars G. are invited to the Cambridge
Poetry Festival in April. Do you have any big brotherly advice to give? I
will write soon.

Your friend   Tomas

18 Feb, 75

Dear Tomas,

This is just a note to say hello! I've been using your poems in an as-
trology class—I can see the flickers of horror running up and down your
spine—as examples of the well-developed Aries, who has overcome the
fear of the unconscious that plagued that other Aries, Frost.

It's time too for your regular fan letter from hysterical American po-
etry readers, this one aggressive with flowers, and pugnacious ferns—

Martin Booth sent me your "Citoyens" in Fulton's translation, which
is not bad. Mine will be a little more Magritte-like.

I'm in the north woods, looking out at a Norway Pine, and a frozen
lake—spending a couple of days circling slowly around a rowboat I found
pulled up on the shore . . . This is not the roof of the world, however, only
the attic floor—snow drifted in through the window . . .

Don Hall sent me a poem—a dithyramb—celebrating in 8 stanzas the virtues of 22 different sorts of cheese—some compared to small dogs, others to cathedrals. I said it was light verse, and a deplorable occupation for a man 44 years old. He is furious, and says it is a deep poem, and that "for you to dismiss it as light verse about cheese is simply nasty, insensitive, ridiculous, grumpy, pig-headed, thoughtless, wicked, and wholly dismissive."

I should have listened to Sheldon!

> Your friend (I was fasting
> the day I wrote him)
> 444 Robert

12 March, 75

Dear Tomas,

This is the first review of our book—a pre-publication review. I don't know why these people always assume Ekelöf is a Russian, and you are a sea pilot—but so it goes!

Your check for the book should be arriving any day—Beacon is sending them to Svensson.

At the Cambridge Poetry Festival, ignore the poets and go to see Joseph Needham, who has written the great book on the history of science in China. It is a great book. He also belongs to the eccentric Episcopal Church in Thaxted (about 30 miles so. of Cambridge) which Carol loves so much. I've never met him, but I want to.

Here is a clumsy version of the short poem, just for you to look at and exclaim over the stupidity of the educated classes, now that it's starting to . . .

> Toward Home?

Homeward

A telephone call ran out into the night
   and shone there over the villages
     and the suburbs.

Afterwards I slept restlessly in the hotel bed.
I resembled the needle in a compass
    that the cross country runner
        on ahead carries with thumping
            heart through the woods.

Questions: Toward Home?
            Call or conversation?
            Does it give off light or only glitter?
            Is there motion after "rann" or does the
                conversation just hang in the sky like a star?
            Why the difference between "pa" and "i"?
            Is it a runner or a skier?

Jim Wright has stopped drinking, at last. He is exhausted, but well. Betty
Kray is expecting both of us (you and me) at the Donnell in the Fall.
    Copies of *Friends* should be on their way to you by ship from Beacon.
I love that "skalbagge"!!!!!
    All's well here. We think of you often. Don't work so hard. After we're
dead, the world will get on well without us.
                            Fondly,
                                Robert with his family

Västerås 31-3-75
Dear Maestro,
        the family is now recovering from a 5-day shock. Paula, who is
now 10 and has long legs, got (I must look in the dictionary) she got THE
MUMPS, which does not sound too frightening, but following that she
had (must look in the dictionary) she had MENINGITIS, violently, and
I think she was in the neighborhood of the Västerås record for high tem-
perature. She had 40.6 (Cel) when she was not too ill and must have had
41 when she was really bad. The turning point was last evening when she
suddenly returned to life again and today she has started to eat small

pieces of fruit etc. and draw very large pictures—but now she is sleeping calmly . . . So I am in a state of stupid euphoria and talking, eating, reading and driving the car at the same time.

Very nice of you to take care of my 3-line poem! I will give the background. I am away from home (but in Sweden), probably in Värmland, and making a telephone call home to Monica. It is about 10 o'clock in the evening. It is a good telephone call, and I suddenly feel how our communication is leaking out into the surroundings, like a glittering river or something—it is not in the air but more on the ground so to say, like glittering ditches here and there. Or like a Milky Way stretched out in the landscape . . . I say *på* landsbygden and *i* förstäderna—the reason for having two different prepositions is the Swedish language which is the real kingdom, or bureaucracy, of prepositions, it is so complicated . . . You have to say *på* about landsbygd but *i* about förstäderna. I suppose in English you have *in* for both. So you could say "in the countryside and the suburbs," or maybe villages (or country fields) is better, I leave it to you. (But not "over.") The cross-country runner is OK, he is not on skies. What do you mean with "on ahead," that is something extra. It is good if it means "on his way" or something, it is wrong if it means that the fellow is leading the running— the competition aspect should not be stressed. This rather romantic, solitary sport is very popular in Sweden. I should add something about the word "landsbygden." The dictionary translation is "countryside"—if the content is the same in both languages I don't know. "Landsbygden" is mostly used as a contrast to "städerna." "Vi på landsbygden har inte samma stress som ni i städerna" etc. It includes both the populated places, the houses etc. and the area around, so you see fields, hills, even woods together with houses when you hear the word. It is a calm word.

It must be refreshing for you to translate a poem of mine with no stones in it.

The Cambridge people have sent me a huge program and the address of a tutor at Christ's College who will keep me "in his spare room." His

name is Mr BUTT. Forssell, I, Harding and Lars G. are reading to-
gether in a Swedish corner. The program is full of for me unknown names
(Englishmen) and also your name, Ginsberg's, Creeley's. But you are not
there in person, only on a film. So they are repeating a previous poetry fes-
tival when you were filmed. In the next poetry festival they don't need the
poets at all, they can just show the films. Very rational.

I hope to meet our enthusiastic publisher Martin Booth. Do you really
mean that there are no interesting English poets at all? What a decline
since the days of John Donne! What a comfort to know that man does not
live of art only, also food is necessary, so I will stick to the Indian restau-
rants. Couldn't you ask Don Hall about some good addresses? In return I
could try to write some subtle poems about cheese. Like this:

> The Archbishop of Gorgonzola
> is giving a sermon today
> in his Cathedral.

Love to you all
Tomas

Runmarö 1-7-75
Dear Robert,
 marvellous gifts dropping from the mailbox yesterday . . . *Old Man
Rubbing* (with the I forgive you, please forgive me—poem at the end, I
have been longing to see it since the reading in 1974), Kabir, Ignatow and
APReview—your poem there immediately called me back to the old trans-
lation desk. I hear the translation trumpet blow again, it is a long time
since . . . Thanks, thanks from us and the island.
 I have been busy with writing a speech. It is completed now. I will de-
liver the speech at Verner von Heidenstam's grave on July 6th (his birthday).
For a moment the idea crossed your mind that a fundamental personality
change has happened to your old friend T.T. admit that! But that is not

true. What happened was that I got the so called Övralid-prize for 1975. Övralid is the place where Heidenstam lived for the last 20 years of his life. He died in 1940. Every year a writer, or scholar, is given 6,000 Sw. crowns. The prize winner has to show up at Övralid (in Östergötland) on Heidenstam's birthday, is met by a brass ensemble from a nearby Health resort, marches together with the 15 old ladies and gentlemen of the Övralid Foundation Board to the poet's tomb, where he (the prize winner) has to give a speech for 20 minutes about Verner von H. Then march to the memorial dinner—the dishes are decided by the corpse himself (salmon, chicken and strawberries).

I wrote to the Swedish Institute and asked for financial support—for the ticket from Sweden–N.Y. this autumn. Yesterday I got the answer: "For bureaucratic reasons I* cannot confirm, but act *as if* I had." ?? He wants to have some more details. I have made myself free from all obligations after Oct 15. When is our N.Y. reading? At the end of Oct. would be fine for me. What is the name and address of that place in North (or South?) Carolina you were planning for me the other year? Can I write to them myself? Don't use your telephone anymore! Don't darken my path with guilt feelings! Give the ladies and the little boys in the Bly human farm my love instead!

Tomas

(I have run out of ink! . . .)

6 Sept. 75

Dear Tomas,

Well, everyone around the U.S. read yesterday that you were a genius . . . The *NY Times Book Review* finally reviewed *Friends*—Helen Vendler reviewed about 12 books, massacring most of them, and saved

---

* Mr John Walldén.

you for the very end, telling American poets they should write like you. So organizing some more readings for you will be easy as duck soup, as of today!! I'll send you a copy of the review in the next letter.

Meanwhile, I need to know what dates you have accepted and what time you have free. I know you are reading for Frannie Quinn in Boston shortly after you arrive. Then we read together in N.Y. Oct 21st, and again on Oct 24th (a Friday) in Bucks County Pa. which is near New York.

Would you like to come out to Minnesota then, to be with us that weekend? or the next weekend? We won't let you get away without a visit to our fireplace and your godson!

I think you'd enjoy reading in Denver—and Peter Martin, who stopped by here the other day, can pay you $250 or $300 plus your air fare from Mpls—

How much more time do you have?

Did Davidson College in North Carolina write you?

It is time to settle all this!!

We are all awaiting your arrival, except of course for the other poets mentioned in the review that praised you, who will probably picket the Donnell Library and burn down the Volvo dealership . . .

Your friend,
Robert

P.S. I like the translation of the Snowbank poem—

"unattached" is a word which is used this way:

"Margaret is not married, she is unattached at the moment."

"Buddhism believes that we should live as far as possible unattached to ambition or society roles."

So the word carries the mood of Meister Eckhart—his "detachment" is close in meaning to "unattachment."

"It" is purposely left vague. You are right in leaving it so.

Fondly, R

8 Sept. 75

Dear Tomas,

A couple of questions on "Båten, Byn."

1. What is "Kolvattnet"?

2. This wave motion, is it being perceived moving across your vision or toward shore?

3. The patience and sadness—are they nouns added to the line giving the feeling of the village, or are the clothes washed in rage *and* patience *and* sadness?

4. Did the meeting break up, or was it broken up?

5. The soldiers guiding the Mercedes—doesn't that imply the speaker was a government man? If so then who "carried the loudspeaker away"?—With us, it was usually the police who did that to break up the rally!

6. Are those "platsidorna" the sides of the Mercedes? Yes, you idiot!

Fondly, your retarded friend,

Robert

12 Sept. 75

Dear Tomas,

Here it is in the *N.Y. Times*
BLESSING!!

Please do write soon—unlike me . . .

I am enclosing a copy of a translation about which you'll *have* to reply! I'll need some new translations to read at the Donnell!

Fondly,

Robert

Västerås 19-9-75

Dear Robert,

The same day 2 letters from you were humming friendly from the mailbox, I felt it already before I got home. 2 days later the "blessing" arrived—is it really that important what they write in the *N.Y. Times Book Review?* I thought Sweden was the country of Cultural Hierarchy. I hate to admit it but I was very glad to have this confirmation that your translations of me dazzle people over there. For ten minutes I felt like Greta Garbo and Björn Borg. Now back to normal. No, it is not normal. This autumn has blessed me with too many activities. I am a teacher, one or two days a week I drive to the University of Uppsala and give lectures in poetry writing to students, in a new experiment for Sweden, a course called "Skapande svenska." 20 persons, mostly ladies, overenthusiastic, flooding me with poems. Translations, questions, attacks and all—I have to put them in small groups of 5 to handle them. It is not academic at all. Last week I gave them for homework to *dream* and to write down their dreams as poems. "I have to go to bed now and do my lesson" one student said to another frightened academic teacher. I still don't believe in Creative Writing as an academic subject (for training people to become authors) but I think the ordinary university courses in Sweden are so dry and dead (e.g. in "Litteraturhistoria") that a wild creative thing is needed as a counter balance.

At the same time the Royal Swedish Stockholm opera boss phoned me and asked me to translate the libretto of Leoš Janáček's *Kátja Kabanová* into Swedish. I was persuaded and found out that that commission was the most funny (and also well-paid) thing I have been ordered to do for years. The opera will be staged next autumn, directed by an East German Demon director. The idea to cooperate with hysterical primadonnas, Demon directors, angry conductors, greedy opera bosses, musicians etc. is exhilarating. And at the same time people went ill in my psychology office so I had to work more there too. Too much, too much. The little U.S. trip will be a good relaxation. And now the schedule for the trip:

I will arrive directly to Boston around Oct 15–16. Two readings in New England. Then New York. I have written to Betty that I agree completely to the "two arias, one duet, plan." A rather structured reading there. We can do what we like in Bucks County on Oct 24th. I have confirmed the letter, writing to the lady what-was-her-name in Bucks County. I also have accepted a reading or two in Denver "in the last days of October." Around Nov 1st I go to Tucson and Phoenix (also confirmed). After that I will probably go to California and then back to Sweden from Seattle, where I have a permanent invitation from Birgitta Steene at the Swedish Department. So there will be a reading in Seattle for certain. After that the North Pole and Sweden. As you know I have a perverse longing for the South and if I get an invitation from there for a reading between Bucks County and Denver it will be difficult to resist. On the other hand I am longing to pester the Bly family again with a visit. I am thinking about you so often and even if we have many days together, you and I, you are not Carol and the godson . . . But it is far away, Madison . . . Anyhow the best time for a Madison visit is between Bucks County and Denver.

About California I don't know for certain. But Bert Meyers thinks he can arrange something for Berkeley maybe—because *Baltics* is printed there (just now). I will *not* read in San Francisco this time—the place is overfed with poets. The whole trip will start around Oct 15 and end around Nov. 8.

Comments about the translations will come very soon.

Love

Tomas

Västerås Sept 21, [1975]
Dear Robert,
    a couple of answers on "The Boat The Village."

"Kölvattnet" is the water, the waves, behind a moving boat. The waves from the boat are going in a fan pattern. My dictionary has the word "wash" for that. I can see translation problems piling up here because in the next stanza you have real washing going on: a village where people are washing clothes etc. So it is unlucky that it is the same word. Maybe there is another word in the U.S.A. for "kölvatten," something like "track waves" or so. Here the boat is not going too fast but sufficiently fast for leaving visible waves which are rolling back or uncoiling the Atlantic . . .

In that village you see women washing and washing, on the beach, by the small streams etc. . . . The act of washing, the movements of the arms, the expressions etc. are at the same time aggressive ("in rage"), patient ("in patience") and also—at least in some of the washers—have a melancholy character. It has been going on for centuries. The Swedish word "vemod" is rather difficult to translate. It is a *tender sadness*. It is a very mild melancholia. I think the Portuguese word "saudade" is very close to it. The sadness of a roe-deer.

"Ett möte som skingrades" . . . the Swedish here can mean both that the meeting was breaking up or was broken up by the authorities. I don't know what would be most accurate. I arrived just when the meeting was finished. I asked what it was about. It was rather confusing but I am almost sure that it was a strike meeting and that an official man, from the government, had been sent to the meeting to persuade the fishermen to go back to work. At that time—as now—the military men were the strong ones. Soldiers (in berets and camouflage-spotted uniforms) were escorting the government man (who was in civilian clothes, sitting there, stiff, looking straight forward, inside his Mercedes after the speech) while the people around were shouting the last arguments against the steel sides of the car. The meeting broke up but there should be no atmosphere of terror in the scene. An atmosphere of disappointment, excitement, unsolved conflict (and also a trace of hope) but no terror. The Portuguese are *not brutal* if you compare them with Spaniards and South Americans. See how they handled the crisis this summer, it has been a civil war almost, but no blood shed . . .

Your old friend
Duck Soup Tommy

P.S. If you look at the stamp on this envelope you will see an old friend.

Västerås Oct 8 [1975]

Old Friend,

I can understand now why your telephone bills sometimes are piling up. The people who arrange readings are not good bureaucrats at all! Yesterday I got a telegram, a long expensive telegram from Phoenix, Arizona where two ladies asked for "confirmation" of a hopeless date (11 Nov), I should answer immediately. But they had forgotten to tell their addresses! Mr Martin from Denver still does not answer. The Georgia man has not written anything. Nothing from Boston. I know by hearsay that Mr Hawley (Oyez boss) is arranging something in Berkeley. I will write to him today. My answer to Phoenix was a telegram to Lois Shelton saying: ARIZONA READINGS POSSIBLE BETWEEN NOV 1 AND 6 TELL PHOENIX PLEASE BEST TOMAS . . . From the Swedish Institute I have confirmation that they will pay a ticket going from Boston-New York-Detroit-Atlanta-Denver-Tucson-Los Angeles-San Francisco-Seattle-home, so I will order that from the Travelers' Bureau here. Enough about this.

Here is a confessional poem about my crisis when I was 15.

May I propose a mixture of the 3 versions of "To Home" / "Homeward"?

A telephone call floated out into the night, and it glittered here and
    there among the fields and in the suburbs.
Then I slept restlessly in the hotel bed.
I was like the needle in the compass that the orienteer has along as
    he runs through the forest with chest thumping.

As you can see you wrote everything (in different versions) except for the word "orienteer" which is, I assume, the correct word. Because I saw in a magazine an article about that particular sport ORIENTEERING. It is from the beginning a Scandinavian sport, spreading out to England, Germany, Canada and in the last years also the U.S.A. It might be rather unknown still but in a couple of years every healthy student in the U.S. will be an orienteer. The need to *run* was clearly demonstrated last time I visited you when students were running naked through the colleges . . .

what was that called? "streaking" or something . . . Is that out of fashion nowadays?

LATE MAY sounds very well in general. The word "airpockets" must be wrong—according to my dictionary it means "turbulence." But what I mean is "life-jacket." Maybe too surrealistic . . . I see the blooming trees as swelling life-jackets (for me? for the trees?), we are safe, life is good after all etc. I think you could say "sweet, dirty May night"—I mean the air was polluted with gas etc. but at the same time a lovely May night, like a beautiful but unwashed girl. Thoughts go "far away" is the meaning. Solomon is there because of the Bible . . . Jesus said: look at the lilies of the valley, they don't work but not even Solomon in all his splendor was as beautiful as they are. I don't remember the exact words. So the blossoming fruit trees know that they are superior in beauty to Solomon, they laugh discreetly at his efforts . . . They bloom also in my tunnel (of depression, which is now disappearing). I need them (the trees) not in order to escape reality (to forget the troubles in the world etc) but to *remember* (to remember that basically there is something good in life, which is real . . .). The message is rather common. You don't have to think about flowers for the dead more than that the flowers of the dead mean the same thing: the corpse is there all right but the flowers tell you that Death does not have the last word. Did you get that message, Master? What a poem for a Sunday school teacher to translate!

About the citoyens Robespierre and Danton—let us sit together on a sofa in New York City and give them the treatment they deserve. Like we did in Runmarö once. I believe in that type of mutual translation.

    I will call you when I arrive in Connecticut. Monica sends her warmest.

Fondly
Tomas

I put some uncommon stamps on the envelope
Trains and planes if someone in the neighborhood is a collector.

Västerås Dec 10 [1975]

Dear Friend,

this is reportage from the Nobel Prize celebration. I am sitting in front of my TV looking at gloomy people coming and going . . . Kings and queens . . . (Where is your Montale article?—I am longing for it . . .) A professor is talking in English with a 100% Swedish accent . . . he is introducing Alfred Nobel (is Nobel going to have the Nobel Prize?) Look, there is Montale—he has a metal star on his coat, he looks dignified in a relaxed way, he will not faint . . . The professor is talking in Swedish now, he is extremely boring, let us talk about your Tranströmer translations instead. *Late May* sounds very good . . . you seem to insist on *"the tunnel where I am"*—if you really think this makes the poem better, OK. But you must be aware that people can misunderstand the situation, they might think I have moved from the town and into a railway tunnel (what the hell is the fellow doing there?). I still prefer "my tunnel."

(Now the orchestra is playing, the professor at last stopped. The conductor looks like an 80-year-old Leonard Bernstein . . . A new professor arrives, talks about molecules . . .)

"Citoyens" Great! The only word I want to rub out is "anyway" (line 3 from the end). Take it away. There are too many anyways in the world . . .

The physicists now get their prizes. Our playboy King smiles fatherly . . . A funny chemistry professor is introducing the prize winners in chemistry—the audience is laughing—what a disaster, no the professor cracked a joke . . . good—these celebrations get more and more relaxed . . . The prize winner has a good name: "professor Vladimir Prelog" . . . "Molecules again" . . . And now mr Montale is given a speech by the 91-year-old Anders Österling (his first book was published in 1902): "The Italian poet Eugenio Montale was born in the province of Liguuuurria . . ." he is shouting . . . Montale has tics now, around his mouth. "His Pegasus is an unquiet spirit that does not want to remain in the honorary stable . . ." Österling goes on and Montale's tics are now more frequent . . . the speech is slowing down, approaching its end . . . "Caro Signor Montale" . . . the victim is standing up now, his body is surprisingly thin, you did not expect that from his round Harpo Marx face, he walks with difficulty . . . and

NOW the King gives away the prize, Montale is saying something to the King, he is smiling, he looks pleased, relaxed again, no tics. Time for the economics prize—you will never get *that* prize Robert but you might get the literary one when you are 80! I will write soon,

Love Tomas

1976

21 Jan '76

Dear Tomas,

Help! An industrious extroverted muscle type named Eva Bruno, from Goteborg, informs me that she has translated all of *Sleepers Joining Hands,* and some weird firm with a Dutch rooster, called Coeckelbergh Förlag, wants to print it in April. She also translated Ted Hughes's *Crow.* Is she any good? What shall I do? This is probably May Swenson's Revenge, a melodrama. Eva Bruno sounds a little like Hitler's mistress—she could still be alive, you know—hiding in Argentina—she probably thought *The Crow* was about her lover . . . somehow it feels gloomy—Goteborg—

Your interview with Rochelle Ratner is lovely!

Fondly, Robert

I never got your Montale article!

Västerås Jan. 22 -76
Dear Robert,

it was a long time ago . . . I remember I started a letter and then was interrupted and could not find it again etc. . . . I will try again. I am longing to go back to the U.S.A. where I am not so persecuted by PAPERS, all these bills, letters, forms, reports, questionnaires, they are a pack of white blood-sucking bats covering me even in sleep. With an arm free I will try to tell you this: we are all well and we hope you are all well, we are often thinking warmly about you and Monica goes so far that she is sometimes showing people the picture of her godson Micah as a baby (but I will not be surprised if he is a pubescent boy with breaking voice by now, time goes fast). Business: I have talked to Börje Lindström about publishing a prose poem book of your work in Fibs Lyrikklubb in Stockholm this winter and spring. As you can see from his own little book *Skenet från den andra stranden* he is so much inside your prose poems that he sometimes does not know how to get out . . . "Hämtar ved" e.g. (page 9) is almost a parody of "Morning Glory." "Old people approaching their breakfast like Viking ships wrapped up in icebergs" etc. But he is also very gifted I think, he will become something. So, our plan is to put our translations together. Do you agree?

"Boat, Town" seems to have got its English version at last, I thought it was untranslatable because of "rullar upp," "fattigravinen" etc. But your solutions are fine. One objection: "military police" is not the word. They were ordinary Portuguese soldiers, farm boys in uniform. Also "escorted" misses the parallel to leading an animal, a horse, oxen etc. Probably the word is "lead." "Walking Running Creeping" is not approved by its author, I mean the Swedish text isn't. The poem got its present shape too fast, it was probably meant to be some other thing. I don't know. "Trän" is a popular plural form of "träd." So the holes resemble the holes from all the invisible trees that have been overturned the last years. Can I use your idea with invisible threads picked out? Not bad. Let us keep our invisible threads unpicked!

Best   Tomas

Västerås 30-1-76
Dear Robert,
     the other day the mail told me to fetch an enormous parcel from the U.S.A., it hardly got into my car and at home I opened it. First I found

a small message telling me to postpone the opening until Christmas, but after some consideration I decided not to wait 11 months and unwrapped the rest. In a silent burst of surprise I looked at your Indian picture book. What a marvelous gift! We will all disappear in these pictures for some time and come back again, a little better.

+ + +

The next day I got your letter about Eva Braun. I was not shaken. Her project does not interfere with our prose poems project, and besides I have the general principle of approving many translators of the same writer. But I cannot tell you if she is good or bad. I will try to find *Crow*. Coeckelbergh is a new publisher, publishing translations of poetry on a large scale— Artur Lundkvist supervises the project. I think Gary Snyder was published recently by them. I think you should exchange a few letters with her and find out if she likes Jung or not.

+ + +

Monica has been fasting for a whole week, in order to get the poisons out of her body and soul. She became very energetic and her eyes became very clear but she did not change much, thank goodness.

+ + +

Justo Jorge Padrón—a Swedish speaking Spanish poet—phoned me and told me that a Spanish publisher has accepted 43 of my poems for a book. Justo is also the best tennis champion of the Canary Islands. He did not mention that when we met but I saw it in a paper. His own poems, translated by Lundkvist, will be published by Coeckelbergh this spring!

Love   Tomas

Västerås 17-2-67 [1976]

Dear Robert, my Spanish translator and your Coeckelbergh colleague Mr. J. Jorge Padrón, who is a good poet, wants to have the address of Hardie St. Martin—he wants to send his books of course.

*

I now appear with my left arm in a cast of plaster after a beautiful somer-sault on the slippery winter ground outside Emma's stable. Life becomes more simple when you have to do everything with one hand.

> Love from
>   slippery Sweden

> Tomas

26 Feb, '76

Dear Tomas,

You'll notice it's your left arm!—the arm of feeling—that means, says Moo goo Gai Pan, the famous Pygmy sorcerer, that you're doing too much bureaucratic work. And since you already wrote me that in your last letter, that proves again the wisdom of wearing overshoes when you walk on ice.

Hardie St. Martin's address is c/o Rodriguez, 166 East 56th St., Apt. 4A, New York 10022.

I must go to El Paso tomorrow for a reading! Hooray—into Mexico for one hour!

I'm overworked like you—it must be something in the stars—
> Your friend, Robert

Hotell Viking: Stay away from this hotel—too expensive
Trondheim
8-4-76

Dear Robert,

I have to send you a few lines from Trønderlag! This is my last stop on a 6-day reading tour in Norway (Bergen-Oslo-Tromsø (!) and Trondheim). Norway is wonderful and exotic. I am reading for students as shy as the Swedish ones but I have made them speak out except in Tromsø where the

North Pole was too close. You seem to be fairly well-known and loved in this country but so far I have not met anyone who knows where your ancestors came from. (I have a vague memory of you pointing at some place just south of Trondheim.) The trip was organized by Willy Dahl (university lector in Oslo), a brave man who recently made people furious—he published a history of modern Norwegian literature. He put me on nonexistent planes etc. so the trip has been chaotic enough. I had a dream one night that I was sent to Greenland by mistake.

Have you translated a poem called "Gullhanen" by Olav H. Hauge? It gave me the best poetic shock I've had for many months. (But it is a sonnet . . .)

Norway is watching you! And your friend   Tomas

Love to
Monica!
And Paula & Emma!

18 May 76

Dear Tomas,

I did my last reading for the year yesterday, and now I can return to being an irascible birds-nest-staring-into introvert again. In New York I corrected a cut version (Frank McShane prepared it) of the conversation you and I had at Columbia. I took some of your sentences and put them under my name, because it seemed you had the best lines! (And I gave you several "urr"—"umm—" "That's not true!" shouts and moans.) The Swedish king has been here and gone—he resembles Dairy-Whip. Carter is exactly like James Dickey. Rolf Jacobsen came to Madison, Wis. (by bus from Austin, Texas) . . . I read with him . . . A fine evening!! Everyone loves to have a decent, sensitive grandfather. We are all well. Carol is papering the inside of her stilts-study. I sold Peanuts (the spotted pony) today for $35. The pound is down to $1.80. We have had no rain *all month*.

I went to the Jung Conference this year, and attacked the Jungians! They were astounded. I tried to get them to promise never to use the word "archetype" again . . .

Your fighter for lost causes—
Robert

Västerås 7-6-76
Dear old companion,
thanks for the new sending of astonishing magazines. I had a good time with your interview, prose poems and with James Dickey's interview. I want to translate "The left hand" too, tell me more about it. What do you mean by PROTECTIVE lamp-lit etc. . . . ?

It is something disarming with Dickey, he lays himself open, probably without knowing it. What is disturbing with most writers is their desire to be BIG at all costs. So when you meet this longing undisguised in this naive muscle-man-way it looks almost like humility. A target so big that you cannot miss.

I was slightly scandalized the other day in the evening paper *Expressen*. Lars Gustafsson was defending me—absolutely with the best intentions—in a review of Lars Bäckström's book *Bildningsroman*. Bäckström had attacked me for being employed by PA-rådet. The organization where I work was once founded by the employers' organization in Sweden but the employers have as little to do with my work as, say, the King has to do with the duties of a postman. But for Bäckström I am a toady of the capitalists. So Lars Gustafsson gave a dramatic anti-picture of that in *Expressen*, describing me as doing "slave work in a subordinate position," in a "module," with "constant attacks of migraine," concealed in spite of my growing reputation in the world etc. I had to go around in Västerås for days with a permanent smile to contradict that gloomy picture. We all end up as laughing-stocks, one way or another, it is comforting to know that. What about attacks on you lately? In America the women seem to be the most aggressive. I heard a story about Adrienne Rich . . . she was giving a reading but refused to start until all the males had left the room! Is that true? I hope not.

My trips to Norway and Denmark have been refreshing. Our publisher Koed Hansen in Aarhus is a young boy, very kind, once a student in Minnesota. One occult thing: when I met him he had his *left* arm in plaster like I had one month earlier. So it is not without risks to touch my writings nowadays.

Rumors tell that you have been translated and described in a new magazine here, called *Ett Tärningskast*. I will try to find it in Stockholm when I go there next week.

Write soon! "They often write to me, but because of my heavy schedule I almost never have the time to answer." (Dickey).

Love
Tomas

[Editor's note: Tranströmer included drafts of two poems in Swedish, with the following commentary:]

1) "Övergångsstället": A relapse in the old Tranströmer style, but less flabby I hope. It was good to be able to *finish* something at last. All my other things now seem to have no end. But summer is before us. We will go to the island 10 days from now.
2) "Hastig promenad": I was very fascinated by this wonderful piece. Should not be kept away from the Swedes. Read this first version and please comment. "Mil" are Swedish miles. "Burning" could be both "brinnande" (burning itself up) or "brännande" (burning others—also you talk about "brännande smak etc.," sharp taste).
A poem about what it is like to be middle-aged?

17 July 76

Dear Tomas,

There are several phrases in this mysterious poem which I don't understand well! That following after is one, and the idea of "skum" is another.

It is Sunday among the pines. Carol and I went for a short sail after breakfast in her new sailboat—a "Laser". . . *Loon #6* is here, a magazine in California named after this place (Cry of the Loon), in it there are two poems of yours, translated by Don Emblen. One poem is about the world going round in circles . . . Bill Booth, who owns this resort, has written a companion to my loon poem. Mine goes:

> From far out in the center of the naked lake,
> the loon's cry rose:
> it was the cry of someone who owned very little.

His companion is:

> From far out in the center of the naked lake,
> the loon's cry rose:
> it was the cry of someone who owned seventeen refrigerators, eight
>   boats, four of whom need repair, nine garbage cans, four cars plus
>   one jeep, whose back tires are bad, one hundred and twenty two
>   sheets, twenty one beds, ten boat motors etc etc. . . .

Love, Robert

P.S. I need help!

Gunnar Harding is doing a new Swedish anthology in English as you know, and has taken lots from the Beacon book of yours—I think he is omitting Martinson!

[------]

Love, Robert

Place to Cross

Ice blows in the eyes, and many suns dance
in the tear-kaleidoscope as I cut across
the street, which comes dawdling after, this street
where Greenland's summer shines in the puddles.

The whole energy of the street seethes around me—
it brings up nothing into the mind, and it never will.
Under the traffic, deep in earth, silently,
the unborn forest waits for thousands of years.

I get the idea that the street can see me.
Its glance is so gloomy that the sun itself
becomes a gray ball in black space.
But for this instant I give off light! The street sees me.

18 July '76

Dear Tomas,

We've just come up to some cool pine woods in Northern Minnesota, oh how lovely it is! Almost as good as Runmarö! Except of course we are not connected to the great belly-button of the Sea, only to the small flat stomach of the inland lake. (A kind of day-care center, I suppose.) But we inland people have lower standards, so a crayfish in fresh water makes us as excited as an octopus in salt water! I caught one yesterday— when I put him on the boat seat, he compressed his tail three or four times and was astounded that he didn't shoot backwards instantly into cool weeds—he just remained where he was on the wooden seat! It is like being a journalist . . .

I'm glad that Gustafsson has told the world that you are only a wage slave of the capitalists—a bug crawling on the wall—rather than one of them. At least you're not the wall.

That story about Adrienne is true, I expect. One has to expect to be singled out at a woman's poetry reading now—*There's one! He's right in the middle!*—I have a wig I take along for such occasions.

I like your translation of "Walking Swiftly" (I'm not sure "promenad" is right—the title refers back to the swiftness with which the konstnaren walks to his ateljé in the last sentence).

The word 2x4's you probably know—it is the standard word for the piece of wood roughly two inches thick by four inches high which are used for the inner skeleton of walls, and all such things. It's there to contrast with stone and granite—and the numbers (2x4's) makes it all still more nervous.

The "kejsaren" should suggest a Chinese emperor.

You can take out the colon after "anda" in the second sentence if you want to—I've done it in the English.

The hens should sound as if they are continuing a patrol (of watchfulness) which they have been doing as a gift for a million years or so. There is a tense change there: Round him the wasps kept guard, the hens continue their patrol (it comes into the *present* now), the oysters open and close all questions. (It is entirely in the present with the oysters.)

"Viljan" is burning in the sense that it is ignited—it is no longer cold, but has heat that it draws from its own burning . . . Savonarola's will was a burning will.

You are right. It is about being middle aged! . . . if the necessary introversion has been held on to! . . .

We all send our love to you and Monica and the children. I notice we have with us one of the cups Monica gave us on our last trip . . . and the other day, poking about my record player, I found a package with 3 records in it! One was of the Västerås Choir!! It must be a gift from you or Monica! Thank you! How strange it was to hear them sing Hallelujah! They have the Swedish pronunciation of the "oo," which transfers the whole song from Palestine instantly to Värmland—

Ingegerd Friberg did send me *Ett tärningskast* and it has my Montale piece in it—which I've been looking for a copy of in English to send you! Thank you and Monica so much for those records!

Love,
Robert

Middle aged American
meditating in the north
woods, trying to forget
2x4's.

P.S. I will send you tomorrow a translation of the new cold wind poem!

Västerås Sept 19 -76
Dear Robert,

this is election day in Sweden, I have voted and I am waiting for the computers to start counting the votes. But 20% have voted by mail so the final outcome will not be clear until the day after tomorrow. I did not vote for Palme this time.

Thank you for working with "Övergångsstället." I have the translation in Runmarö but I remember it, I think. It has a wonderful élan, typical of you. But I think there are slight liberties (misunderstandings?) here and there. That "gatan" . . . "följt mig så länge" does not mean that the street has been "dawdling." I simply mean that 1: I have walked along the street for a long time before crossing it. 2: it is a street I've known since my childhood (actually it is "Skånegatan" in Stockholm South, where I lived as a child), so the street has been with me during my life. It is a day in March, in thaw time, the sun present after many weeks of grey weather. But still cold. Strong light. The traffic in the street is experienced as something almost organic, as a state of mind, full of energy but without purpose. It is a force without memory and without purpose (som ingenting minns och ingenting vill)—it has nothing to do with *my* memories and what *I* want. But the unborn forest under the ground has purpose and is waiting patiently. Then, when I cross, I find that, after all, there is a glimpse of perception in the street too, it is not just blind forces rushing by, it can see me, but only vaguely, because the street is so dim-sighted (like the eyes of certain animals living in caves etc.), it can only glimpse me in the moment when I am on fire with sunshine, and the sun itself is perceived by the street as a grey "nystan," and here is a problem because "nystan" means a ball of yarn in Swedish, the English "ball" is so general. I am thinking of a ball of wool here. Is there an English word for that? Good luck!

What happened to your Sonnevi translations? Did you succeed? Translations, translations . . . I am touchy about that now. It is because of my opera translation, Janáček's *Kátja Kabanová*. The Royal Opera accepted my first translation with pleasure but some singers complained and I had to change a lot of things. Then, 10 days ago, the stage director arrived at last, Herr Joachim Herz aus DDR (East Berlin, or Leipzig, I don't remember . . .) and he started to change my translation without knowing Swedish! once again without telling me. By chance I was aware of it and rushed to the meeting. I was allowed to take part in my own translation for the remaining part—the last act—and I found it possible to work together with the authoritarian Prussian. It was necessary not to fall flat but to be very enthusiastic all the time, then I could convince him. But when I protested about the previous changes he had made he went furious, shouted "NOT ONE SINGLE SYLLABLE CAN BE CHANGED" and ran out. I was in a dilemma: should I withdraw and make a scandal or be patient? I succeeded in sneaking in some alterations in the score of the leading soprano and as almost 100% of my text for the last act was accepted (because I was there and could be enthusiastic in front of him) I decided to stay. I have never been on such a switchback railway as this opera work before—touring the U.S.A. is like living in a sleepy country boarding house compared to that.

I send you a prose piece too. "Mats" is Mats Dahlberg—who has written to you and also got some old *Fifties* from you—and "Laila" is his fiancée. They live in Molkom, Värmland, almost as pleasant as Norway, but a landscape partly destroyed by the big wood companies who clean-cut vast areas and use a lot of poison.

I would love to have a letter from you, Uncle!

Love

Tomas

24 Sept., '76

Dear Tomas,

Thank you for your letter! In the chaos of the summer, I've lost the Swedish for "Övergångsstället." Would you send it to me once more? In return, I'm typing a tiny little *depressing* poem to overcome the good cheer caused by too many Eastern gurus and peanut Christians in this land. (The *debate* starts tonight.)

> Brutal men invading the Farallones with clubs, the psyche in torpor, the Empire dying in its provincial cities, no one to repair the Baths, the judges corrupt. The wagon behind bouncing, breaking on boulders, leaping from side to side empty, slowly being smashed to pieces. All this crumbling darkness is a reality too, the feather on the snow, the rooster's half-eaten body nearby. And other worlds

I do not see . . . the Old People's Home at dusk, the slow murmur
of conversation.

The Farallones are the Farallones islands near San Francisco, whose seals
were clubbed to death in the 19th century. The second image is of a run-
away team of horse pulling a wagon.

Here's another:

Starting Down the Mountain After a Long Climb

In my legs is the trembling of the potassium-embers.
Flowers no one sees sown on limber earth.
I come so slowly to the simple open door.
Around my trembling knees the mountain flowers.

Love from weak legs,
Robert

P.S. I love your Mats prose poem so far! I'm reading it while listening to
the Goldberg Variations!

Igor Kipnis!!!

Västerås 3-11-76
Dear Robert,

       strange, I voted first for Helmut Schmidt in Germany,
then for Fälldin in Sweden and yesterday for Jimmy Carter and I won all
three times.

A young German poet and editor of *Akzente,* the only real literary maga-
zine in West Germany, visited Västerås yesterday. His name is Michael
Krüger. He wants to translate *Baltics* into German (yes, *Baltics*!) and we
talked about the sad fact that *you* are not available in German. He wants

to do something about it and I will remind him about that when we meet next time, in January. He is an honest man. I would like to bring a copy of *Morning Glory* when I visit him there in January, can you send me one? The Germans should read something beside Charles Olson.

My opera adventures never end. The premiere of *Kátja Kabanová* took place two weeks ago. Some days before a journalist in *Dagens Nyheter* had written that the opera had run into difficulties because my translation of *Kátja* turned out to be impossible to use. But a brave team of singers and Mr Joszef Cech had succeeded in the last moment to save the opera by changing my text entirely! Now that was a complete lie—I had from the beginning worked together with Cech and the singers and the problems at the end were caused by the DDR director who wanted changes in details because he did not know Swedish and knew my translation only from a word-by-word translation into his German made by a frightened girl who was good at German. I was furious for two days and wrote to the Information Boss of the opera, asking for an official reaction. He was all excuses but said it was useless to protest to DN. The journalist was a well known well meaning inventor of fables. His name was Marcus Boldeman. At the premiere Monica (in an African dress) and I were approached by a middle-aged lady and the following dialogue was heard.

The Lady: Oh, are you Mr Tranströmer?
Tranströmer: Yes, Madam.
The Lady: Oh, have you met Marcus Boldeman yet, you are supposed to meet him?
Tranströmer: Him! That bastard, who lied about me in *Dagens Nyheter*! Never!
The Lady: I am his mother.

How good to be back in simple surroundings again. No one could hear the text, by the way, the orchestra was too loud and the singers were acting too violently on the stage so they had no energy left for articulation.

It would be wonderful to hear from you again. What happens to my little godson?

> Love
>> Tomas

P.S. Here is a new copy of the street crossing poem.

[8-11-76]

Dear Robert, have a quick look at this! Wonderful poem. "Band" at the end is very general in Swedish. "Ordenband" would mean the ribbon attached to an order sign. Would be fine here.

Do you really mean that Europe is sober? Never been to France? And all that beer they consume in Munich.

>> Cheerio!
>> Tomas

Västerås 11-11-76
Dear Robert,

> it is a long time since you wrote to me. What will the Post Office Department think about you?

Here is a small poem of mine. About Schubert, especially his string quintet in C major and his 4-hand fantasia (opus 103) in f-minor.

I had a meeting yesterday with Roffe Aggestam and Börje Lindström. We decided to translate at least 8 more prose poems of yours. Deadline January 15. The little book will be printed and published in late spring. Translators: Tranströmer, Lindström and Söderberg (Lasse). I want to see a bunch of late prose poems from your hand, can you send me some meant to be published in the camphor gopher book? And very important: you should write a foreword, we would love to translate it (before Jan 15!) and print it. (Your mistranslated foreword to *Krig och tystnad* influenced some freaks over here, as you know.) If you don't write a foreword we will give the offer to Elizabeth Bishop.

> Love
>> Tomas

Gunnar Harding wants badly to know IF you are translating poems from Sonnevi's latest book or not. If not, don't hesitate to tell Harding. You will be discreetly carried away and he will let the poems meet the next gladiator.

18 Nov., '76

Dear Tomas,

I like your translation of "Frost"! The only faint error I notice is "land-stiger"—it isn't a going on land, an embarking, but a disembarking—an image of a boat leaving land in the dead of winter, the sailors' hands freezing as they cast off the ropes holding them to land—

Europe is sober, in that it's always correcting the United States! Now, now, no Vietnam adventures, that's wrong, no you're using the wrong spoon, your accent is wrong, your cars are too big . . . Europe is our superego!

The ribbons are long, I think, perhaps long ribbons girls wear on bonnets, or ticker-tape ribbons, so there are roads crossing roads, as in a frosty window—

Thank you for the new copy of the Street poem! I've already done a new draft.

I'm enclosing a foolish little poem. I'm distracted—I have to leave tomorrow for a poetry festival in San Francisco (Östen Sjöstrand is going to read a couple of poems) and then to AN ANDROGENY CONFERENCE in the Holiday Inn in Evanston, Illinois . . . I'm going—though they don't know it—to represent the unregenerate, unrepentant male.

I'm writing much, and am all excited over some new poems, and sounds!!

There are so many pearls in the ocean, and weeds and "octopuses with un-known Dostoevskyan hands."

Love to your family
and you! Robert

On Top of a Colorado Mountain

Nearly sunset. I walked up two hours, reading as I paused. Now I am at the tree line. All around there are mountain tops with the light on them! The slight delicate Norwegian grass mountain-covering. . . . How I love its uncertain feminine green, all slopes and snow-pulled rolling valleys, all subtlety and no speech, all delicacy and no insistence, all music and no notes, all intimacy and no daydreams, all lovely absences and no angry presences, all faithfulnesses and no divisions . . .

The slate-gray mountain face plunges down, into the early heavy forms, (some snow there) as it dives down so sleekly, so calmly, into union . . . it must be that the descent into the furred ones goes along with the ascent into pure light . . .

I know there are hills inside me like these, and I want to walk on them, where the glad ones prance, holding on to the manes of horses, as the horses fly through heaven and hell, and turn into petals that fall onto the lap of the man with long ears reading . . . "The master is reading Sanskrit texts among falling flowers" . . .

15 Dec, '76

Dear Tomas,

I'm sending you a new draft of the Street Crossing poem, and a first draft of your lovely island poem! It carries several queries with it.

Meanwhile I've read "Schubertiana"! It is a marvelous poem!!! Terr-rr-rr-ific, as the American students would say. Solid and *full of space*.

I've just come back from my December-week-showing-off (the fattest wren ever seen to warble "both high and low") and I found a couple of more places who want you to read this spring—Charleston, South Carolina, and the Transcendental Meditation University at Fairfield, Iowa. There the students know "Allegro" by heart, and it has led to a Haydn revival, I expect. They're having a Festival in early May, around the 9th–12th.

So far there are five:

Charleston, S.C.
Ohio Univ, Athens, Ohio.
Augustina College, Rock Island, Ill.
College of Art & Design, Mpls
Univ of Minn, *Marshall* (nearby)

I've told them all $300 plus expenses (which includes airfare inside U.S.). So if you did 10, you'd go home with $3000 this year.

I'm sending along two books for your friend Michael Krüger.

We saw a Barbara Walters interview last night with Carter and his wife, in which she compared him to Rhett Butler in *Gone With the Wind*! There's no end of wonders. He seems to be a nice man, but more like General Grant than Clark Gable.

I'm home for a whole month. I'll translate all the rest of the poems you've sent me! No, Carter is really a kind of sweet civil servant, as in a Yugoslavian movie . . . there is *no fire coming from his mouth* . . . he is a mammal salamander . . .

Your friend, General Lee

Novel or Romance?

Start of an October Night's Romance

The island boat has an oily smell, and something is always knocking like an obsessive thought. They turn the spotlight on. We are nearing the pier. I'm the only one for this stop. "Do you need a landing board?" No. I take a slow wobbling step right into the night, and am standing on the pier, on the island. I feel soggy and unwieldy, I am a butterfly just crept from the cocoon, the plastic clothes-bag in each of my hands like misshapen wings. I turn around and watch the boat disappear with its lit windows, then grope my way up to the sheltering house that stood empty so long. All the houses around here are uninhabited . . . It is lovely to sleep here. I lie on my back, not knowing if I'm asleep or awake. Some new books I've read sail by like old schooners on the way to the Bermuda triangle, where they will disappear without a trace. A hollow sound is audible, a forgetful drum. A thing that the wind again and again thumps against something that the earth is holding tight. At night not only is absence luminous, at night an object really exists, as this sound exists. The stethoscope sound from a slow heart, it beats, is silent a day, comes back. As if some being moved in zig-zags over the Border. Or someone who beats inside a wall, someone who belongs to the other world, but stays here anyway, beats on, wants to go back. Late. He is not down there, not up there, not on board . . . The other world is also this world. The next morning I see a rusty twig with leaves hanging on, gold and brown. A creeping root. Stones with faces. The forest is full of returned wonders that I love.

version by RB.

Is the one inside the wall a being, a creature, or a heart?
Is it beating *on* the wall, or is its heart beating?

Tomas: Please check especially five details:

> *blasten ater och ater;*   *fravaron av lujus, ar nagot*

> *Hann into dit ner, hann inte dit upp, hann inte ombord*
> "rotvälta" is not in my dictionary!

1977

Västerås 18-1-77

Dear Master,

a wonderful snow is covering Sweden and a blue snow of prose poems leaves is covering my desk. Thanks, thanks. I have 3 days now free and I will really do something with the Bly project. The foreword is perfect. (He was a good translator, a marvellous poet and an unsurpassed writer of forewords.)

I have not been writing letters for a long time. Since early December I have been absorbed in a strange duty: writing an essay about early Swedish literature. The Writers' Publishing house has got into financial difficulties but now everything will be all right (they, we, think) when our real best-seller is completed, called *Författarnas Litteraturhistoria*—Swedish literature from the runestones to Ekelöf, entirely described by us. So Gyllensten has written a chapter about Linné, Lars Gustafsson about Stagnelius, 2 people have written about Strindberg, Lundkvist about Heidenstam etc. etc. But I chose to write about a certain YEAR, and I took the year 1719, which was the year when it finally became clear that Sweden was no super-power anymore. We shrank from the glorious position at the beginning of the reign of Charles XII, to the humble size of 1719, (a half year since) Charles had been shot and we were at the very bottom of everything. I buried myself in history and had a lot of fun. This period is one of the black holes of Swedish literature, no real research has penetrated it since the 1870s and I could walk on lovely overgrown paths right into virginal archives. Oh the welcoming, smiling atmosphere, the fresh air of dusty libraries, the pure athletic joy when you come across a really mildewy print no one has bothered to look at before!

Warmest

Tomas

[Editor's note: Internal evidence indicates that the following is a continuation of TT's letter of 18 January. RB responds on 24 January.]

Comments about "Senhöstnattens roman." I think your translation is very good, especially considering that you misunderstood 50%. The title means "Start of the late autumn *novel.*" I don't know why I called it that, a person here in Västerås congratulated me and hoped that the rest of the novel would be fine. But I want to give the feeling that this is something that can go on for a long time, the island visitor has read the first page of something big he will never understand.

Senhöst could be the last days of October, but the mood here is more of November. So if you hate the words "late autumn," use November. It is of course very autobiographical, a trip to Runmarö during a time of the year when the island is almost deserted. The sound at the beginning is less knocking than rattling, almost ringing (it was probably a loose screw nut vibrating). "The sheltering house" should be "the familiar house" (the house I know so well) . . . that is the meaning of the word "förtrogna." "Again and again" is right. But there is a misunderstanding of "om natten," because "om" is here not a preposition ("at night") but a conjunction ("if the night"). So the meaning is: If (the) night is not only (something more than) absence of light, if the night really *is* something, it must be (is) this sound. "Is silent a day" is wrong. I wrote "ett tag" and that means "for a short while." So the sound beats, is silent for a moment, comes back. As if it were the heartbeat of a person half-way between life and death, going zig-zag over the Border. "Hann inte dit ner" etc. . . . "Hann" is the imperfect of "hinna" meaning "be in time." The creature (or spirit) belongs to the other world but visits "our" world at night. But he must be back in time. Now he was too late, he did not manage to get "down there," not to get "up there" and not to get "on board" in time. He is "akterseglad" (the last line)— så många akterseglade vidunder etc. "Akterseglad" is a sailor's word for arriving too late for the ship, the ship has left the harbor and the sailor remains, "akterseglad." I think the English word is "beached." "Lövruska" is not a twig but a whole branch with leaves on—now most leaves are on the ground but there are exceptional branches. "Rotvälta" is not in my dictionary either. I have to go to the library and look in a bigger one . . . The word was not in any dictionary, NOT EVEN SWEDISH ONES. Strange, everybody here knows what it means but it is not in a book . . .

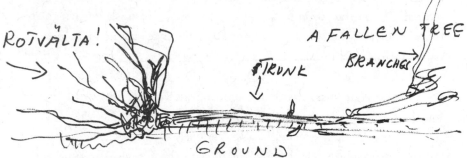

So "rotvälta" means the up-rooted root system of a fallen tree. The butt-end of a fallen tree. Rotvältor can look very strange, like trolls, or devils.

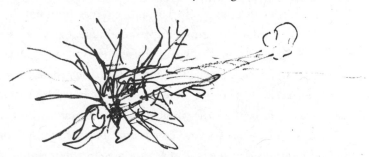

"Street crossing" is now so chewed and digested in your wonderful imagination apparatus that I believe it has become a good Bly poem in English. Maybe it has lost some contact with my version. I would prefer "kaleidoscope of tears" to "tearful kaleidoscope"—I am more baroque. "Is aware" is OK if it is not too abstract, the street should not be aware of my existence by thinking or being told about me, but because the street—like some half-blind cave animal—can see luminous things.

24 Jan, '77

Dear Tomas,

Thank you for the good pile of joyful slips of the brain! We all enjoyed your letter, and Monica's remark will make me good-tempered for weeks . . . I'm glad she likes the Father poem . . . And thank you for your corrections on the Novel poem—it's not so easy to translate when you're blind you know . . . I did realize it was a "romance" in the French sense, that is a roman, I knew at least it was not a *romance* . . . I deserve a little credit . . .

Now to your questions about "Finding the Father." The word "light" on the forehead carries more connotations of "full of light" than it does of "weightless." It is essentially what the visitor sees when he lights the lamp—the eyebrows look dark and heavy, the forehead is apparently rather high, and catches the light.

The whole series of poems could be described as "anti–St. Paul" poems. So they offer various praises of the body he was so suspicious of. For one thing, the body carries us around all day, and charges nothing! That is amazing, when you think of it! I thought of those huge logs that are carried by the sea all the way from the Hawaiian islands to the Oregon coast, floating for months, until left on the Oregon beach. Then there comes an image closely related to those in the Maui poem, which you translated so well. Those crabs might be the same small black hermit crabs, who are listening in Aramaic. A large ocean wave comes and smashes against a boulder half in and half out of water. The crabs are not hurt, but simply slide around the sides of the boulder, and roll around in the water behind it. When it is said the body "wails" with its great energy on certain days—no doubt when the Vitamin E level in the body is very high—it is a good wailing, a kind of joyful humming, as from a big dynamo, or a football player about to go out on the field. (You are right, "longs" are supposed to be "logs.")

The person in the room does not have time to dress properly for the *weather.* He is probably wearing a cotton shirt and pajama bottoms, and not having time to dress, that is put on rain gear with hood, and rain boots, just throws on some old coat and goes out in his tennis shoes.

One of the father's jobs was as a restaurant cook, after work he was an amateur painter . . . not painting walls, but canvases, as I guess is clear.

The last line should have a floating, almost trancelike feeling, with some tenderness thrown forward to "you."

I hope these weighty observations help . . . You haven't answered whether or not you'd like to come this spring. I got another offer last week, from the University of New Orleans. They'll put you up in the French Quarter, in a little guest house, and take you the next day to the area around Lafayette, in the swamps, and take you to a Cajun dance. The Cajuns speak an old form of French, and are the liveliest people left in the south, any thing. They are the direct descendants of the French people deported from Nova Scotia by the English, and described in "Evangeline" by Longfellow . . .

Love, Robert

26 Jan 77

Dear Tomas,

Here are a few comments on "Hastig promenad." Maybe I should type them!! I'm not sure of the implications of "Hastig promenad." The title in English does not mean taking a fast walk, as when one says, I want to take a walk, but I have only five minutes . . . it means walking at a high speed, as when one is excited and wants to get somewhere to begin writing something down, or to paint . . . The colon can be left off after "ändä" . . . the way it reads now in English is simply: "Everything seems calm, and yet somewhere inside I am not calm."

There may be something wrong with "inhägnaden." It's true the sheep are out of their fence, but what I mention here is the *screen* of the screened-in porch that we've added to the house. You remember it. The afternoon before, the children, after peeling a whole bunch of apples (to make into apple sauce for winter), threw the pail of apple peelings out the front door. I'm trying to sleep there, where Carol and I sleep in the screen porch; at six in the morning I hear this ungodly crunch, crunch, crunch, and it is the disobedient sheep who have stumbled upon a positive Paris of goodies . . . that's how the poem begins. Grouchily, I begin to examine the rising sun . . .

"Adelmodet" . . . I don't mean nobility of mind so much as the sort of generosity the good nurse at the hospital has, the one who does so many things for the patients, buys them little things on her off hours, does more than is asked of her . . . it comes not so much from a sense of obligation, as from a human longing to be of use to other humans . . .

The "vanvettig kärlek" should suggest if possible both the Sufi love of God, which they describe as "crazy" or "mad" compared to Lutheranism, and the love of Tristan and Isolde.

"Waves" is not essential in the last sentence. The main thing is that the sound be triumphant and full of energy. The dragon has a mane like this

and the artist decides to bring more curve into them, a deeper rise and fall, so when he's through they will look more like:

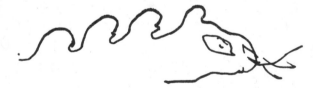

so the noun could be "curve" or "sea-mountain" or "oceanic surf" or almost "tidal waves" . . . or those deep swells that run along at mid ocean . . .

I like the translations, and I'm glad you chose this one! Awful snow here . . .

Love,

Robert

Jan 26 - 77

Dear Robert, have a look at this. As you see I tentatively have left out 6 lines in your foreword, namely the part that starts "It's possible that while a bird . . ." and ends with "big rivers." That part was almost impossible to translate. One sentence I don't understand grammatically ("so there are certain thoughts"). I think the content is more clear without the 6 lines. ??? I have changed some smaller details. You say the pale eyeball creatures want to give poetry *back* to the superego. I have left out "back" because that would mean poetry originated from the superego. We don't believe that, we wild men! The foreword is dynamite, far out!

	Your grounded and
What does	grinded
"stick legs" mean?	friend
	Tomas T.

I am nervous now that the Göteborg ladies will be too quick with translations of you—Rolf Aggestam will push hard to get *our* book published this spring. Title of the book? Proposal . . . TT

31 Jan, '77

Dear Tomas,

Here are a few thoughts, first about the foreword. I do want you to include the second paragraph. I know that it is a bit incoherent, so I'll set down here a version maybe slightly more sensible! It contains the idea, poorly said, I'm afraid, that one advantage of the human being's having invented language is that now, while he's using it, new thoughts occur! I think the calmness of the prose poems helps these "new thoughts" to appear, while the person is writing the prose poem. That's why I used the metaphor of the bird building a nest—he is working . . . Language is the nest human beings make . . .

It's possible that while a bird is building its nest an idea for a song it has never sung rises to its small head. So with us certain thoughts flow upward into our head only when language is being used, and used calmly. Buried impulses toward joy are carried upward on the artesian well of the prose poem that seem not to want to rise in the excited sunlight of the big rivers.

At the end there I'm saying that for strange reasons "big rivers" like *Paradise Lost* contain few of the intimate thoughts of Milton, few tiny quirky joys that make a man suddenly dance a little in his office.

A FEW DETAILS: I meant a *relatively* new form in English, rather than an entirely new form. I can't tell what "bhovande" implies; *needy* is the exact opposite of the adjectives we usually apply to gods. It is used for very old people living in hotels, or women with many children whose husband has abandoned them.

If you want to, just leave out "overjaget" entirely. The sentence would then read: "och ge den till museernas musa." I haven't decided whether in the English version I should keep "superego" or not. Carol suggested dropping it, but it may make a connection for some that "museernas musa" might not. Tell me what I should do!

I made a change in the next sentence. The second draft reads:

> The man or woman writing a poem in this century has to deal with these white shapes, either outdoing them by triping [*sic*] the energy in the poems—Yeats does that—or by doing something they don't notice.

Carol was a little worried about the violence of the example I gave of a "man" as opposed to "humanity"—it is actually a classmate of mine who put in the tiles in our bathroom, and after being kicked out of the house (his house) for being drunk all the time, returned one morning at 6 AM and shot himself in the back yard. I don't know how you feel about that. Another possibility would be: "We have been asked to write about 'humanity,' not about the plumber next door who reads Eckhart and has eight children."

Take whichever you like best.

Later, there seems to be a bit of confusion between "Takes place" which just means "happens" and the longing that each event would have its own space or place in the poem.

I think we should be sure that "Rain in August" is included in the book! Don't you have a translation of it?

"Stick legs" just suggests how the thin legs of an old lady would look to the eye picking them up quickly . . . it comes from a potato with "match-stick legs" . . .

Thank you for doing this! I think you've done it well! Except of course for your grudge against big rivers and artesian wells . . . As I mentioned, artesian wells are simply wells whose water flows upward without being pumped . . . that has never been my luck . . .

Now a few notes on "Tomales Bay." It looks fine! As for the machine, I had the same problem in English as you do in Swedish . . . I wrote it first as "crane," which is our word for a lifting mechanism with a long cable hanging down, used to load ships and such things.

I was then much irritated to realize that we had a bird called "crane" also. So I reluctantly went to "derrick" in order to avoid confusing the reader with the pun on crane. I only realized it was not a machine, when I saw it move. So that is why the exclamation mark appears here . . . it was a shock . . . one could say, "han lever" or even "it is moving . . . alive!" I don't know "gar sen iväg" . . . what happened was that he glimpsed us at the same second, and started to walk away from us, and nearer the shore . . . he was probably in five or six inches of water . . .

We aren't exactly "hjalplost"—we had oars, but the fog came down so quickly we didn't know where we were . . . we couldn't see the shore at all, nor the sea we were heading toward . . .

The first glimpse of the sea lions, when they come up from their "havsk-rubbor," should give a strong fragrance from the birth of Christ in the manger. We rarely use the word "manger" these days, except in reference to that story. The Magi are the Wise Men, all right . . . use whatever trans-lation for these three that would have been used in 19th century Swedish translations of the Bible . . . MAGI—It is such a wonderful, fragrant word in English! The billfold is the ordinary leather folding thing for credit cards and folding money that all Americans carry in their back pockets.

Well enough of this. You already know too much. Poems are best when there are incredible mysteries in them, that is, when you don't understand English. I'm afraid you're not making enough mistakes . . .

I'm not sure whom you mean by the ladies in Göteborg . . . Is that the sleepless translator of *Sleepers*? Ingegerd Friberg wrote me a curious let-ter. She wanted to have exclusive rights on *This Body Is Made of Camphor and Gopherwood,* and had a publisher ready to bring it out right now . . . and I was to tell no one! Of course I was flattered, and imagined flying to Sweden with a trenchcoat and hat brim snapped down over my eyes, passing over the corrections in the garage basement of an expensive apart-ment house at 3 AM . . . But I told her that I had already sent some to you months ago, and in any case, you were my old friend, and had pick of any that you wanted to translate . . . So that ended it . . .

So adieu, I must take the girls to a band concert. . . . .

Love from your friend,

the poetic chauffeur

Robert

Different title?

The Gift the Prose Poem Gives

It's odd but in this century not many original things have been said in an elevated or "raised" voice. It seems that the more original thoughts have appeared spoken in a quiet and low voice. Yesterday I read an Australian poet who writes both "lined" and prose poems, and I noticed that his speech followed more natural rhythms and word order in his prose poems than in his poems. In a prose poem we often feel a man or woman talking not before a crowd, but in a low voice to someone he is sure is listening.

It's possible that while a bird is building her nest an idea for a song she or he has never sung rises to its small head. So there are certain thoughts and impulses to thoughts in us that flow upward and into language only when the psyche is calm, and while language is being used. Buried impulses toward joy are carried upward on the artesian well of the prose poem that seem not to want to rise in the excited sunlight of the big rivers.

The prose poem is for poets in English a relatively new form, but I don't believe a new form in poetry rises accidentally, or only to amuse readers. It arrives because without it some feelings or half buried thoughts in us would remain beneath the consciousness, unsure of themselves, unable to break through.

There are beings made of white marble who watch us whenever we write. They represent the dissatisfaction of the dead with their own poetry. Much stiffness in line poetry is a sympathetic body reaction to these pale, needy divinities, who stand behind the man or woman writing, as pale as those Greek statues in museums, once all brilliant reds and yellows, now a dead white, all the paint flaked off, so that even their eyeballs are white. These white-eyeballed creatures make us nervous, as they try to take poetry away from wildness, and give it back to the superego, to the muse of museums. The man or woman writing a poem in this century has to deal with these white shapes, outdoing them by returning the red and green to the statues—Yeats does that—or by doing something they don't notice. Sometimes when I am writing a prose poem, I have the feeling I can go about my business without these white-eyeball people making so many demands. I don't mean that no one should write poems in lines, but I believe intimacy is important in a poem, and the prose poem helps with that.

Sometimes the spirit even begins to flow upward a little in the language of the prose poem. So prose poems perhaps resemble home or private religion; lined poems are more like public churches. The ancient world had both, and strangely, had different gods for the public religion than for the private, which were appropriately called "Mysteries."

A marvelous thing about the prose poem is how well it absorbs detail. One August day watching a rain shower, I was astounded at how many separate events were taking place, each taking place only once. Each needed to be given space in the poem separately, and I was glad for the prose poem form. The poem is called "August Rain." Even with it I missed most of the events I was watching.

I have a feeling that the contemporary poem longs for what takes place only once. All of us who have passed through the compulsory educational system find ourselves often unable to write the detail for years. We have been pushed too early into generalization. We have been asked to write about "humanity," not about the plumber next door who shot himself in the stomach in front of his own house. A prose poem by contrast does not ask for general statements, it urges us to return to the original perception—before the conclusion rushed in, provided by the mind. For example, one doesn't actually see "people crossing a street." One sees first the glint off the side of some shiny object moving, then the indefinably odd walk a figure with stick legs makes, then a child's red cap, then an arm swinging with some green substance on it, and after a few seconds, the brain reports: "It is people crossing the street when the light went green." In my high school papers I always gave the conclusion before the evidence; I reported, "Humanity wants to be free," or "The dignity of man cannot be corrupted." I like the way the prose poem so easily allows the original perception to live, so that in a good prose poem—just as in a good lined poem—it's possible that every noun could be a singular noun! Not one plural noun in the whole poem! I fail at that again and again, and reading my own prose poems I see that the plural consciousness is still with me, but the prose poem helps us to balance that with what takes place only once.

Robert Bly

Västerås 28-2-77
Dear Robert,
the ornithologists don't agree, but here is a possible translation of the missing part of the foreword:

Kanske händer det medan en fågel är i färd met att bygga sitt bo att idén till en sång den aldrig sjungit förut rinner upp i dess lilla huvud. Hos oss likadant: vissa tankar stiger upp bara när man arbetar med språket, använder det på ett lugnt sätt. Dolda impulser i glädjens riktning strömmar uppåt i prosadiktens artesiska brunn, sådant som inte tycks vilja komma fram i de stora flodernas häftiga solljus.

The rest seems OK. "Ganska" means "relatively" in Swedish—don't think about the German word "ganz" which ist etwas ganz anderes. As for the plumber I think I will ask Aggestam which is the best. Why did you change the sentence about Yeats? I don't like the new version because the word "triping" does not appear in my dictionary. There is a noun "tripe" meaning "inälvor" (intestines) but no verb.

I am leaving on Thursday morning for Germany and Switzerland, AT LAST. I will go by train all the way. The winter is awful here, snow every day.

Can you keep Charleston and New Orleans warm one year, or half a year or so? I don't think I can go this spring but I am longing very much to do a reading trip again, and not too far away in the future. I have had no invitation for a public reading outside Västerås for almost a year. They simply don't want me! Shocking isn't it? I am not even persecuted. And my books are sold out except for the latest 2, but *Stigar* will be sold out this week in the cheap sale drive. So there I am, without books, without platforms,—it is time to cross the Atlantic again.

I will write to you from EUROPE. Write soon. I will be back on March 12.
Love   Tomas

[4-3-77]

on the train . . .

Dear Robert,

Lasse Söderberg is now entering the game so I think there will be a rather FAT book of prose poems at last. They say it will be published by August. Rolf Aggestam knows. I don't know anything anymore, because I am on my way to Europe. If you have some unpublished (and approved!) translations of my poems I think you should let *Ironwood* have a look at them first. I know that the editor (what's-his-name?) is surprised that I never send anything for him. But don't give him too much! Arizona is so far away. Write soon! I will be back on March 11th. I will change trains in Norköping and then in Copenhagen and then sleep and then wake up in Köln.

Have a good time.

Your old friend
Idi Amin DADA

20 March, '77

Just a note to say . . .

Dear Tomas,

Just a note to say hello! Did you receive all my light-headed but faithful comments on your translations of my poems? I worked with astounding speed. (I have a whole cardboard box of mail from 1974 not yet answered.)

I will send a couple translations to *Ironwood,* but not too much. I only half like the man.

I will set up 10 readings for you this fall at $300 each if you will give me a time span, in say OCT, or NOV!

The Swedes may not ask you to read, but your readers over here are faithful, getting more so, positively ravenous. The Swedish book, primarily because of your poems, is one of the best selling books Beacon has had for several years. They are delighted, and watching *Scenes from a Marriage* religiously (it's on TV here now). They probably think it's about you. ("We got ready and showed our home.")

The word is *TRIPLING*—providing 3 times the energy—and so overwhelming the dead eyes that way—

Love, Robert

CARD BY NOAH BLY

[Editor's note: RB wrote the following on a copy of Two Hands News *with an account of this reading:]*

Yes the readings are getting more exciting. At this one, as I was about to begin, six surrealists shoved an enormous cream pie in my face. Then four "street poets" leaped to their feet and decided to beat hell out of the decadent intruders. So it goes!

[Editor's note: RB commented on a copy of the essay "Politics, Poetry and Prophets" by Peter Bates:]

Dear Tomas, You see they are *demanding* I write more political poems! They think seals and billfolds are not enough!

Västerås May 19-77
Dear Robert,
  a large part of this province is underwater. I just returned from a drive through the Strömsholm area where the fields are flooded, the trees standing in a lake, the waves coming closer and closer to the castle—the snow melted too quickly this year, partly because of the ruthless clean-cutting of the woods in the northern part of Västmanland . . . (see my poem for Mats and Laila!) . . . well, spring is here and I have decided to start writing letters again. I have thought it over many times, if I should go to the U.S.A. this autumn and I have found that I should. My poetic ego needs it, my poor poetic ego has shrunk so much that I have to use a magnifying-glass every morning to find it . . .
  You never told me about what has happened to Östen Sjöstrand in California. You sent me a letter telling me the sensational news that you were going to some place to hear Sjöstrand lecture or read or whatever it was. What was it like?

(turn the page softly)

Here are two pieces. The headache piece was not seriously meant, I sent it to Géza Thinsz, who is a fellow sufferer of migraine, as a private message. He translated it into Hungarian, I protested, but he tells me that it is so damned good in Hungarian and many Hungarians have congratulated me. So maybe I should add a note: "written in Swedish but should be read in Hungarian."

In the other piece (I don't know if I should call it "julpsalm" or "minus-grader") is the word "solkatt" (sun cat) which in Swedish means a reflection of the sun . . . If I have a small mirror in the sun I can throw a reflection on a wall, or in your face (you will get dazzled), this bright spot is called "solkatt" in Swedish and it is not in my dictionary but now you know what it means.

On Saturday my old friend the composer Glaser in Västerås will have a "salong" for a couple of friends. He brings people together and then plays his own compositions for them. This time he wants me to read something in the pause between his piano sonata and his symphony nr 1, so I will read prose poems by us. Maybe the hockey poem and some more. Maybe I should also tell them some stories about you.

Love to you all. I have come out from my winter hole, so please send me a letter and say hello!

Tömas

28 June 77

Dear Tomas,

How good to hear from you! Since yesterday I am an inhabitant of my new eight-sided house on my new land on the shore of Kabekona Lake!!!!! Loons all night, harsh crows, woodpeckers, thrushes, weird unidentified chortlings, the unconscious scattered out among a thousand small creatures in the brush! Please write me here: c/o Cry of the Loon Lodge, Laporte, Minn, 56461. The people at the Lodge are friends, and we get our mail there. Carol is here, also Noah and Micah. Mary and Biddy are at a language camp nearby, learning French.

About the lies—in late May I decided I couldn't stand the deceit and unclearness any more and I told Carol what I feel about Ruth and what was happening there. Carol knew with some part of herself, and with some part not. So there has been much grief here. And many old griefs in the marriage, also involving lies—in which, as you say, I live evidently as a fish in muddy water—came to the surface. But for all of us, there is a relief and even a lightness in the clarity at last. It looks as if Ruth will go to the Jung Institute in Zurich this winter, while we all figure out what to do. Don't grieve for us—I tell you this from a similar desire for clarity toward and among the men and women I love—that we love—so I include my love to you and Monica. You should probably not tell Monica yet. Carol may want to do that when she feels the time is right.

Your friend,
Robert

7 July, '77

Dear Tomas,

I'm thinking of you on your island with nothing to read, and so I'm sending you my longest prose poem of recent times! It's all about a piece of wood I picked up in a pasture—thank God there aren't a lot of poets walking around in pastures up here, who knows how many more such objects there may be!

 It looks roughly like this

I am in good shape, only about $10,000 in debt, but I hope to raid the universities this fall to make up some of that.

The order of prose poems planned for the Swedish book is fine. I'm sending the editor a photograph today if I can find one.

I'll write soon about your AMERICAN TOUR this fall, which I'm looking forward to very much! I'll get Mark Strand to introduce you at every reading, with a forty minute talk about "Nothing," then Allen Ginsberg will play several Indian instruments during the reading to provide authentic Swedish flavor, and finally a concrete poet will close with his new poem "Tractor Sounds." As soon as that is finished, he is immediately given a university position, and your books are confiscated by the library, along with your sweater, which you unwisely took off during the reading: that is sold to Texas, and becomes a permanent part of the "Lars Gustafsson Collection."

Do write.   Love, Robert

[undated, 1977?]

Dear Tomas,

A few notes on "August Rain." The towels are from swimming—ones the children left outdoors near the cars when I brought them home the day before from the swimming pool. The "stoop" which you've translated as "pall" is the small wooden platform just outside the screen-door entrance to my study (the schoolhouse). I don't know what you call it. I could have watched the rain from inside the screenporch, but I would have missed some, so I sat outdoors (dragging a chair out with me). (Just an ordinary wooden chair.) "Become crowded" should give the feeling of lots of people on a sidewalk. "Farstu" and "verandan" are in the English both "porch," the little screenporch alongside the schoolhouse. "Livere numarna" I don't recognize. The belts are the simple leather belts a workman might wear—he left for the hospital so quick he didn't get a chance to change it from his "everyday" pants to his "Sunday" pants—"the bachelor" would be a 65 year old farm worker who never had money enough to marry. "Wainscoting" is the old wood boards that used to be put along the bottom of walls. It implies an old farmhouse, never remodeled. The "trunks" are the ships' trunks that get heavier in-between our trips to Europe every four or five years, or even the "suitcases" that get heavier in-between my poetry reading trips. I guess it must be "trunks" because they rub against the side of some old steamer's hold, and somewhere make a hole in the wooden side of the ship. The last sentence is the most important in sound. It should sound triumphant and joyful—water coming in after a long drought!—and only after the reader has taken that in, and is glad, does he notice that it is also an image for the death of the speaker.

If you have one more to do, try "November Day at McClure's" or "Grass from Two Years" or "Windy Day at the Shack."

Love, Robert

Västerås Oct 7 -77

Dear Robert,

strange how encouraging it is to hear your voice on the telephone, even when you have nothing encouraging to say! A good gift. Life is rather calm now. I have returned from a trip to Norway. That small country in the west has received some Swedish culture: from Västerås a boys' choir and the famous writer Lars Gustafsson. I followed in the steps of the boys' choir to Kristiansand—Lars went to Ålesund. I also visited Bergen (together with Jersild and 2 nice ladies who wrote children's books). And alone I went to Stavanger where my offering to give a reading was rejected by the Norwegians but accepted by Robin Fulton, who teaches English there: he gave me one of his lecture hours—we discussed (in English) translation problems and so on with his students. But Kristiansand was very warm and Oslo too. I gave a lecture for the Scandinavian language students. One of them wants to write a thesis about me but the teacher said that he would probably not be allowed to—everything later than Hamsun is regarded as improper there.* Anyway, I am more pro-Norwegian than ever. A country without city culture. "Lutefisk" with bacon. In "Teatercafeét" the waiters are *Indians* nowadays—how exotic to hear an Indian speak Norwegian! In Stavanger there were a few buildings as ugly as the new ones in Sweden. (Oil boom disease.) But the rest is completely Norwegian.

---

* "Especially when written in non-Norwegian dialect."

I will publish a new book next year. Two poems are needed still. They are underway. But some of my colleagues seem to be able to finish a whole book more quickly. I will die as a still-promising poet at 80 . . .

You mentioned Boston. Where in Boston, and who? Our dear sad-voiced Hamburger? Is Boston a good landing place for the Swedish Nightingale? Or should I leave the U.S. from Boston? Maybe I should land in Oberlin—or Minnesota—to get some good and bad advice about what translations to use during the trip. The *Field* people have no hesitations about giving advice. I sent them some translations and they came back with a letter saying that they had 43 proposals for changes in the translation. It would be easier for them to give these proposals face to face.

Maybe this is a good air trip: Stockholm-Minneapolis-Cleveland-Laredo-Boston-Stockholm. Instead of Laredo you could propose other places very far south. The University of Galveston? The Pensacola Poetry Center? (I am looking at my map.) But let us not forget Atlanta. I was moved because they had me so recently and yet want me back.

It is good to know that we have some time to think about that before I rush to the airport. But who knows? You might disappear again, not returning until April 15. In that case I will be in America already, sitting on my suitcase at the Miami airport crying for Betty Kray.

Everybody in your house is warmly hailed

by

Tomas

1978

Jan '78[?]

Dear Tomas,

I started working today on your tour, so I'm not captured by a flying saucer after all!! I want you to get to New Orleans . . . What is happening in Sweden? Here we are waiting for blood transfusions—the poetry is getting worse. I think it must be mercury in the water . . . I've finally finished my Rilke translations I've worked on for 20 years, and Harper & Row has promised me $4,000 for it! We'll be rich!! Right now I'm so broke the children couldn't go to the basketball game tonight—only Carter's brother is rich in this administration. We are all well here, and I'll tell you all that is happening and has happened when you come!

Rip Van Winkle's doctor,
Robert

Västerås Jan 20-78

Dear Robert,

wonderful to hear that New Orleans is possible. And to hear from you, it was a long time ago! Many things have happened and at the same time not very much! We are well but a little overworked. Monica's colleagues in the hospital are a frail sort, often ill, so she has been on duty too much since Christmas. Epidemics are harassing Sweden now. I have been active too, in my job and also writing to Oberlin, to the Swedish Institute and a Yes-reply to Iowa. The Swedish Institute wants to send me to Seattle first. Here is a sketch of my trip.

North pole

Seattle

around
april 1st

preliminary
  sketch.
  Is it
  realistic?

Minnesota
(Minneapolis?
Meeting you)

Iowa
workshop

Oberlin
(We together—
you longer than I)

The South!
(Please help me with these
addresses)
                                   Home

Texas?
(Lars Gustafsson recommends
Austin, a Christopher Middleton . . .)
  Have you any contact
    with them?

My economy now is almost as bad as that of Sweden in general. But on Wednesday I will go to Stockholm and sell my new book! I finished everything except the title (do you have any good titles left over?) two days ago. The most difficult thing to finish was the long poem I include in this letter, a mini-sized Faust, "Ihr naht euch wieder schwankende Gestalten," confessions of a too complicated psychologist. All the people mentioned are my previous clients, including myself 10 years ago: "En konstnär sa: etc." The opening scene is from a motel in Laxå, West Sweden in 1969. That was a bad night! Stop Tomas, you are talking too much. Any difficult words in the poem? "Kohandel" is a funny old fashioned slang word for give-and-take deal, mostly in politics. I find in my dictionary the word "log-rolling," which seems mysterious. "Karbol" is a cheap purifier used in hospitals, probably "carbole" in English. "Det lyhörda huset" means a house that is insufficiently sound proofed, where you can hear what your neighbor is doing.

I remember that I did not thank you for the beautiful Snail-book. How ungrateful! But I was grateful when I read it.

I have seen only one review of our Bly-volume in Swedish. It was Björn Håkansson in *Aftonbladet*, saying some nice words about you and attacking the Publisher for not giving enough information about you (about your service in the navy probably) but the publisher, or rather, Aggestam, thought that you are so well known in Sweden that a presentation is unnecessary. I also met a person who said "I don't agree with your foreword at all"—he thought *I* had written your foreword because my initials were after, meaning that I am the translator. I will send you clippings when something interesting arrives . . .

How is my godson?

Love
Tomas

Västerås Febr 19-78
Dear Maestro,
　　　a short note about what happens here. I had asked the Swedish Institute for a contribution to my U.S. trip, got a half-promise and waited for the definite word. The other week came this message: Sorry, we have spent all our money for this budget year, try again after July 1. Then I wrote

to Betty Kray, who had sent me a nice letter, and asked for 3 days free lodging in her house in New York—I wanted to start in New York because that is the cheapest trip. But the other day I had a preliminary positive answer from another foundation, so I will probably get some travel expenses paid after all. I will probably start with New York anyway, not Seattle . . . Well, that depends. If you have promised me to some place in California it would be a good idea to start in Seattle, but otherwise Boston or other places in the east would be better. Tell me! What I will do is probably this: I'll buy a ticket for New York and back plus a $390 ticket for endless flights inside the U.S.A.—my travel bureau tells me this exists, maybe only for Europeans? Well, send me a small note anyway, I am eagerly waiting for information so I can draw a map. I have always loved maps.

In the meantime, take a look at the two clippings from Sweden. Lundkvist has read the prose poem anthology. He is not included himself. Gyllensten is angry. The article is one of the better volcano eruptions since Strindberg's days. Gyllensten is of course too paranoiac here, the narrow-mindedness and the need to make the great men shrink is not quite so systematic and conspiratory as it is described here. But he has lanced a boil with a carving-knife. Will the patient be better or worse?

Ironwood wants to make a special Tranströmer issue. They sent a Wright-issue with your horse David in it.

Love to all on the farm

Tomas

Västerås March 16 [1978]
Dear friend and Impresario,

I think I will go back to Sweden April 19 and that means that IF somebody between Austin and New York City is interested in a reading on the days 16th–18th I am willing to do it. I can see Georgia, South Carolina, Alabama etc., wonderful states full of universities and poetry freaks . . . And if Austin says no (which I hope it doesn't) I can do readings anywhere south of Oberlin during April 14th–18th.

Your questions about "Galleriet" . . . The faces are pushing forward through the overpainting of oblivion. As if through a wall. Or as seals pop up to the surface to breathe . . . The part with "hissen." It is the same hiss (elevator) as you once traveled in, when we visited my mother's apartment in Stockholm in 1968. In Sweden we have the following system of electric lights in staircases of houses. A button is pushed and then the light lasts for 3 minutes or so, then it is dark and you have to push a switch again. So I arrive (one winter evening) when a previous person has switched on the light 3 minutes before. It suddenly gets dark, except inside the lift, where there is a separate lamp, which is always on. Do you understand? So when the whole house is dark the lift is shining (and rising) like a diving-bell. And as I live on the 5th floor I pass floor after floor and imagine faces looking into the lift when it passes each floor. I am ten years old.

There is a snowstorm today. Horrible. It was spring yesterday. I know so little about your situation now but I am thinking of you. Here is all well. Monica sends her warmest

Tomas

Västerås May 11-78
Dear Robert,

it's unbelievable: cold and windy, a true winter day. And Sweden was beaten by Czechoslovakia (in ice hockey) by 6–1. I am in a miserable mood, trying to feel better by writing to you. You left the coffee shop in Minnesota . . . after a while Keith Harrison arrived, more energetic than ever. I remember nothing from the reading except that I (for once) followed your advice to let the host do part of the reading, Keith in his forceful Australian . . . The party afterwards with an Indian couple: Mr. and Mrs. Ramanujan. I slept in Keith's house. Close to his bathroom in the upper floor is a flight of stairs so steep that an abyss opens. In the middle of the night I went to the bathroom in complete darkness, went back, took a long step and suddenly found myself hurtling into the abyss, but turned miraculously, almost in the air, and was saved, went back to bed, slept, went to Oberlin, hugged the whole Oberlin lot, gave a reading *in a very loud voice* without dropping a single syllable (I questioned the whole audience afterwards). After this the trip went well, my Minnesota (or Louisiana) disease conquered. Two professors met in Austin, both fluent in Swedish, especially Bob Rovinsky, who is also a distinguished marathon runner. During the walk in the Lyndon Johnson part of Austin the following day I happened to meet two dwarves and I also bought some good records. In Atlanta Coleman Barks met me, it was moving to see him again (I met him last time in the U.S.), we went quickly to Troy, had some catfish on the way there, and stayed overnight in Ed Hicks's house. Have you met that man? He is a 2-7-1, an extreme muscle type, a former baseball star, now a Faulkner specialist and also a pilot with his own aeroplane. He is very nice. I found that in Troy I was a sort of test pilot myself—Ed used me to prove that he could make his colleagues and superiors accept a non-Alabaman, non-Southern, even a non-American poet in Troy. They did not want to pay of course. But he forced them to . . . The reading was funny, in a restaurant, with a nice audience including some necktied professors. Next day through a tornado to Indianapolis and Muncie. I don't think the reading went very well there, the audience was like a Swedish one. The flight home was taxing, delayed by tornadoes etc. When we left Kennedy airport a flash of lightning hit the plane, the purser in front of me fluttered up like a rooster in an earthquake, which was more discouraging than the thunderbolt itself . . . I forgot to tell you that I was very happy to have your parcel in Muncie—those wonderful dolls! 2 great *penates*.

Yes, master, that is how it ended. It was a healthful trip for me (especially for my economy) and it was necessary to see you again and find out that, in spite of the tragic complications around you, you are the same person and the same irreplaceable friend.

Important: tell me the full name and address of "Calvin" in New Orleans. I lost it. It is important for Swedish music, I have plans to send him some symphonies he could play on his radio programs.

Emma has quit school and is now working as a horseman in Småland. She will start in a new class this autumn. Love

Tomas

23 May '78

Dear Tomas,

Just a note to tell you that I too returned more or less sane from my reading tour—like you, my last stop was Muncie, Indiana. The audience stared at me as if they had recently seen an inhabitant of a flying saucer, and I was *not* one, but I managed to get through the reading, and get home. Now Noah and Micah and Biddy (sometimes Mary) and I play softball every evening. Micah is an excellent first baseman, with one exception—he never catches the ball. Outside of that he is fine.

I heard of your refusal of Gov Wallace's photograph—that has already become legend in the Red Branch Cycle of stories of visiting poets—and I must say the story pleased me! Southern ladies are insistent!

Calvin Harlan's address is c/o Art Department, University of New Orleans, New Orleans, Louisiana.

Thank you for receiving my grief and my uncertainties and my shadowy complications without running out the door. I enjoyed our reading together and I have heard nothing but good reports of your readings! I'll send you a funny report of the Oberlin reading in the next letter—no enclosures allowed in this one!

Carol has a new job with Farmers Union—$2000 a month for three months. I think that will be very good for her.

With deep fondness always,
Robert

Katrineholm 6-9-78
Dear Robert,
as often when in strange circumstances, I like to write to you. I'm longing for an answer.

I am at the training center for civil defense officers in Katrineholm. I am taught sick-care in general and especially to dig out, rescue and transport wounded civilian people under tumbled-down houses. I wear a helmet and institution clothes and everything is rather military except for the fact that we carry no weapons at all. It is not meaningless. Anyone can happen to meet a tumbled-down house! Didn't you fall from the roof of your chicken house once—if I had had this training I could rescue you very quickly. You would get expert embalming (or what is the word for winding cloth around broken extremities?).

Michael Cuddihy wants to have some letters from me to you but I have to censor them a little first—I mean wipe out things that might insult an innocent reader of *Ironwood*. Of course if you have burned my letters already, then there is no problem. (I will not take away my stupidities, only the worst gossip.)

And, at last, what happens to you? Is it bad? Is it better? Are the children as irresistible as when I saw them.

Here everything is fine, and I suppose they are saying hello, but I can't promise because I live in this civil defense camp . . . I will be back in Västerås 11 days from now. Write!

Your friend   Tomas

21 Sept, '78

Dear Tomas,

Thank you for your letter when out rescuing people from collapsing houses! It's good to know you could rescue me, if you could only get over here in time . . .

I'm happy these days—sometimes positively joyful. My life is arranged this way: The first two weeks of each month I'm at my writing cabin at Kabekona—Ruth and her children are nearby—she is working in a home for 350 mental patients, all considered incurable by the State—no psychiatrist at all for them, not even one—and then on the 15th of each month or so, I come down to Madison, and live in this lovely house I've bought in Madison, at 127 2nd Ave. Madison 56256. I came down here on the 15th of Sept and the boys have been living with me since, and we're in the process of furnishing the rooms for Mary & Biddy. All is going well in that area. Don't worry for your impulsive, prudent friend . . . and Carol, I think, is doing well too. She's going to England in a few weeks, and doing a reading

tour in Connecticut in late October. I'll get to work on that letters prob-
lem, and send any letters chosen to you <u>before</u> *Ironwood* sees them . . . A
hug from the Norwegian owl. Love to Monica!!

Robert

12 Nov, 78

Dear Tomas,

I've finally gotten the letters together for *Ironwood!* I had lots of fun
doing it—you are one of the greatest letter writers in the literary commu-
nity at the moment! It's a community of mumblers, compulsive secret-
keepers, stutterers, verbal limpers, balloon enthusiasts of sin, sailing over
the "poor details of life"—In any case, here are eight chosen half at ran-
dom, half from an eye to humor—they are very funny! Cross out whatever
you don't want in, drop out whole letters if you want to. I think they're all
good. The praise of me
[------]
can't do it in English, because the pun on Sanning and sound-barrier
only exists in Swedish! What can I do? Make up a new title? *At the Edges
of Truth?*—How about *The Railroad Crossing of Truth?*—or *The Customs
Barriers of Truth?* See what I mean?

Do write—your friend
Robert

Love to Monica!

1979

Dear Tomas,

How good to get a letter! You certainly did right to remove that sentence of Monica's . . . my enemies would be sure I had added it in proof anyway. My reputation for modesty is not extreme, since occasionally I rewrite Goethe, and this is—I don't know why—considered immodest by some.

I was most alarmed when you began to plunge into the subject of your health; but relieved to find it is only high blood pressure. That is not serious. And I now understand the Danton poem . . . if I might start a new school of *Medical Imagery Examination* I would say that Danton's being on stilts is a sure diagnosis by the unconscious of high blood pressure. But no one listens to me . . . the poem says you have to become more like Robespierre, take long baths, spend hours on your toilette, etc. My poems say that I spent too much time in the snow, and I must move out of my teepee.

I think I *will* try to use the word "customs" in the title of your book. I'll try to think of a casual expression for those custom benches and desks and check out counters that one finds in the European airports . . . Did I ask you to send me a copy of whatever translation you've been using of the Schubert poem? It will save me many questions of you, but on the other

343

hand . . . I can figure it out if you're willing to correct my stanzas without humiliating me too much. I'm sensitive, being Norwegian . . . By the way, I met that dear man, Lou Camp when I read in Pennsylvania recently . . . (At Wilkes-Barre, when I was being driven back to my bed, I saw a movie theater marquee, with the words

FLOOD INNOCENT

on it. I thought it was a movie about a flood, but it turned out that the famous representative Flood had helped so many in Wilkes-Barre with his numerous crooked schemes that the theater owner put the phrase up there as a sort of primitive magic . . . the verdict is not yet in from the jury.) Lou Camp's wife has left him, Bobbie . . . I was astounded at that, but it seems that she really wanted a career, and felt that Lou's presence was a drawback in that area. He's not very happy at all with the situation. He said something like "Now she has a career, and I am suffering!" He is still at Bucks County Community College.

I am finishing an anthology for the Sierra Club, of "nature poems." I decided to make it a polemical anthology, dividing the poets who believe there is no consciousness outside the human brain from the poets who sense a consciousness out in the trees and countryside. Work on it is very exciting. I've put in Harry Martinson's "Havsvinden." I am going to put in a poem of yours, for sure, but I haven't decided which one yet. Do you have any thoughts on this? Perhaps "A Section of Woods" . . . or an earlier poem?

The situation with the family seems to be all right. I enjoy deeply the two weeks that I spend each month with the children in my new house in Madison. And Carol and I are quite friendly, in literary matters, and in attempts to care for the children, and that is very helpful. She has finished a new story, and has established her crossword puzzle business. It all seems so strange . . . I can't really take it all in yet. I vary between depression and elation. The moods, and even the events, are by no means completely under the control of my will.

I send you both my affection and love.

Robert

April 2, 79

Dear Tomas,

Thanks for the news! It sounds as if Monica is coming *out of retire-ment*. Ellen Goodman is publishing a book of interviews with various American women who have been changing their lives, and one woman said that when she got married, it was like agreeing to *retire*. "I went into retirement right away"—How odd! So they get younger as they leave retirement—how strange!! I think Monica must be doing very well.

I'm enclosing my translation of your marvelous Schubert poem—please pick its poor nappy head for fleas, muskrats, porcupines, whatever creatures are living there unjustly. Is the end right?

I plan to send it to the *New Yorker* just to see what they will do.

We are all well here, quivering a little over the Three Mile Island Nuclear Plant—but otherwise cheerful.

I'm thinking of coming over to Scandinavia during the first two weeks of August. Do you think the Swedes would want me to read anywhere? Was it Svenska Radio who was looking for me last spring?

Saul is sitting here with me, on the lake shore, at Kabekona, and sends his best!!

> Love from your friendly
> "animal helper" as in the
> fairy stories—
> Robert

Västerås April 14 -79
Dear Roberto,

Thanks for a good letter, and a translation which is magnificent in tone (but with minor howlers . . . I will return later to them). Monica is back, after working for almost 3 weeks in Skåne with the Viet Nam refu-gees, or rather not directly with them but with establishing a medicare center for them in Perstorp, where most of the families will be housed. I

visited her once. Perstorp was a gloomy place and could be much helped
with a Chinese part of town. Now she is back in retirement for the next
weeks, and around May 1 we will go to Corfu for a week. And Emma has
left us. She is living together with a young man called Kenneth Karlsson!
She looks happy, so I hope he is a good fellow, but rather shy—he gets very
nervous when he catches sight of me or Monica.

I am happy to hear that you will come to Scandinavia in August. It is not
exactly the season for cultural activities, but the Radio is always open. I
will warn them in advance this time, so you can be invited to talk end-
lessly to the Swedish people, and also get paid for it! John Gardner was
here recently and they had a 2 hour "conversation" with him. I remember
a part that went like this:

Interviewer: And who is, in your opinion, the most important prose
writer in America just now?

Gardner: Well, I know it sounds a little arrogant, but actually I think
it is me.

etc.   It is also possible that a cabaret in Malmö, called "Fredagsbarnen"
(or is it "Mandagsbarnen"?) is active. They have readings and music etc.
I have been a guest there once (in 1974). This cultural cabaret is handled
by Lasse Söderberg and Jacques Werup, and I suppose Lasse would be
happy to have you read there, if you come to Malmö, and the cabaret is
not closed. Write to him! I will figure out who is the best person to warn
at the radio.

Love
Tomas

[Editor's note: Continuation of April 14th letter]

Let me praise you first. The sound, the music the strength in your translation
made me happy . . .

SCHUBERTIANA, comments.

Part I.

There are 2 places where I put a question mark. The first is "holding out a begging cup," which might be too drastic, Oriental, old fashioned, medieval. Maybe the begging of department store windows is more of a modern salesman teasing type. (I don't know how it sounds . . .) I mean, I don't want the reader to see a leprous hermit sitting there in the window, holding out his cup. "Whirlwind" is a little too strong too. Why not "swarm"?

The other thing is "catacombs in motion," which for me sounds almost like "slow motion." What struck me in New York was the violent rushing of the subway cars. Now a catacomb is static, calm, lifeless. A catacomb rushing forward is a paradox, but a ghostly and dangerous paradox. If "in motion" gives that impression it is OK. But the risk is that the motionlessness of the catacombs takes over the word "motion," so it becomes "slow motion." Why not "rushing catacombs"?

Part II

"Treeless" is unnecessary, maybe dangerous. If you mention a tree, even in connection with "-less" you see a tree in front of you, and I don't want to have those trees in my brain!

"Hundred-footed notes" . . . I say "tusenfotingar" which is a small animal, in my dictionary called "centipede" or "millipede."

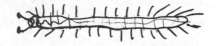

Do you see the similarity??? I want to have the animal kept in your translation. If you are allergic to centipedes you might use your version. But you have to give a reason.

For part V you say "Nor their music," but I suppose "Nor" is a misprint for "NOT."

Part III: perfect.
Part IV:

(Most of it I have to take on trust.) But "the Western Union message" is too Middle West! "Olyckstelegram" is probably untranslatable. It means a telegram with bad news, maybe fatal news. Can you say "calamitous telegram"? Probably not. Charters has "telegram about the accident," which is too long. Well, you have to think more about it.

(The talk about the ax blow from within is probably a presentiment of my high blood pressure . . .)

I am also against the "string musicians." I know that you cannot use "the bows," but maybe you could say "string instruments," or "bow-instruments." I don't want to have *the musicians* talking to me, I want to have the music.

Part V:

The part with our hands moving weights is a little disturbing. First, I don't think you should repeat "It looks," because it sounds as if it belonged to what looked "ridiculous" (previous line). No, the hands moving weights are not ridiculous. (What is ridiculous is the position of 2 men on the same stool, two drivers for the same carriage.) So start with the hands. They are moving weights etc. not in order to make the arm of the balance stand in a position of 50% happiness and 50% suffering. NO, we are trying to change it a little to the happiness side (probably without success). As if we moved the counter-weights, in an effort to alter the frightful equilibrium of the balance arm, where happiness and suffering weigh exactly the same.

Annie did not say "awfully heroic." She said "This music is heroic" (I am, as you know, almost always documentary) and she said it neutrally, or with estimation.

A question mark for "the higher / depths." It *might* be good. Difficult for me to know. But you should know what it means in Swedish

uppför = uphill

djupen = the depths

a paradox here too, or rather an unexpected turn. up / the depths . . .

25 April, 79

Dear Tomas,

Thank you for your letter, and the comments! Goodness, how strange, that Emma has leapt out of the nest! It seems to me they are both children . . . do you mean that my daughters will fly the coop too? Oh dear, that's not right.

There is so much talk here now about the special "TRANSTRÖMER-NUMBER" of *Ironwood*. I'm jealous of course. "No one ever does that for me!" I whimpered that to myself when it came, but I have recovered now, and enjoy greatly the American poets' puzzling as to why you don't fit into the neat categories of American poet-making. You carry some sort of European authority as well, and they believe what you do or say . . . I feel a Goethe-complex approaching.

I've sent "Schubertiana" to the *New Yorker,* and if they accept it, we'll both get a little money! I think you're right on "begging cup" and I'll change that.

"Catacombs in motion" is declared by all hearers as a lucky phrase, full of energy and very ominous. It is the repetition of the long "o" that gives it its mystery, I think. "Catacombs in motion."

I tried "centipede" and it is terrible! In Swedish you actually see the *feet,* in "Tusenfotingar" and I have to have a way in English for the reader to see feet also. If I say *centipede,* he sees a cellar, dirty, with broken linoleum, old orange peels, backed up sewer, etc.

"Treeless" I'm not sure about. I'll brood on it.

"Western Union" I <u>will</u> change!

Your note on the weights is helpful—I believe Sam Charters has it wrong too—I just checked his—I understood you to say exactly the opposite, that suffering and happiness are equally valuable (weigh the same)! I'll work on that passage.

Who is this Annie, the authority on the heroic? I thought she found it too heroic! There I am reading my interpretation of women's consciousness into women.

"upward toward
the depths"   ?

Love,
Robert

29 April, 79

Dear Tomas,

How strange it is! On Friday two unusual things happened, both surrounding you. About two years ago I met a young man at M.I.U. (Maharishi International University at Fairfield, Iowa) who drew well in pencil, and I asked him to do a few drawings for the next book of your translations. On Friday he turned up, with 14 MAGNIFICENT DRAWINGS, inspired by your new poems, copies of which I had sent him . . . they are full of energy, powerful horses, intelligent sheep, a cow floating in the air with a luminous udder (a sort of introverted, Asian cow)—I think you'll like them very much. I'll ask him to do three more—I liked 12 of the 14—then we'll have 15 poems and 15 drawings for *Truth-Borders*. About twenty minutes later, the door opened and Augustin and Brita Mannerheim came in! They stayed overnight, and I took them along to an extravaganza the 4th, 5th, & 6th grades put on at the local school, with Noah as a miner, all the kids singing "American music." Then the next day I found out that he, like me, is determined to write in classical length meters—another sound-fanatic! I liked them both—and they spoke of you two so warmly—cheered my heart—

Love, Robert

31 Oct, 79

Dear Tomas (and Monica)

Well, guess what! I've just finished translating all of *Barriers to Truth*, and Mary is just now typing it. I'll send a copy to you in the next mail, so that you can embarrass me again. I probably translated "dog" as "mouse-seed" and "Paradise" as a lowlevel radiation measuring device.

I had some hurt feelings when you were in the U.S. I guess it was because you hadn't mentioned at all that you were coming, and I heard about it by accident, and interpreted your silence to mean that you didn't want to see me, didn't approve of me, etc. So I was glad to get the broadside you left for me in San Francisco with a cheerful message on it, at least, and a feeling of friendship.

I heard very mixed reports of the doings arranged by the ORTHODOX SWEDES at San Francisco. The Swedish writers apparently insisted on talking all the time about the writer's unions, and collectives, and collaborations with the Government and such stuff; the Americans in the audience wanted desperately to talk about poetry. Finally one young poet stood up, and said to the Swedes: "All of this makes me want to cry." I liked that. I heard that you slipped out of the room whenever possible, and people guessed you must have felt a little of the restiveness over this incessant collective obsession too. Americans long for *soul* and the Swedes somehow didn't understand that.

Please write to me, and tell me what your news is. I have a house in Minneapolis, where I live half the month now (the cabin at Laporte is closed up for the winter). My address in Mpls—I'm going there tomorrow—is 4041 South Vincent, Minneapolis 55410. Please give a big hello to Monica.

As ever,
Robert

Västerås Dec 2nd -79

Dear Robert,

again a little time for my own benefit (the martyr is speaking), a small amount of time to sit down and talk about *Truth Barrier*. Weather is gray, I don't feel healthy and Emma has a crisis with her boyfriend, which shakes the whole family. How good to know that somebody over there takes trouble to translate even

"Street Crossing"

which is untranslatable, so I give it to you—make whatever you can. I hesitate to discuss it, I want to trust you. After all, you are a great poet in English. BUT. I object to the last line. I want to have "But for a second I am luminous (or lit, or shining). The street sees me." In your version here "It" could as well mean "the sun." Or even "the light." I don't know exactly what it means to "be in the light," it sounds symbolic to me. If you insist on "I am in the light," I can take it, but you must add "The street sees me." The line will be a little too long, but never mind.

"The Clearing"

Your secretary made a mistyping in line 2—instead of "be found be those" it should be "be found by those." The whole tone of your translation sounds like a good Bly prose poem tone to me, I am happy for that. I have a few reservations though. "The name sleeps somewhere" should be plural: "The names sleep" etc. . . . I think a whole family has been living in the house. I want to have "the gypsy tribe" instead of "gypsy race." "Race" is a difficult word to use, and in this connection I am not thinking of the gypsies as a race, but as a group with a tradition (non-literate tradition). "This house, where the hired man lived." OK I can understand that for some reason "the croft" is not the right word, but isn't it too much to explain it by saying "where the hired man lived"? What is wrong with croft? Maybe you should say simply "the simple house" or "little house." Or "The cottage"? Think it over. *There is a sentence missing.* After "hums with voices" comes a sentence: "Det är världens centrum." (It is the center of the world.) Did your secretary forget it? (Send my best to her, I hope to see her again soon.)

"First Chapter of a Late Autumn Novel"

I don't know the quality of the word "reek." Does it mean very bad smell? In that case I would like to have a more neutral word, like "smell." I don't like oil but I don't think it stinks. Don't forget to italicize the word "is" in the sentence "if night really *is* something." A point to discuss is the expression "That world is also this one." Maybe it's right. The last sentence: "wonders" is for me a little too positive, I want to have a word more in the monster direction. How is "prodigies"? Good translation probably.

I just got the report from my tax authorities. I got an after taxation of 13,000 Swedish crowns ($3,100), which should all be paid before May 1980. So I propose you look for a very generous publisher for *Truth Barrier*! The moment of truth has arrived. I'll write soon again. Let me hear something from you!

Love
Tomas

11 Dec. 79

Dear Tomas,

Your remarks were all very much to the point, excellent. I made use of every one of them. "Street Crossing" ends "But for a second I am lit. The street sees me."

In "The Clearing," you're surely right about "Where the hired man lived." I do some awkward gymnastics, parallel-bar work, a sort of over-weight Comaneci every once in a while, in order to get an American tone in the language. "Croft" is utterly English, and never caught on here. But the long clause with the hired man didn't work either, so I guess we'll go back to "little house." I also changed "name" to "names," and "race" to "tribe," which I prefer anyway. I added the missing sentence. I don't know why you refer to my "secretary"—I type each of these poems with my own little clawed hands. Occasionally I get Mary or Biddy to retype poems for magazines, etc., but their work goes in spurts, interrupted by washing their hair, etc.—high school girls are not reliable help!

Do you think "monsters" is too strong for "vidunders"? I had it once but it got lost in the various drafts. Please talk a little about "That world is also this one." Am I missing something there? or oversimplifying . . .

Please forgive me for the mess last August, when I said I was coming and didn't. I was much distracted. But one letter of yours evidently didn't arrive. The last letter I had from you said that you hadn't been able to get ahold of the Swedish Radio people, and that Lasse's place was closed in August. I didn't have the money to go there without some help from Radio or a reading, so I abandoned the whole project in that depressed state caused by money shortages. More later!

Love, Robert

1980

Dear Tomas,

Thank you for your new letter about "MINUSGRADER." You cleared up many points that were floating there in doubt with me—thank you! I think I will call it "Below Freezing." I knew that "inte alskar oss" means "doesn't love us," but I can never tell when that might just be some slang phrase meaning the party was no good! Ah well, stupidity, sweet stupidity!

Would you accept: "A spot of sun that moves over the house walls and slips over the unaware forest of faintly lit faces"? Does "faintly lit" seem all right? "gleaming," "glimmering," "flickering" are all very hard to use in English.

GOOD NEWS! Sierra Club has accepted *Truth Barriers* and will publish it in the fall. I asked for and got $1000 for you. I'll try to get it for you before your tax deadline. Was that May 1st?

It is the first book of poems the Sierra Club has ever printed, and an important step for them. You'll be read by all sorts of people climbing glaciers, investigating unknown rivers in Argentina, arguing against capitalists at the Supreme Court—They have published some of the most beautiful books in the U.S., and are prospering when many other houses are in trouble.

Question: Is "furnishings" (furniture, lamps, pictures, etc) OK for "detaljerna"? Question: Does the chalk line say *Someone has scribbled chalk on the car doors* or *A piece of chalk has* scribbled on the car doors? .

Thank you for your helpful letter. Give me your exact dates *[Editor's note: The rest of the letter is lost.]*

Robert

24 Jan '78 [1980]

Dear Tomas,

The American Scandinavian Foundation has a contest for translators, closing in a couple of weeks. I'm going to send in *Truth Barriers,* and so I'd love to have the rest of your corrections soon, so I can add those before sending the Mss. off. Why be caught in embarrassing positions?

I've sent *Poetry East* the new version of "Below Freezing."

There is very sad news here. James Wright has cancer of the throat, and may not live very long. I'm going to New York to see him Feb 1st. He's not responding to radiation treatment and in much pain.

I send my love, as always,

Your faithful friend
Robert

16 Feb, 80

Dear Tomas,

Thank you for your last letter. I gobble the corrections up immediately, like a sort of turkey; and cackle happily afterwards. You must be about half way through now. Sierra Club by the way has assigned the best book designer in the country, a Swiss named Jack Leffenberg, something like that, who will integrate the drawings and type. It's due out in the fall.

I enclosed for your amusement a mad letter from the Oberlin milieu; Stuart and David Young, to my surprise, didn't want anyone to come that they weren't teaching this semester. This man named Wharton asked me to come, and I innocently said yes, if he could find the money. Stuart and David went wild. I don't understand it all, but I did gather that the Tao Te Ching would suggest I not go!

I'm working so hard on poems. It's such a blessing to have some time to work. When I am here, with the children, I do no readings, and so have about three hours a day to write. I am veering back toward form, now, with a new view of it, supported partly by my amateur researches on sound, or repeating sounds. So now I am actually taking new prose poems and putting them into lines . . . exactly reversing what I was doing five years ago, when I took some lined poems, and changed them into prose poems! I am writing at the moment mainly in "twos and threes" . . . that is, a line with two beats, followed by a line with three. The main problem with us is to avoid all iambic rhythms; if we allow any in, the ghosts of English poetry take over; the reader then falls into a schoolboyish trance, and doesn't understand a thing being said to him.

I'll be here in Madison another two weeks. The alternation this year is three weeks and three weeks; three weeks the children stay with me at my bachelor house in Madison, and then three weeks they move out to the farm with Carol. That works amazingly well; and Carol and I are quite friendly in this arrangement. She is doing many lectures, and is doing a book of essays for Harper and Row.

I feel more calm, and more at home in myself and in my poems than I have for many years. And I value my friendship with you, and your poems, very much!

Fondly,
Robert

8 May, 80

Dear Tomas,

You see there's no end to foolishness—this lady translates from a language she doesn't know at all . . . This is chutzpah even beyond mine!

I hope you enjoyed your Cape Cod stay!

Your *Truth-Barriers* is already in proof . . . I must hurry now and do my introduction! I think I'll say you are the *Galsworthy of the North* or some such ringing phrase—how about the *Goethe of the Snow*?

The James Dickey of pacifism . . . the Nabokov of the *uninhabited motel*—

Sierra Club hopes you'll be here (in Berkeley) this fall, so they can show what a barrier to truth looks like . . . all Californians are transparent channels for eternity—

As you can tell, I'm somewhat hysterical and mind-clogged today, having just returned from a 20-day tour. My ego is simultaneously inflated and deformed—it resembles one of those balloons in the Macy Parade—with enormous fingers—held down by ropes . . . The air will start escaping soon. My children insert pins if I remain floating too long.

Please write!! Love to Monica!!

Love,

Robert

3 Oct, 80

Dear Tomas,

This is the first review of our book—pre-publication, as they call it! It says there it will be out in November. I think you'll like the design. You are due to get $1000 then—would you like to have it from the income tax point of view in *this* calendar year, or the *next* (on January 2nd)? Either is fine.

News of the Universe is selling well, getting excellent reviews, and the Sierra Club is licking its paws. You do have a copy of it?

We have moved into a house in Moose Lake, which has a sauna in the woodshed. What health! I'm playing the piano again, and Ruth and I are practicing a Mozart Violin-Piano piece. What a joy!!!!!!

Love to Monica.

Your musical friend

Robert

Västerås 4-11-80

Dear Robert,

   when I *write* this your election has not started, but when you *read* this the show is over, and maybe you are already used to the sad fact that Reagan became President . . . Or? Another strange thing is that people on a planet in the Andromeda galaxy looking at the earth will see the earth as it was 2 million years ago . . .

   It is a black period of 2 weeks for me. First the election. Then to-morrow the TV program, yes I am on TV tomorrow, for 28 minutes, and I don't like it. I have seen the film, the producer cut away everything intelli-gent, so I look as stupid as I probably am, innermost. People will recognize me in the street . . . When Sonnevi was on TV he got 25 letters from un-known people, some saying things like "I understand that you had a diffi-cult childhood." And next week: civil defense training again. I have every opportunity to lose face—I will command a bunch of reluctant samari-tans, and I have forgotten everything I learned, I don't even know how to raise the tent that is my headquarters.

   After the 2 black weeks I will settle down and try to have some fun. Playing chamber music etc. . . . .

   I am very much *for* your prose poem about the old ant mansion. It's an awfully good piece.

   In this letter I send—for your amusement—a "debate" about the reasons for my American reputation. The guilty one is you, as always. What has happened to Lundkvist in America?
                    Love from us all
                         Tomas

                    13 Nov, '80

Dear Tomas,

   Yes, Reagan is President! Ruth went to a dance class the next day, and no one wanted to move. They all stood around, couldn't do the exercises; the bodies were stiff and heavy.

I'll write a note to *Lyrikvännen* if you will send me the address! I want to mention the PLANS—a Sonnevi book etc. I probably should take a vow—as in Alcoholics Anonymous—never to translate another book of yours! But that is too moral—even for me!

Your book will be out next month and the $1000 is ready—shall I send it now or on Jan 2nd?

We are all well. Noah began piano lessons today, and Micah began horn lessons. I got him a cornet last week. Sam is starting the guitar. We'll have a band soon. I'll get out my old saxophone.

Please tell me what the reviewers said about your TV Premiere. You'll probably get offers of marriage. In general, young boys ask me to be their father over here. How can one make *less* impact?

Fondly,

Robert

Västerås 25 nov -80

Dear Robert,

yes please send the Truth Barriers' dollars as fast as possible—the bills are piling up. I need a pair of winter shoes too!

I have been invited to Adelaide for March 1982! The same meeting as the one you visited last year. Tell me everything about Australia!

I will not recommend you to write anything for *Lyrikvännen,* I mean, in this debate about the size of Tranströmer and his contemporaries. Very embarrassing. The address is Lyrikvännen, Box 130, 10121 Stockholm. But don't use it.

Everything is fine. I have almost digested the election. I have survived the latest civil defense training (3 days only) in a healthy sleet. I have survived my TV show too. People liked it, shop assistants and plumbers, even professors. People here have been very generous in an un-Swedish way.

Hope everything is fine with you and your new and old families.

Best

Tomas

1981

6 Feb 81

Dear Tomas,

I was in SF last week, and found out to my surprise that *Truth Barriers* is nearly sold out! That means they'll do another printing, and in the fullness of time (that is, not *in advance* this time) I'll get another two thousand dollars and you'll get another thousand dollars—Sierra Club is very surprised . . .

I was in Michigan also this trip and met your niece! That was another surprise. The teachers standing around immediately got excited, and are longing for you to stop there—at Alma College, or Central Michigan Univ at Mount Pleasant when you come to the Writers' Center at Cape Cod. Do you have any plans for going west? We'd love to see you here, but I'll be out reading during April—My reading times are Oct, January, and April this year—so the best I can hope for is to *meet* you somewhere!

Love to Monica!

Your friend, and
probably one of the
barriers to truth,
Robert

1 Sept, '81

Dear Tomas,

This is just a note to say hello, along with some goodies and baddies, the sort of illiterate babble that passes for reviews in our nation. I hope you are well! Mary is here, helping me answer mail. Did you know that Biddy is going to Harvard this fall also? Two of them! Carol's book, by the way, called *Letters from the Country* (short essays on country life, what Samuel Johnson called "the idiocy of rural life") has gotten marvellous reviews, including one in *Newsweek* in early June. I hope your family is well, and that you had time this summer on the island to write some poems! Yes, Americans think a lot about production, you know . . .

I've just come back from a week-long conference on Pythagoras, in which I was outnumbered by Englishmen, and even more frightening, English numerologists. Plato's solids were talked of a lot, and the arithmetical basis of God. At one point the question was considered: What is the fundamental substance of the universe: a tetrahedron or a horse? I favored the horse, myself, as did Kathleen Raine—she had Blake to guide her, who was very fond of horses—but we were outvoted, and it was decided that the horse is himself made of tetrahedrons.

No one mentioned music for three days, even though Pythagoras always began his instruction with the monochord . . . the instrument with one string, on which one could study harmonies. Luckily I had my dulcimer.

We are all well here. I suppose with your Petrarch Prize you will not write any more to poor Americans, but if you feel like it, your friend here will receive your letters with great pleasure. Don Hall says that he's terribly lonely, and it seems to be spreading. Ruth sends her best. She is working now for the county in the area of child-protection, and has 24 families.

With love,
Robert

1 Sept, '81

Dear Tomas,

I just found a letter of yours from late June! It contained your strange dream, no doubt about your tripartite personality—is this Father, Son and Holy Ghost? If so, which is the Holy Ghost—you or me?

Perhaps I represent the poetry side of you, or—as an American—perhaps the *uncultured* side! Anyway, I'm glad the religious part gave the uncultured part or the poetry part permission to see you! in Västerås!

You can see why I stick to writing poetry rather than becoming an analyst.

The news on the budget looks grimmer every day. The inflation that is causing the huge deficits springs from Johnson's expenditures—without additional taxes—during the Vietnam War. So "inflation" leads to "inflation."

Write soon! Love,

Robert

10 Oct, '81

Dear Tomas,

You know I answer your letters! But by telepathy—that is the newest way. Very elegant.

I miss Sadat. He was an earth father, a little like Frey, always worrying about his children. What if Osiris and Frey were the same?

We're well here, glad and feisty. I've written my first essay on form, and now have to eat all my words praising free verse as the only food conceivable for true Christian folk. Mary and Biddy are both at Harvard, and seem to love it. Sam had his appendix out: it turned out to be only an acid stomach! Noah is practicing the piano; your godson makes models of Spitfires & Messerschmidts!

Love,

Robert

1982

29 june 82

Dear Robert,

you are back from Greece of course? Tell me how you got along with the Olympian gods! It is really time for a good old-fashioned letter from you: cryptic handwriting, encouraging words, sublime gossip. After all we are not so old! With some effort I can almost feel like 38. Or 12.

It is a bitter thing that we could not meet in the U.S.A. The rest was OK for me. The readings went well except in New York—Saul can tell you about that—3–4 stoned people were disturbing the audience and the ladies from the Academy of Am. Poets did not look happy. A Mr Haba from New Jersey called me the next day and was very kind. He is a teacher and knows you—you published a love poem of his.

The worst during the globe trip was the line of people waiting for a bowl of soup in San Francisco.

As soon as we landed in Sweden we had to have an invitation to take part in the Petrarch Prize celebration of 1982—as a previous prize winner I (and Monica) were invited this year too—when the prize was given to Ilse Aichinger. We went to Switzerland, Sils-Maria, Nietzsche's summer resort. They have a big old-fashioned hotel there which could take charge of the strange collection of German professors and literati that compose the gang around the *mecenat* Mr Burda who gives the money. So Monica and I spent 4 days in June in Switzerland and 3 days on trains. We also met

Mr Lars Gustafsson who has left Västerås and his wife Madeleine and now is going to marry a 25-year-old woman philosopher from Texas! She is a specialist in *pre-Socratic* thinking. Lars is still writing 3 books a year. And I am slowly accumulating a new book of poems. This time I will publish it after 5 years, not 4 as usual. So spring 1983 seems to be the time. I was shocked to find—a couple of weeks ago—that I was writing a poem in Sapphic meter, something I did in the early 1950s. Is it Reagan?? Compare with your own development. We will both end up as neo-classicists!!

Tomorrow Monica, I and the dog will go to Runmarö and spend a week there—that is all that remains of our vacation (spent in Australia). Paula will stay in Västerås where she works as a bicycle renter for tourists to rent there. Later, in late July, she will spend her money as a so-called train loafer, "tågluffare" (or is the word "train bum"?)—last summer she went to Greece that way together with 2 friends. Nothing unpleasant happened to the 3 girls. Emma lives in Göteborg and is working as a ticket cashier at Liseberg, the Tivoli of Göteborg.

Monica sends her best to you. We will now go to Stenbro, where you lived in 1968, and fetch some marinated herring my sister-in-law has promised.

Weather is gray but you cannot have everything.

Love

Tomas

30 June, '82

Dear Tomas,

I just got a letter today from some loonies in Madrid, who told me I was invited to a Congress of Poets there in 3 weeks, which was news to me; and then I saw your name on the list too! I've already agreed to go to Russia during those same days . . . oh such excitement!—The group will be Susan Sontag, Arthur Schlesinger, Jr., Gwendolyn Brooks, Studs Terkel and Erica Jong! I wish you would or could come along! We'll go to Kiev for some sort of Writers Conversation, sponsored by Norman Cousins. Are you going to Spain?

I heard marvellous things about your readings in the U.S. earlier this year. We are well here, if somewhat short of money. Everyone is short of money!! The IRS came earlier this month and audited me . . . I told my children goodbye and prepared to go to prison for twenty years—but to my amazement the auditor told me that in general my deductions were "conservative." I could hardly believe my ears. To hear myself described as respectable in my (last?) outpost of outlawry was of course a blow . . . I was elated for days, to realize that I could continue to live with my children and wife . . .

Do write soon!

Love,

Robert

14 July, 82

Dear Tomas,

Thank you for your new letter! Did you get the one I sent to Runmarö? Some other Swedish poets beside your honorable self will get a chance this fall to disturb stoned people in the audience at the Guggenheim . . . five Scandinavian poets—I remember Nordbrandt, and Paal-Helge Haugen (Norway) will be there in late September—along with the COMMUNIST MOZART POET Sonnevi! A small press in New York is going to bring out my translations of his poems to coincide with that visit, which should please the NERUDA WATCHDOG. I'll be there myself to take part in the eternal, never-ending *panel*.

I'm glad to hear news about Gustafsson; I was afraid his production was faltering to only two books a year. I myself am very suspicious of pre-Socratic thinkers from Texas! You know when the Parthenon got set up in Nashville the erosion speeded up tremendously in Athens. It's wrong to read Nietzsche in Oklahoma . . . just asking for trouble. I try to keep Kafka out of Moose Lake . . . some things are just against the grain, and will never work!

Mary is working as a helper to an archeologist in Cambridge this summer; she has typed for months those endless reports, with fractions of inches ostentatiously put on everything. But she is a dear child, and works hard, supporting herself this summer for the first time! Biddy is too, working as a lifeguard in a sort of country club frequented by old people near Boston. Of course most are too old to get into the water, so she has a lot of time for reading! I didn't have money enough to send them to summer school, which is just as well . . .

James Scherer, the eccentric Jungian dentist, has finally made a break with his Past, has sold his business in Madison, and is going to Zurich to throw himself into the Collective Unconscious. I hope there's some money in the collective unconscious, because he, like all dentists, has tended to live high on the tooth. But I must admire his courage in changing careers in midlife. Imagine if we were suddenly to be Oil Importers, or Members of the Israeli Parliament . . .

Noah and Micah are fine; Noah is still car-mad, and will only have posters of cars on his room walls. French chateaus—I tried that—are out; nature in general is considered backward. Micah adores airplanes, and makes models still, working feverishly to bring back the Second World War. Despite all that detailed work, he has a lovely twinkle in his eyes, and a calm, deeply amused smile. I suppose he has so many fools to look at, being littlest, that he is never bored.

I am becoming positively form-mad . . . it must be something in the planets, if it is affecting you too. My latest essay included a poem of Horace's written in Alcaic stanzas . . . I favor that one, rather than the Sapphic . . . but still can't write in it, anyway! Your letter just came, so I haven't brooded— past tense I suppose: brud—over the poems long enough to understand them. More later. Do you have the Beacon Press book *Of Silence and Solitude,* with the photograph of my grandfather? I can't remember if I sent it or not. It reprints an issue of *Poetry East* . . .

Love from the Kafka-Guardian,
Robert

Västerås October 22 -82
Dear Robert,

what a miserable autumn! Of course we get what we deserve: too-good first part of the year, Australia, Hawaii, Switzerland, a warm summer, good health. And then to counterbalance these good things some hardship during September–October.

[------]

Göran Sonnevi had a good time in New York. It is strange that the left-wingers always seem to thrive in the U.S.A.! Tell me about the Scandinavian Circus! When Göran told me about his endless discussions with you about Pythagoras, I felt envy.

Did people understand his qualities? that he is an honest, truth-seeking fellow?

Have a look at the Swedish version of your mysteriously sad and wonderful poem. "Prästen faller på väg från kyrkan" is very concrete: he is walking away from a church building. If I translate "Prästen faller när han lämnar kyrkan kan det också betyda" "The priest lapses into sin when leaving the Lutheran church." [*sic*] If you want to have that meaning too, I have to use the second version. "Hill" means both "kulle" and "berg." What do you prefer? I prefer "berg," it is more Biblical. "Kulle" is too trivial and peaceful. But maybe you are thinking about a real "kulle"?

Did I tell you about my Bible job? I am one of the translation team for the new translation of the Old Testament. My part is David's Psalms. I work together with an old professor in Hebrew. (He is also good at old Arabic etc.) So far we have translated the first 7 psalms.

I go to Holland and Belgium in November, for 5 days only. A Dutch poet, Henk Bernleft, who has worked as a dishwasher in Karlstad, Värmland, translated 60 of my poems instead of the 20 he was asked to translate for a small press in Amsterdam. So it is a real book now, and will be published in a couple of weeks by Marsyas Publishing house.

Monica is doing a district nurse education. Then she will rule over a whole district, from a bicycle.

I have been longing for a letter from you for a long time.

Love

Tomas

P.S. Sensational news! Lars Gustafsson has converted to Judaism! He will marry a Jewish girl in November.

1983

19 July, 83

Dear Tomas,

What a disgrace that I have waited so long to write you! From now on, I'm going to give readings and lectures only in the first half of the year, so that from July 1st on each year I can remain undisturbed in my melancholic, Saturnic mood, and keep my tongue tied up like a bear.

Here you see me, just beginning this wonderful schedule. So we can write again—at least in the second half of the year! Please do send me the news about Monica, and Emma and Paula. Is Paula still in Uppsala? The children here seem to be thriving all right. I took the boys far up into Canada last week on a fishing trip; we caught lake trout, longer than your arm, bass, etc. Your dear godson, who is 12 years old now, caught a 15 pound muskie (muskellunge) and he is wild-eyed. He stops every fisherman he meets in Walker, and asks about muskie fishing on Leech Lake, and has already bought a muskie lure on his own. The lure itself is longer than your hand.

Mary has been in Paris since February, having taken off this term to travel. A few weeks ago a Frenchman stopped her on the street in Paris, and declared he wanted to put her on the cover of a French magazine. Her Celtic beauty apparently surpasses those chain-smoking, depressed, structuralist graduate students France produces these days. So she is working off and on with such things, and hopes to make enough money by Sept 1st for graduate school. Biddy is touring Europe on a bicycle with her boyfriend, mostly Southern Europe. Her postcards are ecstatic.

I suppose you've already settled the details you had wonderment about in the Snowbanks poem. "Prästen faller på väg från kyrkan" is right. The fellow stumbles on the church steps. He has been reading too many liberal theologians and is in trouble. The hill is not exactly a mountain but is a large hill. There's a suggestion of some sort of hill that tourists all like to climb. "Do you think you can make it up, grandpa?" It would take an hour or so to climb, so maybe it is a mountain.

This is terrifying that you are translating the Old Testament. We are trying to get rid of that book in the U.S., and are supporting bad translations for that reason. But the "Psalms" are different . . . You know that David had a lute, and so I think you've put it off long enough . . . you have to get a dulcimer soon. I've traded my dulcimer for a Greek bouzouki. Maybe David had a bouzouki.

If you write me, I'll write you immediately back!

Love from your old friend, mired in inadequacy

and self-pity

Robert

The translation of "Snowbanks" seems to me excellent.

Västerås Dec 22 -83

Dear Robert,

it's months and months since I wrote a letter to you. I sometimes have inner conversations with you, tell you stories, ask questions, laugh etc.

I start with a description of the family situation. Monica and I celebrated our SILVER WEDDING in November, we have been married for 25 years. We are both rather healthy and a little overburdened by duties. Monica has become a District Nurse, and works at a child care center, which means a lot of visits to the homes of newborn babies. There are many Turkish emigrants in her district. And I go on with my psychology. My psalm translation is growing, and I spend a few days every month in Uppsala with the Bible Translation Committee. Emma, now 22, is a shop assistant in a bookshop, selling her father's recent book, among other things. She is both proud and irritated because the book has been well received—I think she finds me overrated. Paula, 19, is a student, a nurse-pupil, in Uppsala. She has a good time, seems to be out dancing a lot with aircraft officers, theologians and other interesting Uppsala men. She is also very idealistic and wants to reform the hospital system. She does not have any plans to marry though, and I am impatient to become a grandfather.

What you wrote about the lack of a positive father figure in our civilization of today is mostly true. What I hope to become is a Zeus-like grandfather.

I have been invited to Texas in April! A former opera singer, now a poet-professor (what a decline!), Cynthia Macdonald, author of *Amputations,* has invited me to the Houston area for a week, and another fellow to Dallas. What can I do but accept that, with gratitude, put on my most European face and bring Monica with me. We will start in Savannah March 29—an organization called AWP wants me to read there. And between Savannah and Houston is New Orleans. Do you think any university in New Orleans has an interest in letting me stop there and mumble a few snowy poems? I have sentimental feelings about the city, I remember so well when we were there: you, I and little Noah.

The magazine *Lyrikvännen* just arrived, I opened it and found that its theme is "The prose poem." There are among many other things 2 pieces by James Wright and your prose poem about looking at a cabbage-worm, well translated by Lasse Söderberg. I almost got inspired. It's such a long time since I wrote something, beside the psalm translations.

What are you doing? New exciting REGULAR poems? Memoirs? Do you happen to spend the first part of April in Texas?

Hugs from Monica and me!

tomas

AND A HAPPY 1984!

New Year's Eve, 1983

Dear Tomas,

It is very seldom that I write anyone back the same day! But I am so glad to hear from you. I thought something was wrong; someone had slandered me, or told you some scandalous remark I had supposedly made about all Swedish poets, etc. But I am glad to see it was just that you had forgotten me.

It is New Year's Eve. Noah, who is a junior in high school this year, and president of his class, which has done wonders for his self-esteem, has his new Christmas cap on, a sort of Welsh farmer's cap, and is off to the movies and some party where everyone will sit around looking embarrassed. Biddy has gone off to Ohio to visit her boyfriend, who has just taken a job selling and buying grain for Cargill; she is a junior at Harvard and a loyal sort of person; she has some wonderful firmness in relationship. Mary is here, and she and Ruth are playing Boggle at the moment—a game in which lettered cubes are rearranged, and the player has two minutes to scribble down four and five letter words that his feverish eyes see on this contained box of cubes. She has spent the vacation writing a paper on Virginia Woolf and T. S. Eliot . . . nothing has changed. The universities still study these old race-horses, now coughing in their stables, covered with old moth-eaten blankets, and on the stable walls the ribbons recalling their old victories: Cleanth Brooks, Northrop Frye, Hugh Kenner, Dinner With Bertrand Russell, Nobel Prize . . .

Ruth is working hard to pass an examination as a psychologist in April . . . naturally it was made up by behaviorists, and instead of studying the unconscious, one studies statistics . . .

So you can see the world is going on in its old way. As for me, I am burdened down with responsibilities, commitments, lectures, seminars and so on. I am writing quite a bit; at the same time preparing a Selected Poems, which gives me an opportunity to rewrite old poems. What fun! I've found about thirty iambic poems written before I took the plunge into free verse, and I like some of them quite well. For me, it was a little like dancing in chains, but sometimes the sound of the chains makes a better music than the silence that surrounds free verse! As you can tell, I am longing for form again, and am not so interested in the prose poem.

Please answer these questions: Did I send you *The Man in the Black Coat Turns*? My translation of Göran Sonnevi? My *Selected Poems of Antonio Machado*?

I will write tomorrow to John Biguenet in New Orleans. I think he can find something; Calvin Harlan is there somewhere too. I think he was there when we all stayed in the French Quarter. I will be in Taos, New Mexico March 29, 30th and 31st. Have you ever seen Taos? It is marvellous. It is the best preserved in some ways of the old Pueblo culture . . . D. H. Lawrence loved the area . . . I'm sure Monica would love to see it. Perhaps we should all meet in Taos the last day of March or the first day of April!

After that I'll go home, where I'll be all through April. We'd love to have you visit Moose Lake, if you plan to come north! You'll have to let me know.

I have your new book, which arrived just as Ruth and I were starting down to Madison to visit my parents, who are now at the Old People's Home . . . I am reading it with deep pleasure . . .

Have I given you news of Micah? He is in the seventh grade, and plays hockey. Each day he straps on his enormous exoskeleton, pulls a T-shirt over it, grabs his long extroverted cane, and is gone . . .

Love to you both,
Robert

1984

[New York, Excelsior Hotel]
25 march -84
Dear Robert,

this is Sunday morning and I'm writing on the single piece of paper the porter reluctantly handed over. Yes, we are here now, not able to go to Taos, because that day (March 29) I give a reading in Savannah, at something called AWP (Associated Writing Programs). After that Atlanta (no reading), New Orleans (no reading), Dallas (!) (Southern Methodist University, reading April 5–6) Houston (a whole week as a visiting writer— April 9–15 at the university there), then Washington (seeing a Västerås friend) and Provincetown (April 18–20, reading). Then home. The trip is determined by invitations and a cheap round-tour ticket, Eastern Airlines, and it starts tomorrow with Richmond, where Greg Orr will pick us up and take us to Charlottesville for a reading which will give me the economic foundation for the rest. (Oh what a boring letter! I'm only writing this to let you know where I am, if IF you happen to be in the neighborhoods during your March–April trips.)

Now something important: A guy in Göthenburg—Göteborg, I mean— will send you a letter inviting you to go there in the beginning of June. He phoned me and asked for your address, also saying that they probably have some organization paying your ticket to and from Sweden. I pray, ask, demand, drum, urge and press you to say YES to that invitation! I will run to

Göteborg and read with you and we could also have 2 hours at the University
threatening the students and professors with all the difficulties of translation
etc. You could come up to Västerås and be our guest for some days. *We could
talk about our frog skins!* I could pester you with my psalm translations.
We both are longing to see you as a living person and not only as a country-
doctor photograph. Monica sends her love—she is here too.

Your friend   Tomas

1985

26 Jan, 85

Dear Tomas,

I had the most wonderful dream last night. I was living by the ocean, and I came back from the ocean to the pier, and could see very clearly into the water near shore. Then somehow I came by surprise on an "ocean man." He was small, maybe four and a half feet tall, with a black beard and black hair. I stroked his hair and beard, and said to myself: "I must call and ask Tomas to fly over immediately." You were the only one I trusted to talk to this "ocean man." So when I woke up I knew that I had to write you today. The ocean man, by the way, asked to go to the bathroom, and I was a little worried about his finding a way back through the pipes, but what can you do? You have to give a (ocean) man privacy. So that was how the dream ended, the conclusion unclear.

But you are to fly over anyway.

Thank you for your last letter. The shock of Sam's death was so extreme, and grievous, that we are still in sorrow. I canceled the talks and lectures I was to give in the fall, and recently have canceled all the spring readings also. So I'll be home until September or October now. As you can imagine, that makes us very poor, but I am doing a new translation of *Peer Gynt*, and that will help. And it feels right to be home . . .

[------]

I'm anxious to have some news from you. And also to find out if you've had any experience interviewing these "ocean men." Ruth and I saw Franco Zeffirelli's new movie of *La Traviata*. Ruth says it is the greatest movie she has ever seen. You are to see it as soon as possible! Love to Monica,

Yours, Robert

P.S. I'm ready to come to Göteborg late spring or summer or fall. Maybe we can see each other!

20 Feb '85

Dear Tomas,

I thought you might like to see these music poems that Bill Holm gave me the other day. I like all the details he has gathered about Liszt!

I hope you're well. Please tell me the gossip from Sweden. Is Göran still writing about Mozart? What if he started on Brahms? John Ashbery is still writing endless poems here, and the Reagan mystique is so powerful no one says a <u>word</u> about politics or the poor. It's just as when in a pond, the frogs suddenly all stop croaking.

Love,

Robert

Västerås 10 March -85
Dear Robert,

it was good to get your letters, even if the content was sad. I think you did the right thing when you canceled the spring readings.

I was moved by the Ocean Man. Maybe the Ocean Man is a part of me?

Monica and I and the girls are well. The girls are both so friendly to their old parents. The other day I brought Paula to a lunch with members of the Bible Commission in Uppsala (I had spent 2 days with them presenting my new version of Psalms 19, 20, 21 and 26). Paula works at the Samariterhemmet Hospital. She works 75% and is saving money for a trip around the world. Emma is studying Ethnology. And they live in Uppsala where I spend a few days every month. Monica is busy organizing medicare for refugees again. Young men from Iran and Iraq mostly. Deserters from the war and the Ayatollah. It is not a popular job among ordinary Swedes. The climate has changed since the 1970s, when working with refugees was glamorous. Now it is eccentric. The mood is more egotistical, provincial and conservative now. The institutions that prosper are the body-building centers. Everybody is jumping up and down on a jumping mattress (we have one too). But also shops for selling sweets are popular.

I did not like the trends during the "political" times, and I don't like the trends now either. I think I am against all sorts of trends.

I wait impatiently for the frogs to start quaking again in the U.S. Pond. What do the new Christian fundamentalists say about obligations to the poor? Do they really read the Bible? Tell me more about this puzzling "Reagan mystique"! Enormous, wide, needle eyes or extremely small camels?

What do you think about Daniel Halpern? He is my new publisher. I mentioned in Provincetown that most of my poems in English are unavailable now. Beacon Press and Ardis—sold out. Somebody told Halpern and I got a nice letter from Ecco Press, asking for the right to do a *Selected Poems* of TT—they wanted to save translations from the previous volumes and also to publish new translations. I proposed Bob Hass as the editor—he does not know any Swedish so he can really judge the translations impartially. I don't know if you have heard from Ecco Press, but if you have, answer.

You will hear from me soon. Dear Stradivarius and Norwegian Zorba we send our love: Monica and Tomas

P.S. Bill Holm's poems gave me much pleasure . . .

30 March, 85

Dear Tomas,

How good it felt to hear from you! I love to have all the news about Emma and Paula and Monica. The climate for compassionate activity has changed in the U.S. too. Now the poor are regarded as riddled with tragedy-bacteria, and one is liable to catch poverty by associating with them. Reagan promises the citizens that they can go back without conscience pangs to the old American selfishness so noticeable in the time of Mark Twain and Mencken. We are experiencing a swing of the pendulum, and people are *immensely grateful* for being allowed to be selfish again. Even the blue collar workers voted against their own future and their children's welfare for the psychic ease of permitted selfishness. I had never seen anything like it—entire towns of laid-off workers, who voted their own joblessness, and now give sad interviews to the papers, talking vaguely about economic unpredictabilities . . .

Something monstrous is coming, or is already here. It has two heads: bad schools, and the collapse of the ability to read texts symbolically, so that the Fundamentalists have *no doubts.*

I took Noah to Mpls yesterday with four others from his French class, and his teacher. They are going to France for ten days! Of course they were wildly excited. Did I tell you Mary and Biddy are graduating from Harvard this spring, and I am to be the Phi Beta Kappa poet, and read a poem at those exercises . . . Now I can show off in front of my daughters, always a precious thing! And have my way paid to the graduation besides!

Bob Hass called the other day, and told me about the project, but said he didn't know if he was the one to do it, since he couldn't read Swedish, etc. I told him I thought he would be perfect for it. He's thinking of taking all of Sam Charters's versions of the *Baltics,* all of mine for *Truth Barriers,* and probably all of Robin Fulton's for the new book. I promised him some advice on that. What do you think of Robin Fulton's translation of the Market Place book? I'm really not prepared to jump into it, but he's very inattentive on sound, and almost all the music and grandeur of the train poem is gone. Has anyone else sent you translations of those latest poems? "Fire-Jottings" on the other hand he does well. I don't know what to advise you. I think I'll stay out of this Market Place book, but Robin's translation of this book does not compare with the clear and fine job that Sam Charters did with *Baltics*. Maybe Sam would translate a few? It should be called *The Wild Market Place,* rather than *The Wild Square.*

Daniel Halpern is a highly alert and responsible publisher, and I think he'll be fine that way. As a poet he's not as good as Lars Gustafsson. (Notice the subtlety of this sentence.)

Do write soon.

Love from us all

Robert

Beijing April 10 -85

Dear Robert,

I think you should have a letter from this country. I arrived yesterday from Bangkok after flying 10 hours + 5 hours. I'm not tired, no jet lag. The program started already this morning. I sat for 2 hours conversing with two silver-haired poets in Mao-dresses and drank four gallons of tea. And suddenly I felt such an enormous longing for you, so I had to write this letter.

In a moment I will go out and have dinner—alone—what a luxury!—I have become fluent in chopsticks and can handle even very slippery noodles.

But I'm longing for Monica. She would have liked this. But she has to stay in Västerås, taking care of Iranian refugees.

The reason why I'm here is that the Professor of Chinese at the University of Stockholm was operated on for kidney stones. When he woke up from the narcosis he got—in his dizzy state—the idea that he should translate my latest book *Det vilda torget* (which he happens to like) into Chinese. He started but it turned out to be too difficult. So he translated it into English (in 3 days—he has lived in Australia for 8 years) and sent it to a young dissident here in Beijing, the gifted poet Bei Dao (remember his name!) who translated 10 poems of mine. 7 of them have been published. [Göran] Malmqvist (the professor from Stockholm) also persuaded the Swedish Institute to send me here, and the Chinese P.E.N. to take care of me. And it is all a great adventure.

Tonight no program. I will take a walk in the bicyclecrowded streets of Beijing, disappear, pop up again, disappear . . .

Tomorrow we will visit the Great Wall.

Best

Tomas

20 April 85

Dear Tomas,

How lucky you are! The closest I get is Arthur Waley and my chopsticks, which get warped from being left too long in the dish-water. I'm longing to go to China. Michael True, from Worcester, Ma, is over there this year, at Nanking, and he's forcing his students to translate *Silence in the Snowy Fields,* so maybe they'll ask me. But I'm enjoying being home so much I don't know if I want to wiggle! I feel you will write a poem about the Great Wall . . . this came to me from an Inspiring Angel . . .

I'm preparing my *Selected Poems* and having a wonderful time, though reading over some old poems is rather humiliating. I sometimes use the image to drill into a mountain, or dive beneath the water, but very often too I find myself in trouble in a poem, surrounded by serious people from inside, who want me to face something, or read some passage they have brought to me, and then I find an image, which immediately becomes a fire-bird, I climb on; we fly out of the forest, and back to my comfortable mediocrity with "nothing accomplished / no important victory won / as if life had never begun" (Robert Frost).

So images can be sly ways of escaping from a poem—oh how sly!

This is my confession for today.

Love,

Robert

Shanghai 22 april -85
Dear Robert—

Must send you something also from this place. I met a woman who translates you. That was in Beijing. Her name is Zheng Min. Strange to sit in a strictly Chinese milieu and hear the names of you and other buddies, like Merwin, being dropped.

The other evening I had the terrible experience of drinking a liquor—something like aquavit—from a bottle with a snake in it. It was a viper, probably brought alive into the bottle with liquor. So I drank its last breath. It tasted worse than I had expected. A long, long aftertaste, somewhat like raw fish but with more scales on it. Ugh! I will never do that again. It is said to be very good medicine.

I am longing for Monica—I get no letters here, I just *write* letters. Shanghai is strange because of the colonial buildings which are now totally taken over by the Chinese. My hotel was very fashionable in the 1930s—the elevator looks like an elevator in early Hitchcock movies. I will step into it now and disappear in the streets. I will walk there together with 11 million Chinese. Sun and dust are wrestling, just now I think dust gets the upper hand. Goodbye now. May peace prevail in Northern Minnesota.

Your friend
Tomas

Västerås 29-9-85
Dear Robert,

The editor of *Lyrikvännen* sent me your latest book which you did not give me, traitor! I could not resist translating the poem "Night Winds" and will probably translate some more.

Just for knowledge I send 2 poems of my own. And, when you read "Shanghai Streets," send a thought to the young poet Zhow Zhenhai alias *Bei Dao* alias Shi Mu who badly wants to have a book of yours. He is one of the most gifted Chinese poets and will publish my poetry in Chinese, a whole volume! (Edith Södergran too.) Now he wants to translate some of your stuff. He visited Sweden, e.g. Runmarö, and Stockholm, around August 1st this year and wrote his name and address on a piece of paper I hereby send to you. Don't try to copy the Chinese handwriting! *Glue* it on the parcel with your book(s)! (And add "Peoples Rep. of China.") I think both *Snowy Fields,* the prose poems and this *Loving a Woman in Two Worlds* will be most appreciated in the Peoples Republic of China. I will write soon again.

Love   Tomas

31 Oct, 85

Dear Tomas,

It is Halloween, and your godson has just finished setting up a horrible sight outdoors—a masked figure with military hat and old coat obviously thinking frightful things—to frighten the little ones coming for Milky Ways. Micah by the way is the only one home now; he is a freshman in high school. Noah is working for the infamous E. F. Hutton stockbrokers in New York, living with Mary in an apartment in the East Village. He loves New York, and is planning to start college next fall. Biddy is in Boston, working for an advertising agency at the moment. I'll see them all in a few days, because my November tour—the only long one this year—is about to begin. I so long to stay home the night before such prospects— every detail of the house looks inviting; why should Ruth get to stay home and not me . . . is this something from a previous life? etc. . . .

I like your translation of "Night Winds" very much! The woodshed is a small building where on the old farms the wood used to be stored— firewood. It is abandoned because people no longer use it for that, or, usually, for anything. Besides, "abandoned woodshed" is a Romantic phrase, primarily in its *sound,* I guess. I rewrote the poem about sixty times but always kept that phrase and the "ant with his small (or narrow) waist." Don Hall hates the "mad and sleepy cork" line, and says mad people don't feel like that at all . . . but of course this is a psychological insight into the feeling life of corks . . . some people just don't sympathize with corks . . .

I will send books to Bei Dao, as suggested. I love the sound in the first stanza of "Alkaiskt." The Shanghai poem looks fine, so far, but I have two copies of Part III and none of Part II—so I must have a Part II!!! Will we see you this year?

Love to Monica . . .
Robert

P.S. I wrote a fan letter to John F. Deane—fine translations of the *Wild Marketplace*!

1986

Västerås 14 March -86

Dear Robert,

I am longing to hear from you. Monica and I are going to the U.S.A. at the end of this month—I have readings in Washington DC and Tucson and N.Y. Maybe you are crossing the country at the same time, ships that pass in the night, whales that swim in the ocean, comets that fly in the sky . . .

Monica needs this trip [worse] than I do. She is too busy with her job here, as a refugee-nurse. Too much for a man, even for a woman. The people come from Iran mostly, some from Iraq and some from Lebanon. Some have invisible holes after bullets. In the evenings we sit together and talk about them. I sometimes feel a little weak from that and was on a thorough health control the other day. I was found absolutely healthy. My blood pressure was better than before (150/100). Don't fall asleep when I am talking about my health!!

Here are 2 poems from your latest book. "Älgen" has got a Swedish version that satisfies me. "Nattgrodor" is immediately interesting, one of your deepest poems, and causes me problems. Something I have not translated and don't understand is why the loons wheel cries THROUGH LOWER WATERS. If you cry "through" water you must sit under, in, the water. Or is "through" an American preposition for "across"? Another word I am not sure about is LANDING in the last stanza. Tell me!

I have showed the 2 translations together with the previous one (Night winds) to the editor of *Lyrikvännen* and he wants to publish them soon. So please give me an opinion.

Here is an American address you can write to if you answer before the end of this month: You can send the letter to Lois Shelton's Poetry Center in Tucson—I suppose you have the address. We will stay there around April 7–10.

We are awfully interested in having you come to Sweden this year. We have so much to talk about! I would love to introduce you to my two grown up lady-daughters.

Monica sends her warmest!

Love
Tomas

P.S. If somebody thought he could destabilize the country by killing Palme he was wrong.

19 March, 86

Dear Tomas,

Thank you for your letter! I have been with you if not in spirit then in error and confusion lately, for I gave a talk at a Conference on Translation in Tempe, Arizona recently using texts of your poems—especially "Right here I was nearly killed one night in February"—and my efforts to avoid *total* error! I found many of your admirers, including Heim, who translates Kundera, and William Arrowsmith, who translates everything . . . lately a marvellous version of Montale.

Wouldn't it be fun if we could meet somewhere in April! I'll be home here until the fifth of April, when I go to Boston, for a Kabir concert with an Indian dancer on the 6th. Then I'll be in Boston and Maine that week before going down to New York on the 14th, where I read at the YMHA

Poetry Center that night. I'll be in New York the rest of that week, mostly at Saul Galin's . . . 212-222-0786. In Boston around the 6th, 7th and 8th I'll be with Biddy in her apartment on the North End. Her tel # is 617-720-3868. I'll call you at Tucson too. *Where will you be before you go to Tucson on the 7th?* And Monica will be with you! How grand! To repeat my plan: (Ruth will be in New York too one weekend)

     Boston, April 6–10 (then Pennsylvania)

     New York, April 14–19

Of course I would love it if you both could come here for a day or two (before 5th or after 19th). Carol is only three or four miles away, so you could see us all at one crack. And your godson Micah is here! He is a freshman now, and just this week got five *A*'s from judges in his "discussion." He is teaching me computers.

I like the two new translations. "Älgen" seems absolutely right as it is. Question about "Night Frogs": "The loons wheel cries through lower waters". . . . This is an odd sentence in English. Loons have a curious cry, which they often give just before diving. So the suggestion here is that they continue this cry while swimming under water, and this image merges with an image of those small flying saucers "wheeling" through the ocean depths, as they are said to do. We also say that a man "wheels" a wheelbarrow. So the loons are "wheeling" the cry ahead of them, as if it were a sack of grain.

In the 5th stanza, the *wire* could be a wire for a musical instrument, a string, as they are called, or an industrial wire. It has been thinned apparently to get a higher pitch. The last line in that stanza should give a sort of blow to the stomach, a deflation. I feel that each time I say the line. Expecting honesty from me is hopeless. *Being honest* is a state of soul; it is not quite the same thing as honesty, which is a noun. I'm sure you understand me.

I think you've got "the landing" right. I am walking up and down the shore of a river, perhaps with muddy banks. At a certain place there is a smoothed down patch of shore where people pull up boats. Maybe it has a wooden platform too.

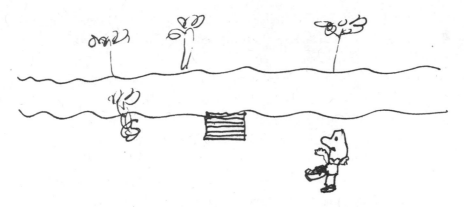

"Robert looking toward the 'old landing.'"

I felt the longing to call you when Palme was shot. It makes everyone feel lonely.

Love to you both,
Robert

August 4, 1986

Dear Tomas,

We are finally home, and more or less recovered from our funny Scandinavian trip. You know we went to Oslo after we saw you, then rented a car in Oslo and parked it in front of an Italian restaurant. Within 15 minutes the Oslo police had towed it away—we are too dense for the subtlety of their No Parking signs—and an hour after that, we had to pay $110 to get it released from its mythological prison somewhere else in that vast city. We then drove up to Jotunheimen to embark on a famous walk, which I had heard of for years, from a Norwegian walking hut over some hills to another. The walk was listed as 7 hours. Little did I know that this was a special listing created by muscle types for other muscle types. Delicate nervous system types deserve a completely different time table—perhaps even a different map. We started out at 8:30 in the morning, laboring uphill with rests every 10 minutes, and were constantly passed by disgustingly healthy types running along under heavy packs, frightening the sheep. By 2 o'clock we had gone only ⅓ of the way, and by 4 o'clock Ruth's knee gave out, so that she had to move it by pulling on the cloth of her trousers to get it to lift. This slowed us down a little, as you can imagine. Now we were being passed by muscle types who had probably started at 2 in the afternoon. One girl actually ran by with her Olympic trainer. By 7 o'clock we were telling these people to warn the cooks that 2 hungry people were slowly approaching. We got in, finally, at 9:30, after 13 hours on the path. This teaches one to read those maps and recommended hours with the sort of suspicion with which one reads political speeches. Actually, we limped around the mountain hut and its environs for two days, and had quite a nice time as the resident invalids. After that we got back out, drove to see my relatives in Hardanger. [------] After that we stayed at an old wooden hotel at Utne for several days, then drove to Oslo and saw Ruth's relatives. One was a marvelous old woman who had been blind since 4, and had taught 38 years in the School for the Blind in Oslo. She reminded me of those people at the end of your car-wreck poem, only instead of being seen too much, she had the most amazingly wrinkled face—intricate and ancient—as if from never having been seen at all. Perhaps we keep wrinkles out of our faces only because we know what we look like in the mirror or in other people's eyes. Perhaps all people before mirrors had astoundingly wrinkled faces. She had a beautiful dignity, and it was grand to see her strong face.

After that we came back to New York and then to Connecticut, where we attended James Hillman's 60th birthday party. This was not so intimate as the party we had out on Gatan. The first day there were 50 people and the second day another 25, and on the third day friends drove in from all the near states, especially New Jersey. 150 people cluttered up the lawn on the third day. It cured Ruth from planning such an event for my 60th birthday. I think she has decided on a quiet dinner for 4. The most astounding event of this extravaganza happened on Saturday night when James, dressed in white shirt and pants with a cane, suddenly appeared on a small stage and, working with his teacher, delivered a 20 minute tap dance to the tune of the St. Louis Blues. It turns out that all his life, since he was 6 or so and saw tap dancing in Atlantic City, he had longed to tap dance in public. For the last six months he had practiced five to six hours a day and he did it. This was a grand inspiration for me, like seeing Michelangelo for the first time.

The dearest thing we did, however, on the entire trip was the visit with you and Monica and the children at Runmarö. We appreciated so much your generosity in wanting us to be there at all, and your hospitality and the opportunity to see the Swedish folk-soul appear under the boat for a moment—the boat of the grass, that is. We especially loved walking past that house nearby and seeing the Swedes in their suits and ties sitting at their tables with the candles lit. So thank you both once more!

I have all sorts of questions to ask you about Robert Hass's suggestions, which in general are excellent. I don't have lots of questions, only 4, and I'll type them in a second onto a special sheet. This letter has been typed by Mary Bly, and I'm sure you've already guessed that someone more clever than I was doing this letter (Yes of course—the typist!)

Ruth often tells the story of mid-summer and how much she enjoyed Monica, the island, the whole warm glad time.

Love
Robert

Dear Tomas:

Here are the four questions: 1. in "Posteringen":

> Jeg stryker längs varma ögonblick . . . This has puzzled even
> Robert Hass's informant. She thinks it may suggest swimming
> in warm currents in a river . . . Suppose I said:
>> "I snuggle up to warm moments,
>> but I can't stay there long."

2. In "Den skingrade församlingen":

> sewage pipes or drainage pipes?
> *sewage pipes* definitely call up shit in English

drainage pipes imply more shower drainage pipes, kitchen pipes, pipes draining a marsh or roof or cellar.

3. "For Matts and Laila":

Resan fortsätter. Robert says my sentence sounds "too translated." Could I say:

Everything keeps moving. ? If I say, the trip goes on, it sounds translated again, and it is as if not only *your* trip continues, but the Date Line and so on.

4. "Minusgrader" . . . "unknowing forest of flickering faces" or "unaware forest of flickering faces." The second, which I found for the Sierra Club edition, is more startling and suggests that something in the faces and bodies of the people is highly unconscious— there's much they are not aware of.

unknowing forest implies that they are a little more like animals, people who have never been to school, with vast areas of total ignorance.

I lay these questions humbly at your feet, and will await your reply! In an hour Noah and I start for the Salmon River in Idaho, for our six day white-water trip . . . Eek! But it's our last time to be together before he leaves for college.

Love to you both

Robert

Uppsala 11 Sept. -86

Dear Robert,

I am here working on Psalms 37 and 38 and I cannot resist writing to you on the impeccable Bible Commission paper . . . First: Monica and I have you and Ruth fresh in our memories, it was a wonderful end of the taxing spring and a good start of the restful summer to have you here. We had the best July for many years. In August problems returned. Monica's sister, Bibbi, had a cerebral hemorrhage, a so called ANEURYSM, got operated on and as a result of the operation had a stroke that caused total aphasia. Now speech gradually returns and I saw her the other day in the hospital. It was not so bad as I expected. In spite of the speech difficulties her personality had not changed. It was like meeting a friend who had a broken leg. Strange that such a handicap does not take away the personality! The prognosis is thought to be rather good.

I am overburdened with DUTIES and also with gratitude to Bob Hass. He has been working a lot. At least I could answer your questions about

STRYKER LÄNGS VARMA ÖGONBLICK

"Stryker" means pass, stroke, sometimes rub. What do you say when you describe a bird flying close to a hillside. Or a cat touching your legs. Or a hand stroking a fur. Choose what you like. "I pass along warm moments" is possible, but maybe a little too abstract. It should be a sensuous touch too.

KLOAKTRUMMOR

probably "sewage pipes" is the right word. Should be pipes with large diameter, the kind of pipes you have under the streets, under a city.

RESAN FORTSÄTTER   I don't mind if the reader has the impression that not only my trip goes on. Primarily it is my trip, but secondarily it is the dateline, the world, History, galaxies etc. etc.

OVETANDE SKOGEN As you describe the difference between "unaware" and "unknowing" I find that "unaware" is probably the right word.

I have to hurry. Let us write more letters this autumn! Monica is in Västerås, but I send her love too to you and Ruth. We want to hug you both soon again!

Tomas

October 3, 1986

Dear Tomas,

Thank you for your letter and the four details about translations. To my surprise, I got a request the other day to translate some Psalms. This thing must be catchy, and we will lose our amateur status if this keeps up. What would our Sixties friends think of us? Mary is home with us this week and she is typing this letter to you (hello Tomas!) in her free time between work on her new detective novel. Biddy has gone to Barcelona to teach English to short dark-haired foreigners. Micah has been giving me instruction today on the new computer that a Bush grant in Minneapolis purchased for me. All of this enormous technological machinery—and I use it simply to run off eighty-five-syllable poems. I'll enclose the first two poems I ran off. The dragon poem has 85 syllables, but I haven't counted the other. I heard rumors that you're going to join me on April 11th in San Francisco—that would be nice. The audiences in San Francisco are so enthusiastic that they believe they understand Swedish. This must be a common human failing, because I noticed that the people in Stockholm pretended that they understood English. Ruth is away today, teaching for the first time at a women's Conference—She refuses to be pulled in by all those extroverts, however, so she is teaching dream interpretation woman by woman in a house with a smoky fireplace. Noah is at Harvard, just beginning, with the same teacher for Samuel Johnson that I had 37 years ago. Is there anything I can send you from those of us with such long life here in the land of milk and honey?

Love to you both,
Robert

1987

June 28, 1987

Dear Tomas,

Summer has begun at last! I suppose you are out on the island, you and Monica. Last year almost at this exact time we were with you enjoying every moment of the visit. This year we are at home and it is probably better than being in the hands of those reckless Norwegians who are unable to add up figures. We also enjoyed tremendously our visit in San Francisco and the dinners at the various elegant cafes we managed to find. Let's see what news there is of the family: Biddy has come back from Spain (hello! the typing mistakes can be put at my door). She will be here some of the summer and will help me (what???!!) on some of my literary tasks. [------] Mary called from San Francisco two days ago and reported that she had been accepted by Christ Church College at Oxford and has been offered a $10,000 loan without Interest by an eccentric old couple somewhere in the U.S. who are spending their declining years in such restful activity. Micah and I are going up fishing soon to the cabin. Ruth and I just spent a week on the Lake Superior shore, which is our mini ocean, and we had the most wonderful time for one week. I said: this is what Monica and Tomas have all summer. I finally heard by the way from those eccentrics who organized our reading in San Francisco. These street people always find a way to out-flank you somehow. I insisted on 50% of the gross for you and me to divide and I knew that that would amount to something around $1400. They got the money and I waited. I got a check for $920 with the explanation that since none of the other poets taking part in the conference were being paid for the seminars, etc., these poets amounting to 80 or so, they paid by giving free tickets to our conference. There you go, outflanked again . . . I therefore have $460 dollars here to send you in genuine American greenery and I will send one little piece of it now and then you will never know when the rest is going to come. You are to consider it as a gift from the American economy, fading fast.

What other news—Gary Snyder and Robert Creeley and I were taken into the American Academy of Arts and Letters in a stupendous Swedish-type ceremony last month, during which Jacques Barzun gave a stupefying lecture criticizing the grammar of art reviewers in small towns. All these small birds of course fell off their branches immediately upon hearing his harsh words. Afterward, Robert Creeley said to me, "Robert, we have about two years to change this place and if we don't, we are in big trouble." I said, "Forget it. We are in big trouble." Franny Quinn from Boston came down for the ceremony and when we went out afterward, someone had stolen his car. By the way, I heard that someone went up to John Updike in an airport the other day and asked if he were Tomas Tranströmer (sorry, no . . .). I went into a rug shop in Santa Barbara and the rug merchant asked me if I were Steve Martin. I guess I had better quit. Next time I will send you a poem or two. Meanwhile, I send our love to you both.

Robert

Runmarö 13 July -87
Dear Robert,
    wonderful to hear from you! Monica and I have been thinking often of you and your family, [------] and I called Monica at once to tell her the latest good news. She is in Västerås, had to leave the island yesterday because her vacation was over (most of her vacation was spent in the U.S.A.

and Canada, in March–April . . .). Also we had a week in Italy in June, when the PETRARCH PRIZE was delivered again—this time to a novelist, Hermann Lenz, very nice man, whose problem is that he is not Siegfried Lenz, who is more well-known; they are both writing about life in Nazi Germany. So we spent a renaissance period of 3 days in the little city Asolo, n.w. of Venice. We drank some champagne, which makes you think very clearly—my head turned into an aquarium with goldfish who were mumbling sentences of Marcus Aurelius.

Here in Runmarö life is more simple, but luxurious too, as you know. When I am alone, I am supposed to CONCENTRATE, to write without the distractions of a happy family life. Today I had a very long nap.

Thank you for the 100 dollars,* which is what 2 people of the enormous audience that was crying in front of us in San Francisco, paid for entrance. I did not expect the fellow who arranged the reading to pay anything at all. So I am pleased.

Thank you for the review too. Stratis Haviaras is the man who is responsible for the whole project—he told me to ask Robert Hass to edit the book. And Roger Skillings (p-town) is responsible too—he told Halpern that I had no publisher in the U.S. Perhaps Stratis will be the only person writing a review of the book. There is some logic in that. He started the book, and the book will end up in his arms.

Our next trip will be to Poland, in early October. Our ambassador in Warsaw, Örjan Berner, is a writer and he has sent me a xerox of a lot of my poetry that has been translated into Polish—I was shocked to see how much it was. So I go. Can you send your "selected" to me? I want to give it to a reliable Pole.

Love to Ruth from us both. And to you

Tomas

---

*I hope it does not come from Iran. I am pleased you did not send it to the Contras.

Aug 31, 87

Dear Tomas and Monica,

It is the end of summer! How awful! The children go somewhere else, the grownups stand around like bare trees . . . The poetry fanatics wake up from their long sleep, and want me to cut off bits of my hair again and give it to them. I would prefer they just gave me the money I need because I am such a good person, and can type so well. Your godson has gone out for football but hopefully will not play much . . . He must have some muscle type in him. I did too at his age, but my shame overcame it and I was afraid the girls would laugh at me. Noah has decided to take the term off before he goes back to the STRESS of Harvard and I'm very glad about that. He and I have had some sweet weeks here at Moose Lake painting the log cabin, and putting screens on, making walks and such things. Mary leaves for Oxford in a few weeks; she is wildly excited. Maybe she will come to visit you. Wouldn't that be nice! Biddy's boyfriend, Raffael, is going back to Spain this week. She is brooding about graduate school in linguistics, but the world seems to have no place exactly right for her. She is too healthy and too normal, that's why. Ruth and I are going dancing more than we have for years, and carrying on with bicycles, and even got a sail boat this summer! She turned it over yesterday. We think of you two often and fondly. Will you be coming to Ollie North country this year? If so we will meet you somewhere! Of course we'd love to have you here or in Minneapolis where we'll have an apartment . . .

Your friends,

Robert & Ruth

Västerås 21 Dec -87
Dear Robert,

before it is too late for 1987 I have to write a few lines. Is everything well? [------] Is Minnesota surviving this winter?

About us. Monica has fought with the bureaucrats and superiors as usual and at last felt that she was "burned out" with the organization, not with the refugees. So she resigns in January 1988. The refugees say moving goodbyes. The next year she will probably return to child care center jobs. But first—in middle January—we will spend 2 weeks in Madeira together. An old (93-year-old) relative died and left Monica a small inheritance, so we are going to spend that.

I have to report 2 late autumn trips. First Poland. After 24 hours in Poland I had 1: performed a program at the University of Warsaw. 2: been robbed at the railway station at 6 o'clock in the morning, and 3: transformed myself into a black market currency dealer in Krakow. 3 is a consequence of 2.

What happened was that 2 gangsters emptied my pants pockets, where I had all my money (1,100 Swedish crowns and a lot of ZLOTY). I was squeezed between the two in a corridor, I did not understand what was going on—I thought *I* was squeezing *them,* two claustrophobic Poles trying to get out of the train in time. I felt sorry for them. But everything changed when we arrived to the hotel in Krakow and discovered that all my money had gone. There was only one thing to do. Monica had 200 Swedish crowns. We went out in the magnificent main square in Krakow and after 30 seconds a fishy character appeared and asked if we had anything to change. For the 200 Swedish crowns we got more zloty than the Scandinavian language professor got paid in one month.

After Poznan, Gdansky and Warsaw again, we returned to Sweden. I left 50% of my collected poems, translated into Polish, in Krakow, with a publishing house that is well thought of, but usually needs 2–5 years to print a manuscript. I don't even know if they want to print the poems at all. But the translations were well-received by audiences (students)—the translator is a Solidarnosc-refugee in Stockholm.

Poland was a strong emotional experience. It was not a comfortable trip but memorable.

Comfortable was the latest European visit: Amsterdam and Münster (West German town with a huge Scandinavian Department).

Emma is well. She has a most agreeable boyfriend—we call him Stefan 2, because her previous boyfriend had the same name (Stefan 1). Paula is in Denpasar, Bali. She is making a tour around the world. She has survived Burma and Thailand. In April she will be in the U.S.A., like us, but we will not meet—perhaps on the plane home.

Right now I have a headache, one blue leg and a slight limp after badminton. Monica does not like my badminton playing, she thinks that I should choose a sport better suited to my age—like golf. But golf is for the ruling classes, we all know that . . . Well, I was elevated to a more dignified level in the eyes of the public 2 weeks ago when Nobel Prize winner Brodsky mentioned my name in a TV interview. People hurry to me in the streets "did you see the interview with hrmm what's his name . . . the NOBEL PRIZE WINNER on TV—HE MENTIONED YOUR NAME!!"

It is now your turn to give me a report of recent events in the Bly surroundings. Give Ruth and other family members a hug and have a happy new year!

Best
Tomas

1988

January 10, 1988

Dear Tomas,

Thank you for your lovely letter. I have been writing an essay on the naive male and I think you must qualify for one with your heart-wrenching tale of being sorry for two Poles whom you unmercifully pressed against in the train corridor. They probably have a girlfriend now, working at the Swedish embassy getting the names and photographs of other Swedes coming to Poland. I, of course, am not naive. I don't know where I get all the information I put into my lecture on naiveté. Let's see what the news of the family is . . .

Biddy is in the room at this moment. She is studying psycholinguistics at the University of Minnesota. I expect the people in her department are eating the special Chomsky-chocolates perfected by the master. She likes very much to study the processes of learning, which that sort of linguistics emphasizes, and she is hoping to go to Chicago or Stanford next year. Micah is doing well at St. Paul Academy. He is turning out to be a good writer, with essays that are beautifully grounded in physical details. I wanted you to know that your godson has just bought his first car. It looks very different from anything I have ever owned. As you know, I tend to own middle-class middle-browed Toyotas with rust holes of forgetfulness here and there, but the other day Micah, determined to have a car that fits his nature, brought me out to a huge car lot north of town where he knew there was a brilliant, red, confident, bizarre Mazda RX7—positively Tibetan in its self-confidence, with eyelids that slowly open when needed and two bucket seats in the front to keep the rest of the family out. It has a rotary engine. It is actually a 1979, but in perfect shape; so he leaped far ahead of me at one stroke there. Of course the penalty is that he has to type for me to earn the money that he didn't have at the moment. [------] Mary is at Oxford. Her address is simply Christ Church, Oxford, England. I'm sure she would love to have a note from you. She will be there another year and a half. I'm glad to have news of Emma and Paula. I don't understand how the Swedes can afford to go around the world— maybe they don't have Reagan as a president.

I'm sending you my schedule for April. You'll see I am working only about 5 days in March, but 10 in April. I hope that we can get together. Please do reciprocate by sending me your April schedule. We're all living in an apartment in Minneapolis now, at an address you will see on the outside of the envelope. Our telephone number is 612-339-1952. Please call us as soon as you get into the country, so we can arrange another dinner as in San Francisco, maybe with Ruth this time. She's working hard on her novel, and of course, forced by that to think about her mother and grandmother. Probably that's why you and I write poetry. Give a hug to Monica and get a new haircut now that you are famous through Mr. Brodsky.

Your friend, as always and as ever,

Robert

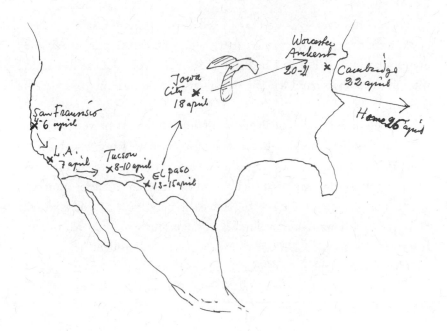

Västerås 19 March -88

Dear Robert,

here is my schedule. It is sad that we can only collect memories of each other—you in SF and I in Cambridge. My hosts are: in SF the Press Club, in L.A. Ross Shideler, in Tucson the Sheltons, in El Paso Leslie Ullmann, in Worcester Frannie Quinn, in Cambridge Diana Der-Hovanessian. Perhaps I will see some of your children in Cambridge. The reading is in the New England Poetry Club on April 22. (Tel. 617-864-2224)

I am suffocating under 400 unanswered letters. America has become BUREAUCRATIC. For the single reading at UCLA they sent me 5 papers to fill in. It was necessary to get a special visa called "I-1." The Swedish Institute called the embassy and asked what would happen if I gave a reading in the U.S. without that visa.

—Is he paid?

—Yes.

—If he is paid and does not have a I-1, we will not allow him to enter the United States for 10 years!

No one has ever told me that I needed this type of visa. Actually it could have been an interesting experience to be exiled from the United States for 10 years. But as I had signed so many contracts at this time I went to the embassy and had my new visa stamped into my passport. No problem.

Robbed in Poland. Exiled from the United States. A naive man.

I am handwriting this because I have been looking at a bad TV program—2 ladies are talking about the relation between men and women; you would have been spellbound by this, but I cannot stand it, I switch it off . . . but am too lazy to fetch the typewriter. Can you read this? Have you written any new volumes? Is there much snow in Minnesota? Are you going to Paris? Who is your candidate for President?

I have your telephone number. Give Ruth our love.

Your old friend

Tomas

1989

May 3, 89

Dear Tomas,

What fun to have your new book! And I have some time! Oh what a pleasure. Here is a draft of the church poem. "Överblick" is a problem for me . . . I don't know if I should be looking down from above or just have some sort of wide cultural point of view . . . which I usually don't have. Ruth is fine, and sends her best. Politically we are all very shocked here.— Bush has fallen asleep, and he's dreaming of the Cold War as some people dream of the Middle Ages. More, as soon as I finish (stumbling over) another poem.　　Love

Robert

A hug for Monica!

Runmarö 14 May -89

Dear Robert,

oh I was happy to get your letter . . . And your translation of "Romanska bågar" seems to have the right tone. You are probably the only one among my—now rather numerous—translators who has the right feeling for this poem that embarasses certain readers and makes others happy. You understand that this poem is not sentimental, but emotional, and of course documentary.

(You can easily see your Swedish friend, blinded from tears, tottering out from San Marco in Venice, supported by his faithful bodyguard Monica, after suddenly realizing that the human soul is built in ROMANESQUE style.)

Your translation carries the emotion wonderfully (that is how I feel without knowing English . . .) but there are a few objections.

I share your doubts about "no point of view." The Swedish word "Överblick" does not stress the above position. You can have ÖVERBLICK of something in front of you. The word can be used both very concretely and symbolically, you can have no ÖVERBLICK of the landscape and no överblick of a situation. Is the word "overview" possible to use in the same way? Or "survey"? In the poem you have to start with the simple fact that in a romanesque church you cannot grasp the interior—in a Gothic church you can see most of what is inside in a single glance, but a romanesque church is more like a labyrinth.

Line 6. "human being" sounds a little cliché-like. Of course it would be dangerous to say "Do not be ashamed to be a MAN!" Can you say "a human"? Well, this is a question for someone who knows English.

At the end: "Herr Tanka" should be "Mr Tanaka." If you say "Herr" in an English text it will mean that Mr Tanaka is a German. But of course he is Japanese—Tanaka is one of the most common Japanese names. "Herr" in Swedish is "Mr" in English.

"Sunblazing" might be wrong. Or right. "Sjudande" in Swedish means literally almost boiling, but not quite. You can also say "sjudande av vrede, entusiasm etc." (Tea is best when it has been "sjudande" but not "kokande.") I don't know the English word and I think you should be allowed some freedom here. "Blazing" sounds OK, but should not be a cliché.

I have been here in Runmarö for 3 days and I am returning tomorrow to Västerås. It has been a laborious spring, but things are getting better. I will be free for 2 weeks, to do Bible translations.

Love to Ruth and the children you manage to get hold of. Hope to hear from you soon . . .

> Love from Monica
> Tomas

May 27, 89

Dear Tomas,

Thank you for your letter! Sjudande might be "seething"—I'll have to see. My notes are up in Moose Lake. I'd like to tackle that Alcaic poem too, but it looks hard. Both of us admire that Romanesque poem a lot. I was translating it for Ruth on the way down to Mpls the other day by car, and she thought the whole idea very fine!

I'll have time this summer. For the first time in about fifteen years, I have all of July and all of August free! Wow!

I'm enclosing a piece from the *NY Times* describing a strange phenomenon: people looking at great art tend to become disoriented, or feel slightly crazy. Someone has to lead them out into the sunlight I think.

I've had some fun this week, putting together all my polemic articles on poetry from *The Sixties* and *The Seventies* . . . I'll make a book out of them, called *American Poetry: Wildness and Domesticity.* I have the urge to do some more of that . . . maybe I'll start the magazine again . . . Do one issue of *The Eighties* and then on to the NINETIES!

These Chinese students are beginning the Nineties . . . Please give a big hug to Monica, and write soon!

> Your capital L liberal friend
> Robert

1990

Runmarö 30 April (and 5 April) [May] -90
Dear master and buddy,

why do I always have to write to other people than you? So many letters nowadays are written for practical reasons. I am buried under a pyramid of unanswered letters. I wake up under them, I go to sleep under them.

I hope all is well with you and the close people. Here the mood is good. Monica and I have returned from a 3-week period as inhabitants in Venice. We were able to borrow a flat there, a real ghost house, and of course the experience of Venice was overwhelming. We returned slowly by train. When we woke up in Stockholm we bought the first Swedish newspaper in almost a month. We read it between Stockholm and Västerås. Suddenly Monica said: "I faint." She had come across a small note saying that I had gotten the so called "Neustadt Prize." I turned gray. I had gotten the so called "Nordiska Priset" one month earlier, we had both been to Iceland to receive it. And now this new one. I had the feeling that I had to travel around and apologize the rest of the year. "Forgive me for getting too many prizes . . ." After half an hour I could see the positive aspects—I had been lifted up from a rather humble existence to something approaching wealth. For the next year.

The Nordic Prize gets a lot of publicity here, but the Neustadt Prize not. The Swedes probably are confused because it is an unheard-of American prize with a German name. "Neustadt"—the Swede shakes his head. This lack of publicity is good for me, but I think Ivar Ivask is disappointed. He wants Norman, Oklahoma, to be known as the cultural center of the Western world. And I want to hide here in the incredibly early green spring—Sweden is the warmest part of Europe right now. Everything is upside down.

(I have the feeling that Ivar Ivask doubts my ability to behave properly during the solemn ceremonies.)

I must tell you a strange episode. In the beginning of February I visited Oslo, for one day and one night. In the morning I hurried to the Oslo railway station—and there—I saw—YOU. Or rather, an old relative of yours. It must have been one of your Bleie relatives. I passed very near, but the person did not show any sign of recognition, so I stopped my impulse to run and greet him, You, or whatever it was . . . I was tempted to ask the man if he was a relative of yours. But it was too early in the morning for such an attack. Perhaps it was your apparition? But he looked 5 years older than you. Perhaps you have a shamanistic method to fly to the Oslo railway station now and then and relax for a couple of minutes while you are sleeping in Minnesota, or lecturing mankind somewhere . . .

The other day I had a conversation with Fran Quinn's automatic telephone answerer. From Bill Holm I recently had a letter. So it is time to hear from you too.

> Love from us both.
>
> among daffodils
> Tomas

P.S. Would you like your letters to me to be stored by the Uppsala University Library? They want to take care of my papers. Gloomy librarians . . .

Appendix 1

Letters

Letter from Monica Tranströmer to Robert Bly on the translation of "Vermeer," August 6, 1995

Dear Robert,

Thank you for your letter and for your Vermeer translation. Tomas has pointed out what he does not find perfect in the translation. Then it's my job to understand what he means and describe the problem in my bad English!

And now to Vermeer!

Stanza 1 line 4. "The murderer" is stronger than "the death-bringer." He makes you unhappy—he makes you feel ill. But he does not kill you!

Stanza 2 line 2. "canals." In the dictionary "redd" is called "roadstead." What is sure is that the boats are anchored. And in Swedish "redden" even gives association to "bredden" which means "the breadth." Could Delft have any real harbour? Only canals I suppose.

Stanza 2, line 2. "ultimatum" seems stronger than "demands"
"   line 4. Tomas has written that the flowers are "sweating premo-
nitions of war"
Stanza 4 line 1. "airy" Is there any problem with "clear"?
"   line 3. Stopped "smack"—it sounds too funny!
Stanza 5, line 1. I think Tomas prefers "ears sing, from depth or height."
Stanza 6, line 1. "human beings" is a little too general. Tomas says "It hurts
to go through walls, it makes you ill."
Stanza 6 line 3. "Now to the walls" I do not think Tomas wants to teach
us something about the wall! Just tell us that it is there and it's the same
for him, me and for all of us.
Stanza 7, line 1. "airy." Maybe "clear"?
"   line 2. Maybe emptiness instead of "what is empty"?

We have a very busy time now. It's a lot of coming and going in Runmarö.
But the only thing we think of is Emma's wedding party on August 12. At
least 50 guests and maybe rain—help! But after the 12th life will be a little
more normal again. Do you have any plans to come to Sweden? We should
love that. We think very often on you.

    A hug to you both and to the whole family from both of us!

                                    Monica

I send this as a fax to U.S.A. too.

Letter from Robert Bly to Torbjörn Schmidt, February 3, 2000

Dear Torbjörn,
    Thank you very much for sending me back the original copies of the
letters. I was becoming alarmed at the gap in our correspondence, and I
wasn't sure what was happening. Don't hesitate to write me about the de-
tails in the letters that are not clear.
    About my Norwegian origin: My great-grandfather came from Bleie

on the Surfjord in Hardanger Fjord. It's a little settlement between Odda and Utne on the west side of the Surfjord. The family is still there. A whole group from that settlement came to Illinois in 1855 and then around 1888 moved up to western Minnesota where I was born. As was typical with second generation immigrants the parents did not teach their children Norwegian. I got a Fulbright Grant in 1955 with the aim of translating Norwegian poetry into English. They sent me three months early to the Oslo summer school for an intensive Norwegian course. I remained there the rest of the year translating Olaf Bull, Rolf Jacobsen, Claes Gill, Paul Brekke, and so on. Brekke published a small anthology of European poets in which I found Gunnar Ekelöf and Harry Martinson. When I got back to the United States, a man named Bill Duffy and I started a magazine called *The Fifties*—first issue in 1958—which took as its task the introduction of Ekelöf, Georg Trakl, César Vallejo, Pablo Neruda, Montale, Pasternak and various others to the American poets of my generation. Bill Duffy's wife was a Swede Christina Bratt, whose grandfather I think instituted the Bratt liquor rationing. I've mentioned her in another letter to you. She and I did the first translations in English of Gunnar Ekelöf, called *I Do Best Alone at Night*.

A few years later I heard about a young poet named Tranströmer and a new book called *Den halvfärdiga himlen*. The University of Minnesota has an excellent Scandinavian collection, so I drove the 150 miles or so to Minneapolis from the farm to find the book, and when I got home there was a letter from Tranströmer on my desk actually addressed to James Wright who often visited, as it happened. Tomas had seen some poems of James' and mine in the *Times Literary Supplement* and as he later said to me, he felt closer to those poems than to any poems by members of his generation in Sweden. So there was an instant kind of communion. On my side, when I began to publish English translations from *Half-Finished Heaven,* my oldest friend in poetry, Donald Hall, wrote me a note saying "How much does it cost to have a mail drop in Stockholm?" He was playful but serious. He thought I had written the poems and then they had been sent to American editors from Stockholm. So Tomas and James and I remained a little community. At about the same time I was, in order to earn money, translating Scandinavian fiction. I did Hamsun's *Hunger* and then *The Story of Gösta Berling* and then some stories of Strindberg. So I got to know Swedish fairly well, but Tomas would make marvelously subtle comments to me about the mood of my English in his poems—he knew English very well—and occasionally he saved me from embarrassing and disastrous things. I recall that it was during the seven-day Jewish war, Europeans had a fear of the atomic bomb being used. Tomas was thinking about that fear one morning while he was shaving, I think in the late 60s. It's called "Det oppna fonstret." It goes this way:

> I shaved one morning standing
> by the open window
> on the second story.

The next line said: "Knappte igång rakapparaten." I was aware that he was imagining a rocket taking off from the Near East. Later in the poem there's a helicopter and a pilot's voice saying "You're seeing this for the last time." So this word "rakapparaten" which I didn't remember from Strindberg or Lagerlöf I translated as "the rocket." After I sent the poem to Tomas, he wrote back, "No, Robert, it's an electric razor!" So you can see how he saved me from hideous errors, and made it appear as if I actually knew Swedish. But I think it was something unexplainable, something water-like or flowing in our approach to poetry that made our translations of each other full of feeling even with occasional mistakes.

I think I've answered your question there about the arrival of Tomas's letter. Eric Sellin was not connected with this exchange. I'll look over Tomas's letters to James Wright in the Wright archives here in Minneapolis and see if I can find that first letter.

About photographs: I think it was probably Carol Bly, my first wife, who took the photograph of Tomas and me standing by the sea. I'll ask her if she has a copy of that or any other photographs. I'm sure we can find something. If I do find them, I will send them on to you.

I love those doodles of Tranströmer, the kerosene lamps, the memories of Africa. If I were you I would include tons of those, as many as you can. They are really wonderful!

I'm going to send on to you a couple of books about my august self. Maybe you'll find something there helpful. In one of them, *Of Solitude and Silence,* Leif Sjöberg has an essay called "The Poet as Translator: Robert Bly and Scandinavian Poetry." And there's a photograph next to it of myself and my two daughters on Hardanger Fjord with Bleie in the background. And then four drafts of Tomas's poem "Övergångsstället" with a letter from Tomas from Västerås dated December 2nd, 1979, commenting on that and other translations. Do you have that letter of December 2nd, 1979 in your book so far?

I do have a couple of such books, and I'm going to try to find extra copies to send to you. If I succeed, I'll ship them by air next week. I'm glad you're back to work again on the book. I think we have a good chance of publishing a version of it in English as well.

> With good wishes as ever,
> Robert

P.S. Please give my love to Monica and Tomas.

Appendix 2

Poems

Snowfall in the Afternoon

I

The grass is half-covered with snow.
It was the sort of snowfall that starts in late afternoon,
And now the little houses of the grass are growing dark.

II

If I reached my hands down, near the earth,
I could take handfuls of darkness!
A darkness was always there, which we never noticed.

III

As the snow grows heavier, the cornstalks fade farther away,
And the barn moves nearer to the house.
The barn moves all alone in the growing storm.

IV

The barn is full of corn, and moving toward us now,
Like a hulk blown toward us in a storm at sea;
All the sailors on deck have been blind for many years.

—Robert Bly, from *Silence in the Snowy Fields*

Three Presidents

Andrew Jackson

I want to be a white horse!
I want to be a white horse on the green mountains!
A horse that runs over wooden bridges, and sleeps
In abandoned barns. . . .

Theodore Roosevelt

When I was President, I crushed snails with my bare teeth.
I slept in my underwear in the White House.
I ate the Cubans with a straw, and Lenin dreamt of *me* every night.
I wore down a forest of willow trees. I ground the snow,
And sold it.
The mountains of Texas shall heal our cornfields,
Overrun by the yellow race.
As for me, I want to be a stone. Yes!
I want to be a stone laid down thousands of years ago,
A stone with almost invisible cracks!
I want to be a stone that holds up the edge of the lake house,
A stone that suddenly gets up and runs around at night,
And lets the marriage bed fall; a stone that leaps into the water,
Carrying the robber down with him.

John F. Kennedy

I want to be a stream of water falling—
Water falling from high in the mountains, water

That dissolves everything,
And is never drunk, falling from ledge to ledge, from glass to glass.
I want the air around me to be invisible, resilient,
Able to flow past rocks.
I will carry the boulders with me to the valley.
Then ascending I will fall through space again:
Glittering in the sun, like the crystal in sideboards,
Goblets of the old life, before it was ruined by the Church.
And when I ascend the third time, I will fall forever,
Missing the earth entirely.

—Robert Bly, from *The Light Around the Body*

Preludes

I

I shy from something that comes scraping crossways through the
   blizzard.
Fragment out of what is to come.
A wall gotten loose. Something eyeless. Hard.
A face of teeth!
A wall, alone. Or is a house there,
even though I can't see it?
The future . . . an army of empty houses
feeling their way forward in the falling snow.

II

Two truths approach each other. One comes from inside, the other
   from outside,
and where they meet we have a chance to catch sight of ourselves.

The man who sees what's about to take place cries out wildly: "Stop!
Anything, if only I don't have to know myself."

And a boat exists that wants to tie up on shore—it's trying right
   here—
in fact it will try thousands of times yet.

Out of the darkness of the woods a long boathook appears, pokes in
   through the open window,
in among the guests who are getting warm dancing.

III

The apartment where I lived over half my life has to be cleaned out.
It's already empty of everything. The anchor has let go—despite the
continuing weight of grief it is the lightest apartment in the whole
city. Truth doesn't need any furniture. My life has just completed a big
circle and come back to its starting place: a room blown out. Things
I've lived through here become visible on the walls like Egyptian
paintings, murals from the inside of the grave chamber. But the scenes
are growing fainter, because the light is getting too strong. The win-
dows have got larger. The empty apartment is a large telescope held
up to the sky. It is silent as a Quaker service. All you can hear are the
doves in the backyard, their cooing.

> —Tomas Tranströmer, from *Night Vision*,
> translated by Robert Bly

C Major

As he stepped out into the street after a meeting with her
the snow whirled in the air.
Winter had come
while they were making love.
The night was white.
He walked fast from joy.
The streets slanted down.

Smiles passed—
everyone smiled behind turned-up collars.
How free it all was!
And all the questionmarks started to sing about God's life.
That's how it seemed to him.

Music was free at last
and walked through the blowing snow
with long strides.
All things around him on the way toward the note C.
A trembling needle pointing toward C.
An hour risen above anxieties.
How easy!
Everyone smiled behind turned-up collars.

> —Tomas Tranströmer, from *Den halvfärdiga*
> *himlen,* translated by Robert Bly (unpublished)

Notes

About These Notes

Endnotes take up twenty-two pages in the original Swedish edition of *Airmail* edited by Torbjörn Schmidt. I had hoped to make do with substantially fewer notes in this American edition, and perhaps proportionately I have achieved that goal. But it soon became clear to me that an American edition would call for numerous clarifications not needed by the Swedish audience. Also, the significant additions to the present edition opened up many more questions and issues to be resolved.

We live in an age of powerful search engines, and my policy has been not to include a note for anything a curious American reader can readily find online. This has spared me many, many elucidations of the obvious. On the other hand, I found it essential to a general comprehension of this book to do everything I could to help the reader understand casual but meaningful allusions to works, published, unpublished, or in progress, of the two poets that form the consistent connective tissue and ostensible subject matter of their conversation. I have also chosen to illuminate what the reader might otherwise assume to be offhanded whimsy on the part of

Bly or Tranströmer. For instance, when the latter tosses off, on March 24, 1984, "We could talk about our frog skins!" he is in fact referring to a piece Bly has recently published in the *New York Times Book Review* discussing the Russian fairy tale "The Frog Princess," though no mention of it by its author has been preserved in the correspondence.

My impulse as editor has consistently been to facilitate the story these letters tell, to fill in gaps where parts of the correspondence are obviously missing, and, frankly, to make *Airmail* the best read possible given the available surviving materials. Even the more trivial bits preserved here help us grasp the spirit of liveliness and fun that kept Bly and Tranströmer, collegial considerations aside, writing back and forth to each other for more than a quarter century.

Of course I had allies in these enhancements of the text. Torbjörn Schmidt did meticulous pioneering work on the original edition, from which I have gratefully drawn. Where the letters frequently venture out beyond the scope of Schmidt's work, I've benefited from the informed consultation of Roland Thorstensson, professor emeritus of Scandinavian studies and Swedish at Gustavus Adolphus College in St. Peter, Minnesota. (In December 2010, Professor Thorstensson shared a stage with Robert Bly at Plymouth Congregational Church in Minneapolis, where he read the Swedish originals of Bly's Tranströmer translations.) I indicate where I've adopted his wording with the initials "RT." Bly scholar Mark Gustafson has also given me good help on recondite Bly matters, as has Robert Bly himself. Monica and Tomas Tranströmer have very graciously replied to my queries at a busy time for them indeed. I should note that unless otherwise attributed, all translations of Tranströmer's (and other Scandinavian poets') titles are Bly's. In several cases, Bly has translated a book title for reference though not the book itself. Most of the Tranströmer poems mentioned by Bly can be found in *The Half-Finished Heaven,* in consultation with which this book is best read. Most of Bly's own poems alluded to in the text are readily available in his own volumes, though I have included a few around which more than the usual amount of discussion revolves in these letters.

—Thomas R. Smith

RB April 6, 1964

Halvfärdiga himlen—Tranströmer's 1962 poetry collection, translated by RB into English as *The Half-Finished Heaven.*

RB May 15, 1964

Allen anthology—*The New American Poetry: 1945–1960,* edited by Donald M. Allen, 1960.

TT September 3, 1964

"Snowfall"—"Snowfall in the Afternoon," *Silence in the Snowy Fields.*

RB October 23, 1964

Nå, her er vi alle i Paris!—The first two sentences are in Norwegian. RB translates: "Here we all are in Paris! Who could imagine such a strange thing!"

Another man I admire greatly—Georg Groddeck (1866–1934), German physician from whose *The Book of the It* Freud derived the concept of the Id.

That newspaper out in the weather—"Om Historien" translated by RB as "About History."

RB March 18, 1965

I enjoyed *Hemligheter på vägen*—TT's 1958 collection, title translated by RB as *Secrets on the Road.*

"Efter Anfall"—Translated by RB as "After the Attack."

this mole is an old friend—Reference to mole in TT's "Resans formler" (translated by Robin Fulton as "The Journey's Formulae"). RB also references his own "Laziness and Silence" and "The Mole" by John Haines.

RB March 31, 1965

Ord och Bild—Swedish cultural and literary journal founded in 1892.

RB July 8, 1965

old Heimat! old Bleie—"old home" in Bleie, ancestral home of Blys.

I just wrote Jim Wright—Letter to James Wright, July 8, 1965: "We stopped at a farmhouse—[Tranströmer] asked for some sort of key—we went to this huge red barn and he opened the door with the gigantic old key—it was a Moose Museum! Yes, it had a complete moose skeleton, hundreds of moose teeth for sale, everything in the whole building was moose. It was probably the only building in Sweden completely pervaded by moose and moosiness."

that calm and grotesque St. George—This sculpture by Bernt Notke became the subject of RB's poem "St. George, the Dragon, and the Virgin," *Meditations on the Insatiable Soul,* 1994.

RB December 1, 1965

Leif Sjöberg—Sjöberg's article in the *American Swedish Monthly,* 1965:5, was titled "Poetry: A Pretty Hopeless Product to Market."

RB February 7, 1966

urgammel Bleie gard—According to RB, "longstanding Bly farm."

låsa—"lock."

TT March 1, 1966

Viet-Nam poem about the ghost train—"Asian Peace Offers Rejected without Publication," in *The Light Around the Body.*

RB March 18, 1966

Sweden Writes—Anthology of contemporary Swedish writers, 1965, edited by Lars Bäckström and Göran Palm.

RB April 10, 1966

Herr Across-the-River—RB seems to be playing here on an incorrect translation of the name "Tranströmer." According to RT, "ström" does indeed mean "stream," but "tran" in Swedish is not related to our English root meaning "across." Instead it means "fish oil." "Tranströmer," says RT, is "one of the many last names in Swedish where two seemingly different objects are combined."

TT April 10, 1966

BLM—*Bonniers litterära magasin,* influential Swedish literary journal.

TT June 4, 1966

Klanger och spår—Translated by RB as *Resonance and Tracks,* 1966.

TT July 20, 1966

poem about the Oyster—"Opening an Oyster," in *The Light Around the Body.*

RB August 8, 1966

"I det fria"—Translated by RB as "Out in the Open."

"As the Asian War Begins"—Later version published in *The Light Around the Body.*

TT September 1966

Bonniers—TT's longtime publisher.

MRA—Moral Re-Armament, a conservative Christian revivalist movement founded by Protestant evangelist Frank Buchman in 1938.

"Lamento"—Translated by RB as "Lamento."

TT October 1, 1966

Ducks—Tiny chapbook of a three-line poem by RB, hence the playful reference to *Gone with the Wind.*

RB October 8, 1966

Dagens Nyheter—(Daily News) Largest morning newspaper in Sweden, founded in 1864.

Hjorth—Daniel Hjorth, chief editor at BLM.

Calvinols resa genom världen—Novel by Swedish author P. C. Jersild.

TT October 29, 1966

Aftonbladet—A leading Swedish daily tabloid, founded in 1830.

RB November 20, 1966

Thursday about 10 of America's—See Donald Hall's marvelous account of this event in his interview with Peter Stitt, *Paris Review,* Fall 1991.

TT April 5, 1967

Carroll—Donald Carroll, publisher of Rapp & Carroll.

RB June 10, 1967

wall-stumbling-along-in-the-street poem—"Preludier" by TT, translated by RB as "Preludes."

TT July 11, 1967

I'm enclosing a poem—"Med älven," translated by RB as "Going with the Current."

TT August 8, 1967

My own poem—"Andrum juli," translated by RB as "Breathing Space July."

Myrdal's articles—Jan Myrdal, critical commentary on U.S. involvement in Vietnam.

TT September 30, 1967

The Lion's Tail and Eyes—Reference to RB's collection of that title (with James Wright and William Duffy), Sixties Press, 1962, in which Bly posits a poetry of evocative imagery rather than literalistic "pictures."

RB October 2, 1967

Strountes—Title of Gunnar Ekelöf's 1955 collection, translated by RB as *Nonsense*.

TT October 7, 1967

you're getting two letters at once—The other may be TT's letter of September 30.

your dispute in *The Sixties*—RB, "The Collapse of James Dickey," *The Sixties* 9, Spring 1967.

TT December 18, 1967

Stanza 2—RB's poem "Melancholy" in *The Light Around the Body*.

RB December 27, 1967

Also a copy of my play—*The Satisfaction of Vietnam: A Play in Eight Scenes*, unpublished.

"Direktörens död," etc.—RB's poems "The Executive's Death," "Those Being Eaten by America," and "Smothered by the World," from *The Light Around the Body*.

TT February 19, 1968

Sinyavsky trial—Andrei Sinyavsky, Russian dissident.

RB April 23, 1968

Ord om Vietnam—Anthology edited by Benny Andersen, 1967.

TT June 9, 1968

the enclosed poem—"Trafik," translated by RB as "Traffic."

golden wings—Reference to RB poem "Laziness and Silence" in *Silence in the Snowy Fields*.

TT July 12, 1968

Mamma in the hospital—TT's mother, Helmy Tranströmer, was being treated for cancer.

Mr. Hall—Donald Hall.

TT August 8, 1968

Unicorn—American literary journal featuring RB's translations of Martinson.

Miami Beach—Site of the Republican convention at which Nixon was nominated.

RB October 21, 1968

George—George Hitchcock, editor of *Kayak*.

TT December 10, 1968

Harry Smith—Editor of the literary magazine *The Smith* (not the Beat Harry Smith), writing in *The Sixties* 10, 1968: "I don't even doubt that lovely poems are written in China, but I am unaware of any Chinaman who has done as well as John Donne."

RB December 30, 1968

the two lovely poems—"The Open Window" and "Outskirts" (RB translation).

RB January 15, 1969

cement piping poem—"Outskirts."

TT January 18, 1969

Misan—Emma Tranströmer.

TT June 14, 1969

"sitting on some rocks"—"Sitting on Some Rocks in Shaw Cove, California," in RB, *The Morning Glory,* 1969.

RB June 24, 1969

first drafts of two translations—"Outskirts" and "The Open Window."

TT July 30, 1969

Issa—*Issa: Ten Poems,* self-published pamphlet of RB translations of Japanese haiku poet Issa, given away at poetry readings: "This booklet is a gift, and is not to be sold."

Bly magazine from Tennessee—Special RB issue of the *Tennessee Poetry Journal,* 1969.

Comrade Zhdanov—Andrei Zhdanov, chairman of the Soviet of the Union, infamous for his purges of musicians and stance toward "incorrect art" as ideological diversion.

TT November 17, 1969

very strong poem of yours—"The Teeth-Mother Naked at Last."

politrucs—"Politically appointed civil servant" with connotations of "bureaucrat" (RT).

exiled Hungarian poet—Géza Thinsz.

RB December 10, 1969

The Shadow Brother—Early title of *Sleepers Joining Hands,* 1973.

Doing Nothing for a Thousand Years—Published in 1979 as *This Tree Will Be Here for a Thousand Years.*

TT January 4, 1970

a new poem—"Upprätt," translated by RB as "Standing Up."

RB January 16, 1970

the Barn in Devon—"Walking on the Sussex Coast."

the rocket-shaver poem—"The Open Window." See RB's letter to Torbjörn Schmidt, p. 418.

RB January 20, 1970

your Hen Poem—"Standing Up."

TT January 30, 1970

The reconstruction of this long letter is something of an educated guess. The Swedish draft, as translated by Judith Moffett and Lars-Håkan Svensson, is incomplete, ending with the sentence "Or I can stand anything except not to . . ." Weighing date and context, I've taken the risk of combining this with the partial letter in *Ironwood* (see end note for RB November 12, 1978), originally written mostly in English, dealing with poems from *Night Vision,* and which begins "And there is a boat trying to put in." (JM and L-HS have also translated the part of the first paragraph of the last section beginning "The boathook is something totally foreign.")

RB February 9, 1970

Would you check this translation—TT's "Balakirevs dröm (1905)," translated by RB as "Balakirev's Dream (1905)."

TT February 27, 1970

Crunk—RB's pseudonym for critical essays in *The Fifties* and *The Sixties.*

TT April 19, 1970

"walking in spring ditches"—Published as "Walking in the Ditch Grass" in *Jumping Out of Bed,* Barre Publishers, 1973.

2 poems "Telpas"—"Open and Closed Space" and "About History."

"våra istidsateljéers röda djur"—translated by RB as "red beasts of the ice-age studios."

new "book"—*Mörkerseende,* translated by RB as *Night Vision.*

"Författarförlaget"—A left-leaning writers' cooperative formed in 1969.

RB April 26, 1970

"Till vänner bakom en gräns"—Translated by RB as "To Friends behind a Border."

ordene sum "visar tänderna"—words baring their teeth.

Enclosed with the letter was a clipping of newspaper article on RB and Sen. McCarthy.

TT May 2, 1970

Voznesensky—Andrei Voznesensky, Russian poet.

TT August 11, 1970

a very LONG poem—"Östersjöar," 1974; "Baltics," not translated by RB, but English versions by Samuel Charters and Robin Fulton.

poem about roads—"Längre In," translated by RB as "Further In."

TT September 7, 1970

Canadian Thistle—Published as "Looking at a Dry Canadian Thistle Brought in from the Snow" in the first edition of *The Morning Glory,* 1969, revised to "Looking at a Dry Tumbleweed Brought in from the Snow" in later editions.

RB September 14, 1970

"Renaissance Painting"—Published as "Leonardo's Secret" in *The Morning Glory,* 1969.

"The Hunter"—Published in *The Morning Glory,* 1969.

"Helicopter"—"Going in a Helicopter from Riverside to the L.A. Airport," published in *The Morning Glory,* 1969.

RB November 12, 1970 (first letter)

"The Bookcase"—TT's "Bokskåpet."

"Skiss i oktober"—TT, "Sketch in October."

Jag är jordens—"I am of the earth" (RT).

RB November 12, 1970 (second letter)

References are to "Namnet," translated by RB as "The Name."

TT November 18, 1970

The letter from the professor—Stephen Mooney, editor of the *Tennessee Poetry Journal*. Mooney had apparently reported being harassed by the Ku Klux Klan.

RB November 24, 1970

The letter included drafts of "At the Riverside," later "Going with the Current" ("Med älven") and "Breathing Space July."

TT November 29, 1970

the Buckleys—William F. Buckley, conservative writer and pundit.

holy barbarian—Possibly a reference to Lawrence Lipton's book on the Beats, *The Holy Barbarians,* 1959.

RB December 14, 1970

I know the power—RB's solution is "identity books" in "The Bookcase."

TT December 20, 1970

stakhanovite—A category of Soviet industrial worker rewarded with special privileges for productivity beyond the ordinary.

RB December 28, 1970

The concrete has a cement-headed foreman—Playful reference to TT poem "Summer Grass" (RB translation): "Grass and flowers—we are landing. / The grass has a green foreman. / I go and check in."

RB January 21, 1971

cleaning oil off birds—On January 19, two tankers collided off Golden Gate, spilling 840,000 gallons of oil into San Francisco Bay. An estimated 10,000 birds and millions of sea creatures were killed.

TT April 2, 1971

A book is planned—*Poesi från USA,* 1972, included TT's translations of RB, James Wright, and W. S. Merwin.

TT May 21, 1971

Din gamle vän—Your old friend.

RB May 30, 1971

She gave birth—Micah Bly.

TT June 4, 1971

George Young—editor of the journal *Granite.*

RB July 22, 1971

my brother—James Bly, born 1925.

National Guard Camp poem—"Posteringen" translated by RB as "Guard Duty."

RB July 27, 1971

"Spiritual Death" and "Sleeping Woman"—Unpublished. Described in 1999 RB note to Torbjörn Schmidt as "Two rejected poems."

your Snowmelt poem—"Från snösmältningen—'66" translated by RB as "Snow-Melting Time, '66."

TT August 4, 1971

a woman I had been very close to—Gun Bergman, born 1916, translator of Slavic languages.

RB September 1, 1971

The Vladimir Mayakovsky quote is translated by Judith Moffett and Lars-Håkan Svensson.

TT September 13, 1971

"Sverige-Amerika-stiftelsen"—Sweden-America Foundation.

What is absurd—Refers to prose that became introduction to RB's translations of Göran Sonnevi, *The Economy Spinning Faster and Faster*, SUN, 1982. RB sticks to his story that Sonnevi's poem on the Vietnam war caused Swedish prime minister Olof Palme to change his position on the war.

TT September 25, 1971

Thank you for the 20 poems—*Twenty Poems*, The Seventies Press, 1970, featured a cover drawing by Franz Richter. In his notes, RB writes that TT is one of "three powerful poets in Sweden so far in this century."

RB November 23, 1971

4-4-4 generalizations—4-4-4 refers to a balanced physical/personality type in psychologist William Sheldon's body typology.

The letter included a clipping from the *Daily Iowan*, "Famed poet Bly condemns Writers' Workshop makeup."

TT November 26, 1971

Martinson—*Dikter om ljus och mörker*, title translated by RB as *Poems on Light and Dark*.

RB December 12, 1971

"Hair"—Published in RB's *Sleepers Joining Hands*, 1973.

This is Senator Kennedy's plane—Senator Ted Kennedy, while campaigning in 1964, survived a harrowing small-plane crash.

RB January 1, 1972

I took a long walk—This experience is recorded in RB's prose poem "Opening the Door of a Barn I Thought Was Empty on New Year's Eve" in *The Morning Glory*, 1975 edition.

the troll poem—Translated by RB as "The Hill in the Woods."

TT January 18, 1972

"företagsdemokrati"—A democratic workplace organizational principle that gave workers a greater part in decision making. "The aim was to do away with a top-down, hierarchical system" (RT).

RB January 29, 1972

Alan Ross—Publisher of London Magazine Editions.

TT February 8, 1972

Håkan Berggren—Swedish ambassador to the United States; at that time head of the Swedish Information Service in New York.

the dentist Scherer—James Scherer, friend of RB.

RB March 12, 1972

Worm Digging Poem—RB's "Digging Worms," published in *This Tree Will Be Here a Thousand Years,* 1979.

TT April 5, 1972

your wonderful Hawaiian crab—RB's prose poem "On the Rocks at Maui," in *The Morning Glory,* 1975.

RB April 8, 1972

a Hindi poem—This undated clipping has TT's typed note: "Please, ask KABIR, next time you meet him. What poem of mine is this, translated into HINDI?"

TT May 1, 1972

the CDU—Christian Democratic Union, conservative party in Germany.

I was making some arm movements—Playful reference to RB's habit of gesturing while reading poems.

take this shorter poem—"Markgenomskådande," translated by RB as "Seeing Through the Ground."

"jump-issue"—*The Seventies* 1, Spring 1972, featured material that became the Beacon Press volume *Leaping Poetry,* 1975. It contains TT's "Out in the Open."

RB May 24, 1972

"Pa Mauis Klippor"—"On the Rocks at Maui."

TT July 8, 1972

My Pittsburgh coronation ceremony—TT received a prize from the International Poetry Forum.

the Swenson book is out—*Windows and Stones: Selected Poems,* translated by May Swenson with Leif Sjöberg, University of Pittsburgh Press, 1972.

RB August 4, 1972

up here in Steinshylla's hytte—up here in the tourist hut (RB).

TT August 9, 1972

my next "book"—*Stigar,* 1973 (*Pathways,* RB translation), also included translations of RB and János Pilinszky.

RB September 1, 1972

Kjell Heggelund—Influential Norwegian publisher, poet, editor.

TT November 21, 1972

Keith Harrison—Australian poet and teacher living in Minnesota.

Franklin—Franklin Brainard, Minnesota poet ill with leukemia.

RB November 26, 1972

Keith Gunderson—Minnesota poet and philosopher, author of *3124 Lyndale Ave. So. Apt 24,* published by the Minnesota Writers' Publishing House.

TT January 9, 1973

the terror bombings—Nixon's infamous "Christmas" bombings of North Vietnam.

a small despair poem—TT's "December Evening, '72" ("Decemberkväll -72").

RB January 10, 1973

the next Beacon book—Published as *Friends, You Drank Some Darkness,* 1975.

TT January 28, 1973

Mr Booth—Martin Booth, British publisher.

the October poem—"Sketch in October."

RB March 17, 1973

"Namnlöst"—Translated by RB as "No Name for It."

Färjesång—RB renders as *Ferryman's Song.*

"Etyder"—Studies.

RB March 24, 1973

hear the stones roll—Reference to TT's poem "Allegro."

TT March 29, 1973

November birch—Reference to RB's "Solitude Late at Night in the Woods."

RB July 4, 1973

fruit-poem—"Sena maj," translated by RB as "Late May."

TT August 18, 1973

Your poems in *Stigar*: "Late Night in the Woods," "Six Winter Privacy Poems," "Walking in the Ditch Grass," "Digging Worms," "On the Rocks at Maui."

RB January 30, 1974

the kamikaze poem—"Längs radien," translated by RB as "Along the Lines."

TT February 13, 1974

Mr Galin—Saul Galin, literature professor at Brooklyn College, New York.

the rushingwaterpoem—"Snow-Melting Time, '66."

RB March 12, 1974

Ruth says—Ruth Counsel, who became RB's second wife in 1980.

RB March 15, 1974

according to Daniela—The letter includes a brochure from Daniela Gioseffi.

RB March 30, 1974

APR—*American Poetry Review,* Jan./Feb. 1974, with RB's essay "The Network and the Community."

TT April 30, 1974

the book of seal poems—*Point Reyes Poems,* Mudra, Half Moon Bay, California.

2 Danish pamphlets—RB's poems in translation from Husets Forlag.

I have recommended the book—*Earthwalk* by Philip Slater, discussed in "The Network and the Community."

RB July 16, 1974

a thesis on my poems—Published as *Moving Inward: A Study of Robert Bly's Poetry,* 1977.

TT August 22, 1974

footnote: Jag gillar Jung, tvivla inte på det.—"I like Jung, be sure about that" (RT).

Another of your fads—See *Leaping Poetry,* "The Three Brains," on the ideas of American neurologist Paul MacLean.

RB September 3, 1974

the Danton poem—"Citoyens."

RB October 16, 1974

NFO farmers—The National Farmers Organization staged dramatic protests against the low prices of farm goods.

RB November 24, 1974

"The Poet's Friend"—Reference to the name of the Swedish journal *Lyrikvännen.*

TT February 4, 1975

Hemåt—Translated by RB as "Calling Home."

And the other one—"Gläntan," missing from this letter, was translated by RB as "The Clearing."

RB February 18, 1975

This is not the roof—Reference to TT's "Along the Lines."

RB March 12, 1975

Svensson—Georg Svensson of Bonniers publishers.

"skalbagge"—Beetle in the last paragraph of "The Clearing."

TT July 1, 1975

Old Man Rubbing—The final poem in *Old Man Rubbing His Eyes,* Unicorn Press, is "Passing an Orchard by Train."

RB Septemer 6, 1975

the Snowbank poem—"Snowbanks North of the House" in *The Man in the Black Coat Turns,* 1981.

RB September 8, 1975

"Båten, Byn"—"Båten—Byn," translated by RB as "Boat, Town."

TT September 19, 1975

"Skapande svenska"—Creative Swedish (or creative writing in Swedish) (RT).

TT October 8, 1975

Mr Hawley (Oyez boss)—Robert Hawley, cofounder of Oyez Press.

Here is a confessional poem—"Från vintern 1947," translated by RB as "From the Winter of 1947."

TT January 22, 1976

Skenet från den andra stranden—"The light from the other shore" (RT).

"Hämtar ved"—"Fetching Firewood" (RT).

Can I use your idea—RB had mistakenly translated TT's "trees" ("träd") as "threads."

TT June 7, 1976

"The left hand"—"The Left Hand" in RB's *This Body Is Made of Camphor and Gopherwood,* Harper and Row, 1977.

Ett Tärningskast—Throw of the dice.

"Övergångsstället"—Translated by RB as "Street Crossing."

"Hastig promenad"—RB's "Walking Swiftly" in *This Body Is Made of Camphor and Gopherwood.*

RB July 17, 1976

the idea of "skum"—RB translates as "gloomy" in the attached draft titled "Place to Cross."

Cry of the Loon—Near Laporte, Minnesota, where RB bought a house the next year.

TT September 19, 1976

I send you a prose piece—"Till Mats och Laila," translated by RB as "For Mats and Laila."

RB September 24, 1976

Brutal men invading—Published in verse form as "Visiting the Farallones" in *The Man in the Black Coat Turns,* 1981.

TT November 8, 1976

Wonderful poem—"Frost on Window Panes" in RB's *The Morning Glory.*

TT November 11, 1976

Here is a small poem of mine—"Schubertiana."

Not to be confused with the earlier poem, "C Major," which appears for the first time in RB's translation in Appendix 2 of this book.

RB January 24, 1977

"Finding the Father"—In *This Body Is Made of Camphor and Gopherwood.*

TT January 26, 1977

have a look at this—See "The Gift the Prose Poem Gives" in RB January 31, 1977.

RB January 31, 1977

a few notes on "Tomales Bay"—"Sunday Morning in Tomales Bay" from *Point Reyes Poems*.

TT March 4, 1977

The letter is written on some typed information about the Nobel Prize, on which Saul Bellow's name is crossed out and RB's written in, with the year 1976 changed to 1996.

what's-his-name?—Michael Cuddihy.

RB March 20, 1977

seals and billfolds—See "The Dead Seal" in *The Morning Glory*.

TT May 19, 1977

The headache piece—"The House of Headache," translated by John Matthias and Lars-Håkan Svensson in the *New Yorker,* October 17, 2011.

In the other piece—"Minusgrader," translated by RB as "Below Freezing."

Glaser—Werner Wolf Glaser.

Maybe the hockey poem—"The Hockey Poem" in *The Morning Glory*.

RB July 7, 1977

my longest prose poem—"Finding an Old Ant Mansion" in *The Man in the Black Coat Turns*.

"Lars Gustafsson Collection"—Gustafsson lectured at the University of Texas, Austin in the 1970s and subsequently lived there 1983–2003.

TT January 20, 1978

the long poem I include in this letter—"Galleriet," translated by RB as "The Gallery."

the beautiful Snail-book—RB's *This Body Is Made of Camphor and Gopherwood* is embellished by pencil drawings of snail shells by Gendron Jensen.

our Bly-volume in Swedish—*Prosadikter,* 1977.

TT February 19, 1978

a Wright-issue—*Ironwood* 10, 1977, featured Carol Bly's photo of James Wright on the horse David, mentioned in Wright's poetry.

TT May 11, 1978

penates—In both Spanish and Latin, household gods.

RB May 23, 1978

Gov Wallace's photograph—George Wallace, governor of Alabama and segregationist.

TT September 6, 1978

Michael Cuddihy wants to have some letters—Published in special TT issue, *Ironwood* 13, 1979.

RB November 12, 1978

Ironwood—The *Ironwood* issue included TT's letters of: January 30, 1970 (partial, seems to belong to letter of that date translated here by JM and L-HS, though written mostly in English), February 27, 1970, February 8, 1972, January 18, 1977, May 19, 1977, May 11, 1978. The originals of all these letters are missing, so the versions here may incorporate transcription errors.

RB February 5, 1979

in the title of your book—In 1980, RB published a full translation of TT's *Sanningsbarriären* as *Truth Barriers,* Sierra Club.

I am finishing an anthology—*News of the Universe,* 1980.

"Havsvinden"—Translated by RB as "The Sea Wind."

TT April 14, 1979

"Fredagsbarnen" (or is it "Mandagsbarnen"?)—"Friday's Children" or "Monday's Children"; TT is playing on an old proverb here.

Annie did not say—Ann Charters.

RB April 29, 1979

I met a young man at M.I.U.—Joseph Stubblefield.

RB December 2, 1979

This letter originally appeared in *Poetry East* 4/5, 1981, and was reprinted in *Of Solitude and Silence: Writings on Robert Bly,* edited by Richard Jones and Kate Daniels, Beacon Press. Since the original, written in English, is lost, transcription errors may be built-in, as with the *Ironwood* letters.

RB February 16, 1980

the Oberlin milieu—Stuart Friebert and David Young, editors of *Field* at Oberlin College, Oberlin, Ohio.

Wharton—Bob Wharton.

RB October 3, 1980

The review from *Publishers Weekly,* September 26, 1980, was enclosed with the letter.

TT November 4, 1980

the TV program—"Tomas Transt234mer—ett möte sommaren 1980."

In this letter I send—On a photocopy of the article, TT has written: "Means that you don't have to worry about the Nobel Prize and I don't have to worry about membership in the Swedish Academy."

RB September 1, 1981 (first letter)

your Petrarch Prize—German annual literary award.

Enclosed is the April 26, 1981, review of *Truth Barriers* from the *New York Times.* RB has captioned photo of TT: "I once read a Kafka book and have never been the same since."

RB September 1, 1981 (second letter)

a letter of yours from late June—This letter is lost.

RB October 10, 1981

Enclosed with the letter is a newspaper clipping about a man who shot his TV thirty-one times.

TT June 29, 1982

A Mr Haba—James Haba.

mecenat—A generous patron, especially of literature and the arts (RT).

The letter included poems titled "Postludium " and "Svarta vykort," with TT's note, "Sapphic!"

RB July 14, 1982

the NERUDA WATCHDOG—Artur Lundkvist.

My latest essay—"Form That Is Neither In Nor Out," *Poetry East* 4/5, Spring/Summer 1981.

Enclosed with the letter is a flyer for "A Conference on Form August 7–11, 1982," and "Love Poem in Twos and Threes," published in *Loving a Woman in Two Worlds,* Dial Press, 1985.

TT October 22, 1982

your mysteriously sad and wonderful poem—"Snowbanks North of the House."

my Bible job—TT's versions of the Psalms were published as a part of a new Swedish translation of the Bible in 2000.

RB New Year's Eve, 1983

I have your new book—*Det vilda torget,* 1983.

TT March 25, 1984

We could talk about our frog skins!—RB discusses the Russian fairy tale "The Frog Princess" in "In Search of an American Muse," *New York Times Book Review,* January 22, 1984.

RB January 26, 1985

The shock of Sam's death—Sam Ray, son of Ruth Bly and David Ray, was killed in an accident in September 1984.

a new translation of *Peer Gynt*—The play was finished and staged at the Guthrie Theater, Minneapolis, in 2008.

RB February 20, 1985

Included with the letter were Bill Holm's poems "Liszt" and "Playing Bach's *Orgenbüchlein* on the Piano"; also a *Minneapolis Tribune* story with photo of RB in jail for protesting arms manufacturer Honeywell.

RB March 30, 1985

the Market Place book—*Det vilda torget*.

TT September 29, 1985

your latest book—*Loving a Woman in Two Worlds*.

RB October 31, 1985

the first stanza of "Alkaiskt"—in *För levande och döda*.

TT March 14, 1986

"Älgen"—"The Moose."

"Nattgrodor"—"Night Frogs."

by killing Palme—Swedish prime minister Olof Palme was assassinated in Stockholm on February 28, 1986.

RB March 19, 1986

"Right here I was nearly killed"—"Ensamhet," translated by RB as "Solitude."

Heim—Michael Henry Heim.

RB August 4, 1986

your car-wreck poem—"Ensamhet."

I have all sorts of questions—Robert Hass was then editing his *Selected Poems* of Tranströmer (1987), incorporating a number of RB's translations. RB includes the revisions occasioned by Hass's queries in *The Half-Finished Heaven.*

Here are the four questions—The four poems are translated by RB as, respectively, "Guard Duty," "The Scattered Congregation," "For Mats and Laila," and "Below Freezing."

TT September 11, 1986

STRYKER LÄNGS VARMA ÖGONBLICK—In "Posteringen," translated by RB as "Guard Duty."

RB October 3, 1986

eighty-five-syllable poems—RB's invented form, the *ramage,* several examples of which appear in *Talking into the Ear of a Donkey,* W. W. Norton, 2011.

RB January 10, 1988

an essay on the naive male—Part of RB's work in progress, *Iron John,* Addison-Wesley, 1990.

RB May 3, 1989

What fun to have your new book!—*För levande och döda (For the Living and the Dead).*

Here is a draft—"Romanesque Arches."

TT April 30–May 5, 1990

Neustadt Prize—Annual prize sponsored by the University of Oklahoma, publisher of *World Literature Today,* edited by Ivar Ivask. WLT featured a special section on TT in its Autumn 1990 issue.

Index

About the Authors

Robert Bly is the author of numerous books of poetry, nonfiction, translation, and cultural criticism, including *The Light Around the Body*, winner of the National Book Award for poetry, and the international best seller *Iron John: A Book about Men*. His many volumes of translation include *The Half-Finished Heaven: The Best Poems of Tomas Tranströmer*. His most recent book of poems is *Talking into the Ear of a Donkey*. He lives in Minneapolis, Minnesota.

Tomas Tranströmer was born and educated in Stockholm and worked as a psychologist. One of Sweden's most distinguished poets, he received the Nobel Prize for Literature in 2011. He is also the recipient of the Neustadt International Prize for Literature, the Bonnier Award for Poetry, Germany's Petrarch Prize, the Bellman Prize, and the Swedish Academy's Nordic Prize. He has written twelve books of poems. He lives in Stockholm, Sweden.

About the Editors

Thomas R. Smith is an internationally published poet, editor, essayist, and teacher. His six books of poems include *Waking Before Dawn* and *The Foot of the Rainbow*. He edited *Walking Swiftly*, a festschrift for Robert Bly's sixty-fifth birthday, and *Robert Bly in This World* (with James P. Lenfestey), proceedings of a conference at the University of Minnesota in 2009. He lives in western Wisconsin and teaches poetry at the Loft Literary Center in Minneapolis.

Torbjörn Schmidt, born 1955, is Master of Arts at the University of Stockholm and currently preparing a doctoral dissertation on Tomas Tranströmer's poetry. In 1998 he was appointed editor of the original Swedish edition of *Airmail* (2001), a book that was followed by an enlarged Danish edition in 2007. From 1981 to 1994, Schmidt worked as editor-in-chief of the major Swedish poetry magazine *Lyrikvännen* ("The Poet's Friend").

Book design by Rachel Holscher. Composition by BookMobile Design & Digital Publisher Services, Minneapolis, Minnesota. Manufactured by Friesens on acid-free 100 percent postconsumer wastepaper.